STUDIES

IN

MEANING

STUDIES IN MEANING: EXPLORING CONSTRUCTIVIST PSYCHOLOGY

Edited by
Jonathan D. Raskin
State University of New York at New Paltz

and

Sara K. Bridges
The University of Memphis

Pace University Press
2002

Library of Congress Cataloging-in-Publication Data

Studies in meaning : exploring constructivist psychology / edited
by Jonathan D. Raskin and Sara K. Bridges.
    p.cm.
Includes bibliographical references and index.
ISBN 0-944473-57-1
    1. Personal construct therapy. I. Raskin, Jonathan D. II. Bridges,
Sara K.

RC489.P46 S785 2002
616.89'1--dc21

                                                   2001055412

Table of Contents

PART III
EXPLORATIONS IN CONSTRUCTIVIST RESEARCH

PART IV
NEW DIRECTIONS IN CONSTRUCTIVIST PSYCHOLOGY

Contributors

Marla Arvay, Department of Educational and Counselling Psychology, and Special Education, University of British Columbia, Vancouver, Canada

Sara K. Bridges, Department of Counseling, Educational Psychology and Research, The University of Memphis, Tennessee, USA

Christopher R. Erbes, Department of Psychology, Texas Tech University, Lubbock, Texas, USA

Joseph Eron, Catskill Family Institute, Kingston, New York, USA

April J. Faidley, Meridian Psychological Associates, Indianapolis, Indiana, USA

Stephanie Lewis Harter, Department of Psychology, Texas Tech University, Lubbock, Texas, USA

Marie Hoskins, School of Child and Youth Care, University of Victoria, Canada

Larry M. Leitner, Department of Psychology, Miami University, Oxford, Ohio, USA

Thomas Lund, Catskill Family Institute, Kingston, New York, USA

Sheila McNamee, Department of Communication, University of New Hampshire, Durham, USA

Robert A. Neimeyer, Department of Psychology, The University of Memphis, Tennessee, USA

Nancy Pike, Department of Psychology, Miami University, Oxford, Ohio, USA

Jonathan D. Raskin, Department of Psychology, State University of New York at New Paltz, New York, USA

Mark Schlutsmeyer, Department of Psychology, Miami University, Oxford, Ohio, USA

John Shotter, Department of Communication, University of New Hampshire, Durham, USA

Caroline M. Stanley, Department of Psychology, State University of New York at New Paltz, New York, USA

Thomas Szasz, Department of Psychiatry, State University of New York Upstate Medical University, Syracuse, New York, USA

Beverly Walker, Department of Psychology, University of Wollongong, Australia

William George (Bill) Warren, Faculty of Education, The University of Newcastle, New South Wales, Australia

Preface

In the warm afterglow of a successful conference, we are pleased to present you with a volume that reflects some interesting directions in the burgeoning area of constructivist psychology. The conference we speak of is the Ninth Biennial Conference of the North American Personal Construct Network (NAPCN), which was held on the campus of the State University of New York at New Paltz from July 12-16, 2000. The volume at hand consists almost exclusively of papers that first were presented at this conference.

The conference theme, "Constructivist Psychology at the Millennium: Future Directions in Research and Practice," seemed to convey the widespread enthusiasm of the participants as they worked to further their constructivist work in a variety of psychological arenas. However, it became apparent as the conference proceeded that the precise boundaries of constructivist psychology seemed to be expanding even more rapidly than most of us attending had previously anticipated. Given NAPCN's history as an organization of professionals primarily interested in examining George Kelly's personal construct psychology (PCP), it was not surprising that PCP was at the center of much of what was presented at the New Paltz conference. However, as had been the trend at recent NAPCN and international personal construct psychology gatherings, a multitude of other constructivist and related perspectives seemed to powerfully intermingle with the usual PCP material: social constructionism, narrative psychology, radical constructivism, phenomenology, qualitative methodologies, and so on. The result was that many conference attendees experienced constructivist psychology undergoing fascinating, challenging, exciting, and sometimes even intimidating transformations as the many disparate constructivist approaches came into prolonged contact with each other.

Of course, an obvious advantage of this contact is the rich intellectual exchanges that occur. A disadvantage is that many folks, constructivists included, end up feeling a bit lost amidst the ever-expanding constructivist landscape. This volume, without expecting to fully remedy this situation, marks an effort to provide examples of the many new voices expressing themselves in a more integrated and collaborative way in constructivist psychology. Thus, some of the chapters come from a PCP vantage point, while others develop social constructionist or radical constructivist themes. Many, if not most, of the chapters combine a variety of constructivist approaches. The impact of these approaches is apparent in a variety of psychological areas. As editors, we have broken the volume into four sections, none of which is mutually exclusive. The first examines theory and practice issues. The second explores notions about psychological disorder. The third examines the role of constructivism in research. The last ponders future directions.

On a more personal note, we are thankful to a variety of people who helped us tremendously as we developed this volume. First, we want to thank Mark Hussey and Kerry Morris of Pace University Press for their tireless assistance in the preparation of the manuscript (not to mention the occasional necessary nagging!). As two editors with young children, we appreciated their prolonged patience with us during this undertaking. We also wish to thank Katy Sampson and Stephanie Insko (whose assistance with indexing was invaluable) and Dave Strauss (for designing the cover). Further, Sara would like to acknowledge Susan Slate Mathews for her insightful comments about Sara's closing chapter. She also wants to thank her husband Eric for his love, support, and patience during the completion of this volume. Finally, Jon wishes to thank his wife, Shay, and his daughters, Ari and Noa, for their ongoing love, support, and willingness to hear about the intricacies of subject indexing on a semi-regular basis.

Whether you are a committed constructivist psychologist or a skeptical newcomer to PCP and constructivism, we think that you will find this volume useful in its efforts to overview constructivist psychology and to present papers that examine constructivist theory, practice, and research. It is our aspiration that this volume will serve as the start point for a variety of conversations among and between constructivist and non-constructivist psychologists.

Jonathan D. Raskin   Sara K. Bridges
New Paltz, New York   *Memphis, Tennessee*

December, 2001

PART I

CONSTRUCTIVIST
THEORY AND PRACTICE

CHAPTER 1

Constructivism in Psychology: Personal Construct Psychology, Radical Constructivism, and Social Constructionism[1]

Jonathan D. Raskin

In this introductory chapter, I discuss three theories of psychological constructivism: personal construct psychology, radical constructivism, and social constructionism. I evaluate these theories in connection with Chiari and Nuzzo's classification scheme, which uses the categories of epistemological constructivism, hermeneutic constructivism, and limited realism. Given the different types of constructivism used by the contributors to this volume, I suggest that making connections among theories of psychological constructivism is a potentially beneficial endeavor.

INTRODUCTION: ONCE UPON A CONSTRUCTION

The constructivist psychologies theorize about and investigate how human beings create systems for meaningfully understanding their worlds and experiences. I refer to these "constructivisms" using the plural because there are many varieties of constructivism (Neimeyer & Raskin, 2001) and they have been described in various constellations (Botella, 1995; Chiari & Nuzzo, 1996a, 1996b; Lyddon, 1995; Mahoney, 1988, 1991, 1995; Rosen, 1996; Sexton, 1997). Depending upon how one chooses to carve out categories of constructivism, one finds differing areas of commonality and divergence. Regardless, the constructivist psychologies have grown immensely in quantity and influence over the past fifty years, originating in a variety of theoretical and research venues that have slowly developed greater contact with each other and with psychology at large. In fact, as the twenty-first century begins, constructivist psychologists find themselves standing at the crossroads,

---

[1] A version of this chapter also appears online in the 2002 volume of the *American Communication Journal*, [Available on the World Wide Web: http://acjournal.org]. The author thanks Jay Efran for his feedback on this chapter.

ready to make their mark on the broader discipline of psychology. However, despite their steadily growing influence, constructivist psychologies have not evolved into a single, coherent, theoretically consistent orientation. Given numerous theoretical differences, there is not even agreement among constructivist psychologists that arriving at a singularly recognizable orientation is desirable. Nevertheless, some constructivist psychologists' efforts to form a loosely confederated constructivist theoretical orientation have made inroads into mainstream psychology, as evidenced by the publication of several constructivist-themed volumes by the American Psychological Association (Neimeyer, 2001; Neimeyer & Mahoney, 1995; Neimeyer & Raskin, 2000). Even so, constructivist psychologists— perhaps due to their different historical and theoretical ancestries— have yet to make the same impact on psychology as earlier movements, such as psychoanalysis, radical behaviorism, cognitive psychology, and humanistic psychology. It seems that many American psychologists and students are still unfamiliar with constructivism, as evidenced by its exclusion from most psychology textbooks. This exclusion can at least in part be attributed to confusion about what constitutes constructivism. One comes across so many varieties of constructivist psychology that even the experts seem befuddled. Terms like "constructivism," "constructionism," and "constructive" are employed so idiosyncratically and inconsistently that at times they seem to defy definition. If the precise differences between the constructivist psychologies escape those who identify themselves as being "in the fold," one can only imagine how bewildered non-constructivist psychologists must be. This is unfortunate because it undermines the possibility that constructivist ideas will attract a larger audience.

In light of these concerns, this paper attempts to clarify similarities and differences among three key constructivist psychologies. I describe "personal construct psychology," "radical constructivism," and "social constructionism." I suggest—as has Lyddon (1995)— that the commonalities among these approaches outweigh the points of divergence. Highlighting this common ground should be useful to both psychologists and non-psychologists. I contend that all three approaches center on human meaning making as psychology's primary focus of inquiry. In comparing and contrasting these approaches, I try to overcome some of the convoluted jargon that has inhibited communication about the larger meaning of the constructivist movement.

2

THE CHANGING NATURE OF KNOWLEDGE

When psychologists use the term "constructivism" in its most general sense, what do they mean? In his historical analysis of the changing nature of knowing, Sexton (1997) divides human history into three distinct eras: premodern, modern, and postmodern. Each of these periods emphasized a particular ontological perspective that shaped how people dealt with events, problems, and solutions. The premodern era (from the sixth century B.C. through the Middle Ages) emphasized dualism, idealism, and rationalism. Faith and religion played central roles, and "effective change efforts were prayer, faith, thinking, and/or reasoning" (Sexton, 1997, p. 5). By comparison, the modern era (roughly from the Renaissance to the end of the nineteenth century, though modern thought still dominates much of current discourse) stressed empiricism, logical positivism, scientific methodology, the identification of objective truths, and validity. One consequence of the modern era

> was to solidify scientific and professional knowledge as the legitimate source of understanding the world. Through the logical process of science we could discover that which was true. . . . Scientific knowledge was assumed to be a mirror image of objective reality. (Sexton, 1997, p. 7)

Sexton (1997) labels the third (and present) era as postmodern/constructivist and depicts it as accentuating the creation, rather than the discovery, of personal and social realities. The postmodern/constructivist era stresses the viability, as opposed to the validity, of knowledge claims. It also pays special attention to epistemological issues. Investigators and theorists become concerned with how people know, as well as what they know. Compared to modernism (wherein truths independent of subjective bias are revealed to neutral scientists), postmodernism/constructivism highlights human participation in the construction of knowledge:

> The perspective of the observer and the object of observation are inseparable; the nature of meaning is relative; phenomena are context-based; and the process of knowledge and understanding is social, inductive, hermeneutical, and qualitative. (Sexton, 1997, p. 8)

Because constructivism focuses on ways in which persons and societies create (rather than discover) constructions of reality, its adherents often exhibit varying degrees of skepticism about whether persons have direct and accurate access to an external world. In other words, constructivists see reality as

> noumenal—that is, it lies beyond the reach of our most ambitious theories, whether personal or scientific, forever denying us as human beings the security of justifying our beliefs, faiths, and ideologies by simple recourse to "objective circumstances" outside ourselves. (Neimeyer, 1995, p. 3)

Thus, all constructivist psychologies share the belief that none of the many ways of understanding that people have developed provide a God's Eye (i.e., purely objective) view of the world. All constructed meanings reflect a point of view. However, constructivists often disagree among themselves about the implications of this position, particularly regarding the nature of reality, the origin of constructed meaning, and the best way to conduct psychological research.

EPISTEMOLOGICAL AND HERMENEUTIC CONSTRUCTIVISMS

Chiari and Nuzzo (1996b) argue that all constructivist psychologies attempt to conceptually bridge realist and idealist approaches to knowledge. Realism holds that "material objects exist externally to us and independently of our sense experience," while idealism maintains that "no such material objects or external realities exist apart from our knowledge or consciousness of them, the whole world being dependent on the mind" (p. 166). Building on the idea that constructivist approaches grapple to overcome the realism-idealism dichotomy, Chiari and Nuzzo (1996b) distinguish two broad categories of constructivism—epistemological and hermeneutic. Particular theories of constructivism can presumably be located within one category or the other.

Epistemological constructivism.

Epistemological constructivists are not purely idealists because they believe in the existence of an external reality that is independent of the observer. However, they also believe that it is not possible for observers to know that independent reality except through their constructions of it. Therefore, knowledge is a compilation of human-made constructions. Such constructions are heuristic fictions useful for understanding the world. In this regard, epistemological constructivism sees knowledge schemes as being classifiable as more or less viable rather than more or less accurate. People cannot know for certain if their constructions correspond to an independent reality, but they can know if their constructions work well for them. In this regard, people are cognitively closed systems: "In fact, it is really with the idea of a closure of cognitive systems that the subject/object dichotomy is substantially overcome and traditional realistic perspectives are actually abandoned" (Chiari & Nuzzo, 1996b, p. 171). Von Glaserfeld's radical constructivism seems to most clearly exemplify epistemological constructivism, although Kelly's personal construct psychology also fits nicely.

Hermeneutic constructivism.

Hermeneutic constructivists do not believe in the existence of an observer-independent reality. They consider knowledge a product of the linguistic activity of a community of observers. Thus, there can be as many knowledge systems as there are groups discursively negotiating them. In hermeneutic approaches to constructivism, the roles of language, discourse, and communication become central in understanding how knowledge systems are developed and maintained. There are many forms of hermeneutic constructivism, but they all share certain fundamental premises.

> Although their historical backgrounds are different, all these approaches share a view of knowledge (and truth) as interpretation, an interpretation historically founded rather than timeless, contextually verifiable rather than universally valid, and linguistically generated and socially negotiated rather than cognitively and individually produced. (Chiari & Nuzzo, 1996b, p. 174)

Gergen's social constructionism can be considered an example of hermeneutic constructivism and Maturana's radical constructivism appears to contain hermeneutic elements.

Limited realism.

Chiari and Nuzzo (1996b) discuss a third approach to bridging the realism-idealism dimension. They call it limited realism. Limited realists believe that an external reality exists. They also contend that it is possible to know that reality directly. However, because human perception is fallible, limited realists assume that the correspondence between knowledge and reality is imperfect. According to Chiari and Nuzzo, cognitive psychologists such as Albert Ellis and Aaron Beck should be considered limited realists because they emphasize the correction of erroneous thinking that distorts reality or is illogical (DeRubeis & Beck, 1988; Dryden & Ellis, 1988). Thus,

5

despite Ellis' recent claims to being a constructivist (Ellis, 1997, 1998), Chiari and Nuzzo's (1996b) criteria imply that his rational emotive therapy is a form of limited realism.

Some constructivists, such as Mahoney (1991), at times seem to espouse limited realism (Chiari & Nuzzo, 1996b). A case can even be made that Kelly's personal construct psychology—considered by many the first systematic use of constructivism within clinical psychology—is a form of limited realism (Stevens, 1998). Chiari and Nuzzo (1996b) contend that limited realist approaches should not be considered constructivist because such approaches claim that subjective representations mirror, with varying degrees of accuracy, an independent reality. Chiari and Nuzzo (1996b) suggest

> that the label *psychological constructivism* should be limited to the set of theories and approaches that strive to transcend the traditional opposition between realism and idealism by adopting the metatheoretical assumption that the structure and organization of the known—the knower as known included—are inextricably linked to the structure of the knower. The link may be in the form of an ordering and organization of a world constituted by the person's experience (epistemological constructivism) or in the sense that operations of distinctions in language constitute the generation and validation of all reality (hermeneutic constructivism). (Chiari & Nuzzo, 1996b, p. 178)

I have outlined Chiari and Nuzzo's (1996b) distinction between hermeneutic and epistemological constructivism to provide a framework for discussing three distinct psychological constructivisms: personal construct psychology (PCP), radical constructivism (RC), and social constructionism (SC). I do not consider this framework to be a "final" classification, but it does constitute one potentially helpful way to map the extensive constructivist terrain.

PERSONAL CONSTRUCTIVISM: MAKING YOUR OWN MEANING

KELLY'S THEORY

Personal constructivism, also referred to as personal construct psychology (PCP) or personal construct theory (PCT), originated with the pioneering work of George Kelly (1955/1991a, 1955/1991b). Kelly proposed that people organize their experiences by developing bipolar dimensions of meaning, or personal constructs. These hierarchically interrelated constructs are used to anticipate and predict how the world and its inhabitants might behave. By inventing dimensions of meaning that account for events, people organize psychological experience. Further, they continually test their personal constructs by tracking how well they predict life circumstances and by revising them when they are judged deficient. PCP uses the metaphor of the knowing individual as a personal scientist who continually puts his or her constructions to the test. Closely tied to the ideas of personal science and personal construing is the concept of constructive alternativism, the foundational philosophical premise of PCP. Constructive alternativism postulates that there are infinite possibilities for conceptualizing events (Kelly, 1955/1991a). As their previous sets of constructions prove unsatisfying, people are free to creatively develop entirely new dimensions of meaning.

The extent to which the external world influences a person's constructions is given a great deal of attention in PCP. Both the viability and validity of constructions is valued. To many (but not all) personal construct theorists, some constructions are indeed better than others because of their predictive utility or better approximation of events in the world (Kelly, 1955/1991a, 1955/1991b; Landfield, 1980; Stevens, 1998; Walker, 1992; Warren, 1992, 1998). Personal construct theorists use Kelly's concept of "hostility" to describe those who hang onto faulty constructions in the face of invalidating evidence—in other words, hostile people try to force the world to fit their preferred constructions rather than altering their constructions to better fit the world. Although people can always feel free to construe events in novel ways, some PCP scholars see the world itself as unyielding in its essential qualities, rendering constructions that effectively reflect these qualities as intrinsically more useful than others.

In PCP, the self is commonly viewed as constructed, not discovered (Burr, Butt, & Epting, 1997; Epting & Amerikaner, 1980). It is generated by the way a person successively construes himself or herself. Often, deeply embedded and intransigent constructions of self—most often developed early in life, especially prior to the development of language, become impermeable to self-reflection and alteration. The person usually sees these elements, called core constructs, as unfiltered truths rather than constructed realities (Kelly, 1955/1991a, 1955/1991b). Because core constructs are so basic, it is a long and arduous task for people to reconstrue these aspects of themselves. Even in psychotherapy, enduring senses of self, the "I-me-mine" aspects of individual identity, are the hardest to modify. In Kelly's approach, social and relational factors play a role in the constructive process. However, individual persons are still seen as the prime source of their own constructions.

The formation of close relationships is based upon what PCP psychologists call sociality, which requires people to construe the constructs of others with whom they wish to interact. When done effectively, sociality leads to *role relationships*, in which individuals are able to intimately understand one another (Kelly, 1970, 1955/1991a, 1955/1991b). Kelly developed his theory of personality with psychotherapy in mind. While eclectic in the sense that he encouraged clinicians to draw from a variety of clinical approaches, Kelly did develop an important therapeutic tool of his own called *fixed role therapy*. In this procedure, the client is asked to act out in everyday life the role of someone psychologically different from himself or herself. By prior agreement a client is encouraged to experiment for a set period of time with new modes of behaving and construing. Moreover, because of the experimental context, the client can do so without directly challenging his or her own sense of self; after all, the client is only acting! As a client experiments with these new ways of being, he or she has opportunities to incorporate new perspectives and possibilities into his or her sense of self. New possibilities are potentially opened. Fixed-role therapy is explicitly constructivist in the sense that it sees trying out new vantage points as central to change. It is a way to encourage the revision of personal constructions that have kept the individual stuck in ineffective problem-solving modes. For expanded descriptions of fixed-role therapy, see Epting (1984) and Kelly (1991/1955b).

COGNITIVE OR HUMANISTIC?

To Kelly's amusement, personal constructivism has been claimed by many different theoretical orientations in psychology, including the psychoanalytic, behavioral, humanistic, and existential perspectives (Kelly, 1970). Within PCP's ranks, there is often disagreement over whether Kelly's approach is more closely related to cognitive-behaviorial or humanistic-existential perspectives. Certainly, the "person as scientist" metaphor that Kelly used fits nicely with the cognitive paradigm's emphasis on rationally examining experiences as a basis for improving knowledge. The fact that Kelly structured PCP around a fundamental postulate and twelve corollaries (making it sound very logical, formal, and mathematical) makes it easy to see the theory as basically cognitive. When PCP is included in undergraduate personality texts, it most often appears as part of the cognitive section. Moreover, the just published second edition of the *Handbook of Cognitive-Behavioral Therapies* includes PCP as part of a chapter on constructivism(Neimeyer & Raskin, 2001).

Nevertheless, a variety of PCP scholars persuasively argue that PCP is basically a humanistic theory. They point to the theory's emphasis on free choice and the creation of personal meaning. They also point to Kelly's strong distaste for anti-humanistic diagnostic traditions (Butt, 1998b, 2000; Epting & Leitner, 1992; Johnson, Pfenninger, & Klion, 2000; Raskin & Epting, 1993, 1995; Raskin & Lewandowski, 2000). Humanistically oriented personal construct psychologists see the postulate and corollary style in which Kelly wrote his theory as a decoy originally intended to throw off Kelly's more traditional colleagues, who—in 1955 when the theory was first published—might not have been receptive to an overtly humanistic presentation style. Humanistic PCP'ers believe that those reading Kelly's theory as a cognitive approach are responding more to the presentation style than the underlying content, which includes a heavy emphasis on personal agency and self-determination (Epting & Leitner, 1992). Furthermore, Kelly consistently railed against paradigms that construe human subjects as passive objects of inquiry rather than active creators of their own personal meanings. Interestingly, at the time of his death, Kelly was in the process of rewriting his theory in a more accessible form (Maher, 1969), which some believe would have revealed humanistic underpinnings.

EPISTEMOLOGICAL CONSTRUCTIVISM
OR LIMITED REALISM?

The cognitive versus humanistic debate leads to whether PCP is best viewed as an epistemological constructivist theory or a limited realist theory. PCP's emphasis on meaning as a primarily personal endeavor supports classifying it as a form of epistemological constructivism. That is, personal construct psychology generally conceptualizes people as more or less locked within their own personal meaning systems. Some interconnection between meaning systems is possible, based on the notion of sociality mentioned earlier (Kelly, 1955/1991a). However, despite sociality, the person in PCP is often seen as existing within a closed, idiosyncratic web of personal meanings. This easily allows PCP to be classified as a form of epistemological constructivism.

On the other hand, a case can be made that PCP contains elements of limited realism. Numerous PCP researchers argue that some constructions are indeed better than others if they conform more adequately to the contours of external reality. (Howard, 1997; Landfield, 1980; Stevens, 1998; Walker, 1992; Warren, 1992, 1998). Whereas epistemological constructivists emphasize the viability of knowledge structures, limited realists believe that some correspondence can be established between constructions and external reality, even if it is imperfect. Various PCP theorists consider PCP a version of limited realism, even though in Chiari and Nuzzo's (1996b) terms this implies that PCP is not a genuine constructivist approach. Fay Fransella, one of the leading personal construct psychologists and director of the Centre for Personal Construct Psychology, most vocally expresses concerns about classifying PCP as a type of constructivism. She sees constructivism as a passing fad and worries that it might absorb PCP. Fransella (1995) argues, "if personal construct theory is allowed to be subsumed under the umbrella of constructivism as if it were *nothing but* constructivist, Kelly's philosophy may well survive, but his theory will sink without trace" (p. 131, italics in original). While not all PCP'ers share Fransella's concern—instead arguing that PCP can only be enriched by greater contact with other constructivist approaches—her anxiety highlights unease about integrating constructivist approaches into a single orientation.

RADICAL CONSTRUCTIVISM: YOUR OWN PRIVATE TAKE ON REALITY

Kelly's personal constructivism is often seen as related to, but less extreme than, types of constructivism categorized as radical. It is to the radical constructivist theories of von Glaserfeld (1984, 1995a, 1995b) and Maturana (1988; Maturana & Varela, 1992; Varela, 1984) that I turn next.

VON GLASERFELD'S THEORY

Von Glaserfeld's radical constructivism emphasizes the ability of human beings to use the understandings they create to help them navigate life, regardless of whether or not such understandings match an external reality. Borrowing heavily from Darwinian evolutionary theory and Piagetian cognitive developmental theory, von Glaserfeld asserts that human perception is adaptive—it evolved to help people survive. However, von Glaserfeld distinguishes adaptation from accuracy, stating that for radical constructivists, "adaptation does not mean adequation to an external world of things existing-in-themselves, but rather improving the organism's equilibrium, i.e., its fit, relative to experienced constraints" (1995a, p. 63). Von

Glaserfeld sees human cognition as a closed system. People are capable only of knowing when their constructions of events fail, but are never capable of knowing truth in any kind of direct, objective manner. In other words, von Glaserfeld replaces an emphasis on the validity of human perception with an emphasis on its viability. He neither denies the existence of an outside world, nor does he believe that people can ever have ontological access to that world: "Constructivism, thus, does not say there is no world and no other people, it merely holds that insofar as we know them, both the world and the others are models that we ourselves construct" (von Glaserfeld, 1995a, p. 137).

For von Glaserfeld, people only brush up against the real world when their constructions of it fail. External reality constrains people's constructions of it; constructions need to aid adaptation to a world that is not directly knowable. Von Glaserfeld relies extensively on the writings of Piaget in advancing the idea of cognitive adaptation. However, von Glaserfeld (1984, 1995a) contends that Piaget is often misunderstood by American psychologists, who interpret the Piagetian notions of accommodation and assimilation as evidence of Piaget's commitment to a realist epistemology. By contrast, von Glaserfeld argues that assimilation and accommodation are basically constructivist concepts. Assimilation is constructivist in that it entails taking information and adapting it to one's current experiential understandings. That is, it involves reducing "experiences to already existing sensorimotor or conceptual structures" (1995a, p. 63). This ties into Piagetian schema theory because von Glaserfeld sees mental schemes as involving assimilation. That is, the first part of a scheme involves recognizing (or re-presenting to oneself) a particular circumstance, the second part involves taking an action associated with that circumstance, and the third part involves the expectation that the action taken will produce a predicted result. Understanding schemas in this way helps make understandable how von Glaserfeld sees accommodation in constructivist terms. Rather than defining accommodation as altering one's schemas to more accurately reflect the world (as accommodation is commonly understood), von Glaserfeld (1995a) sees accommodation as a process "largely determined by the cognizing agent's unobservable expectations, rather than by what an observer may call sensory 'input'" (p. 66). In other words, it is the failure of one's internalized mental schemes, rather than the direct impact of external reality, that leads to accommodation. Further, von Glaserfeld is interested in the rela-

11

tionship between linguistically mediated human social interaction and accommodation. He argues that perturbation of a schema does not arise primarily from bumping into reality, but from internal and interpersonal transactions. As a result, von Glaserfeld does not assume that accommodation necessarily leads to increasingly accurate portrayals or representations of reality.

Von Glaserfeld thinks of people as operating in their own very private, self-constructed worlds. Language and social interaction allow for interpersonal communication, but never permit an individual to escape from encased isolation as a knowing being. While people accommodate within the framework of social interaction, they ultimately remain cognitively isolated.

> There is no doubt that these subjective meanings get modified, honed, and adapted throughout their use in the course of social interactions. But this adaptation does not and cannot change the fact that the material an individual's meanings are composed of can be taken only from that individual's own subjective experiences. (von Glaserfeld, 1995a, p. 137)

In this respect, "radical constructivism considers absolute meanings for words unattainable—that is, all speakers use private languages. Although specific words may be familiar, personal histories influence users to create unique meanings" (Loria, 1995, p. 156). Because people are locked inside their own subjective experiences, radical constructivists are interested in the ways that human beings establish and maintain communities. For instance, Efran and Fauber (1995) talk of the "communal choreography" made possible by language (p. 277). The characteristics of the social "dance" that people use to choreograph their lives is central to the radical constructivist views of biologist and cyberneticist Humberto Maturana, whose work I discuss next.

MATURANA'S THEORY

Maturana maintains that "problems do not exist apart from the observers who language them—they are created, or brought forth, in language" (Loria, 1995, p. 158). Such statements brand Maturana as even more radical than some of the others who fall under the radical constructivist heading (Efran & Fauber, 1995; Efran, Lukens, & Lukens, 1990; Kenny & Gardner, 1988). Central to Maturana's work is the concept of *autopoesis*—the notion that organisms are, by definition, self-creating and self-sustaining systems. Maturana calls his position *structure determinism*. It presumes that any and all changes in organisms "are determined by their structure" (Maturana & Varela, 1992, p. 96). Like von Glaserfeld, Maturana sees living systems as cognitively closed. When living systems think they are mapping an external world, they are simply experiencing and processing their own structurally determined responses. Features of the external (or internal) environment enter into the equation by "triggering" changes in a living being's structural dynamics. However, the environment never directly "instructs" the system about how to behave. Depending on differences in structure, particular organisms are uniquely sensitive or totally unresponsive to particular kinds of environmental stimulation. A closed system never comes into direct contact with reality. What is "outside" never gets "inside." Rather, the organism's existence consists of ongoing structural changes in relation to the surrounding medium in which it operates. Maturana refers to this history of accommodations as a *natural drift*. The drift is without intrinsic meaning or purpose and it lasts until a "disintegrating" event occurs—something that destroys the organism's autopoietic structure. At a more general level, no particular adaptation is "objectively" better or worse than any other. All values (and evaluations) are products of human language exchanges. It is only through such language operations that meanings arise.

Central to autopoiesis is the concept of *structural coupling*, wherein two systems (or unities) recurrently interact in such a way as to form a unity of their own called a second-order unity. This happens on the basic biological level—the structural couplings of many smaller biological unities, for example, constitute higher evolved organisms. At the social level, individuals couple to form communities that, in turn, enhance their own survival. These are referred to as *third-order couplings* (Maturana & Varela, 1992). The social phenomena we associate with such couplings often develop within a *linguistic domain*. While many living organisms can operate within linguistic domains (e.g., Maurana and Varela [1992] discuss parrots, which use their songs to sustain mating rituals), human beings are relatively unique in their ability to harness self-reflexivity to create genuine languages. Using language, human beings are able to examine their own origins and to evaluate their own formulations of knowledge. However, it is important to keep in mind that despite the enormous human accomplishments that language makes possible, "every world brought forth necessarily hides its origins" (Maturana & Varela, 1992, p. 242).

Maturana's work is of interest within constructivist psychology because it provides a framework for examining how human beings come to interact within social domains using language, creating and sustaining particular forms of knowing—what Maturana (1988) calls *explanatory domains*. Different explanatory domains legitimize different ways of validating experience. Maturana (1988) cites "games, science, religions, political doctrines, philosophical systems, and ideologies in general" (p. 33-34) as examples of explanatory domains. A person chooses to operate in different explanatory domains because "of his or her preference . . . for the basic premises that constitute the domain in which he or she operates" (Maturana, 1988, p. 33). For Maturana, the purpose in formulating autopoietic theory is not only "to understand the regularity of the world we are experiencing at every moment, but [to do so] without any point of reference independent of ourselves that would give certainty to our descriptions and cognitive assertions" (Maturana & Varela, 1992, p. 241). From Maturana's perspective, "we are continuously immersed in [a] network of interactions, the results of which depend on history" (Maturana & Varela, 1992, p. 242).

EPISTEMOLOGICAL OR HERMENEUTIC CONSTRUCTIVISM?

The epistemological constructivist label seems to more readily apply to von Glaserfeld than to Maturana. Von Glaserfeld and Maturana both see human beings as closed systems that cannot directly access external reality. This is in keeping with epistemological constructivism. However, both theorists also emphasize the role of language in sustaining social realities, implying a more hermeneutic constructivist approach. Von Glaserfeld, though, seems to root his ideas about language squarely within a paradigm that sees communication as imperfect—that is, unable to fully provide an individual with the meanings expressed by others.

> Every learner of a language must construct his or her word meanings out of elements of individual experience. . . . There is no doubt that these subjective meanings get honed, modified, and adapted . . . in the course of social interactions. But this adaptation does not and cannot change the fact that the material an individual's meanings are composed of can be taken only from that individual's own subjective experience. (von Glaserfeld, 1995a, p. 137)

This proposes an even more isolated status for knowing than Kelly (1955/1991a, 1955/1991b) envisioned. In PCP, there is at least the concept of sociality, which holds that people can form relationships by successfully construing each other's constructions. Even so, both von Glaserfeld and Kelly can readily be categorized as epistemological constructivists. Both posit an isolated knower who indirectly bumps into external reality. The resulting perturbations lead the knower to revise his or her constructs to make them more instrumentally viable. Von Glaserfeld and Kelly's similarities are highlighted further in that both of them (as well as Maturana) outline approaches in which people are considered self-organizing systems whose ability to construe the world is determined by their psychological structures (Kenny & Gardner, 1988). Despite these theoretical similarities, Kelly's followers often conceive of his theory as a form of limited realism (Noaparast, 1995; Stevens, 1998; Walker, 1992; Warren, 1998). This perhaps explains why personal construct psychologists generally seem to be more tentative about the issue of external reality than their radical constructivist counterparts, who more outspokenly repudiate realist positions. Of course, despite von Glaserfeld's (1984, 1995a) outright rejection of realism (as compared to Kelly [1955/1991a, 1955/1991b], who was often coy on this topic), Kelly and von Glaserfeld are certainly "more realist" than Maturana. They both remain committed to the idea of a reality independent of the knower, even if the knower cannot ever access it completely. It is this feature of their thinking that leads to my classifying both of them, in the final analysis, as epistemological constructivists rather than hermeneutic constructivists or limited realists.

Classifying Maturana is another matter. Maturana rejects representationalism, the idea that knowledge results from direct inputs from the external world. However, he also rejects the alternative, a kind of solipsism that ignores "the surrounding environment on the assumption that the nervous system functions completely in a vacuum, where everything is valid and everything is possible" (Maturana & Varela, 1992, p. 133-134). Nevertheless, Maturana frequently asserts, "there is no independently existing reality. We literally create the world by living in it" (Kenny & Gardner, 1988, p. 15). Maturana addresses this apparent contradiction by advocating sailing "between the Scylla monster of representationism and the Charybdis whirlpool of solipsism" (Maturana & Varela, 1992, p. 134). As a result, Maturana and Varela (1992) propose that people must distinguish two different kinds of explanation. The first kind is useful in studying the internal dynamics of a system; in such explanations, the external world is irrelevant in causing changes in the system because all such changes are determined solely by the organism's structure, not by external inputs. The second kind of explanation is useful when people function as observers in studying other living beings; in these explanations, people posit ways in which environmental and organismic changes are interrelated. In other words, for Maturana, the truths one "discovers" vary in accordance with the positioning of the observer, which is always a matter of preference. Rather than seeing people as trapped in a set of private meanings expressed through language (and thus lacking the ability to fully comprehend each other's communications), Maturana emphasizes the role of third-order couplings. Such couplings produce social unities. From this perspective, social systems are not merely collections of isolated individuals brushing up against one another but never legitimately coming into contact. Rather, social systems are emergent forms of organization created through third-order couplings. They sustain themselves because they foster the autopoiesis of their members. Social systems (i.e., communities) "bring forth" particular realities through the ways that they make and "language" distinctions. In this sense, reality is not something external. It is the result of a community's elaborate attempts to coordinate its own activities:

> 'Reality' is wheeled on stage, not as an independently existing source of validation, but as a step in an argument to try to re-establish [a] lost co-ordination. In other words, 'reality' is employed as a compelling proposition to try to make the other person 'see sense'. (Kenny & Gardner, 1988, p. 17)

Because Maturana refuses to talk about a reality independent of the observer, his theory seems best classified as a hermeneutic constructivism. Maturana's notion of "bringing forth" the world as we make distinctions typifies the hermeneutic posture.

SOCIAL CONSTRUCTIONISM: THE DISCURSIVE, CONTEXTUAL, AND SOCIALLY CONSTITUTED PERSON

Unlike personal constructivism and radical constructivism—whose origins are generally credited to Kelly, von Glaserfeld, and Maturana—no single author has been given credit for originating social constructionism. In a recent article, Hruby (2001) delineates three models of social constructionism that derive, respectively, from (1) the sociology of knowledge research, most notably Berger and Luckmann's (1966) classic book, The Social Construction of Reality; (2) postmodern and poststructuralist perspectives in social psychology, with Kenneth Gergen's (1985, 1994) work being an examplar; and (3) new realist perspectives, which hold that "there is a coherent and dependably consistent reality that is the basis for our sensations, even if our sensations do not resemble the causative phenomenal bases, or 'onta' that prompt them" (Hruby, 2001, p. 57). Most of the following discussion focuses on the second of Hruby's (2001) three models—with a particular focus on Kenneth Gergen's work, which is significantly influenced by his social psychology background.

Despite the many forms of social constructionism, virtually all those who identify themselves as social constructionists favor using the term "constructionism" rather than "constructivism." This distinction reflects the social constructionist's aversion to the notion of an isolated knower. Gergen, for example, has criticized radical constructivism as being too fully "interiorized" and, as a result, condemning human beings to imprisonment in their own, individualistic experience (Gergen, 1995b). By contrast, social constructionists emphasize the "primacy of relational, conversational, social practices as the source of individual psychic life" (Stam, 1998, p. 199). Social constructionists take issue with the traditional, Western individualism of American psychology, not to mention the rationalism of cognitive-behavioral perspectives—which some see as implied in PCP's "person as scientist" metaphor. In this context, it is interesting to note that Gergen once referred to Kelly's PCP as "perhaps the capstone theory of rationality" (Gergen, 1991, p. 40). On the other hand, whereas Kelly's theory is often applauded for its humanistic, existential, and phenomenological leanings (Butt, 1998a, 1998b; Epting & Leitner, 1992; Holland, 1970; Raskin & Epting, 1995), social constructionist approaches have been criticized for being excessively anti-humanistic (Burr, 1995; Gergen, 1995a). Further, social constructionism is relativistic in emphasizing how contextual, linguistic, and relational factors combine to determine the kinds of human beings that people will become and how their views of the world will develop. In social constructionism all knowledge is considered local and fleeting. It is negotiated between people within a given context and time frame. What constitutes personhood one day may change the next, based on shifts in social surroundings and currently accepted interpersonal boundaries.

In a social constructionist paradigm, people are not considered to have any sort of stable and essential personality (Burr, 1995; Gergen, 1991, 1994). As Burr (1995) puts it, "there is no objective evidence that you can appeal to which would demonstrate the existence of your personality" (p. 21). Personality is a socially constructed idea. Gergen (1991) and other social constructionists contend that there are as many realities as there are cultures, contexts, and ways of communicating. The same goes for selves. Social constructionists often deconstruct the very idea of coherent selfhood (Sampson, 1989). Each of us has multiple, "multiphrenic" selves, which are socially constituted within the boundaries of culture, context, and language (Gergen, 1991). Personhood becomes a matter of how people are talked about, the social practices they engage in, and the particular relationships they find themselves in. Thus, "in order to account for the things you find yourself and other people doing . . . you have to come up with the idea that people have a thing called a personality that is responsible for this behaviour" (Burr, 1995, p. 21). Rather than emphasizing enduring qualities of each person from which human action springs forth—something akin to Carl Rogers' (1959, 1961) innate self—social constructionists speak of "identity." The ways in which someone is identified, talked about, and treated all contribute to creating a particular identity for the individual. Because a person is likely to be identified, talked about, and engaged by others in a variety of specific contexts, the person may actually come to live out different identities in each of those settings (Gergen, 1991). In their focus on constructed identities over essential selves, social constructionists categorically reject the very notion of an inherent human nature existing across persons. Each of us has a multitude of identities that are negotiated and defined within specific interpersonal relationships and cultural contexts. Human identity is fluid and constituted within the parameters set forward by social surroundings (Gergen, 1991, 1994).

The role of language is critical in social constructionism. How people talk about themselves and their world determines the nature of their experiences. For example, because Americans live in a society that employs the language of agency and selfhood, freedom and independence become experientially real for Americans (Gergen, 1991). Of course, there are many different ways of talking about the world within any society's many subcultures. Because some ways of constructing reality through language become dominant over others, social constructionists are interested in the origins of power relations. How do some accounts become dominant while others are ignored or suppressed? In other words, why do some accounts *warrant voice* (i.e., get listened to and valued widely) while others do not (Burr, 1995; Gergen, 1989)? In examining this question, social constructionists draw extensively from Michel Foucault's writings on power relations (Rabinow, 1984). They have also been interested in the performative aspects of language. That is, people use words and symbols not just descriptively, but persuasively to accomplish goals (Burr, 1995). As a minor example, when I tell my spouse that I am tired, I am not simply describing my biological state. I am encouraging her to turn out the lights!

As I have mentioned, social constructionists argue that reality is socially negotiated. This is in contrast to the more isolated forms of personal knowing that characterize Kelly's and von Glaserfeld's theories. Further, social constructionism's reluctance to privilege knowledge developed in one context over knowledge developed in another make it a more relativistic approach than either personal or radical constructivism, which at least pay lip service to the idea that some constructions are better than others. Psychology as a whole has generally shown a lukewarm reception to social constructionism, perhaps because in many ways it directly challenges some of the discipline's most cherished assumptions. Through most of psychology's history, psychologists have focused on the individual. They have often ignored or minimized contextual and cultural factors. Psychology's laboratory studies have generally been designed to "control for" and eliminate "extraneous variables" —the very contextual factors that most interest social constructionists (Burr, 1995)! Social constructionism is about relationships. The focus is on what social constructionist John Shotter once called *joint action* (Shotter, 1993)—the cooperative development and implementation of shared functional meanings that arise when two or more people interact.

SOCIAL CONSTRUCTIONISM AS HERMENEUTIC CONSTRUCTIVISM

With the possible exception of the new realism that Hruby (2001) describes, social constructionism seems a clear example of Chiari and Nuzzo's (1996b) hermeneutic constructivism. Its emphasis on reality as constituted in language exemplifies the hermeneutic viewpoint. Reality, in social constructionism, is usually viewed as dependent on how groups of people collectively elaborate their ideas. Thus, there are an infinite variety of socially constructed realities. In this context, Gergen (1991, 1994) has repeatedly pointed to the possibilities and complications of the current age, with its abundance of ultra-sophisticated communication technologies. Due to computers, cell phones, and other emerging forms of high tech communication, people can participate in a multitude of social contexts virtually simultaneously. As the number of contexts in which people participate expands exponentially, they often notice the contextually bound nature of truths that previously seemed enduring and universal. Gergen (1991) uses the terms *saturated self* and *multiphrenia* to describe the psychological experience of enacting so many different, socially constituted selves in such a short span of time. In premodern and modern times people interacted in precious few contexts. With few alternative intelligibilities to challenge the truth of these contexts, their socially constructed aspects remained masked. By contrast, in the postmodern psychological world people mix and match realities and identities in an increasingly complex array of circumstances. This expands possibilities, but makes judging one context's knowledge as superior to others a less than clear-cut endeavor.

The confusion this produces perhaps explains why many people criticize social constructionism for encouraging anything-goes relativism (Gillett, 1998; Held, 1995; Matthews, 1998; Parker, 1999). Critics suggest that without a single, stable reality on which to rely, people tend to feel lost and ungrounded. Interestingly, several social constructionists have argued the reverse position—that this inherent relativism is one of the strongest assets of the postmodern perspective, generating a less dogmatic and righteous society that is more open and flexible (Edwards, Ashmore, & Potter, 1995; Gergen, 1994; Raskin, 2001). Gergen (1994) has been especially vocal in defending the relativism of social constructionism, contending that it moves people toward interpersonal collaboration and the beneficial reexamination of sometimes stifling cultural practices.

CONSTRUCTIVIST INTEGRATION: PROBLEMS AND PROSPECTS

There is a great deal of room for cross-fertilization among the various constructivist psychologies. For example, I previously discussed how social constructionists prefer the term "constructionist" to signal their rejection of individualist and rationalist accounts, which they see as isolating and solipsistic. Yet Maturana's concept of third order coupling seems to echo, in many ways, social constructionism's effort to shift psychology's emphasis from decontextualized selves to socially constructed identities. From both perspectives, the social unit can be targeted for study. Although it is beyond this manuscript's purview to detail all the potential linkages among types of constructivism, these perspectives do not seem as incommensurate as their devotees sometimes imply. Connections among constructivist approaches warrant further exploration. After all, even when they disagree about specifics, all varieties of constructivism challenge psychologists to refocus their attentions on the critical importance of the human meaning making process.

REFERENCES

Berger, P. L., & Luckmann, T. (1966). *The social construction of reality: A treatise in the sociology of knowledge*. Garden City, NY: Doubleday.

Botella, L. (1995). Personal construct theory, constructivism, and postmodern thought. In R. A. Neimeyer & G. J. Neimeyer (Eds.), *Advances in personal construct psychology* (Vol. 3, pp. 3-35). Greenwich, CT: JAI Press.

Burr, V. (1995). *An introduction to social constructionism*. London: Routledge.

Burr, V., Butt, T., & Epting, F. (1997). Core construing: Self discovery or self invention? In G. J. Neimeyer & R. A. Neimeyer (Eds.), *Advances in personal construct psychology* (Vol. 4, pp. 39-62). Greenwich, CT: JAI Press.

Butt, T. (1998a). Sedimentation and elaborative choice. *Journal of Constructivist Psychology, 11*, 265-281.

Butt, T. (1998b). Sociality, role, and embodiment. *Journal of Constructivist Psychology, 11*, 105-116.

Butt, T. (2000). Pragmatism, constructivism, and ethics. *Journal of Constructivist Psychology, 13*, 85-101.

Chiari, G., & Nuzzo, M. L. (1996a). Personal construct theory within psychological constructivism: Precursor or Avant-garde? In B. M. Walker & J. Costigan & L. L. Viney & B. Warren (Eds.), *Personal construct theory: A psychology for the future* (pp. 25-54). Melbourne: Australian Psychological Society Imprint Series.

Chiari, G., & Nuzzo, M. L. (1996b). Psychological constructivisms: A metatheoretical differentiation. *Journal of Constructivist Psychology, 9*, 163-184.

DeRubeis, R. J., & Beck, A. T. (1988). Cognitive therapy. In K. S. Dobson (Ed.), *Handbook of cognitive-behavioral therapies* (pp. 273-306). New York: Guilford.

Dryden, W., & Ellis, A. (1988). Rational-emotive therapy. In K. S. Dobson (Ed.), *Handbook of cognitive-behavioral therapies* (pp. 214-272). New York: Guilford.

Edwards, D., Ashmore, M., & Potter, J. (1995). Death and furniture: The rhetoric, politics and theology of bottom line arguments against relativism. *History of the Human Sciences, 8*, 25-49.

Efran, J. S., & Fauber, R. L. (1995). Radical constructivism: Questions and answers. In R. A. Neimeyer & M. J. Mahoney (Eds.), *Constructivism in psychotherapy* (pp. 275-304). Washington, DC: American Psychological Association.

Efran, J. S., Lukens, M. D., & Lukens, R. J. (1990). *Language, structure, and change: Frameworks of meaning in psychotherapy*. New York: Norton.

Ellis, A. (1997). Postmodern ethics for active-directive counseling and psychotherapy. *Journal of Mental Health Counseling, 19*, 211-225.

Ellis, A. (1998). How rational emotive behavior therapy belongs in the constructivist camp. In M. F. Hoyt (Ed.), *The handbook of constructive therapies: Innovative approaches from leading practitioners* (pp. 83-99). San Francisco: Jossey-Bass.

Epting, F. R. (1984). *Personal construct counseling and psychotherapy.* New York: John Wiley.

Epting, F. R., & Amerikaner, M. (1980). Optimal functioning: A personal construct approach. In A. W. Landfield & L. M. Leitner (Eds.), *Personal construct psychology: Psychotherapy and personality* (pp. 55-73). New York: Wiley-Interscience.

Epting, F. R., & Leitner, L. M. (1992). Humanistic psychology and personal construct theory. *Humanistic Psychologist, 20,* 243-259.

Fransella, F. (1995). *George Kelly.* London: Sage.

Gergen, K. J. (1985). The social constructionist movement in modern psychology. *American Psychologist, 40,* 266-275.

Gergen, K. J. (1989). Warranting voice and the elaboration of the self. In J. Shotter & K. J. Gergen (Eds.), *Texts of identity* (pp. 70-81). London: Sage.

Gergen, K. J. (1991). *The saturated self: Dilemmas of identity in contemporary life.* New York: Basic Books.

Gergen, K. J. (1994). *Realities and relationships.* Cambridge, MA: Harvard University Press.

Gergen, K. J. (1995a). Postmodernism as a humanism. *Humanistic Psychologist, 23,* 71-82.

Gergen, K. J. (1995b). Social construction and the education process. In L. P. Steffe & J. Gale (Eds.), *Constructivism in education* (pp. 17-39). Hillsdale, NJ: Lawrence Erlbaum.

Gillett, E. (1998). Relativism and the social constructivist paradigm. *Philosophy, Psychiatry, and Psychology, 5,* 37-48.

Held, B. S. (1995). *Back to reality: A critique of postmodern theory in psychotherapy.* New York: Norton.

Holland, R. (1970). George Kelly: Constructive innocent and reluctant existentialist. In D. Bannister (Ed.), *Perspectives in personal construct theory* (pp. 111-132). London: Academic Press.

Howard, G. S. (1997, July). *Constructive realism.* Paper presented at the Twelfth International Congress on Personal Construct Psychology, Seattle.

Hruby, G. G. (2001). Sociological, postmodern, and new realism perspectives in social constructionism: Implications for literacy research. *Reading Research Quarterly, 36*(1), 48-62.

Johnson, T. J., Pfenninger, D. T., & Klion, R. E. (2000). Constructing and deconstructing transitive diagnosis. In R. A. Neimeyer & J. D. Raskin (Eds.), *Constructions of disorder: Meaning-making frameworks for psychotherapy* (pp. 145-174). Washington, DC: American Psychological Association.

Kelly, G. A. (1970). A brief introduction to personal construct psychology. In D. Bannister (Ed.), *Perspectives in personal construct psychology* (pp. 1-30). San Diego: Academic Press.

Kelly, G. A. (1991a). *The psychology of personal constructs: Vol. 1. A theory of personality.* London: Routledge. (Original work published 1955)

Kelly, G. A. (1991b). *The psychology of personal constructs: Vol. 2. Clinical diagnosis and psychotherapy.* London: Routledge. (Original work published 1955)

Kenny, V., & Gardner, G. (1988). Constructions of self-organizing systems. *The Irish Journal of Psychology, 9,* 1-24.

Landfield, A. W. (1980). The person as perspectivist, literalist, and chaotic fragmentalist. In A. W. Landfield & L. M. Leitner (Eds.), *Personal construct psychology: Psychotherapy and personality* (pp. 3-17). New York: Wiley.

Loria, B. R. (1995). Structure determinism and script analysis: A bringing forth of alternative realities. *Transactional Analysis Journal, 25,* 156-168.

Lyddon, W. J. (1995). Forms and facets of constructivist psychology. In R. A. Neimeyer & M. J. Mahoney (Eds.), *Constructivism in psychotherapy* (pp. 69-92). Washington, DC: American Psychological Association.

Maher, B. (1969). Introduction. George Kelly: A brief biography. In B. Maher (Ed.), *Clinical psychology and personality: The selected papers of George Kelly* (pp. 1-3). New York: Wiley.

Mahoney, M. J. (1988). Constructive metatheory: I. Basic features and historical foundations. *International Journal of Personal Construct Psychology, 1,* 1-35.

Mahoney, M. J. (1991). *Human change processes.* New York: Basic Books.

Mahoney, M. J. (1995). Continuing evolution of the cognitive sciences and psychotherapies. In R. A. Neimeyer & M. J. Mahoney (Eds.), *Constructivism in psychotherapy* (pp. 39-67). Washington, DC: American Psychological Association.

Matthews, W. J. (1998). Let's get real: The fallacy of post-modernism. *Journal of Theoretical and Philosophical Psychology, 18,* 16-32.

Maturana, H. R. (1988). Reality: The search for objectivity or the quest for a compelling argument. *The Irish Journal of Psychology, 9,* 25-82.

Maturana, H. R., & Varela, F. J. (1992). *The tree of knowledge: The biological roots of human understanding* (Rev. ed., R. Paolucci, Trans.). Boston: Shambhala.

Neimeyer, R. A. (1995). An invitation to constructivist psychotherapies. In R. A. Neimeyer & M. J. Mahoney (Eds.), *Constructivism in psychotherapy* (pp. 1-8). Washington, DC: American Psychological Association.

Neimeyer, R. A. (Ed.). (2001). *Meaning reconstruction and the experience of loss.* Washington, DC: American Psychological Association.

Neimeyer, R. A., & Mahoney, M. J. (Eds.). (1995). *Constructivism in psychotherapy.* Washington, DC: American Psychological Association.

Neimeyer, R. A., & Raskin, J. D. (Eds.). (2000). *Constructions of disorder: Meaning-making frameworks for psychotherapy.* Washington, DC: American Psychological Association.

Neimeyer, R. A., & Raskin, J. D. (2001). Varieties of constructivism in psychotherapy. In K. S. Dobson (Ed.), *Handbook of cognitive-behavioral therapies* (2nd ed., pp. 393-430). New York: Guilford.

Noaparast, K. B. (1995). Toward a more realistic constructivism. In R. A. Neimeyer & G. J. Neimeyer (Eds.), *Advances in personal construct theory* (Vol. 3, pp. 37-59). Greenwich, CT: JAI Press.

Parker, I. (1999). Against relativism in psychology, on balance. *History of the Human Sciences, 12,* 61-78.

Rabinow, P. (Ed.) (1984). *The Foucault reader.* New York: Pantheon.

Raskin, J. D. (2001). On relativism in constructivist psychology. *Journal of Constructivist Psychology, 14,* 285-313.

Raskin, J. D., & Epting, F. R. (1993). Personal construct theory and the argument against mental illness. *International Journal of Personal Construct Psychology, 6,* 351-369.

Raskin, J. D., & Epting, F. R. (1995). Constructivism and psychotherapeutic method: Transitive diagnosis as humanistic assessment [Annual Edition]. *Methods: A Journal for Human Science,* 3-27.

Raskin, J. D., & Lewandowski, A. M. (2000). The construction of disorder as human enterprise. In R. A. Neimeyer & J. D. Raskin (Eds.), *Constructions of disorder: Meaning-making frameworks for psychotherapy* (pp. 15-40). Washington, DC: American Psychological Association.

Rogers, C. R. (1959). A theory of therapy, personality, and interpersonal relationships, as developed in the client-centered framework. In S. Koch (Ed.), *Psychology: A study of science: Vol. 3. Formulations of the person and the social contact* (pp. 184-256). New York: McGraw-Hill.

Rogers, C. R. (1961). *On becoming a person.* Boston: Houghton Mifflin.

Rosen, H. (1996). Meaning-making narratives: Foundations for constructivist and social constructionist psychotherapies. In H. Rosen & K. T. Kuehlwein (Eds.), *Constructing realities: Meaning-making perspectives for psychotherapists* (pp. 3-51). San Francisco: Jossey-Bass.

Sampson, E. E. (1989). The deconstruction of the self. In J. Shotter & K. J. Gergen (Eds.), *Texts of identity* (pp. 1-19). London: Sage.

Sexton, T. L. (1997). Constructivist thinking within the history of ideas: The challenge of a new paradigm. In T. L. Sexton & B. L. Griffin (Eds.), *Constructivist thinking in counseling practice, research, and training* (pp. 3-18). New York: Teachers College Press.

Shotter, J. (1993). *Cultural politics of everyday life: Social constructionism, rhetoric and knowing of the third kind.* Toronto: University of Toronto Press.

Stam, H. J. (1998). Personal-construct theory and social constructionism: Difference and dialogue. *Journal of Constructivist Psychology, 11,* 187-203.

Stevens, C. D. (1998). Realism and Kelly's pragmatic constructivism. *Journal of Constructivist Psychology, 11,* 283-308.

Varela, F. J. (1984). The creative circle: Sketches on the natural history of circular-ity. In P. Watzlawick (Ed.), *The invented reality: How do we know what we believe we know? Contributions to constructivism* (pp. 309-323). New York: Norton.

von Glaserfeld, E. (1984). An introduction to radical constructivism. In P. Watzlawick (Ed.), *The invented reality: How do we know what we believe we know? Contributions to constructivism* (pp. 17-40). New York: Norton.

von Glaserfeld, E. (1995a). *Radical constructivism: A way of knowing and learning.* London: The Falmer Press.

von Glaserfeld, E. (1995b). A constructivist approach to teaching. In L. P. Steffe & J. Gale (Eds.), *Constructivism in education* (pp. 3-15). Hillsdale, NJ: Lawrence Erlbaum.

Walker, B. M. (1992). Values and Kelly's theory: Becoming a good scientist. *International Journal of Personal Construct Psychology, 5,* 259-269.

Warren, B. (1992). Subjecting and objecting in personal construct psychology. In A. Thomson & P. Cummins (Eds.), *European perspectives in personal construct psy-chology* (pp. 57-66). Lincoln, NE: European Personal Construct Association.

Warren, B. (1998). *Philosophical dimensions of personal construct psychology.* London: Routledge.

CHAPTER 2

Constructions of Abuse: Understanding the Effects of Childhood Sexual Abuse

Christopher R. Erbes and Stephanie Lewis Harter

This chapter discusses the implications of personal construct psychology for research and treatment with sexual abuse survivors. Constructivist theory provides a heuristic frame for understanding sexually abusive experiences, including meaning making efforts of survivors of the abuse and of researchers and therapists working with those survivors. Child sexual abuse (CSA) represents a potentially traumatic experience that violates personal constructions of self and others and culturally shared assumptions. CSA occurs within social ecologies, including the family environment and larger sociopolitical systems. These systems provide contexts for personal constructions that may, in turn, participate in the evolving ecology of meanings. Historically, voices of sexual abuse survivors have been relatively silenced within this larger discourse.

The application of personal construct psychology to the study and treatment of CSA requires a reconceptualization of the stance of the therapist and researcher that reaches beyond the use of categorical labels and corresponding cookie-cutter approaches to treatment. Harter and Neimeyer (1995) described the long-term effects and treatment of CSA from a developmental, systemic, constructivist framework, reviewing research programs that have consistently implicated the importance of personal constructions for current psychological functioning, social relationships, and therapeutic outcomes for adult survivors of CSA. The present chapter extends that work. It includes discussion of the political and professional systems within which we confront CSA, as healers, researchers, and survivors; relevance of constructivist theory for understanding personal constructions of abusive experiences and the social contexts within which abuse occurs; and empirical research validating and extending constructivist models. The chapter concludes with a discussion of meaning making efforts of adult survivors within social and cultural contexts, including implications for therapeutic relationships and further constructivist research.

PROFESSIONAL CONSTRUCTIONS OF ABUSE AND POLITICAL CONTEXTS

The study of CSA within the social sciences has led a cyclical course, with periods of intensive interest followed by deliberate ignorance (Herman, 1992). When confronted with events and experiences that shatter our shared myths regarding childhood, family, and gender, professional colleagues and society have historically opposed researchers who struggled to understand the prevalence and implications of CSA. Political forces in the past two decades have both encouraged and opposed such research (Herman, 1981). During that time, there has been an enormous increase in the amount of research and clinical attention devoted to CSA and to its immediate and long-term implications for survivors. This expansion of knowledge and attention has not been without response, however. Both researchers and therapists working with sexually abused populations have been sued and otherwise attacked as a result of advocacy by an organization purporting to defend parents falsely accused of abuse. Some prominent psychologists have joined efforts to control the activities of therapists and researchers striving to meet the needs of abuse survivors (Pope & Brown, 1996).

In this heated climate, researchers have nonetheless consistently documented that sexual abuse of children is all-too prevalent and that survivors of abuse are at increased risk for a wide range of negative long-term effects. Studies have shown that sexual abuse is surprisingly common, affecting approximately 20-40% of women and 10-20% of men (Finkelhor, Hotaling, Lewis, & Smith, 1990; Peters, Wyatt, & Finkelhor, 1986; Russell, 1984). Long term correlates of CSA include, but are not limited to, depression, anxiety, eating disorders (particularly bulimia nervosa), substance abuse, dissociation, interpersonal and personality difficulties, self-injurious behaviors (including suicidality), and revictimization (for reviews see Beitchman et al., 1992; Briere, 1992; Briere & Runtz, 1993; Browne & Finkelhor, 1986; Finkelhor, 1990; Jumper, 1995; Polusny & Follette, 1995; Rind & Tromovitch, 1997). However, these group comparisons mask considerable heterogeneity in individual outcome. Responses to abuse vary from survivor to survivor and some survivors function at levels comparable to those with no history of CSA.

28

Traditional nosology has been of limited benefit in understanding the sequelae of childhood sexual abuse (Harter, 1995; Harter & Neimeyer, 1995; Harter, 2000). The *Diagnostic and Statistical Manual of Mental Disorders* (DSM-IV; American Psychiatric Association, 1994) defines psychological syndromes by symptom presentation, with a focus on current and observable symptoms. Such diagnosis by observer focuses on external behaviors that are present in a given period of time, and thus decontextualizes symptomatic behavior from lifespan development and personal meaning. From a nosological perspective, sexual abuse may be described as a nonspecific stressor, given that survivors are at risk for increased distress across the range of DSM-defined pathologies. In listening to survivors' accounts of abusive experiences, we have not found such experiences to be described as nonspecifically stressful. Rather, both the experiences and each person's responses to them are intensely particular and personal, often leaving survivors with a sense of such anomaly as to be irrevocably alien from others.

Recently, traits such as "hardiness," "resilience," and "problem-focused" coping have been explored to explain individual variation in response to childhood abuse along a continuum from pathology to health (e.g., Binder, McNeil, & Goldstone, 1996; Dilillo, Long, & Russell, 1994; Himelien & McElrath, 1996; Lam & Grossman, 1997; Leitenberg, Greenwald, & Cado, 1992). Although more dimensional than DSM categorizations, reification of such equally nomothetic constructs may create a complementary nosology of wellness analogous to the DSM system of pathology. Both approaches risk imposing culturally laden, often circular, professional constructions that lack relevance to persons struggling to make meaning of their experiences.

Researchers are beginning to make progress in understanding the tremendous variation in the type and severity of difficulties experienced by abuse survivors. Abuse-related factors, such as intrusiveness of the abuse, use of force, and paternal perpetrators have been consistently linked to more negative outcomes (Beitchman et al., 1992; Browne & Finkelhor, 1986). Functioning of the family of origin has also been consistently linked to outcomes of abuse, both when the abuse occurred within and outside the family (Alexander & Lupfer, 1987; Harter & Vanecek, 2000). However, research has also suggested that the personal constructions of abuse survivors may be more closely linked to long term functioning than external characteristics of the abuse or the context within which it occurred (Harter,

Alexander, & Neimeyer, 1988; Harter & Neimeyer, 1995). The idiographic, developmental analyses that are the hallmark of constructivist approaches seem particularly suited for continued exploration of the heterogeneous outcomes of abuse.

CONSTRUCTIVIST THEORY AND CHILDHOOD SEXUAL ABUSE

Kelly (1955) reached beyond nosological and deterministic explanations of his day, to propose that behavior is channeled by anticipatory personal attempts to make meaning of experience.

> The human personality, being a course of events that keeps flowing along, is not well adapted to receptacles. Only after one is dead is it possible to make a relatively static classification of his personality. Even then the unfolding of subsequent events may throw his life role into a new historical perspective and change many of the meanings previously assigned to it. (p. 453)

Kelly (1955) described persons as essentially in process, abstracting similarities and differences from the flow of events that allow them to anticipate and control their experiences. The person is embedded within a physical and social ecology that both affords infinite constructions of experience and constrains viable constructions. When constructions are not useful in anticipating experience, this invalidation leads to revision of the constructions. Constructions available to people are also constrained by their prior construing of events. Thus, people are both free to construct a world of experience and constrained by that construing. The meaning making system that evolves through successive construing of events both provides and limits alternatives for future behavior.

CONSTRUING ABUSE WITHIN A SOCIAL CONTEXT

Social relationships, particularly early relationships with caregivers, provide an important ecology within which we develop our systems for construing ourselves and the world. Constructions of early relationships become core to subsequent construing of the self and others. Although such core constructions may also evolve in light of ongoing experience, their implications to all subsequent constructions make them relatively resistant to change (Harter & Neimeyer, 1995). These core constructions, in turn, provide the means to meaningfully relate to others throughout the lifespan.

Central to our ability to relate to others is sociality, described by Kelly (1955) as the ability to anticipate another's constructions.

These anticipations of others' behaviors are built on past relational experiences. They require us to abstract similarities and differences between current and past relationships and between our own constructions and the presumed constructions of others. Commonality of constructions refers to similarities in the manner in which events are construed, rather than the events themselves. Although each person's system of meaning is unique, common themes can be extracted across construct systems, particularly for persons with similar histories of experience. However, the necessity to construe a stream of events quite anomalous from those experienced by others may create divergent axes of meaning, divergent constructions of subsequent events, and constructions of self as markedly different from others. The resulting lack of commonality in construing may make it more difficult for the survivor to anticipate and understand others' behaviors, particularly in nonabusive relations, and also render the survivor's behavior unpredictable and incomprehensible to others (Harter et al., 1988; Harter & Neimeyer, 1995).

Abusive family environments are difficult contexts in which to progressively evolve constructions of self and others that will be viable outside the family. Constructivist and family research supports prior clinical descriptions of incestuous families and suggests that similar family environments may also increase risk for abuse outside the family (Draucker, 1996; Harter & Neimeyer, 1995; Nash, Hulsey, Sexton, Harralson, & Lambert, 1993). Behavior within the family may be quite divergent from surrounding social mores and also from the family's own verbalized moral constructs. In addition to violation of sexual taboos, the family environment may be rigidly organized, authoritarian, and conflictual. Sexual abuse often co-occurs with other physical and emotional abuse. In a reversal of assumed social roles, both within the society at large and as verbalized within the family, children are used to meeting parents' needs, emotionally and sexually (Gelinas, 1983). The abuse and related family environment may be maintained by isolating family members, particularly the abused child, from those outside the family. Enforced secrecy regarding the violation of sexual taboos and other social expectations for family relationships may limit opportunities to verbalize or otherwise explore these contradictions. There may be little nonsexual affection, empathy, or communication, so that intimacy becomes equated with sexual intrusion and parental nurture becomes equated with use of force to control (Harter et al., 1988; Harter & Neimeyer, 1995; Harter & Vanecek, 2000; Herman, 1981; Meiselman, 1978).

In families such as this, the child's emotional response to the environment and to abusive events may be repeatedly invalidated, as family members impose their own constructions of abusive experiences, rejecting and punishing any contradictory expression. Thus, the child may have difficulty learning to verbalize constructions of abusive events, including emotional and physiological responses to those experiences. Emotional responses may continue to be construed at a preverbal level and emerging self-constructions may be influenced by physiological distress as well as derogatory constructions offered by family members (Harter et al., 1988; Harter & Neimeyer, 1995; Harter & Vanecek, 2000).

Whether abuse occurs within or outside the family, the family's ability to foster the child's meaning making process influences the impact of abuse on subsequent construing. If the family cannot tolerate the child's response to the abuse, it may not only invalidate specific constructions of experience, but the child as a construing person. Thus, the child becomes even more vulnerable to meanings offered within the family or similar relationships, which may deny, minimize, or blame the child for the abuse. The child anticipates that efforts to construe some alternative meaning from the abuse will be painful and unsuccessful. While this construction may be repeatedly validated within an abusive family, it also limits efforts to reconstrue the abuse, relationships, and the self outside abusive contexts.

CONSTRUING THE TRAUMATIC EVENT
OF CHILD SEXUAL ABUSE

Traumatic aspects of sexually abusive experiences also have a continuing impact on evolving constructions of self and the world. DSM-IV defines traumatic experiences as those that threaten our life or physical integrity and includes sexual experiences for which a child is developmentally unprepared within this definition (American Psychiatric Association, 1994). Personal construct researchers focus on the personal meaning of events, rather than independent characteristics of the events, defining trauma as an experience that invalidates or disrupts the basic processes or assumptions through which we participate in life (Harter & Neimeyer, 1995).

The severity and circumstances of sexual abuse vary tremendously; however, sexual abuse can be violent, horrifying, and—by definition—invasive (Finkelhor, 1987). Researchers and clinicians have speculated that the impact of traumatic events occurs through the failure of a person's meaning-making system to integrate or construe the event (Horowitz, 1986; Sewell, 1997). Janoff-Bulman (1992), for example, suggested that traumatic events contradict our basic assumptions about the world, the self, and others to the point that these assumptions are "shattered." It is the lack of these basic assumptions, according to her model, that leads to the commonly observed difficulties of trauma survivors. Horowitz (1986) suggested that traumatic events cannot be assimilated into existing schema and that this results in the traumatic material being maintained separate from the rest of a person's cognitive (meaning-making) system. Because the traumatic events are not integrated into the larger construct system, they are cyclically intrusively re-experienced or avoided to the point of partial amnesia. Briere (1996) has suggested that intrusive recollections in sexual abuse survivors represent attempts to desensitize themselves to the traumatic material, reducing the overwhelming affect associated with the experience so that it can be incorporated into their meaning systems.

All of these perspectives share a common focus on meaning making. They discuss the meaning attached to a traumatic memory and the ways in which that meaning does or does not fit into existing construct systems. Thus, it can be seen that the traumatic nature of CSA has an impact in at least two central ways. First, the experience of trauma can alter an individual's overall construct system so that negative, anomalous, or threatening meanings are attached to events throughout the survivor's life. This is the shattering of assumptions discussed by Janoff-Bulman (1992). As an individual attempts to incorporate knowledge of abuse experiences, it is difficult to construe a worthy self, benevolent universe, or just world. Although constructions of the world as negative and threatening may be realistic constructions of the survivor's childhood experience, they may help to maintain a defensive stance toward new experience that isolates the survivor from potentially nonabusive relationships. Self-blame or constructions of the self as unworthy may actually buffer constructions of the world as threatening and uncontrollable. Unfortunately, they may also contribute to continued distress and reduce opportunities for more elaborative self-construction. As reviewed in a subsequent section, research from constructivist traditions has confirmed differences in both content and structure of construing in sexual abuse survivors.

The second important aspect of the constructions of CSA involves the difficulty in trying to construe traumatic events. Because traumatic events lie outside the range of convenience of individual and, indeed, societal construct systems, it is difficult to make meaning of them at all. According to Kelly (1955), no experience can exist as an experience if it is not, on some level, construed. Because traumatic events do lie so far outside the range of convenience of construct systems, however, they are likely to be poorly elaborated and may be constructed on very basic, nonverbal, preconscious, physiological levels. In work with survivors of combat and of violent civilian trauma Sewell, Cromwell, and their colleagues have shown that survivors of traumatic events who suffer from post-traumatic symptoms are more likely to have poorly elaborated constructions of these events (Sewell, 1996, 1997; Sewell et al., 1996). Inability to elaborate constructions of abusive experiences that can be integrated with evolving constructions of self and the world may result in fragmented self constructions. Our recent work suggests that sexual abuse survivors may have highly differentiated but poorly integrated self constructions (Erbes & Harter, 1999; Erbes, 2000).

THE DIALECTIC OF TRAUMA AND FAMILY ENVIRONMENT
There has been some debate among researchers regarding whether the effects of abuse manifest because of the traumatic nature of the event itself, or because of the family environment in which the abuse occurs (Boney-McCoy & Finkelhor, 1996, 1998; Nash et al., 1993; Nash, Neimeyer, Hulsey, & Lambert, 1998). Some contend that family contexts that allow or foster sexual abuse of children are dysfunctional to the point of leading to the effects found in survivors. Others contend that sexual abuse, like rape in an adult, is a traumatic experience that leads to the development of post-traumatic symptoms. It would seem that a dialectic has been formed, with one side involving the impact of discreet events of abuse and the other encompassing the broad familial and social environment in which survivors develop. One advantage of a constructivist approach to this area of study is that it can accommodate, indeed seems to pull for, a synthesis of these two positions.
There is no reason to assume that abuse survivors have difficulties only because of either their family environments or only because of specific abuse events. The development of abuse survivors is assumed to emerge from aspects of both the family and the potentially traumatic nature of the abuse. The studies reviewed below, and research from other labs, have shown consistently that the effects of abuse are related to characteristics of both family environments and the abuse itself (e.g., Alexander, 1993; Harter & Vanecek, 2000; Nash

et al., 1993). Because the impact of abuse will depend on how that event is construed, and because family environments play a key role in the development of construct systems, it is clear that both of these aspects of a survivor's history will play pivotal roles in development and later functioning (Harter et al., 1988; Harter & Neimeyer, 1995; Harter & Vanecek, 2000). This is a true synthesis, then, in that social context and the trauma of abuse do not make simple additive contributions to later difficulties. Instead they interact in complex, recursive ways so that social context influences how abuse is construed and abuse, simultaneously, influences how the social context is constructed. It is worth noting that the term "constructed," in this sense, refers both to the process of experiential construction and to the process of influencing familial and other interpersonal relationships. As the process of construing abusive events changes a child's construct system, her or his interactions with others will be altered as well.

CONSTRUCTIVIST RESEARCH AND CHILD SEXUAL ABUSE

Personal construct psychology has made extensive contributions to elaborating models of traumatization and recovery following an abusive experience and towards empirical refinement of those models (Harter, 1995; Harter & Neimeyer, 1995). This research has consistently documented that long term functioning of sexual abuse survivors is closely linked to constructions of the self and of important others (Erbes & Harter, 1999; Harter, 2000). Kelly's (1955) Repertory Grid methodology has been useful in investigating the dimensions that survivors use in organizing their social world, in contrast to limiting investigation to dimensions provided by the researcher (Harter, 2000; Harter, Erbes, & Hart, 1999). More recently personal construct efforts are extending towards more elaboratively narrative methodologies, such as accounts of abusive or other traumatic experiences and self-characterization sketches (Erbes, 2000; Rigsby, Harter, & Wagner, 2000).

To summarize some of the findings from this methodologically diverse research area, personal construct and cognitive constructivist researchers have confirmed that survivors of both sexual and other types of abuse are likely to perceive themselves as distant from both their ideal selves and from other people. Negative and extreme perceptions of the self appear particularly related to long term distress and social maladjustment (Harter et al., 1988; Fisher et al., 1997). However, rather than more negative self-statements producing distress, preverbal constructions experienced as symptom distress may be primary to more explicitly verbalized constructions of the self (Harter, 2000; Harter & Vanecek, 2000). Survivors are vulnerable to perceiving their selves and their bodies as fundamentally damaged and inadequate (Nash et al., 1993). Perceived stigmatization and self-blame accompany continued long-term negative effects (Coffey, Leitenberg, Henning, Turner, & Bennett, 1996; Hazzard, 1993; McMillen & Zuravin, 1997; Wyatt & Newcomb, 1990). In contrast, survivors who perceive that they have grown stronger or wiser as a result of abusive experience are less distressed (McMillen, Zuravin, & Rideout, 1995). Constructions of the self as different from important attachment figures, such as the parents, also appear closely related to continued distress and social maladjustment (Harter, 2000).

A controlled outcome study has also documented the helpfulness of a constructivist approach to treating this population (Alexander, Neimeyer, Follette, Moore, & Harter, 1989). In group therapy treatment, perceptions of the self as different from other members and therapists are related to more negative outcome. Early in treatment, differentiated positive perceptions and a sense of commonality with other group members appear particularly important. In the later stages of treatment positive differentiated perceptions of and identification with group therapists becomes more important than perceptions of other group members (Neimeyer, Harter, & Alexander, 1991).

Research also supports the role of family environment as a context for evolving constructions of abuse survivors. Harter and Vanecek (2000) found family environment to be more closely related to assumptions about others and the world, whereas reports of abuse itself are more directly related to symptom distress, possibly through traumatic processes discussed previously. Both family environment and abuse are related to self-assumptions, possibly, in part, through influencing assumptions about others and symptom distress, respectively. Thus, constructions of self are built in the context of construing others and are also influenced by internal distress and personally traumatic events.

Together, these findings suggest that adults with a history of sexual abuse are prone to negative valence and extremity in construing, particularly construing of the self, and to perceiving themselves as lacking commonality with others. Opportunities to share with others in an affirming atmosphere, fostering an increasing sense of commonality, may be an important element in treatment. It may also be important for the therapist to identify the emerging wisdom in the survivors' life struggles, rather than focusing exclusively on the deleterious effects of abuse.

Emerging research also suggests that experiences of abuse may alter the types of constructs used by survivors to organize their social worlds. When constructs are elicited with the Repertory Grid, sexual abuse survivors offer fewer constructs related to emotional arousal and more concrete, factual descriptions that those with no abuse history (Harter et al., 1999). In self-characterization sketches, sexual abuse survivors also generally use fewer constructs expressing affect, particular anxiety or fear, than those without a history of abuse. However, those who have experienced the most intrusive abuse, at the hands of family members, express increased affect in their self-characterizations, including increased anxiety or fear, sadness or depression, and optimism or energy (Erbes, 2000).

While traditional clinical descriptions of abuse survivors have included developmentally immature and global interpersonal perceptions, constructivist research has suggested that self-constructions of sexual abuse survivors are at least as complex or differentiated as those without a history of abuse (Erbes & Harter, 1999; Fischer et al., 1997). Thus, while abuse survivors may have been confronted with events that their developing cognitive skills and social context poorly equipped them to construe, they have not necessarily contented themselves with simplistic frameworks for understanding themselves and their social worlds. Those who have been more severely abused particularly appear to be more differentiated, or possibility fragmented, in their perceptions of self. When describing themselves in self-characterizations, abuse survivors show a positive relationship between self-differentiation and anxiety or fear in their narratives. This relationship is opposite in those who are not abused. This suggests that differentiated constructions of abuse survivors may be qualitatively different from those without similar experiences, perhaps reflecting affectively laden struggles to integrate fragmented self-constructions (Erbes, 2000).

CONSTRUCTIONS OF ADULT ABUSE SURVIVORS WITHIN CLINICAL AND BROADER SOCIAL CONTEXTS

CURRENT INTERPERSONAL AND SOCIAL CONTEXTS

The preceding discussion illustrates that sexual abuse survivors may find themselves constructing realities in ways that are divergent from those of non-survivors. They may construe their worlds in highly negative or threatening terms. They may have key aspects of their childhood experiences that are poorly elaborated, leading to unstable or fragmented constructions of themselves and their worlds. Often, their construct systems have been established in enmeshed, threatening, or conflictual family systems that color their anticipations of future relationships. Based on this, it is easy to see how adult survivors can have difficulty in adult life.

An understanding of the constructed worlds of CSA survivors requires that we move beyond simply considering past contexts and developmental history. It is important to consider the implications of a survivor's constructions on his or her daily interpersonal interactions. Constructions of our worlds and selves are continually being reinforced or altered by current events and interactions, however much they may have been influenced by the past (Strupp & Binder, 1984; Mahoney, 1991). Thus, understanding the current implications and alterations of survivors' construct systems is a central part of work in this area. Recent theoretical work has pointed out that construing takes place at varying levels of interactions (ranging from the bio-genetic through personal-agentic, dyadic-relational and cultural-linguistic; Mascolo, Craig-Bray, & Neimeyer, 1997) with interactions also occurring between the various levels. Abusive experiences illustrate this synergy between levels of construing ranging from physiological through personally verbalized meanings to culturally shared assumptions.

Past research has documented an array of interpersonal difficulties faced by survivors of abuse (Browne & Finkelhor, 1986; Harter et al., 1988; Lipovsky & Kilpatrick, 1992; Polusny & Follette, 1995). Perhaps because abusive experiences are so anomalous from public myths of childhood and relationships, survivors have described themselves as feeling irrevocably different from others (Harter & Neimeyer, 1995; Herman, 1981,1992; Janoff-Bulman, 1982). The highly anomalous construct systems that can emerge from abusive experiences can lead to considerable challenges in relating to others. People who have suffered from abuse may be con-

38

structing realities that are based on trauma and conflict and that do not work well in nontraumatic situations. The meanings they derive from their experiences may be quite different from the meanings that other individuals would derive, or even understand, based on their less traumatic backgrounds. The resulting interpersonal conflicts can be bewildering both to the survivors and to those with whom they try to relate. Some survivors may find themselves entering into relationships and situations more suited to their specialized, abuse-focused construct systems. Thus, it is no surprise that survivors of CSA are much more likely to be victims of sexual assault as adults (Messman & Long, 1996).

The present challenges of abuse survivors extend beyond family and other intimate relationships into more public realms. As childhood abuse has become more openly acknowledged in the media, public stories may further enforce survivors' feelings of isolation, due to unique aspects of their own abuse, the context in which it occurred, and their subsequent struggles for meaning. Witnessing reactions to public disclosures may be further invalidating to survivors, as other survivors' stories are met with skepticism or accusations of misguided, self-serving, or malicious motivations. Pre-emptive attention to abusive experiences may also limit possibilities for self-construction open to survivors, by failing to respect other individual uniqueness or by assuming that survivors will be invariably marred by the abuse. Survivors may be seen as less qualified for roles such as relationship partner, parent, or health professional.

This public aspect of construction, which can be so challenging for abuse survivors, extends to areas of psychological discourse as well. The politics of pathology and of victimization both risk assigning survivors to pre-emptive categories that separate them from their "normal" peers. Persons who have experienced childhood sexual abuse may be faced with the alternatives of being construed as pathological, without reference to their abusive experiences, or of being stereotypically construed as "only a victim" or even as "only a survivor" (Harter & Neimeyer, 1995; see also Pope & Brown, 1996; Briere, 1996). Respect for the uniquely personal aspects of abusive experiences and their context within the person's unfolding life story is an essential element of a personal construct approach to understanding abusive experiences, whether as a researcher or as a consultant to survivors in their meaning-making processes.

THE CLINICAL CONTEXT

Given the prevalence and correlates of CSA, it is easy to see that it is an issue arising in many psychotherapeutic encounters. From 50 to 90 percent of clients report histories of sexual abuse, depending upon the population sampled (Harter & Neimeyer, 1995). Research suggests that therapists also have frequent histories of abuse. National surveys have found 23% of male and 32% of female psychologists reporting histories of CSA (Polusny & Follette, 1996) and 43% of female mental health professionals reporting histories of CSA (Elliott & Guy, 1993). Thus, like our clients, we are often simultaneously both subject and object of our struggles to understand abusive experiences. With its reflexive stance, encompassing construing of both therapist and client, constructivism has a great deal to offer therapists working with survivors of abuse. Because constructivist therapy is not a technically prescriptive approach (Blowers & O'Conner, 1995; Harter & Neimeyer, 1995; Neimeyer, 1995), this discussion will highlight general themes and issues rather than specific techniques.

Constructivist therapy with abuse survivors is likely to put a great deal of focus on the therapeutic relationship as a vehicle of change. This relationship should embody a deep respect for the individuality of the client and the utility of her or his constructions, a non-authoritarian approach to therapeutic intervention, and an elaborative, rather than corrective, approach. The relationship provides a dialogue in which new interpersonal meanings can be experienced, with resulting changes in a client's construct system. Further, if a safe and elaborative relationship is present, it may provide a context for survivors to reconstrue their abuse experiences and the meanings of those experiences for their lives.

Constructivism has actively focused on the co-creation of reality, that is on the ways in which individuals' construct systems are developed through interactions with broader interpersonal, familial, and societal systems of construction (Mahoney, 1991; Neimeyer, 1998b, 2000). Survivors develop constructions of self and others through participation in family systems that are frequently hostile, closed, or invalidating. Participation in an interpersonal system—a relationship—that provides safety and validation may offer the best chance for revision of these construct systems. If the therapist is able to maintain a consistent stance of support, respect, and validation of the client as construer, this can provide new material that the survivor must incorporate into his or her construct system. In this way, the therapeutic relationship can serve both as an environment in which new construction is fostered through exposure to novel experiences and as a forum in which clients can safely explore new means of construction.

Painful experiences of the active misuse of power and influence leave survivors very sensitive to power issues and invalidation in a therapy relationship. While construing the therapist as a powerful, more expert other may be a familiar theme, it may also maintain constructions of the client as unable to make meaning of his or her own experience, thus invalidating the client's construing process. The client may alternate between acquiescence to the constructions of the therapist and awareness of the deep invalidation of self it entails. Relating to the client in a new manner, absent in the family of origin, may result in uncomfortable invalidation of the client's expectations. At the same time, this therapeutic relating offers a deeper validation of the client as a construing person. This tension between opportunities to invalidate outdated constructions and validation of the client's construing process requires courage and creativity on the part of both client and therapist. Such therapeutic relationships offer opportunities for the client to reject previously dominant constructions imposed by abusive relationships or the larger social context, to enact new constructions of self and relationships, and to validate these new constructions. In contrast, imposing prescriptive meanings and remedies on the client (such as an idea that "all survivors" will deal with a specific set of issues in a given order) can be experienced as a reenactment of invalidating abusive relationships (Harter, 1995; Pope & Brown, 1996). Constructivism's respect for the idiographic meanings people create is thus particularly salient for this population. The understanding that no two abuse situations, no two family contexts, and no two construct systems will be identical precludes the use of rigid "blueprints" for conceptualization or treatment.

The need to avoid invalidating therapeutic relationships and to respect the constructions of a client prompts a non-authoritarian style on the part of therapists. This follows from both the tenets of constructivism (Mahoney, 1991) and from the needs of an abused population (Briere, 1992, 1996). Personal construct psychology, and constructivism in general, acknowledges that clients and therapists alike struggle to make meaning of their experiences through individualized, nonverifiable construct systems. Once this is acknowledged, it no longer makes sense for therapists to hold themselves up as arbiters of the truth or directors of healing. Rather, there is a focus on developing a collaborative relationship in which client and therapist work together to foster the individual's exploration and selection of the most viable constructions of the client's experiences and relationships. A key implication of this collaborative stance is a deep respect for the construct systems survivors bring to the therapy setting. An abuse survivor's construct system was created to deal with situations for which the public discourse offers, at best, superficial meanings. The resulting constructions may differ from more privileged models of health, but cannot be labeled as "dysfunctional" or "pathological." They represent the best alternatives formerly available to the client—constructions that allowed them to survive past abuse. The therapist joins with the client in creating new possibilities. This respect for the constructions of a survivor can help to avoid a major form of invalidation that easily occurs in therapy— telling clients that they are "thinking wrong" (Neimeyer, 1998a).

In the context of a therapeutic relationship, exploration of traumatic narratives may be particularly useful. Again, we are not advocating a prescriptive stance and would not suggest that clients must "relive," or even fully remember, their abuse experiences in a therapeutic context in order to "recover." Participation in a therapeutic relationship (or indeed, similar relationships outside of the therapeutic context) that differs from previous abusive contexts may provide ample material and opportunity for constructive elaboration without the need for deliberate exposure, re-living, or memory techniques. Inevitably, as the client construes the therapy, that relationship will be contrasted to past experience, casting past experience into a new context. At the same time, the therapist provides an inviting context within which painful, previously silenced, content can be shared. However, the pacing and extent of that disclosure is primarily the client's choice. While the therapist may offer opportunities to integrate past with current and future experience, the relative orientation to past, current, or future experience is chosen by the client and may vary through the course of therapy. Telling the personal story of the abuse may be an important beginning to elaborate its implications for the continuing life story. This storytelling may provide narrative coherence to the fragmented views of self that may result from struggles to meaningfully construe traumatic events.

FUTURE IMPLICATIONS

As our appreciation for the prevalence, implications, and complexities of sexual abuse in clinical populations grows, we must continue to develop further conceptualizations, research paradigms, and treatment approaches. The model outlined here represents one attempt at construing the complex issues, experiences, and dynamics faced by adult survivors of childhood sexual abuse. Like all such constructions, it will need to develop to incorporate new information and to better accommodate clinical and research experiences.

Kelly's (1955) Repertory Grid Technique has been useful in eliciting personal constructions of abuse survivors and measuring changes in these constructions within therapy. Narrative methodologies are more recently being used to assess constructions of abuse survivors as contextual meaning making processes unfolding through time. Narrative paradigms are both exciting and daunting as they offer incredible richness of information limited only by the development of methods for reliably extracting and tabulating that richness. Standardized content analysis procedures such as the word-count program developed by James Pennebaker and colleagues (Pennebaker & Frances, 1998) offer an initial starting point for abstracting common themes across narratives of abuse. However, personal construct and other more individualized content coding procedures (Landfield, 1971; Viney, 1983) offer more context-sensitive, richer analyses of idiographic meanings. Such coding by skilled raters is more sensitive to the idiographic content of abuse and other trauma survivor's constructions and more predictive of distress and social relating (Erbes, 2000; Harter et al., 1999; Rigsby et al., 2000).

Perhaps the most important role that the personal construct researcher and therapist can play is to create a safe context in which previously silent narratives can unfold. This offers similar challenges to both researchers and clinicians: to approach CSA survivors from a respectful, validating stance that affords expression and elaboration of idiographic, personal constructions, rather than imposition of the professional's own pre-emptive constructions.

REFERENCES

Alexander, P. C. (1993). The differential effects of abuse characteristics and attachment in the prediction of long-term effects of sexual abuse. *Journal of Interpersonal Violence, 8,* 346-362.

Alexander, P. C., & Lupfer, S. L. (1987). Family characteristics and long-term consequences associated with sexual abuse. *Archives of Sexual Behavior, 16,* 235-245.

Alexander, P. C., Neimeyer, R. A., Follette, V. M., Moore, M. K., & Harter, S. L. (1989). A comparison of group treatments of women sexually abused as children. *Journal of Consulting and Clinical Psychology, 57,* 479-483.

American Psychiatric Association. (1994). *Diagnostic and statistical manual of mental disorders* (4th edition). Washington, DC: Author.

Beitchman, J. H., Zucker, K. J., Hood, J. E., DaCosta, B. A., Akman, D., & Cassavia, E. (1992). A review of the long-term effects of child sexual abuse. *Child Abuse and Neglect, 16,* 101-118.

Binder, R. L., McNeil, D. E., & Goldstone, R. L. (1996). Is adaptive coping possible for adult survivors of childhood sexual abuse? *Psychiatric Services, 47,* 186-188.

Blowers, G. H., & O'Connor, K. P. (1995). Construing contexts: Problems and prospects of George Kelly's personal construct psychology. *British Journal of Clinical Psychology, 34,* 1-16.

Boney-McCoy, S., & Finkelhor, D. (1996). Is youth victimization related to trauma symptoms and depression after controlling for prior symptoms and family relationships? A longitudinal, prospective study. *Journal of Consulting and Clinical Psychology, 64,* 1406-1416.

Boney-McCoy, S., & Finkelhor, D. (1998). Psychopathology associated with sexual abuse: A reply to Nash, Neimeyer, Hulsey, and Lambert (1998). *Journal of Consulting and Clinical Psychology, 66,* 572-573.

Briere, J. (1992). *Child abuse trauma: Theory and treatment of the lasting effects.* Newberry Park, CA: Sage.

Briere, J. (1996). *Therapy for adults molested as children: Beyond survival* (2nd ed.). New York: Springer.

Briere, J., & Runtz, M. (1993). Child sexual abuse: Long-term sequelae and implications for assessment. *Journal of Interpersonal Violence, 8,* 312-330.

Browne, A., & Finkelhor, D. (1986). Impact of child sexual abuse: A review of the research. *Psychological Bulletin, 99,* 66-77.

Coffey, P., Leitenberg, H., Henning, K., Turner, T., & Bennett, R. T. (1996). Mediators of the long-term impact of child sexual abuse: Perceived stigma, betrayal, powerlessness, and self-blame. *Child Abuse and Neglect, 20,* 447-455.

Dilillo, D. K., Long, P. J., & Russell, L. M. (1994). Childhood coping strategies of intrafamilial and extrafamilial female sexual abuse victims. *Journal of Child Sexual Abuse,* 3(2), 45-65.

Draucker, C. B. (1996). Family-of-origin variables and adult female survivors of childhood sexual abuse: A review of the research. *Journal of Child Sexual Abuse,* 5(4), 35-63.

Elliott, D. M., & Guy, J. D. (1993). Mental health professionals versus non-mental-health professionals: Childhood trauma and adult functioning. *Professional Psychology: Research and Practice,* 24, 83-90.

Erbes, C. R. (2000). *Child sexual abuse and the self: Affect and differentiation.* Unpublished doctoral dissertation, Texas Tech University

Erbes, C. R., & Harter, S. L. (1999). Domain-specific cognitive complexity in survivors of child abuse. *Journal of Constructivist Psychology,* 12, 215-238.

Finkelhor, D. (1987). The trauma of child sexual abuse: Two models. *Journal of Interpersonal Violence,* 2, 348-366.

Finkelhor, D. (1990). Early and long-term effects of child sexual abuse: An update. *Professional Psychology: Research and Practice,* 21, 325-330.

Finkelhor, D., Hotaling, G., Lewis, I. A., & Smith, C. (1990). Sexual abuse in a national survey of adult men and women: Prevalence, characteristics, and risk factors. *Child Abuse and Neglect,* 14, 19-28.

Fischer, K.W., Ayoub, C., Singh, I., Noam, G., Maraganore, H., & Raya, P. (1997). Psychopathology as adaptive development along distinctive pathways. *Development and Psychopathology,* 9, 749-779.

Gelinas, D. J. (1983). The persisting negative effects of incest. *Psychiatry,* 46, 312-332.

Harter, S. L. (1988). Psychotherapy as a reconstructive process: Implications of integrative theories for outcome research. *International Journal of Personal Construct Psychology,* 1, 349-367.

Harter, S. L. (1995). Construing on the edge: Clinical mythology in working with borderline processes. In R. A. Neimeyer & M. J. Mahoney (Eds.), *Constructivism in psychotherapy* (pp. 371-383). Washington, DC: American Psychological Association.

Harter, S. L. (2000). Quantitative measures of construing in child abuse survivors. *Journal of Constructivist Psychology,* 13, 103-116.

Harter, S. L., Alexander, P. C., & Neimeyer, R. A. (1988). Long-term effects of incestuous child abuse in college women: Social adjustment, social cognition, and family characteristics. *Journal of Consulting and Clinical Psychology,* 56, 5-8.

Harter, S. L., Erbes, C. R., & Hart, C. C. (1999, February). *Use of the Role Construct Repertory Grid to assess the personal constructions of sexual abuse survivors.* Paper presented at the 32nd Annual Comparative Literature Symposium, Narrative and Consciousness: Literature, Psychology, and the Brain, Lubbock, TX.

Harter, S. L., & Neimeyer, R. A (1995). Long term effects of child sexual abuse: Toward a constructivist theory of trauma and its treatment. In R. A. Neimeyer & G. J. Neimeyer (Eds.) *Advances in personal construct psychology* (Vol. 3, pp. 229-269). Greenwich, CT: JAI.

Harter, S. L., & Vanecek, J. (2000). Cognitive assumptions and long-term distress in survivors of childhood abuse, parental alcoholism, and dysfunctional family environments. *Cognitive Therapy and Research, 24,* 445-472.

Hazzard, A. (1993). Trauma-related beliefs as mediators of sexual abuse impact in adult women survivors: A pilot study. *Journal of Child Sexual Abuse, 2*(3), 55-69.

Herman, J. L. (1981). *Father-daughter incest.* Cambridge, MA: Harvard University Press.

Herman, J. L. (1992). *Trauma and recovery.* New York: Basic Books.

Himelein, M. J., & McElrath, J. V. (1996). Resilient child sexual abuse survivors: Cognitive coping and illusion. *Child Abuse and Neglect, 20,* 747-758.

Horowitz, M. J. (1986). *Stress response syndromes* (2nd ed.). Northvale, NJ: Jason Aronson.

Janoff-Bulman, R. (1982). Esteem and control bases of blame: Adaptive strategies for victims versus observers. *Journal of Personality, 40,* 180-192.

Janoff-Bulman, R. (1992). *Shattered assumptions: Towards a new psychology of trauma.* New York: Free Press.

Jumper, S. A. (1995) A meta-analysis of the relationship of child sexual abuse to adult psychological adjustment. *Child Abuse and Neglect, 19,* 715-728.

Kelly, G. A. (1955). *The psychology of personal constructs* (2 vols.). New York: Norton.

Lam, J. N., & Grossman, F. K. (1997). Resiliency and adult adaptation in women with and without self-reported histories of childhood sexual abuse. *Journal of Traumatic Stress, 10,* 175-196.

Landfield, A. W. (1971). *Personal construct systems in psychotherapy.* Chicago: Rand McNally.

Leitenberg, H., Greenwald, E., & Cado, S. (1992). A retrospective study of long-term methods of coping with having been sexually abused during childhood. *Child Abuse and Neglect, 16,* 399-407.

Lipovsky, J. A., & Kilpatrick, D. G. (1992). The child sexual abuse victim as an adult. In W. O'Donohue & J. H. Geer (Eds.), *The sexual abuse of children: Clinical issues* (Vol. 2, pp. 430-476). Hillsdale, NJ: Lawrence Erlbaum Associates.

Mahoney, M. J. (1991). *Human change processes: The scientific foundations of psychotherapy.* New York: Basic Books.

Mascolo, M. F., Craig-Bray, L., & Neimeyer, R. A. (1997). The construction of meaning and action in development and psychotherapy: An epigenetic systems perspective. In G. J. Neimeyer & R. A. Neimeyer (Eds.), *Advances in personal construct psychology* (Vol. 4, pp 3-38). Greenwich, CT: JAI.

McMillen, C., & Zuravin, S. (1997). Attributions of blame and responsibility for child sexual abuse and adult adjustment. *Journal of Interpersonal Violence, 12,* 30-48.

McMillen, C., Zuravin, S., & Rideout, G. (1995). Perceived benefit from child sexual abuse. *Journal of Consulting and Clinical Psychology, 63,* 1037-1043.

Meiselman, K. C. (1978). *Incest: A psychological study of causes and effects with treatment recommendations.* San Francisco: Jossey-Bass.

Messman, T. L., & Long, P. J. (1996). Child sexual abuse and its relationship to revictimization in adult women: A review. *Clinical Psychology Review, 16,* 397-420.

Nash, M. R., Hulsey, T. L., Sexton, M. C., Harralson, T. L., & Lambert, W. (1993). Long-term sequelae of childhood sexual abuse: Perceived family environment, psychopathology, and dissociation. *Journal of Consulting and Clinical Psychology, 61,* 276-283.

Nash, M. R., Neimeyer, R. A., Hulsey, T. L., & Lambert, W. (1998). Psychopathology associated with sexual abuse: The importance of complementary designs and common ground. *Journal of Consulting and Clinical Psychology, 66,* 568-571.

Neimeyer, R. A. (1995). An appraisal of constructivist psychotherapies: Contexts and challenges. In M. J. Mahoney (Ed.), *Cognitive and constructive psychotherapies: Theory, research, and practice* (pp. 163-194). New York: Springer.

Neimeyer, R. A. (1998a). *Lessons of loss: A guide to coping.* New York: McGraw-Hill.

Neimeyer, R. A. (1998b). Social constructionism in the counseling context. *Counseling Psychology Quarterly, 11,* 135-149.

Neimeyer, R. A. (2000). Narrative disruptions in the construction of the self. In R. A. Neimeyer & J. D. Raskin (Eds.), *Constructions of disorder: Meaning-making frameworks for psychotherapy* (pp. 207-242). Washington, DC: American Psychological Association.

Neimeyer, R. A., & Harter, S. L. (1988). Facilitating individual change in personal construct therapy. In G. Dunnett (Ed.), *Working with people: Clinical uses of personal construct psychology* (pp. 174-185). London: Routledge.

Neimeyer, R. A., Harter, S. L., & Alexander, P. C. (1991). Group perceptions as predictors of outcome in the treatment of incest survivors. *Psychotherapy Research, 1,* 148-158.

Neimeyer, R. A., & Stewart, A. E. (1996). Trauma, healing, and the narrative emplotment of loss. *Families in Society, 77,* 360-375.

Pennebaker, J. W., & Francis, M. E. (1998). *Linguistic inquiry and word count, the second version: SLIWC.* Unpublished manuscript and software program. University of Texas, Austin, TX.

Peters, S. D., Wyatt, G. E., & Finkelhor, D. (1986). Prevalence. In D. Finkelhor (Ed.), *A sourcebook on child sexual abuse* (pp. 15-59). Beverly Hills, C.A.: Sage.

Polusny, M. A. & Follette, V. M. (1995). Long-term correlates of child sexual abuse: Theory and review of the empirical literature. *Applied and Preventive Psychology, 4,* 143-166.

Polusny, M. A. & Follette, V. M. (1996). Remembering childhood sexual abuse: A national survey of psychologists' clinical practices, beliefs, and personal experiences. *Professional Psychology: Research and Practice, 27,* 41-52.

Pope, K. S., & Brown, L. S. (1996). *Recovered memories of abuse: Assessment, therapy, forensics.* Washington, DC: American Psychological Association.

Rigsby, J., Harter, S. L., & Wagner, K. (2000, July). *Trauma narratives as personal construing.* Paper presented at the Ninth Biennial Conference of the North American Personal Construct Network, New Paltz, New York.

Rind, B., & Tromovitch, P. (1997). A meta-analytic review of findings from national samples on psychological correlates of child sexual abuse. *Journal of Sex Research, 34,* 237-255.

Russell, D. (1984). *Sexual exploitation: Rape, child sexual abuse, and workplace harassment.* Beverly Hills, CA: Sage Library of Social Research.

Sewell, K. W. (1996). Constructional risk factors for a post-traumatic stress response after a mass murder. *Journal of Constructivist Psychology, 9,* 97-107.

Sewell, K. W. (1997). Posttraumatic stress: Towards a constructivist model of psychotherapy. In R. A. Neimeyer & G. J. Neimeyer (Eds.), *Advances in personal construct psychology* (Vol. 4, pp. 207-235). Greenwich, CT: JAI.

Sewell, K. W., Cromwell, R. L., Farrell-Higgins, J., Palmer, R., Ohlde, C., & Patterson, T. W. (1996). Hierarchical elaboration in the conceptual structures of Vietnam combat veterans. *Journal of Constructivist Psychology, 9,* 79-96.

Strupp, H. H., & Binder, J. L. (1984). *Psychotherapy in a new key: A guide to time-limited dynamic psychotherapy.* New York: Basic Books.

Viney, L. L. (1983). The assessment of psychological states through content analysis of verbal communications. *Psychological Bulletin, 94,* 542-563.

Wyatt, G. E., & Newcomb, M. (1990). Internal and external mediators of women's sexual abuse in childhood. *Journal of Consulting and Clinical Psychology, 58,* 758-767.

CHAPTER 3

Nonvalidation vs. (In)validation: Implications for theory and practice

Beverly M. Walker

This chapter will examine some aspects of the concept of validation as it is formulated within personal construct psychology (PCP). To begin with there will be a discussion of what the term means and how it differs from other notions with which it is frequently confused. Validation will be viewed in a more complex, less unified way than has often been the case, one that is not a unilinear mechanistic process, but multidetermined and multi-faceted, linking to other key processes such as the metaphor of the scientist. That linkage alerts us to the neglected possibility that people sometimes engage in neither validation nor invalidation by their actions. Further, the steps entailed in Kelly's scientist metaphor, it will be demonstrated, provide a way of bringing together these nonvalidation strategies. Past writers have gone some way in recognizing these points, but have confused the issue by widening the meaning of hostility to encompass nonvalidation and thus, losing the utility of the term nonvalidation in its own right. Finally, the implications that this elaboration of Kelly's notion of the validation cycle provides for an understanding of psychological disorder will be explored.

This chapter follows from a 1999 presentation in Berlin at the Thirteenth International Personal Construct Psychology Congress, where I presented a paper written with a number of colleagues about validation (Walker, Oades, Caputi, Stevens & Crittenden, 2000). That paper contains many ideas, the exploration of which had initially been triggered by discussions within the Wollongong Personal Construct group over many years. We feel it has many important implications for both theory and practice. The present discussion takes the part of that paper for which I was primarily responsible and develops it further to focus on some of those implications.

However, while preparing this paper I realized that there were several papers, one by Lorenzini, Sassaroli, and Rocchi (1989) and two by Pfenninger and Klion (1994, 1995), which in some respects took up similar issues. Those papers contain many points relevant to this discussion, although they are presented in the context of a discussion of hostility, using that term in a variety of ways, some of which seem at variance with Kelly's (1955) own definition as I will indicate. Nevertheless these, together with papers by Button (1996) and Landfield (1988), represent both an important clarification as well as an elaboration of validation from a Kellian perspective.

CLARIFYING THE FOCUS OF THE CHAPTER

As we pointed out previously (Walker et al., 2000) Kelly used the term "validation" to refer to two things, which, not surprisingly, can cause confusion. Primarily, he writes about the validation cycle, whereby people test out their construing systems. The cycle begins with the formulation of a hypothesis, conduction of an experiment to test out that hypothesis, and finishes with the evaluation of the outcome. Has the hypothesis been supported or not? As you will note, this cycle is closely linked to the metaphor of the scientist. The second usage is with reference to one of the outcomes of the experiment (i.e., when the hypothesis has been supported). The contrast to this (i.e., when the experiment fails and the hypothesis is not supported) Kelly termed invalidation. This chapter is predominantly concerned with the primary use of the expression validation in terms of the validation cycle, the process whereby construing is put to the test.

Unfortunately, there are some important ways in which validation has been misrepresented. To begin with, it is very tempting to view the validation process and the related scientist metaphor as a unilinear causal mechanistic process in the form of "if you do X and Y results then Z will follow." But the reality is not so simple.

Button (1996) points to one complication when he reminds us of the origins of the word validation in the Latin verb "valere"— to strengthen. Validation, he suggests, implies more the strengthening and weakening of theories of the world, rather than unequivocal confirmation or disconfirmation. It is unlikely in any single test or interaction that any part of the construction process is either conclusively validated or invalidated for much of our construing. Indeed, it is probably a cumulative process over many situations, rather than the critical experiment that scientists look for in their work.

Additionally we (Walker et al., 2000) pointed to another complication, suggesting that it might be useful to distinguish at least three different aspects of construing that might be validated or invalidated at one and the same time: the content of construing, the structure of construing, and the process of the construer. By content we included examples of both the application of a construct to an element (e.g., people are boring) as well as the utility of the construct as a whole (e.g., whether construing people as boring-interesting is useful). Structure refers to the nature of the existing assumed hierarchical system of construing. It was illustrated by the features of Hinkle's "implicative network," which may include the hierarchical place, whether relatively superordinate or subordinate, or the relationships to different subsets of the construing system (e.g., the most important determinant of whether I spend time with people is whether they are honest or dishonest, not whether they are boring or not.)

While writing this chapter I discovered that Lorenzini et al. (1989, p. 421) had made similar distinctions whereby they contrasted two sorts of invalidations, "the *true/false* type and the *connection* type with a third, the *applicability* type. The true/false type is of the form 'people are boring.'" The connection type related to the structure of construing and might take the form of "given that people are boring they are not worth taking trouble over." Applicability is illustrated by whether or not people can be usefully construed in terms of the construct boring-interesting.

There was a third area of construing that we proposed, an area that broadens the focus of validation beyond what might be considered the largely cognitive perspective of Lorenzini and his colleagues, the process of the construer. Here the wider approach to exploring the problem may be the focus, so that what is validated is one's way of experimenting—for example, whether the way one is experimenting is loosely linked or tightly framed, operating within a narrow area (constricted) or over a vast expanse (dilated), emotionally loaded or logically framed, drawing in others or tested in solitude.

There is a further illustration of a mechanistic interpretation of validation that deserves attention. Kelly thought it important to differentiate between validation and reinforcement, a distinction that subsequently has been ignored too frequently. This distinction has implications for a theme to be taken up later in this chapter, the notion of a psychological disorder. Those who conflate the two assume that a validated prediction (in the sense of a confirmed prediction) amounts to positive reinforcement, an invalidated one to

51

punishment. The assumptions are that with punishment change should result, whereas with positive reinforcement the behaviors and related constructs would continue, strengthened as a consequence. But Kelly indicates many instances where invalidation does not result in change, whereas validation does. This is not inconsistent with his view that the confirmation of predictions is generally less problematic to the person than invalidation. Walker et al. (2000) take up this issue in detail, suggesting that the experience cycle provides a way of resolving this problem because of its emphasis on investment and commitment.

Thus, the validation cycle is more complex than is usually presented. Simple cognitive or mechanistic accounts do not usefully characterize its key features. Its complexity bears important relationships to many other processes, not only those of an intrapersonal nature. This is further illustrated by considering in detail its linkage to the scientist metaphor.

THE INCIPIENT SCIENTIST AND THE VALIDATION CYCLE

If one reads many secondary PCP sources, one is repeatedly told that Kelly's metaphor of the person is of a scientist. Indeed, at times Kelly himself states this, particularly when he is painting a picture of his theory with a broad brush, as he tends to in the orally presented papers (e.g., Maher, 1969). But as previously pointed out, a more careful reading of his position is that he saw people as "incipient scientists," potential scientists (Walker, 1990).

My understanding of this differentiation is that in part we are born as explorers, seeking to know more about the world and ourselves as part of it. Here Kelly's position appears very similar to that of the ego psychologists, with their focus on active, coping processes present from birth. Mair (1977) suggested that the flavor of this concept could perhaps best be captured by seeing people as adventurers, risk takers, like the pioneers who crossed the vast expanses of the American continent in their covered wagons, setting up settlements and farms.

Kelly goes further than simply suggesting that people can behave as adventurers by advocating exploration as a way of life, as one of the "shoulds" proposed by his position. The very fact that he pushes this position indicates that many people do not avail themselves of their potential in this direction. They retreat to the safety of what they know, what is familiar.

But the scientist metaphor has implications beyond the advocacy of exploration as a desirable way to live. It suggests a particular form of that process. It proposes a staged sequence of events that corresponds to the ideal or stereotype of science. This sequence entails formulating a theory, developing hypotheses based on that theory, constructing an experiment to test out the theory, carrying that out, analyzing the results, and revising the theory in the light of those results.

Those of you who know even a little about science will realize that possibly most science does not follow this kind of sequence. However, this is the ideal of scientific process that is so inaccurately taught in many different contexts, especially in psychology.

THE SCIENTIST DE-RAILED

But if we are only incipient scientists, and hence the process can go wrong, what happens then? At the broader level the adventuring spirit may fail us. For whatever reason, after whatever circumstance, with whatever construing, we cling to what is rather than reach for what might be. At its most extreme we might find people who feel so traumatized that they shut down their meaning making altogether, as Leitner (1999) has pointed out. Those diagnosed as catatonic may be in this category.

But problematic processes that subvert our smooth and effective exploration extend into the details of our engagement with the world. This is, however, most readily to be understood in terms of the processes of ideal science. Figure 1 is reprinted from Walker et al. (2000), with minor modifications. Processes reflected in stages of the scientist metaphor are summarized, the parallels when we consider construing are proposed, and examples of how each stage of scientific experimentation may be de-railed given. We used the term nonvalidation to refer to instances of noncompletion of the ideal validational process, the opposite pole to validation as a process. The nonvalidation strategies are not necessarily exhaustive, though clearly the scientist metaphor provides us with a way of ordering them. Many of the examples of nonvalidation strategies have been outlined in previous PCP writing, but often they have been unconnected to the validation cycle or the scientist metaphor, and have remained unrelated across theorists. Efran (2000) captured the overall feel of nonvalidation: "If you can't win, then avoid losing. If you can't be right, avoid being wrong." I will elaborate some examples to illustrate each stage.

With regard to stage 1 Landfield (1988) posed the problem of the person who remains trapped in circumspection, avoiding anticipations, showing "reluctance in defining situations, person, or validating evidence" (p. 241). Kelly (1955) wrote about this in terms of the breakdown of the CPC (circumspection-preemption-control) cycle. It was this cycle that Kelly linked to effective decision-making, such that the stages of the cycle are moved through in order to reach the resolution. By remaining endlessly exploring options the circumspectionist is frozen, unable to move further, with essential problems remaining unsolved.

Figure 1. Parallel processes for the scientist metaphor, validation cycle and nonvalidation strategy examples (adapted from Walker et al., 2000).

STAGE	SCIENTIST METAPHOR	CONSTRUING EQUIVALENT	TYPES OF NONVALIDATION STRATEGIES
1	Develop component(s) of a theory	Form a construct	Circumspect endlessly
2	Formulate hypothesis	Make predictions about how the construct applies to elements	Make predictions loose
3	Devise experiment to test it out	Behave or observe others behaving in line with the construct and its applications	Be hostile — "cook the books"
4	Analyze and interpret the data	Evaluate outcome of such behaving	Misread or ignore others' reactions
5	Revise hypotheses or continue further experimentation along the same lines	Act on the basis of that outcome	Be dogmatic or "literal assuming"

Concerning stage 2, Bannister's (1965) arguments concerning the impact of serial invalidation are illustrative of such a nonvalidation strategy. He suggested that those who find themselves in situations where their construing is repeatedly invalidated, as is the case in many dysfunctional families, might develop a coping strategy that entails loosening the relationships between constructs. The result is that specific predictions can no longer be made and invalidation is consequently avoided.

The illustration given at stage 3 is of Kellian hostility. A recent example I observed exemplifies the processes involved. I will discuss it in depth, as hostility has frequently been misrepresented in the construct theory literature and this example brings out the essential features.

An academic raised the issue with his colleagues that they, as a department, were giving the wrong message to students about the importance of deadlines. Policy about this needed to be formulated, he argued. When it was pointed out that the department did have a policy, which was quite punitive concerning deadlines and, further, that the policy was implemented, the academic still persisted to push this issue. Meeting after meeting was devoted to it, with the staff increasingly being attacked for their lack of professionalism by their colleague. Students at all levels were given hour-long lectures on the importance of meeting deadlines. Month after month it was put on the agenda for departmental meetings, with the staff becoming increasingly angry at both the waste of time and the attack on them as professionals. Eventually, the academic was forced to formulate a revision to the policy so that a vote could be taken, something he had been avoiding. Curiously his revision was less stringent than the one in the policy document. When put to the vote it lost overwhelmingly and the issue was not raised again.

This series of events remained unexplained until the faculty member lodged a complaint against a student whom he wanted removed from his class for disruptive behavior. In discussion with the student, it transpired that she had first had a confrontation with the faculty member after he had granted her an extension on an essay. He had subsequently announced in class that extensions would not be granted. She went to him to clarify if her extension still held. In the course of the conversation he had indicated, "the most important thing in life is keeping deadlines." She, mistakenly assuming that this was a conversation between two adults, responded: "If that's what you think I feel sorry for you."

This example clearly indicates how, when this academic's core construct about the critical nature of meeting deadlines was invalidated, he made sure that everyone, but everyone, had to spend considerable time and energy with the importance of meeting deadlines preoccupying them. He had dragged the discussion out by avoiding resolution of the issue for months on end. The staff and students felt assaulted and undermined, but he had orchestrated events so that his core construct had been massively validated. He had fudged the data to provide the desired outcome. I will return to a discussion of hostility later in the chapter.

At the fourth stage of the scientist metaphor things can go array when we misread others' reactions, or perhaps ignore them. Other people and their reactions are the principal sources of validational evidence (Walker, 1992). Kelly wrote about the importance of the construing of others' construing and basing our relationships with others on that foundation. This he termed sociality. If sociality is not our strong point, then the gathering of evidence may be haphazard or inaccurate. This is not the same as being hostile, as there is no attempt to manipulate the outcome. It is just that at times people do not readily construe the construing of others.

The final stage is illustrated by another approach pointed to by Landfield (1988). He contrasted people who play literal assuming roles with perspectivist roles. Those adopting the literal assuming approach feel that they are "no longer in need of validational evidence" (p. 241) in that they assume that their views have been validated once and for all, without question. Such an approach involves people engaging in experiments to the extent that they behave according to their hypotheses, but ignore the outcomes of them. By contrast one can approach the world "hypothetically and metaphorically. Experience, at any point in life, becomes the base for new experience and learning" (Landfield, 1988, p. 241). By so doing one adopts a stance that invites the likelihood of invalidation and hence leaves open the possibilities of potential change.

While it is tempting to use the term "strategy" to refer to problematic nonvalidation illustrations, this should not be taken to mean that they are necessarily consciously adopted or that we have control over them. This would be a misrepresentation. It may be that our skills are not well developed in, for example, construing others' construing. Sometimes we may be driven to these activities, such as might characterize Freudian defenses. Kelly (1955), for example, links hostility to what the psychoanalysts call reaction formation.

There are other situations where the very nature of the problem precludes completion of the validation cycle. A person may be in situations where there is a lack of feedback provided about the situation. Feedback might be contradictory (as in double bind situations), it might be inconsistent or largely absent (as for young children in many malfunctioning families), or it may be that the project one is engaged with may be a long term one (as when writing a novel) (Stevens, 1999). Take, for example, the situation of those diagnosed with a potentially life threatening disease. Many of the most important things on which their behaviors are contingent cannot be, with certainty, predicted. The completion of the cycle is denied them. They remain "people living with cancer," not people cured of cancer. Such situations are fraught with anxiety, fear and looming possibilities of threat.

Note also that I have avoided the assumption that nonvalidation behaviors are necessarily trait-like or type-like, such that certain people possess them. I have deliberately used verbs (action words) rather than nouns as much as possible. This raises the issue of whether forms of nonvalidation can become habits and, if so, how habits can be considered within construct theory. Landfield's literal assuming approach may be relevant here.

Because of Kelly's stress on people being effective scientists, the implication is that the non-completion of experimentation is undesirable. The examples I have given fall into that category. But nonvalidation strategies can have positive effects, which is not all that surprising when you think about it. Why else would they persist? However the question then becomes; "Positive for whom?" "Positive for what?" In general nonvalidation may have short-term gains for the non-experimenter. People feel better, more in control, less threatened or anxious. They solve the immediate problem, particularly by protecting the status quo from change and its associated distress. But Kelly's position is less about the short-term than the long haul, as a discussion of the implications of this for psychological disorder will elucidate.

Before exploring this issue, however, I want to make a small diversion to discuss Pfenninger and Klion's (1994, 1995) work on hostility. Many of the points they make are similar to those I have made, but the impact of their work, which is important, is obscured by their use of the term "hostility" to refer to a variety of things.

HOSTILITY OR NONVALIDATION?

The papers of Pfenninger and Klion (1994, 1995) contain many keen observations and ideas, but at times appear inconsistent, particularly in the definitions they give of hostility. Further they ascribe ambiguity to Kelly's use of the term. To refresh your memory, Kelly defined hostility as "continued effort to extort validational evidence in favor of a type of social prediction which has already been recognized as a failure" (Kelly, 1955, p. 533). Pfenniger and Klion (1995) claim that "many of the clinical examples Kelly provides in his writing do not involve extortional threats or intimidation" (Pfenniger & Klion, 1995, p. 271), though they give no supportive illustrative examples. However, Kelly did not write about "extortional threats or intimidation" (italics added) but about extortion, and uses this term consistent with the dictionary definition of "extract forcibly" (*Concise Oxford Dictionary*, 1952, p. 421), which is importantly different.

It is this action of forcible extraction from others that is the defining characteristic of hostility, as the extended example I used earlier in the chapter clearly demonstrated. When Kelly proposed constructs like hostility and aggression he was aiming to look at the phenomena from the perspective of the person committing the actions, rather than from that of the recipients of them. Thus, the person whom others find to be hostile is attempting to create a situation in which those others are coerced to confirm his/her predictions, to act in ways that conform to his/her invalidated view. To define hostility as "the refusal to change an invalidated construct" (Pfenninger & Klion, 1995, p. 271) excludes its most central quality, its impact on the actions and experiences of others, a view that later in the paper Pfenninger and Klion (1995) also seem to reach (c.f., p. 281).

Subsequently they proffer another view, a different definition: "a commitment can be considered to be hostile when it becomes so central and permeable that it is habitually applied beyond its range of convenience and leads to frequent social invalidation" (Pfenninger & Klion, 1995, pp. 282-3). Once again what is lost is the actions that impact on others, the coercion of their behavior to produce the desired outcome, and hence their resultant experience of the protagonist as hostile. Pfenninger and Klion are not the only ones using hostility in idiosyncratic ways. Lorenzini at al.'s (1989, p. 418) definition of "incompatibility between two subjectively construed predictions," which more appropriately should be termed fragmentation, has similar problems.

When I looked at the sorts of things that people were using the term hostility for, it seemed to me that they were applying it beyond its range of convenience because they lacked a term like nonvalidation to link together the outcomes of the failed scientist. Further recognition of this may lead us to revise the ways Kelly characterized disorder.

PCP AND PSYCHOLOGICAL DISORDER

A defining characteristic of Kelly's approach is that it "is designed around the problem of reconstruing life, but it is not a system built upon psychopathology" (Kelly, 1955, p. 830). He advocates an approach to psychological disturbance that rejects the kinds of entities entailed in DSM-IV diagnosis in favor of an approach involving diagnostic dimensions concerning construction and transition. In this context he presents a definition of disorder: "we may define disorder as any personal construction which is used repeatedly in spite of consistent invalidation" (p. 831). When he returns to this question he presents another definition: "it represents any structure that appears to fail to accomplish its purpose" (p. 835).

While this latter definition may appear, at first sight, to differ substantially from the former one, this is not so evident with careful comparison. The structure is presumably "any personal construction," the purpose of which is to help the person make sense of things in ways that correspond to reality and move us forward in our quest to know more. But the first definition includes "repeatedly," while the second does not. And the second definition uses the word "appear," raising the issue: appear to whom? Kelly recognizes the problems of using such a "flexible" definition, and comments:

> Appear to whom? What purpose is its purpose? What is failure? The answers are; anybody; anybody's; and whatever you like. In other words, we are content to let 'disorder' mean whatever is ineffectual from the viewpoint of the client, from the viewpoint of his therapist, from the viewpoint of his stuffy neighbors, from the viewpoint of history, or from the viewpoint of God. Perhaps the proper question is not what is a disorder but where, and the therapist's question is not who needs treatment but what needs treatment....we are working with a definition that is both provincial and heuristic. (p. 835-6, italics in original)

Pfenninger and Klion (1995) raise an issue with the original definition in that they consider the behavior of people such as social reformers, who persist with their vision despite repeated invalidation. It would only occur to me to challenge the definition of validation if we consider that validation-invalidation is some objective process. Clearly it is not. It is construed. The vision for the future of someone like Gandhi may have been derided and rejected by those in authority and even by numbers of his own people, all sorts of obstacles put in his way, but Gandhi would have expected such opposition. Indeed that may have been validation for his position in itself. Gandhi received lots of validation from those whose opinions he valued and considered relevant, both at home and overseas.

However, while it certainly is the case that any construction used repeatedly in spite of consistent invalidation is problematic, psychological disorder generally—and indeed as discussed by Kelly—is broader. The individual mentioned early, who circumpects endlessly, never formulating any testable hypotheses, is an illustration. I would like to suggest that disorder could be related more directly to a breakdown of one or more stages of the scientist. I propose that disorder be considered as "any nonvalidation strategy that is repeatedly used to apply to either much of what we construe or to core/superordinate areas of our lives."

What consequences for researchers and practitioners follow from this analysis? The delineation of nonvalidation, a key aspect of a PCP analysis of psychological functioning and the opposite pole of validation as a process, should help us clarify the nature of our area and its differences from other theoretical positions more clearly. It also may alert us to other problematic ways of functioning not yet explored within the area that link to those spelled out in Figure 1. Hopefully, too, the term hostility can be rehabilitated from its current diffuse usage, thereby allowing us to explore more fully its implications and relationships to other key processes.

In conclusion, the use of the term nonvalidation allows us to more readily talk about a range of issues that follow from Kelly's theory and to pursue them further. Previously, people seem to have resorted to the term "hostility" to encompass some of these. As a result it should be recognized that it is these nonvalidation strategies, exemplifying our failure to reach our potential as scientists, that Kelly considered problematic in people's construing processes. Hence, it might be useful to revise his working definition of psychological disorder.

REFERENCES

Bannister, D. (1965). The genesis of schizophrenic thought disorder: Re-test of the serial invalidation hypothesis. *British Journal of Psychiatry, 111*, 377-382.

Button, E. (1996). Validation and invalidation. In J. W. Scheer & A. Catina (Eds.) *Empirical constructivism in Europe: The personal construct approach* (pp. 142-148). Giessen, Germany: Psychosozial-Verlag.

Concise Oxford Dictionary of Current English (1952). Oxford: Clarendon.

Efran, J. (2000, July). A context-centered therapist's toolkit. Paper presented at the Ninth Biennial Conference of the North American Personal Construct Network, New Paltz, NY.

Hinkle, D. N. (1965). *The change of personal constructs from the viewpoint of a theory of construct implications.* Unpublished doctoral dissertation, Ohio State University.

Kelly, G. A. (1955). *The psychology of personal constructs* (2 vols.). New York: Norton.

Landfield, A. W. (1988). Personal science and the concept of validation. *International Journal of Personal Construct Psychology, 1*, 237-249.

Leitner, L. M. (1999). Levels of awareness in experiential personal construct psychotherapy. *Journal of Constructivist Psychology, 12*, 239-252.

Lorenzini, R., Sassaroli, S., & Rocchi M. T. (1989). Schizophrenia and paranoia as solutions to predictive failure. *International Journal of Personal Construct Psychology, 4*, 417-432.

Mair, M. (1976). Metaphors for living. *Nebraska Symposium on Motivation, 24*, 243-290.

Maher, B. (Ed.). (1969). *Clinical psychology and personality: The selected papers of George Kelly.* Malabar, FL: Krieger.

Pfenninger, D. T., & Klion, R. E. (1994). Fitting the world to constructs: The role of activity in meaning making. *Journal of Constructivist Psychology, 3*, 151-161.

Pfenninger, D. T., & Klion, R. E. (1995). Re-thinking hostility: Is it ever better to fight than switch? *Advances in personal construct psychology, 3*, 271-289.

Stevens, C. D. (1999). *Crooked paths to insight: the pragmatics of loose and tight construing.* Unpublished doctoral dissertation, University of Wollongong.

Walker, B. M. (1990). Construing George Kelly's construing of the person-in-relation. *International Journal of Personal Construct Psychology, 3*, 41-50.

Walker, B. M. (1992). Values and Kelly's theory: Becoming a good scientist. *International Journal of Personal Construct Psychology, 5*, 259-269.

Walker, B. M., Oades, L. G., Caputi, P., Stevens C. D., & Crittenden, N. (2000). Going beyond the scientist metaphor: From validation to experience cycles. In J. W. Scheer (Ed.). *The person in society: Challenges to a constructivist theory* (pp. 100-113). Giessen, Germany: Psychosozial-Verlag.

CHAPTER 4

Narrative Solutions:
Toward Understanding the Art of Helpful Conversation[1]

Joseph Eron and Thomas Lund

The narrative solutions approach developed at the Catskill Family Institute (CFI) integrates concepts and techniques from strategic, solution-focused, and narrative therapy. The conceptual basis for the approach was first presented in an article that proposed a framework for how problems evolve and dissolve (Eron & Lund, 1993). Its principles and practices were further elaborated in a book entitled *Narrative Solutions in Brief Therapy* (Eron & Lund, 1996), and several chapters (Eron & Lund, 1995, 1998a and 1998b, Lund & Eron, 1998).

In the 1980s, we were drawn by the simplicity and practicality of the brief therapy approach developed at the Mental Research Institute (MRI) in Palo Alto, California (Watzlawick, Weakland, & Fisch, 1974; Weakland, Fisch, Watzlawick, & Bodin, 1974). The MRI approach differed from the structural family therapies of the 1970s and 1980s in its inherent optimism about the nature of problems and solutions.

The work at MRI represented a shift toward a constructivist position about psychotherapy. Problems were seen as arising from the mishandling of ordinary life difficulties. For problems to develop, there was no assumption made that something was to be inherently wrong within or between people, no pathology or disorder. Instead it was what people did about their predicaments, and how they viewed them, that started problems and kept them going. Therapy was brief, practical and problem focused. The emphasis was simply on interrupting problem-maintaining interactions, and getting people back on course, on to and over the next hurdle in life.

---

[1] Portions of this chapter are adapted from J. B. Eron and T. W. Lund (1996), *Narrative Solutions in Brief Therapy*

An important assumption of constructivism is that meaning and action are interwoven. How people view their predicament is intimately connected with, in fact inseparable from, what they do about it. As Goolishian and Anderson (1989) state: "Problems are no more than a socially created reality that is sustained by behavior and coordinated in language" (p. 534). Epstein and Loos (1989), in proposing what they call an alternative conceptualization of family therapy based on a dialogic constructivist position, note that "language is the vehicle for the development of meaning," and that "languaging" entails "not only the denotations of objects with linguistic symbols but also the action taken with respect to that notation" (p. 412). Narrative therapists White and Epston (1990) say that it is not the "underlying structure or dysfunction" that "determines the behaviors and interactions of family members;" rather, "it is the meaning that members attribute to events that determines their behavior" (p. 3).

Paul Watzlawick articulated the constructivist underpinnings of the MRI approach, authoring several books on the subject of meaning, including *The Invented Reality* (1984), *The Language of Change* (1978), and *How Real is Real?* (1976). In all these accounts, consideration was given to the idea that meaning was socially constructed, that truth was relative, and that reality was invented, not discovered. Watzlawick (1984) distinguished between first-order realities that had to do with the properties of objects, and second-order realities that had to do with meaning, significance, and values—the stuff of human affairs. "Relationships," he said, "are not aspects of first-order reality, whose true nature can be determined scientifically. Instead they are pure constructs of the partners in the relationship, and as such they resist all objective verification" (p. 238). Watzlawick reminded us that the "map is not the territory; the name is not what it names; and interpretation of reality is only an interpretation and not reality itself. Only a schizophrenic eats the menu instead of the food listed on the menu" (p. 215).

In an interesting elaboration of Watzlawick's constructivist ideas to the process of problem maintenance, Jeffrey Bogdan (1986) emphasized the connection between meaning and action. "It cannot strictly be the case," he said, "that behaviors, problematic or otherwise, are maintained by other behaviors. I have no access to your behavior per se, only to my representation, or interpretation of it. Therefore, it must be my interpretation of your behavior per se, that maintains my own actions" (p. 35). In terms of actual clinical practice, the only foray that MRI therapists made into the realm of meaning came through the application of an intriguing technique called "re-framing." By experimenting with this technique, we developed ways to merge the realms of meaning and action that, for all practical purposes, had been kept separate from each other.

In the early development of our approach, we were intrigued by the technique of "reframing" and tried to improve upon its effectiveness (Eron & Lund, 1989). Introduced by the MRI group as a "gentle art" (Watzlawick et al., 1974) reframing was a way "to change the conceptual and/or emotional setting or viewpoint in relation to which a situation was experienced and to place it in another frame which fits the 'facts' of the same concrete situation equally well or even better" (p. 95). Although reframing was originally described as a technique to alter the meanings people ascribe to events and behavior, this important cognitive element got lost in an emphasis on strategic intervention. MRI became known as the bastion of strategic therapy; its practitioners emphasizing the use of behavioral tasks and directives to interrupt stuck interactional patterns, often with a paradoxical or uncommonsensical bent. Also, MRI brief therapy applied reframing to the *immediate interactional context that surrounded the problem.* Watzlawick and his colleagues offered a typical example of reframing in which the nagging behavior of a wife is relabeled as being protective of her withdrawn husband. By sacrificing her own image, she is helping him to "look good" in the presence of others. It was felt that by shifting the meaning of the wife's nagging behavior, but still within this narrow interactional context, the couple's stuck behavior pattern might be interrupted.

Haley (1976, 1980) also applied reframing to the immediate situation. For example, in an attempt to negotiate a "solvable problem," a therapist encouraged the exasperated parents of a troubled teenager, whom they considered mentally ill, to develop a plan for motivating their "lazy" son (Haley, 1980). These therapeutic twists of meaning—from mad to bad, crazy to lazy, one-down to one-up— as applied to the narrow confines of a stuck situation, relegated reframing to a technique, a form of spin-doctoring, designed to get people to go along with therapeutic directives aimed at changing here-and-now patterns of behavior.

We discovered, however, that altering the meaning of a client's predicament was helpful in and of itself. We noticed swift and dramatic shifts in interactional behavior when people found new ways of understanding their stuck situation and how these took shape over time. Once we helped clients revise their perspectives on their problems, they often figured out for themselves what to do differently (Eron & Lund, 1989). Our shift away from the perspective practices of strategic family therapy paralleled the growth of the solution-focused and narrative therapies in the late 1980s and 1990s. The solution-focused approaches of Steve de Shazer and Insoo Kim Berg (de Shazer, 1985; de Shazer et al., 1986) and William O'Hanlon and Michele Weiner-Davis (1989) shifted the therapist's focus away from talk about problems and toward talk about solutions. Solution-focused therapists reoriented family members to exceptions to the present problems and to the future without the problem by emphasizing people's strengths and competencies.

Narrative therapists Michael White and David Epston (1990) also spoke about problems in a different way than their predecessors. They observed that as problems came to dominate people's lives, the stories they told themselves became negative and problem saturated. "Externalizing conversations" were designed to separate persons from problems and help them marshal their own resources against the problem. The broad spectrum of life experiences—times when people fell under the influence of problems and when they did not—were incorporated into helpful conversations.

Over the past 20 years at the CFI, we studied conversations between CFI's therapists and the families they tried to help. We attempted to discern the key ingredients of helpful conversations that brought out the best in people and inspired solutions across the life span. The result was an approach that interweaves elements common to strategic, solution-focused, and narrative therapy that empower people to access the resources needed to resolve problems efficiently.

TOWARD A THEORY OF PROBLEM CONSTRUCTION

In order to plan helpful conversations, it's important to understand how problems are constructed. Steve de Shazer (1985), the codeveloper of solution focused therapy, acknowledged the importance of clarifying one's own assumptions about complaint development.

> Therapists need to make some assumptions about the construction of complaints and the nature of solutions to do their job. . . .The assumptions can be seen to operate like rules for mapping complaints and problems. If a therapist uses a certain set of assumptions, say "Y," then a certain type of map will develop. (p. 22)

In our approach, mapping how people become fixed on problematic views of self and other leads to an understanding of how to affect change. Therapists need not wander around in the narrative dark, not knowing what stories to look for or what views to change. Paul Watzlawick (1984) offered a useful metaphor that depicts how we see the haphazard, although not entirely accidental, route to problem development.

> A captain who on a stormy night has to sail through an uncharted channel, devoid of beacons and other navigational aids, will either wreck his ship on the cliffs or regain the safe open sea beyond the strait. If he loses ship and life, his failure proves that the course he steered was not the right one. One may say that he discovered what the passage was not. If, on the other hand, he clears the strait, this success merely proves that he literally did not at any point come into collision with the (otherwise, unknown) shape and nature of the waterway; it tells him nothing about how safe or how close to disaster he was at any given moment. He passed the strait like a blind man. His course fit the unknown topography, but this does not mean that it matched it. (p. 14)

There is no precise route through life that steers us away from problems. We continue to bump against unforeseen obstacles along the way. It is the meaning we ascribe to these bumps, and to the actions of people affected by them, that determines our ultimate course. These ascriptions of meaning give shape and contour to our journey and lend to it some measure of predictability. Because there is no predetermined route to problems—or solutions—we must begin with people's own constructions and understand how they took shape to create the configuration of ideas and actions that constitute the problem. If we listen carefully to people we are trying to help and track their experience of events significant to them, we will arrive at an understanding of their own peculiar path into the straits of problem construction. Once we have this map, we, the navigators of the conversation, can help them steer back into the open seas.

An extremely articulate 14-year-old girl named Jean, whose independent spirit was being spent in seemingly endless battles with her father, helped shed light on this process of problem construction. We use her story to elucidate our assumptions.

PROBLEM CONSTRUCTION: A CASE OF UGLY ARGUING

When Jean's mother called to make an appointment, she defined the problem in terms of the "constant, ugly arguing" that went on between Jean and her father. Recently, their verbal battles had turned into pushing and shoving matches. Through tears, Mrs. Ryan spoke about her own feeble attempts to referee the two combatants and how this was tearing her apart. Lately she lapsed into siding with whoever seemed "least unreasonable," more often than not, her daughter. After all, she said, with just a hint of sarcasm, her husband was the adult and should have more self-control than his 14-year-old daughter. After several tries, Mrs. Ryan convinced her unyielding husband and defiant daughter to come to counseling to help her with her upset. Repeated attempts to convince the combatants that it was their problem had not worked.

In the first therapy session, family members related an example of a typical scene from their lives. Mr. Ryan came home from work and noticed Jean sitting on the couch eating popcorn and watching TV. She ignored him. Father commented, "I told you not to eat in the living room...besides, don't you have homework to do?" Jean sighed theatrically and continued to watch TV, deliberately not looking at her father. Finally she muttered, "Lighten up, Dad. Are you stressed out from work or what?" Mr. Ryan called Jean lazy and hopeless; she responded with an obscenity; Mr. Ryan started yelling; Mrs. Ryan entered the room and asked her husband to please calm down, saying, "You just walked in the door. Do we have to start in already?"

A typical evening in the life of the Ryan family had begun, culminating in everyone going off into their separate corners with an icy silence in the air. The only calm member of the family was Jean's brother, John, who managed to stay out of the fray. When things heated up, he would talk to his friends on the phone or close his bedroom door and quietly do his homework.

This vignette typified a more-of-the-same cycle of behavior that perpetuated the problem. The more disrespectful Jean acted, the more Mr. Ryan yelled at her, and the more Mrs. Ryan criticized her husband for overreacting. The ensuing conflict promoted emotional withdrawal among family members, punctuated by outbursts of ugly arguing. By tracking this repeated sequence of behavior, the goal of therapy became clear.

If Mr. Ryan were to calm down and join with his wife to set realistic expectations for Jean's behavior, Jean would probably act less defiant and the ugly arguing would stop. This behavioral goal is similar to what a structural family therapist looks for in realigning the hierarchy or reinforcing system boundaries. The goal is also similar to what an MRI brief therapist aims for in disrupting the father's problem-maintaining solution of coercion and exhortation.

After family members gave us a clear picture of the behavioral interaction, Jean asked the therapist an interesting question. "Dr. Lund," she said, "my brother did the same thing last week and nothing happened. I'd like to know why." She went on to describe how her brother was told to mow the lawn as soon as he came home from school. Instead, he invited some friends over to watch a tape of a basketball game, and they all ate sandwiches in the living room. Jean described how she waited around to watch the fireworks, expecting to see her brother get the brunt of her father's anger for once. To her dismay, Mr. Ryan did not say or do anything about the matter. The following interaction ensued over the question of the father's nonreaction.

Mr. Ryan:	(looking thoughtful) I seem to remember that I did say something to John like, "You know you guys shouldn't be eating in the living room."
Jean:	Yeah. And that is all you said. You didn't *do* anything about it.
Lund:	(to Mr. Ryan) Do you remember what John said to you?
Mr. Ryan:	Yeah. He said he was sorry and promised they would clean up when they were through.
Jean:	(rolling her eyes) But he was supposed to be mowing the lawn, and you never said anything about that!
Mr. Ryan:	I seem to remember that John apologized for forgetting to mow the lawn. Maybe that's why I didn't say anything. [John verified this story.]
Jean and Mrs. Ryan:	(in unison) But you let him eat in the living room, and he never did mow the lawn that day.

John remained quiet, while his father looked puzzled. What emerged in this conversation was that everyone in the family agreed about a key difference. John did many of the same things that Jean did, but with very different results.

Objectively speaking, eating popcorn in the leaving room is not much different than eating sandwiches in the living room, yet Mr. Ryan's *reaction* to the two situations was dramatically different. Obviously his contradictory response had something to do with how he *viewed* the two situations and the people involved in them. This relates to our first assumption about problem evolution and problem maintenance.

Assumption 1. *How people feel and how they act in a situation depends on how they construe the situation.*

This first assumption is about the self exclusively. It follows the thinking of personality theorist George Kelly. Salvatore Maddi (1968), in a comparative analysis of different theories of personality, wrote that "for Kelly, events have an actual existence separate from man, but do not achieve importance for understanding personality until they are construed by him" (p. 114). Ultimately, we must take into account how each individual caught in the web of problematic interaction *construes* the actions of others. In this case, Mr. Ryan's reaction to the event of eating popcorn in the living room set in motion the emotionally charged responses that followed.

To fully comprehend Mr. Ryan's construction of the event, however, we must consider how he viewed others around him. The event itself seems innocuous. The meaning father assigned to the events must be based on how he had come to see his daughter's actions and intentions, which was quite different from how he had come to see his son's actions and intentions. This leads to our second assumption.

Assumption 2. *Peoples' constructions of events or situations, and consequently how they feel and act, depend largely on their views of others. This includes their constructions of other peoples' motivations and intentions and their view of others' views of them.*

R.D. Laing (1969) wrote extensively about how individual constructions about self and other affect family interaction. He observed, "the person whom we describe . . . is not the only agent in his 'world'. How he perceives and acts towards the others, how they perceive and act towards him, how he perceives them as perceiving him . . . are all aspects of the situation" (p. 66) Laing and his colleagues previously described how peoples' self-identities are a composite of their views of themselves and their views of how others see them (Laing, Phillipson, & Lee, 1966).

Mr. Ryan's ideas about Jean's intentions contrasted with his ideas about John's intentions. He felt that Jean did things to "intentionally provoke him," that she had "no interest in cooperating," and that she clearly "disrespected" him. On the other hand, he saw John as "basically a good kid" who "cared" for him, "respected" him and valued his advice. Thus, this construction of how Jean saw him was very different from his construction on how John saw him. In his mind, his daughter regarded him as an unworthy father, undeserving of her respect, and his son saw him as decent father whom he still valued. Obviously, John's apology for eating in the living room and Jean's sassy response reinforced these preexisting constructions.

Jean and her brother, John, filled the therapist in on their own ideas of Dad's behavior and shed more light on why he responded differently to the two eating incidents. With a hint of sadness in her voice, Jean said that her father treated her brother with far more "respect" that he treated her. As the therapist expressed interest in Jean's point of view, she burst into tears. "He thinks I'm stupid, or retarded, and he doesn't respect me at all as a person," she said. John chimed in with his perspective on the father-daughter conflict. He felt that neither one had respect for the other. "You're just like Dad," he said. "You can't let anything go. You know he can be picky. I just let it ride, and that's what you should do."

Now that we had these perspectives on the two "eating" events and the people involved in them, we could explain why one situation triggered a problematic interaction and the other did not. Mr. Ryan's differing reactions were an outgrowth of differing viewpoints about Jean and John's actions and intentions, and how he felt they viewed him. Similarly, Jean's defiant behavior became more explainable once we understood her perspective about her father's actions and intentions and how she thought her father viewed her. John, too, helped us understand why Father's reaction to his eating sandwiches in the living room was so mild. Although he saw him as "picky," he did not attribute any negative intention to his actions. He simply felt, "That's just him." Because he saw his father seeing him as a "good kid" who was competent and worthy of respect, he was better able to accept his father's ways.

The basis for the emotional intensity of people's reactions to events relates to the next assumption.

Assumption 3. *People have strong preferences with regard to how they would like to behave, how they would like to see them-selves, and how they would like to be seen by others. We refer to this constellation of ideas about self as a person's "preferred view."*

This concept of preferred view appears in different shapes and forms in the writings of prominent self psychologists and family therapists. For example, the concept of preferred view was implied in the client-centered therapy developed by Carl Rogers, whose ideas bear a marked resemblance to postmodern, nonimpositional concepts about therapy and change. Rogers (1961) proposed that people experience distress when there is a gap between their ideal self and self as perceived. Successful therapy closes this gap. "During and after therapy," Rogers said, "the perceived self would be more positively valued, i.e., would become more congruent with the ideal or valued self" (pp. 234-235). William James (1890/1984) made a similar distinction between the "immediate and actual and the remote and potential selves" (p. 315).

More recently, Hazel Markus and Paula Nurius (1986) introduced the notion of "possible selves" to "represent individuals' ideas of what they are afraid of becoming" (p.954). Similar to our concept of preferred view, possible selves serve both a motivational and evaluative function. People are motivated to achieve their possible or desirable possible selves and to avoid their negative or undesirable possible selves, and to evaluate their own behavior in relation to these standards. In our terms, people compare events in their lives against constructions of preference and are motivated to reconcile gaps between how they would like things to be and how they think events turn out. Like our concept of preferred view, the concept of possible selves implies that there is no "real" singular representation of self. We are not describing schemas lodged inside our psyches, but rather a constellation of evolving possibilities by which we measure our life experience and construct who we are.

Strategic family therapists also recognized the therapeutic importance of understanding how people want or prefer to be seen by others. For example, in their seminal article presenting the MRI approach, Weakland, Fisch, Watzlawick, and Bodin noted that they determined early in treatment "what approach would appeal most to the particular patient—to observe where 'he lives' and meet his need, whether it is to believe in the magical, to defeat the expert, to be a caretaker of someone, to face a challenge, or whatever" (1974,

p. 156).   Narrative therapists Michael White and David Epston (1990), touching on the concept of preferred view, emphasized how "preferred outcomes" or "preferred stories" are drawn out in the course of therapeutic conversation to open up alternative possibilities for change. They noted that often these preferred stories and preferred outcomes were hidden, buried under "problem-saturated" accounts of the self. This clinical observation squared with the research findings of Markus and Nurius (1986), who pointed out that a person's possible selves are less obvious to other people than their active, "real" self-representations. Thus, people might act in ways that are out of sync with their own preferences, but their wishes might not be apparent to others they are close to. As you will see in our case example, both Jean and her father ultimately reveal that they would like to have a close relationship. They are both unhappy, even saddened, by their current interaction. These preferences would not be obvious, however, if one looked only at their current actions or listened to their problem-saturated accounts of their present situation.

Let us be clear that we do not see "preferred view" as a "thing" that people "have" and cannot get rid of. Rather, we are talking about a host of possible views or preferences that suit people, that fit with who they wish to be. For example, "I'm clever," "I'm a good mother," "I'm a good thinker," and "I'm sensitive and caring," may all represent preferred attributions of self. People also may have preferred explanations for actions they take.

For example, "I did X because I love my child," or "I did Y because I would do anything for a friend," might constitute preferred explanations. On the other hand, the thought that "I did X to be manipulative or controlling," might violate a person's preference. In general, we regard "preferred view" as a narrative concept—a fluid, evolving set of ideas about the self that embraces past, present, and future dimensions. Preferred views are inferred by the stories people tell about their lives.

Gleaning a person's preferred view can be a slippery business. There is no simple, direct route, such as asking, "How do you prefer to be seen by others?" or "What is your preferred view, anyway?" that yields a clear and accurate answer. Furthermore, although we may react emotionally when we do not act as we would like or when we feel that others do not see us as we want them to, we may not be clear about our wishes and intentions. Even when we are clear, we do not often communicate our preferences to others. We rarely say things such as, "You know, I prefer to be seen as a brilliant therapist. That's why my vein popped when you questioned my approach to helping that client."

Preferred views of self are inferred by asking a host of preference questions. For example, we asked Jean's father how he felt when he lost his temper. Did he feel good about himself or bad about himself? We also inquired about how he thought his wife regarded his interactions with Jean, and whether her response to him was preferred or not. We asked how he felt about earlier times in his relationship with Jean, when things were going better. Further, we inquired about current aspects of his life such as his work as a teacher. Did he enjoy teaching? How did he think his students and coworkers regarded him? We also asked how he felt about how his own parents dealt with him as a teenager. Was he acting like his father? Did he prefer to act like his father?

Out of this inquiry, we gleaned that Jean's father preferred to see himself as a good teacher and a caring and involved father. It mattered a great deal to him that he was respected and that his advice was valued. He did not like himself when he lost his temper, and he was not at all happy with how he thought his wife regarded him. He wanted to be different from his own father but was beginning to wonder whether he was. He was most comfortable with his son's view of him. John was the only member of the family who he felt regarded him with respect, who saw him as he wanted to be seen. Conversations with Jean revealed that she preferred to be seen as smart, capable, competent, and independent. She was pretty sure that her father did not see her in these ways. These discrepancies in viewpoint bring us to our next assumption about problem evolution.

Assumption 4. *People experience negative and unsettling emotions such as frustration, sadness, and anxiety when (1) they behave in ways that are discrepant with preferred views of self, (2) they see themselves in ways that are discrepant with preferred views, and (3) they imagine that others see them in ways that are discrepant with preferred views.*

An assumption of Carl Roger's client-centered therapy was that people experienced unsettling emotions when there was a gap between their ideal self and their actual self, or self as perceived. Effective therapy occurred when the therapist assumed a critical position or stance that helped the client to experience "unconditional positive regard." Thus, the client's view of the therapist's view of her was seen as key to closing the troublesome gap between ideal self and self as perceived. Rogers was an individual therapist who focused on internal conflicts. Although Rogers described how "conditional positive regard" of parents and influential adults affected children's emotional development and shaped problems, he did not involve parents or family members in the actual therapy (Rogers, 1951).

The work of R. D. Laing and his colleagues (Laing et al., 1966) added what we call a "cognitive-interactional" dimension. Although Laing never touched on the concept of preferred view, one of his most important, yet neglected, contributions to the field of family therapy was the notion of "disjunctive attributions." Laing wrote eloquently about the pain people experience when they perceive a gap between their own intentions and the attributions others assign to their motives. He said "there is a strong tendency to feel guilt, anxiety, anger and doubt, if self attributions are disjunctive with attributions made about the self by other" (p. 152). According to Laing, disjunctive attributions are experienced from three vantage points. These include one's view of self, one's view of the other, and one's view of the other's view of self. When one's view of self grows out of sync with one's view of the other and with one's view of the other's view of self, emotional distress results. To Laing (1970), people experienced these gaps as internal "knots" that, on occasion, literally drove them crazy. One of Laing's most poignant portrayals of this process appeared in an evocative book called *The Divided Self*, which depicted the dark descent into schizophrenic thinking spurred on by the entangling web of disjunctive knots (Laing, 1960). What Laing described experientially as a "knot," we portray graphically in a problem cycle.

In describing our approach, we will use the term "disjunction" or "disjunctive attributions" to refer to the gap between how people prefer to be seen by others and how they see others seeing them. The experience of disjunction supplies the fuel that gets problem cycles going and keeps them going. We will consider how problems evolve as this gap widens and how problems resolve as this gap narrows. In this sense our definition of the concept of "disjunction" combines the individual-experiential contributions of Rogers with the interactional-experiential contributions of Laing to portray how people become stuck in their socially constructed predicaments.

Laing suggested that people experience disjunctive attributions, as if tied up in twisted knots that they can't loosen. William James (1890/1984) also described the painful experience of disjunction quite eloquently many years ago:

> Those images in the minds of other men are, it is true, things outside of me, whose changes I perceive just as I perceive any other outward change. But the pride and shame which I feel are not concerned merely with those changes. I feel as if something else had changed too, when I perceived my image in your mind to have changed for the worse, something in me to which that image belongs, and which a moment ago I felt inside of me, big and strong and lusty, but now weak, contracted and collapsed. (p. 97)

The emotional effects of disjunctive attributions bring us to our next assumption about problem construction.

Assumption 5. Problematic behavior often emerges as one or more people begin to see others seeing them in ways discrepant with how they prefer to be seen. This often happens at times of family transition, when views of self and other are changing, fluid, and unsettled.

Events that occur during these times in families are significant to problem construction, because they awaken a search for new meaning. At these times of flux, family members may begin to reconsider how those close to them see them. The idea that relationships change when people notice something different about important others was discussed in depth by Gregory Bateson (1988). According to Bateson, shifts in interactional patterns occur when people respond to "news of difference" (p. 28). What may seem at first glance to be an ordinary event, such as eating popcorn in the living room, staying out beyond a curfew, choosing a new friend who rides motorcycles and sports tattoos, or not coming home on time for dinner, supply the raw material for problem formation. If an event construed as "different" challenges how people prefer to be seen and alters how they think others see them, new action is likely to emerge. This new behavior may set in motion problematic interactions.

Ironically, there are many occasions in which what may appear to be a more grievous or upsetting event, such as the onset of major illness, may not lead to problems beyond the illness itself. A person may draw on existing strengths to "tough the illness out," or "not give in to it," so that intimate others continue to perceive the person as unchanged. The person's preferred view in this sense remains intact, unshaken by the event and the ensuing actions of others, so that the idea of a problem (beyond the upsetting event itself) never materializes. Life is actually filled with such nonproblem scenarios, although we tend not to notice them.

This assumption about problem evolution expands upon a basic premise of the MRI model mentioned earlier, that problems develop from the mishandling of ordinary life difficulties. From this perspective, people "slip into" problem maintaining patterns more by accident than by structural or systemic design. Jeffrey Bogdan (1986) referred to this process as "accidentalism" (p.35) to convey the random, not entirely predictable path to problems in the MRI approach. Steve de Shazer (1985) touched on a similar theme in describing how problems evolve out of "damned bad luck" (p. 18). A seemingly trivial event can trigger the onset of a major problem by jostling the preexisting views of those affected by the event. Whether a life event or an "accident" turns into an enduring problem hinges not only on how the event is construed but also on whether disjunctive views of self and other emerge in the wake of the event. Although events that we cannot control or predict happen in life, there is some predictability as to whether problems develop. If an event challenges a person's preferred view and alters how he or she sees others seeing him or her, there is an increased probability that problems will develop. Beyond randomness, there is a method to this process of problem construction.

In order to understand how transitional events affect problems, it is essential to know something about life before the event. When the conversation with Jean and her family turned to the preproblem past, more clues to the mystery of problem construction were found. The following conversation took place between the therapist and Jean, with her brother present.

Lund: Was there a time when you believed your dad thought well of you?

Jean: He used to think I was smart.

Lund: When was that?

Jean: A few years ago.

Lund: What were you two doing differently then?

Jean: He used to take me skiing.

Lund: I don't think I get it. How did that indicate that he
       thought you were smart?

Jean: Because he taught me to ski, and I learned so fast that he
       used to joke about it to his friends.

Lund: How was that for you?

Jean: That was fun. We did it with golf, too.

Lund: You did it with golf?

Jean: He taught me. I did good....he would tease his friends
       about how I was going to beat them all before I left jun-
       ior high school.

Lund: Do you still do things together?

Jean: No.

Lund: What happened?

Jean: I don't know. . . he just got mean. . . (tears).

Lund: Do you think Dad thinks you are at all smart now?

Jean: No...I thought he would be happy that I got good
       grades in school.

Lund: He's not?

Jean: All he does is question how I get such good grades
       when I can't remember to do things that he asks me at
       home. . . . I can't stand him anymore.

Lund: Would you mind if I asked your dad about the skiing
       and golf and told him what you told me about that? I
       would really like to know how that was for him.

Jean: That's fine with me.

This conversation revealed how Jean interpreted the changes
in her relationship with her father over time. She used to feel good
when her father saw her as "smart," but she thinks he no longer
does. She expresses sadness about this gap between how she would
prefer to be seen and how she now imagines that her father thinks
of her. She also speaks about her preferences. She prefers not to be
fighting with her father and recalls longingly the times when they
were close, when he taught her skiing and complimented her to his
friends. All this would be news to Dad, who had not the faintest idea
that his daughter respected him or valued his input. Once upon a
time, Jean's father experienced his daughter's love, trust, respect, and

admiration. The typical adolescent transition of growing up and away from parents was made more painful by his perception that Jean lost all semblances of love and respect for him.

The intensity of Jean's apparent movement away from her father was fueled by disjunctive attributions, by her assumptions that her father regarded her in a negative light. She was furious that her father saw her as "stupid" and incompetent, and she entertained little hope that her father would ever see her as she preferred. The effect of current behavior was that Jean refused to go along with her father's requests and would never apologize for forgetting about a family rule, as her brother did. The more convinced Jean became that her father thought her to be stupid, incompetent, and unworthy of his respect, the more she wore her defiance like a badge, concealing her preference for closeness and masking her sadness with sarcasm and anger. The conversation with Jean's parents went as follows:

Lund:	I enjoyed talking with your children. Jean was telling me about some fun that you and she had.
Mr. Ryan:	(looking confused) She told you about us having fun?
Lund:	I was a bit surprised myself...she mentioned that you taught her to ski and golf and that she had the sense that you enjoyed it, too...she seemed pleased that you enjoyed it.
Mr. Ryan:	That's what you talked about?
Lund:	That was part of what we talked about...do you folks talk much about that?
Mr. Ryan:	(Mrs. Ryan smiling and looking on) No, I'm very surprised she brought that up. I thought she forgot anything I did that might be good....how did that come up?
Lund:	I was asking her about when things were going well...can I ask you both the same thing?
Mr. Ryan:	Well, I guess I would have to agree with Jean for a change. Things were very good then.
Lund:	What made them good for you?
Mr. Ryan:	She was interested in what I had to say.
Lund:	You mean she cooperated?

Mr. Ryan:	Pretty much. She was always a bit challenging.
Lund:	I don't think I understood what you just said about her interest in what you had to say.
Mrs. Ryan:	I think what he means is that she used to show more interest in her father and want to learn about things he did.
Lund:	Is that accurate?
Mr. Ryan:	Yeah, I think so...she doesn't seem to care for me or anything about me.
Lund:	How is that for you?
Mr. Ryan:	It hurts.
Lund:	When did things change?
Mr. Ryan:	When she went to her new school, made some new friends, and had no interest in spending time with the family.
Mrs. Ryan:	She spent less time with her dad and used the wise guy humor that he had taught her on him...he didn't like it.

Mr. Ryan seemed surprised that Jean might have anything good to say about him, or that she might speak of occasions in which she saw him as he wished. He, too, expressed hurt about the changes in their relationship. He and his wife recalled with nostalgia the times when Jean showed an interest in what he had to say. As Jean approached adolescence, went to a new school, and made new friends, she *acted as* if she did not respect her father's advice anymore. Her father's temper outbursts were an outgrowth of the experience of disjunction. The more convinced he became that his daughter found him unworthy of regard the more he attempted to command her respect through force. His preferences for closeness and for being a helpful guide in Jean's quest for independence were no longer visible to Jean.

Jay Efran and his colleagues said, "Objectivist therapists want to know what *really* happened in the past; constructivist therapists are more interested in 'history' as a key to the unfolding family narrative that gives contemporary events their meaning" (Efran, Lukens, & Lukens, 1988, p. 28). It is important to understand how past stories or narratives of people's lives help to give meaning to events in the present. These stories affect how people view "news of difference" in relationships. As Mr. Ryan looked back, he remembered his own troubled adolescence. He recalled constant arguing with his father, who never understood him and died before they had a chance to resolve their conflicts. He vowed to do things differently and remain close to his daughter. Mr. Ryan perceived changes in Jean, as she became an adolescent. He interpreted these changes to mean that she was moving away from him, a worrisome construction shaped by this past narrative. Mrs. Ryan's story of her own adolescence was similar to Jean's. Although she too had conflicts with her parents, they resolved as family members negotiated this challenging life transition. Mrs. Ryan viewed Jean's new and different adolescent behavior as "normal," a nonproblematic construction shaped by her past narrative.

Thus, what emerged from conversation with Jean and her family was a story of misunderstanding and conflict emerging during a time of family transition. As Jean reached adolescence, she showed more interest in friends. As she grew more independent, she appeared to disregard her parents' input. Jean's mother took these developments in stride. As she noticed news of difference, she perceived no challenge to her preferred view. Jean's father, on the other hand, felt threatened. He questioned whether these changes meant that Jean no longer loved or needed him. This unsettling view of self in the eyes of an important other propelled problem-maintaining behavior into motion.

Assumption 6. As problem cycles evolve, views of self and other become more fixed and actions more restricted. Repetitions of the cycle reinforce disjunctive attributions, escalate negative emotions, and promote more-of-the-same behavior.

As Mr. Ryan increased his efforts to give "input" to Jean in ways that undermined her sense of independence, she grew more defiant. He began to feel his daughter's shunning him, which heightened his hurt, then anger, and fueled his futile attempts to command respect. The more upset and critical he became toward Jean, the more Mrs. Ryan acted in ways that suggested that she, too, disrespected him. Now he felt his wife regarded him in ways discrepant with his preferred view.

As the gap widened between how Mr. Ryan preferred to be seen and how he saw others seeing him, his distress and volatile behavior increased. He failed to notice occasions in which Jean treated him as he wished. Memories of Jean's respect for him, of skiing lessons and other happy times, faded. It was hard to imagine a future in which Mr. Ryan might once again be an important part of his daughter's life.

Disjunctive attributions also limited the range of behavior shown by Jean and her mother. Mrs. Ryan preferred to see herself as a competent mother and a loving wife, yet she felt that she could not get through to her daughter or her husband to stop their ugly arguing. Her failure to help caused her to doubt her own virtues as partner and parent. Shuttle diplomacy became Mother's only hope to remedy an increasingly hopeless situation. Meanwhile, the more coercive and critical Dad became, and the more conciliatory Mom became, the less Jean gave an inch. She refused to apologize even to her mother for misdeeds and stopped asking either parent for assistance in any way that might indicate to them that they mattered, even just a little. The problem evolved into something fixed and static. It became a real "thing" that everyone noticed and that organized day-to-day life of the family. This "thingification" of the problem captures our final assumption about problem construction.

Assumption 7. As problematic interaction comes to dominate family life, family members become more convinced that a problem really exists and locate its cause in perceived deficiencies of self and other.

INTEGRATING STRATEGIC AND NARRATIVE CONCEPTS

In the 1970s and 1980s, strategic therapists maintained a narrow focus on immediate interaction and downplayed the importance of people's constructions about the past and future. Narrative therapists added the broad sweep of time to our understanding of human predicaments. Understanding how the broad narrative landscape shapes the narrow immediate situation and how the narrow immediate situation shapes the broad narrative landscape is integral to understanding problem construction and problem deconstruction.

Cloé Madanes, a leader in the development of the strategic approach, described therapy in a way that captured this integration of past, present, and future. Note her emphasis on narrative in this passage from her book, *Sex, Love and Violence* (Madanes, 1990):

> If a therapist must have a theory of personality, then the most helpful one is that of an identity as a mental, abridged antholo-

gy of stories, any one of which can be replaced by a story from the total collection. Therapy thus involves editing the abridged edition of perceptions of the present and past. A change in these perceptions is a change in the personality, and a change of shared perceptions is a change in the relationship. (p.247)

Stories from the past, whether they are told or not, influence the development and maintenance of present interaction in ways that may not be known to the current protagonists. Unbeknownst to Jean, her mother and father looked back on their own adolescences with very different perspectives. Mr. Ryan's story of his relationship with his own father and how this changed for the worse as he approached adolescence is relevant to his present "framing" of Jean's behavior. Similarly, Mrs. Ryan's story of her "normal" relationship with her mother during adolescence, and her sense that things went well during that transition, fits with her present "framing" of her daughter's behavior. Past narrative accounts affect how transitional events are interpreted and shape how people respond to "news of difference."

When problematic interaction comes to dominant family life, the lens through which people view self and other narrows. Certain features of the broad narrative landscape are not noticed, whereas those that are emphasized reinforce negative feelings. Mr. Ryan does not notice present actions that might indicate that Jean respects him. Jean overlooks current behaviors that might imply that her father thinks well of her. Similarly, preferred stories from the past are forgotten or recast in light of current negative views. While embroiled in problematic interactions, people do not see a preproblem past, do not notice current exceptions to problems, and do not envision a future without the problem.

The integration of narrative and strategic concepts brings together past, present, and future dimensions of individual and family life. Psychotherapists tend to emphasize one to the exclusion of the other, which obscures the exquisite interplay of time. For example, psychodynamic therapists often criticize behavior therapists and strategic family therapists for focusing only on here-and-now symptoms and ignoring their roots. Here-and-now therapies are regarded as "not deep enough." Similarly, present-oriented therapists, who emphasize brevity and practicality, are often intolerant of detours into the past. By linking narrative and strategic concepts, we suggest that key stories from the past inform the present predicament, which in turn informs how people recall their pasts and envision their futures. By understanding the process of problem construction in terms of all three-time dimensions, we are better able to select key stories to talk about in therapy that will alter the present predicament, as well as reorient people to their pasts and futures.

Let us examine a case in further detail to show problem construction that elucidates how to map the path to and find creative solutions to difficult symptoms.

A 65-YEAR OLD MAN OVERCOMES PSYCHIATRIC SYMPTOMS

Don was 55 years old when he was first hospitalized for depression. Now 65, this was his seventh admission to a psychiatric inpatient facility. He had received numerous shock treatments, a variety of psychotropic medications and different psychotherapies, but felt that nothing had helped. His most recent symptoms included violent head shaking movements, which he felt were out of his control. Don was told that his symptoms were psychologically based, but he did not accept this diagnosis. He believed that his head movements were neurological despite the fact that tests proved negative.

Don was seen as a difficult patient. He did not take his medication reliably. He did not go along with many of the regimens prescribed by the treatment team (group activities, occupational therapy, and counseling). He often refused to take showers, grumbled about morning wake ups and arrived late for activities and meals.

The clinical director of the inpatient facility invited us to train the entire staff—psychologists, social workers, nurses, psychiatrists and line staff—in the narrative solutions approach. He felt that Don would be a good test case because he was making life difficult for the treatment team, and was particularly challenging to staff in positions of authority. The psychiatrists were frustrated with Don because he defied their recommendations and challenged their expertise, and the clinical director was constantly receiving complaints about him. Don's wife called regularly, expressing her dismay with his lack of progress and her despair over 10 years of taking Don to the best of places and getting poor results. Line staff had mixed experiences with Don. Some felt they could reach him and had little difficulty motivating him to participate in activities. Others said he was driving them crazy; one commenting in jest that he might benefit from the medication Don refused.

Before talking with Don, we were shown videotape of him sitting alone on a couch by a window in one of the day treatment rooms. The scene portrayed Don at his worst. He looked like a backward mental patient, his face expressionless, his head suddenly erupting into strange sideways movements while he tried desperately to hold it in place. Don did not look like a man who was once a high paid executive with an insurance company (as we were told). We wondered where that person was and how he might be reached.

Our aim was to conduct an initial interview with Don that would provide a blueprint for helpful conversations for the entire treatment team. We asked the staff to review the videotape of the interview. They were to jot down the qualities and attributes that fit with Don's preferred view, then discern whether there was a gap between the person Don wished to be, how he saw his own behavior (and symptoms) and how he felt others regarded him. This assessment would offer clues as to how to address a variety of issues affecting the staff, for example.

HOW TO TALK WITH DON ABOUT HIS HEAD SHAKING SYMPTOMS

- how to talk with Don about medication and promote compliance
- how to plan activities that might engage Don's interest and participation
- how to develop an aftercare plan that might suit Don's preferences
- how to engage the line staff, counselors and supervisors in a coordinated approach to helpful conversations
- how to involve family members (i.e. Don's spouse) as a resource in motivating change

The conversation between Dr. Eron and Don began as follows:

Eron: I understand Dr. Martin (the clinical director) talked with you about us having this conversation today. He hoped it might be helpful?

Don: He said you're the expert. You wrote a book that everyone's reading here. I'm sorry I haven't had a chance to read it yet. I hope you can help, but I think I'm a hopeless case.

Eron: Don, I was curious about how you wound up at this hospital. Was it your idea to come here?

Don:	Not really. My wife thought this might be the place. I've been to a lot of other institutions before this one. She hoped they might cure me? (Sounds sarcastic)
Eron:	Your wife's name is?
Don:	Julia
Eron:	How were you with Julia's idea?
Don:	I didn't like it. I hate these places.
Eron:	But you came anyway. Julia must be very important to you. She felt it was a good idea and you cooperated, despite hating these places.
Don:	(Looks upset) My wife's been through a lot with me (head starts to shake).
Eron:	Why did Julia think it was a good idea to come here?
Don:	I've put her though a lot. She feels I'm very sick and that maybe these people will have the answer. I am very sick.
Eron:	What are your thoughts on how you wound up in this place and the other places you mentioned.
Don:	I don't know. The first time I was depressed. Then they said I was crazy, schizophrenic. I've had every diagnosis you can imagine.
Eron:	What do you think?
Don:	I think it's neurological. But the doctors can't figure it out.
Eron:	What did your wife think happened to you Don? How does she feel you wound up here?
Don:	(Don's head movements intensify, then as they slow down a little he says with sadness,) She's disappointed with me. We used to have a great life.
Eron:	Can you tell me about that life? When were things at their best?

DON'S IDEAS

Note that the interview does do not begin with a discussion of Don's diagnosis, condition or symptoms. Instead the therapist is curious about what Don thinks about being at this facility. Was it his idea to come to an inpatient facility or someone else's? If someone else's idea, what does he think of his or her idea? The therapist relates to Don as an independent thinker and writer of his own life script. If the discussion were to begin around Don's psychiatric condition or out of control symptoms, it would appeal to Don at his worst and to the negative ways that he feels many important others have regarded him over the past ten years. Such a discussion is more likely to invoke defensiveness, passivity, and perhaps even a display of symptoms.

The discussion of Don's ideas about being in an inpatient facility orients the interview around his preferences, hopes, and intentions. Don says that being in an inpatient facility does not suit him; it violates his preferred sense of himself. Don mentions that his wife, Julia, wanted him to go to the hospital and he went along with her preference. When describing how Julia sees him ("she's been through a lot with me"), Don's head begins to shake.

The emergence of symptoms at this point in the interview suggests that he experiences a gap (painfully so) between the person he has become in the eyes of his wife (sick, helpless, needing hospitalization) and through his own eyes ("I'm very sick," he says). When the discussion shifts back to Don's point of view about this place and other similar institutions, his head shaking subsides. By consulting Don's opinion and respecting his know how, Don is more likely to see the therapist seeing him as capable and competent. As the gap narrows, Don acts more competent and in control. As the gap widens, he becomes symptomatic.

At the close of this segment, Don is asked about his wife's opinion of how he wound up at this place. He stops talking, and his head shaking symptoms intensify. Not wanting to linger with Don in the gap, the focus shifts to Don at his best, inviting him to recall his life with Julia before the problem began.

Shifting the focus to the preproblem past has several advantages. Don may tell stories of his life that contrast with his current circumstances and offer clues to preferred qualities and attributes. This process of noticing strengths and attributes helps to build an alliance between therapist and client, minimizing resistance and opening possibilities for change. Don's attention is drawn to other people in his life who noticed these positive attributes. For example, was there a time when Julia saw him as competent and in control of his life? What was that like for him? What was that like for her? Through Don's own narrative we may also get clues as to what went awry. How did Don go from being at his best to being at his worst?

What transitional life events or circumstances underscored this transformation?

DON'S STORY

When Don spoke about his life before the 10 years of hospitalizations, he perked up. His head did not shake nor did he seem conscious of controlling its movements. He spoke of his life as an executive for a large insurance firm, his success as a salesman, and his accumulation of material wealth. While proud of his achievements, his story had another side. He referred sarcastically to his ability to "sell sand to an Arab," and refer with disdain to the "three martini" lunches that were part of his life routine.

What mattered most to Don during this time was how well he and Julia got along. They traveled a lot, ate at fine restaurants, and bought a beach house. Julia admired Don's talents and looked up to him. Don had helped bring her into the company and she had moved up the ladder. She now relished her own executive position and enjoyed the corporate life style.

When Don was asked how he met Julia, he filled in other important pieces of his life story. They met as teenagers, both coming from what Don called "dysfunctional" families. Don's family was poor. His mother was alcoholic and his father worked several jobs and was not around much. Julia grew up in a family where both parents drank. Julia looked to Don for guidance. He was four years older. Don liked being seen as helpful, as a leader, and as someone Julia admired.

The therapist expressed curiosity with the theme of alcoholism that appeared in Don's story—the three martini lunches, the corporate life style, his mother's drinking, and his wife's background. He learned that Don had become sober during the ten years of repeated hospitalizations. It was a fact that seemed discrepant with a life of nervous breakdowns and out of control symptoms, and this contradiction peaked the therapist's curiosity.

Don was then asked a mystery question. How was it that he made a decision to take control of his life (seeking sobriety) at a time when things seemed out of control (being hospitalized, receiving shock treatments for depression)? Mystery questions invite clients to explain the gap between the people they want to be and how it is they have been acting. Responses to these questions often provide clues to how problems evolve, which in turn provide clues to solutions. The discussion with Don about drinking and sobriety went as follows.

Eron: What led you to make a decision to stop drinking—at a time when you were feeling pretty bad (after Don's first hospitalization and a series of shock treatments)?

Don: It was just *common sense* I guess. I didn't like the effects anymore. Drinking didn't taste good. It didn't feel good anymore.

Eron: But what was your motivation?

Don: As I said it was just common sense.

Eron: Decisions like those require *self-control, determination.* Don't they?

Don: Drinking no longer had a pleasurable effect. It wasn't working anymore.

Eron: I'm curious Don. Why at that particular time in your life did you make this choice? You said this was after your first hospitalization. And you gave up something that was part of your life style, — the three martini lunches, and all that. Were you trying to take a stand?

Don: After I got out of the hospital I went back to work. I was dysfunctional. I showed up at 11:00. I was abstinent, no caffeine, no alcohol, but I felt terrible. I recognized that if alcohol was my problem I should have felt better.

Eron: But you persisted with sobriety despite not feeling better. Why?

Don: I don't know. I knew I had to change my life style.

Note that several preferred qualities and attributes reveal themselves through this conversation about sobriety (common sense, determination, persistence, self-control). Don is helped to notice these qualities. As he sees the therapist seeing him as in control and as an initiator of important life changes, his head movements cease. The therapist expresses particular interest in the transformation Don underwent at this time in his life. He appeared to be questioning his old life style, which involved material success, impressing people in authority and drinking heavily. Although he seemed determined to do something different with his life, his efforts were not being rewarded. He lost motivation to go to work. His ambition waned. He later said that he went to Alcoholics Anonymous (AA) meetings, but did not share this important part of his life with Julia. Julia continued to live the corporate life, to work hard and move up the ladder. Don seemed to be on a different path, but it was not something he talked about with people close to him. This preference to live a sober, less material, and perhaps more spiritual life seemed submerged. Looking at himself through the eyes of his wife, boss and co-workers, Don appeared as a disappointment, a failure, and not a man on a spiritual mission.

The therapist asked Don more about his travels with his wife to see if this valued aspect of their life together fit within this new (preferred?) lifestyle.

Don:	That fall (after Don's first hospitalization) Julia and I went to the Middle East. It was fantastic. The cross section of civilizations and religions inspired me. (As Don talked about his trip, he suddenly shifted to Dr. Eron.) You're Jewish, aren't you?
Eron:	Yes
Don:	Surely you've been to Jerusalem. What did you think?
Eron:	Actually, Don, I've never been.
Don:	(Incredulous) You're Jewish and you've never been to Jerusalem!
Eron:	I'm afraid so, Don.
Don:	You must go. It's important to do these things in your life. I don't think you can live a full life until you've been to that part of the world. This is where all the major religions of the world meet. If you're a spiritual person, and I sense you are, then you must go.

Don was now asking the therapist mystery questions and helping him to notice gaps in his own life narrative. "How is it that someone who's interested in me and my inner aspirations, and who also appears to be a spiritual person, would not have visited this important part of the world?" As Don turned therapist, he grew animated, energetic and anything-but-depressed. The therapist thanked him for his insights, as their conversation drew to a close.

Two weeks after meeting with Don, a session was scheduled with Don's wife, Julia, to pursue her ideas about how the problem evolved and what she would like to see for their future. Although the therapist's preference was to meet with Julia alone, Don did not like

90

that idea. Given Don's desire to be in control and his concern about how his wife regarded him, his wish to sit in on the meeting was not surprising. Thus, Don sat in the corner of the room while the therapist talked with Julia, respecting the therapist's preference to talk with her individually by not interrupting. Every time Julia expressed her frustration with Don and his symptoms and the misery of their lives over the past 10 years, Don's head shook violently. When Julia described Don at his best, his symptoms subsided.

The most interesting piece of information came toward the end of the interview. Julia corroborated Don's account that he was at his best during the time between his first and second hospitalizations. It was then that Don sought sobriety and attended AA. It was then that the couple traveled to Israel and Don maintained a leisurely work schedule. Julia mentioned that Don's boss was a bit frustrated with Don's semi-retirement schedule. He appealed to him to increase his hours and do more work-related travel and sales. Julia said that Don agreed. Two weeks later he was in the hospital again, having suffered a second "nervous breakdown," setting in motion a pattern that would continue for 10 years. The interview concluded as follows:

> Eron: (Looking over at Don with puzzlement) I got the impression from you both that Don was content working less hours, and traveling. In fact you both seemed to feel that Don was at his best during this time. Did I get that right?
>
> Julia: Yes.
>
> Eron: Is that like Don to do what his boss wanted rather than what he wanted?
>
> Julia: That's Don all right. (Don looks at the floor; his head is not shaking but he appears sad, forlorn)
>
> Eron: (To Julia and Don) That's interesting. I'll be talking with the staff about my conversations with you both. Don helped me see that I need to get in touch with my spirituality and go to Jerusalem. One thing I'll be encouraging people to do here is return the favor and help Don figure out what he would like for his life. You've been very helpful in giving us some clues, Julia. Thank you.

CLUES TO SOLUTIONS

Based on this initial interview with Don and Julia, we made several recommendations.

> (1) Consult Don's expertise about the effectiveness of medication. Ask him, what medications have been helpful? What medications have not been helpful? What does he think about taking medication? What are his preferences?

Why? Don's skepticism about medication may be linked to his preference for sobriety, and aversion to using drugs as a solution to his life difficulties. Furthermore, Don prefers to be seen as competent and in control. Taking a prescriptive, directive stance about what is best for Don medically, then suggesting that he is a noncompliant patient, challenges his preferred view and invites resistance. Asking Don's opinion about what works for him confirms his preferred view, minimizes resistance, and also helps to determine what medications have actually been useful.

> (2) Talk further with Don about his thoughts about lifestyle changes, sobriety, and his emerging spirituality.

Why? These preferences appear to be submerged. Don has not spoken to intimate others or staff about what he would like for his life. The primary focus of conversation has been on his symptoms and what to do about them. Hopefully, as Don is helped to notice his own preferences, he will be more likely to talk with others about what he would like for his life.

> (3) Do not talk with Don and his wife about his head shaking symptoms or his progress (or lack of progress) in controlling them.

Why? These conversations challenge Don's preferred view as a competent, in control person. Don and Julia's lives have become immersed in symptom talk, which has blocked discussion of preferences and possibilities.

> (4) Consult Julia's expertise about how the problem evolved.

Why? Don sees Julia as the most important person in his life. They helped each other grow up and leave dysfunctional backgrounds. At one time, Don saw himself as helpful to Julia. Now he sees himself as a miserable disappointment. In talking with Julia, it became clear that her construction of how the problem evolved corroborated Don's account, and offered clues about how to talk with Don about his unspoken preferences.

(5) *Design activities on the treatment unit that appeal to Don's talents and abilities.*

Why? Don was at his best when he functioned as an executive leader. Because he is older and has more life experiences than most of his fellow inpatients, he may feel more comfortable as a group discussion leader, advisor, and confidant. Don prefers to be seen as helpful to others and this attribute may be put to good use on the treatment unit.

(6) *Determine which conversations with the line staff are helpful and which are not, and promote more of these helpful conversations.*

Why? Staff members described varying results in working with Don. Some found him to be compliant, others defiant. By mapping these conversations, we may find that those staff who are effective with Don appeal to his preferred view, and others do not. This may help staff to become more aware of their conversational approach and coordinate their efforts to bring out the best in Don.

NEW CONVERSATIONS, NEW POSSIBILITIES

Randall, one of the staff members who had been most effective with Don, began talking with him more about his hopes and aspirations. Don confided in Randall about his disaffection with the corporate lifestyle, his desire to change his life and help others, and his concern about whether Julia would approve of these changes in him. One reason Randall was helpful was that Don saw him as a "regular guy" who talked with him as a regular person. Randall did not express interest in Don's symptoms and how they interfered with waking up in the morning and attending activities. Randall's approach was to tell Don to "get off his butt and get moving; that he was needed; that people were waiting for him." Counseling staff began to see the wisdom of talking with Don about his life and tapping into his knowledge about that life, rather than monitoring his symptoms. Counseling sessions became focused on Don's wish to be helpful to others, past stories of this attribute, and a future focus on putting this attribute to use.

Staff members also became creative in designing activities that suited Don. Jenny, an activities coordinator, insisted that Don

play the piano and lead sing-alongs during the Christmas holiday.
Afterwards, Don delivered an emotional speech about connection
and caring for others and what the holidays meant to him, recognizing Randall, Jenny and the staff for their kindness and kinship.
The activities staff encouraged Don to lead discussion groups focused
on philosophy and spirituality. Don and Randall began chatting
about what he might do when he left the facility, focusing on retirement, travel, volunteer work, and creative ways to use his leadership
skills to help others.

The clinical director and counselors sought Don's expertise
about medication, what had worked and what had not. They asked
Don what medications might help him access his inner potential, as
opposed to dulling his senses and blotting him out. Don acknowledged that he experienced anxiety and that the anti-anxiety medications in moderate doses helped him to feel more competent and in
control. Don began taking this medication reliably, stopped second-
guessing the psychiatrists, and reported positive results.

Within a month after the interview with Don and Julia, Don's
symptoms dramatically improved. The head shaking gradually subsided and eventually stopped once Don stopped looking at his symptoms as a statement of who he was. He began paying less attention
to whether his head shook and more attention to what he wanted to
do with the rest of his life. Don became clear that he wanted to leave
his job and devote his time to volunteer work and travel. He discussed these plans with Julia, who was pleased with his progress and
accepting of his change in lifestyle.

In six weeks, Don returned home and maintained regular
contact with Randall during the first year following his discharge.
Randall let us know that Don remained symptom free and was enjoy-
ing his retirement and being helpful to others. After 10 years of
being a mental patient, Don has not been readmitted to an inpatient
facility.

CONSTRUCTIVISM APPLIED

Constructivism is not merely an esoteric philosophy useful in
academic debates about reality and social convention. How we see
people and how they see themselves and their predicaments has profound implications for how we talk with them and help them with
their predicaments.

Don and the people close to him had become fixed on the
idea that there was something deeply wrong with him, that the right

expert and medication had not been found, or worse, that he was a hopeless case. Over a ten-year period, Don had adopted the mindset of being a mental patient, referring to himself as "sick," "hopeless," "undiagnosable," and a burden to his wife—his head shaking violently in synchrony with these negative attributions.

On the other hand, seeing Don as a competent, capable person with a long history of achievements, and seeing his "condition" as a curiosity that commanded an explanation, led to very different conversations, and ultimately, a different "treatment" outcome. Seemingly, severe and difficult-to-diagnosis-and-treat psychiatric symptoms improved once we consulted the person experiencing these symptoms and tapped his expertise about the path to problem construction. Despite ten years of repeated hospitalizations, we made no assumption that anything was intrinsically "wrong with Don." Instead the focus shifted to what was "strong with Don" and to the mystery of how these strengths and attributes got lost during an important time of transition in his life.

Don's own story of how the problem evolved offered clues to narrative solutions. We learned from Don and his wife about a time in his life in which he began to reconsider his priorities, but had difficulty assimilating this shift into a new (and coherent) construction of self. Symptoms emerged as Don continued to conform to the perceived wishes of others (working hard, making more money, doing corporate sales) and failed to speak up about his own preferences (for sobriety, spirituality, travel, helping others). Once Don helped us map the path to problem construction, the path to problem deconstruction (and change) became clear. We could pinpoint what kinds of conversations might be useful to Don in motivating change and what conversations would not be useful.

Don's symptoms resolved when he (1) became more keenly aware of the person he wanted to be; (2) noticed the gap between this preferred vision of self, how he was acting, and how he imagined important others regarded him; and (3) felt capable of bridging the gap by acting more in line with his preferred view. Don left "treatment" with a personal construct theory that could be applied to everyday life. He now had a clear understanding of his qualities and attributes, how he had gotten stuck, what his symptoms meant in the context of these attributes, and a blueprint for how to live his life in a more fulfilling, nonsymptomatic way.

REFERENCES

Bateson, G. (1988). *Mind and nature.* New York: Bantam.

Bogdan, J. (1986). Do families really need problems? Why I am not a functionalist. *Family Therapy Networker, 10*(4), 30-35, 67-69.

deShazer, S. (1985). *Keys to solutions in brief therapy.* New York: Norton.

deShazer, S., Berg, I.K., Lipchik, E., Nunnally, E., Molnar, A., Gingerich, W., & Weiner Davis, M. (1986). Brief therapy: Focused solution development. *Family Process, 25,* 207-221.

Efran, J. S., Lukens, R. J., & Lukens, M. D. (1988). Constructivism: What's in it for you? *Family Therapy Networker, 12*(5), 27-35.

Epstein, E. S., & Loos, V. E. (1989). Some irreverent thoughts on the limits of family therapy: Toward a language based explanation of human systems. *Journal of Family Psychology, 3,* 405-421.

Eron, J., & Lund, T. W. (1989). From magic to method: Principles of effective reframing. *Family Therapy Networker, 13*(1), 64-68, 81-83.

Eron, J. B. & Lund, T. W. (1993). How problems evolve and dissolve: Integrating narrative and strategic concepts. *Family Process, 32,* 291-309.

Eron, J. B. & Lund, T. W. (1995). The overresponsibility trap: Helping "co-dependents" create a new life story. *Family Therapy Networker, 19*(6), 61-70.

Eron, J. B. & Lund, T. W. (1996). *Narrative solutions in brief therapy.* New York: Guilford.

Eron, J. B. & Lund, T. W. (1998a). Narrative solutions couples therapy. In F. M. Dattilio (Ed.), *Case studies in couple and family therapy: Systemic and cognitive perspectives* (pp. 371-400). New York: Guilford.

Eron, J. B. & Lund, T. W. (1998b). Narrative solutions in brief couples therapy. In J. M. Donovan (Ed.), *Short term couples therapy* (pp 291-324). New York: Guilford.

Goolishian, H., & Anderson, H. (1987). Language systems and therapy: An evolving idea. *Psychotherapy, 24,* 529-538.

Haley, J. (1976). *Problem-solving therapy.* San Francisco: Jossey-Bass.

Haley, J. (1980). *Leaving home: The therapy of disturbed young people.* New York: McGraw-Hill.

Lund, T. W. & Eron, J. B. (1998). The narrative solutions approach for retelling children's stories: Using preferred views to construct useful conversations. In M. F. Hoyt (Ed.), *The handbook of constructive therapies: Innovative approaches from leading practitioners* (pp. 358-379). San Francisco: Jossey-Bass.

James, W. (1984). The principles of psychology. In B.W. Wiltshire (Ed.), *William James: The essential writings* (pp. 44-161). Albany: SUNY press. (Original work published 1890)

Laing, R. D. (1960). *The divided self.* London: Tavistock.

Laing, R. D. (1969). *Self and others.* London: Tavistock.

Laing, R. D. (1970). *Knots.* London: Tavistock.

Laing, R. D., Phillipson, H., & Lee, A. R. (1966). *Interpersonal perceptions: A theory and method of research.* London: Tavistock.

Madanes, C. (1990). *Sex, love and violence: Strategies for transformation.* New York: Norton.

Maddi, S. (1968). *Personality theories: A comparative analysis.* Homewood, IL: Dorsey Press.

Markus, H., & Nurius, P. (1986). Possible selves. *American Psychologist, 41,* 954-969.

O'Hanlon, W. H., & Weiner-Davis, M. (1989). *In search of solutions: A new direction in psychotherapy.* New York: Norton.

Rogers, C. R. (1951). *Client centered therapy.* Boston: Houghton Mifflin.

Rogers, C. R. (1961). *On becoming a person: A therapist's view of psychotherapy.* Boston: Houghton Mifflin.

Watzlawick, P. (1976). *How real is real?* New York: Random House.

Watzlawick, P. (1978). *The language of change.* New York: Basic Books.

Watzlawick, P. (Ed.). (1984). *The invented reality.* New York: Norton.

Watzlawick, P., Weakland, J., & Fisch, R. (1974). *Change: Principles of problem formation and problem resolution.* New York: Norton.

Weakland, J. H., Fisch, R., Watzlawick, P., & Bodin, A. M. (1974). Brief therapy: Focused problem resolution. *Family Process, 13,* 141-168.

White, M., & Epston, D. (1990). *Narrative means to therapeutic ends.* New York: Norton.

PART II

CONSTRUCTIVIST CONCEPTUALIZATIONS OF DISORDER

CHAPTER 5

Disorder, Diagnoses, and the Struggles of Humanness[1]

Larry M. Leitner and April J. Faidley

To illustrate the relationships between disorder, diagnoses, and the struggles of humanness, consider this exercise. Write a phrase, of four words or fewer, that describes a problem with which you are currently struggling. Now write a second phrase, of three words or fewer, that describes an enduring and problematic characteristic of your personality. You may think carefully about these phrases or write down the first phrases that come to your mind. Now, put the paper aside. We will return to it later.

John presented for psychotherapy as quite anxious and depressed. His wife, Rachel, had ceased relating to him emotionally, sexually, and verbally for the last 12 months. She denied that there was anything wrong with their relationship, explaining instead that she was thinking about "things," including what she wanted for herself and her marriage. John felt stuck, "dangling in the wind," while he endeavored to patiently wait until Rachel decided what she wanted. If he asked any questions or expressed any feelings about his situation, Rachel would tell him that he was driving her away. He did not feel that he could end the relationship, as Rachel was the only woman he had ever loved. He wanted the return of the intimacy they had before. His therapist could feel both John's anxiety and his great dependency on Rachel. It seemed that no choice John could make would relieve his anxiety and, at the same time, assuage his dependency. However, John's therapist faced choices of her own. It is these choices that are the thrust of this chapter.

In essence, as therapy begins, the therapist needs to conceptualize John's personality and problems. Typically, this decision is made through the preemptive application of a diagnosis of mental

[1] The clinical material in this paper has been falsified to protect client confidentiality.

disorder to John from the *Diagnostic and Statistical Manual of Mental Disorders* (4th Edition, Text Revision; *DSM-IV-TR* [American Psychiatric Association, 2000]). For example, the therapist might choose "Generalized Anxiety Disorder in a Dependent Personality Disorder." It is our contention that, rather than describing a "disorder," a good diagnosis captures, at least in part, the lived *struggles of humanness* in which this particular human being is engaged. In other words, John does not suffer from a "generalized anxiety disorder in a dependent personality disorder." He is, like all of us, engaged in the complex, ambiguous, terrifying journey through the relational complexities that are the bases of psychological life.

We will make this point in three ways. First, we will describe George Kelly's (1955/1991) concept of transitive diagnosis, his alternative to the DSM. Transitive diagnosis carries within it certain implicit requirements that we will attempt to spell out. In the process of clarifying these requirements, we will look at some of the ways the DSM fails to meet Kelly's requirements. Next, we will briefly focus on the excessively reductionistic aspects of the term "disorder" and the ways that diagnostic systems that employ such reductionistic assumptions injure clients more than help them. Finally, we will introduce a non-reductionistic approach to diagnosing human meaning making (Leitner, Faidley, & Celentana, 2000).

TRANSITIVE DIAGNOSIS AND THE DSM

Process.

Kelly (1955/1991, pp. 153-155) makes it clear that, for a constructivist, diagnosis is the planning stage for psychotherapy. He specifically states that he uses the term "transitive diagnosis" because diagnosis is an attempt to conceptualize "bridges between the client's present and ... future" (p. 153). He goes on to describe the ways that psychoanalysis, despite its flaws, attempted to arrive at diagnoses of *inner life* as opposed to objectively describing a Greek statue – frozen, unchanging, and, therefore, for the purposes of psychotherapy, hopeless. "Like psychoanalysis, the psychology of personal constructs also registers its protest against nosological diagnosis and all the forms of thinking which distract our attention from the fact that life does go on and on" (p. 154). In other words, a viable diagnostic system has its primary focus on the ever-evolving process of meaning making, not on fixed categories in which to stick clients.

The DSM is not a system focusing on process. Returning to John, for example, does knowing that he suffers from an "anxiety disorder in a dependent personality disorder" tell us much of relevance about him? Does the diagnosis tell us anything about his hopes, his fears, his courage as he struggles, the places where he feels so threatened that he acts in ways that lead him to hate himself, and so on? Does the diagnosis tell us why he has these hopes and fears? Does it capture ways that he sometimes acts more on the basis of his courage than on his despair? These questions, among others, get us to the process of John's life rather than mere "facts."

Treatment implications.

Transitive diagnosis also requires that diagnoses have treatment implications. "In transitive diagnosis the clinician…attempts to formulate the decisive issues at the outset and forthwith directs his [her] diagnostic examination towards resolving them" (p.154). In other words, a diagnostic system, no matter how reliable, objective, or accurate, is worthless absent treatment implications.

Treatment can be understood as the application of theory to distress (Leitner, et al, 2000). Thus, in order to generate implications for treatment, a diagnostic system must be theoretically relevant. Clinicians who are Rogerian in their orientation, for example, would need diagnoses descriptive of the areas in which the client has experienced conditional positive regard and developed conditions of worth. Rational emotive therapists would need diagnoses of the client's irrational cognitions. Freudian analysts would need diagnoses of the client's ego defense mechanisms, areas of superego harshness or weakness, and so forth. Constructivists need diagnoses of the client's process of meaning making.

The DSM, by definition, fails to generate treatment implications. The authors of the DSM take great pride in the system being "atheoretical." Implicit in this assertion is the *theoretical* position that certain ways of categorizing human struggles can be "atheoretical." There is, in this theory, an assumption that "objective truths" transcend theories and exist outside of any theoretical understanding of them. Such a position is obviously incompatible with constructivist understandings of the interrelationship between theory and reality.

Returning to John, knowing he "has" (a term with its own implications) an "anxiety disorder" does not tell the Rogerian anything about the areas where John has experienced conditional positive regard. It does not tell the rational emotive therapist about the types of irrational cognitions John has. It does not tell the psychoanalyst anything about John's defense mechanisms or areas of super-ego harshness. Finally, and most importantly for constructivists, it does not tell us anything about his process of meaning creation. Thus it is little wonder that, when a system so realistic (Rychlak, 1968) in its orientation is used as the basis for understanding psychopathology, the treatment approaches that share its realistic meta-theoretical premises (e.g., biological and cognitive-behavioral) wind up being the dominant approaches in the field today. As a final thought here, given that different theories have different and incompatible assumptions about the nature of persons, we believe it is impossible to develop one diagnostic system that all clinicians, no matter their theoretical orientation, can use.

Experience and reality.

Kelly also implies that transitive diagnosis requires that the diagnostic system be descriptive of the client's experience, as well as honor certain realities. In so doing, Kelly is being true to his critical constructivist position that meanings are created and re-created in the dynamic interaction between the person and a real world. For example, he states that, when deciding what diagnostic understanding to use, "we need to be guided by what we want to do about the events *as well as* by their reality" (p. 153, emphasis added). Later he describes the ways that the clients' current interpersonal realities (e.g., socio-economic resources or lack thereof, the ways that a spouse may construe the client's need for psychotherapy, etc.) are vital in a transitive diagnosis (pp. 174-176).

Further, a transitive diagnosis should "embrace the realities of the client's life" (p. 153). Because these "realities" are construed ones, this statement makes it clear that the diagnostic system has to honor the client's inner "truths." A system that ignores, minimizes, or demeans inner experience, therefore, cannot be a transitive diagnostic system. Similarly, a system that takes the client out of the contextual realities of life fails Kelly's requirements.

Returning yet again to John, his "anxiety disorder in a dependent personality disorder" tells the clinician little about his experience of the world. It says that he is anxious and dependent on people. It does not tell us anything about the exact nature of his fears, the reasons that his world seems so dangerous to him, or the ways in which his rural and impoverished upbringing created certain realities for him. It also says nothing about how a wife leaving might be experienced in John's particular African-American subculture. Therefore, yet again, the DSM fails as a transitive diagnostic system.

The presence of the therapist.

Finally, a transitive diagnosis that encompasses process, has treatment implications, and acknowledges experience and reality implies the presence of the person or persons participating with the client to bring about change. After all, once a professional has been consulted, that person becomes part of the client's process of meaning making. The professional's presence alters the client's experience and the client's reality, and the meanings that may be created and re-created in the interaction between the client and the therapist will have treatment implications. A maximally effective transitive diagnosis anticipates the dynamics of the treatment milieu. As a nosological system focused on encapsulating entities of disorder, the DSM does not touch this vital aspect of transitive diagnosis. To take just one example of this weakness, knowing John's DSM diagnosis tells us little about aspects of John's personality that the therapist might like or the ways his "anxiety disorder" might effect the process of connecting with him in therapy.

REDUCTIONISM, DISORDER, AND DIAGNOSES

In part, the DSM fails as a transitive diagnostic system because its theoretical approach to psychology assumes that the struggles of persons can be reduced, through a diagnostic label, to a disorder. This, obviously, is a theoretical assumption, not a statement about an objective "Truth." For example, the DSM reduces John's entire life to an eight-word phrase—Generalized Anxiety Disorder in a Dependent Personality Disorder.

Now, let us return to the phrases you wrote to describe yourself. In contrast to the DSM, your description is based upon your own personal, idiosyncratic, meaning system. Construct psychologists know that your own personal description of yourself and others will be experienced as more meaningful and important than descriptions provided by others. (Landfield, 1977, reviews a huge literature on this issue.) Based upon this research, we believe it is reasonable to hypothesize that your personal description of yourself is more meaningful to you than any DSM (or any other external) description could be.

Now, with the foregoing as background, let us return to the exercise of the introductory paragraph. How would it be for you if your life were reduced to those two phrases? To what extent do they capture the essence of who you are? To what extent are there important aspects of your personality that would be distorted and trivialized if they were seen through the lenses of those two phrases? Do they capture your important strengths? In what ways do the phrases honor or discount important contextual realities in your life (e.g., being brought up in abject poverty, being lesbian or gay in a homophobic subculture, being female in a society that is still sexist, etc.)? Do these descriptions, albeit richer than a DSM diagnosis, honor your personal struggles?

Most likely, rich as these two phrases might be, they still fail miserably at providing a rich conceptualization of you. Even if they captured the essence of your problems, we are much more than our problems. Reducing a human being down to a few words distorts and impoverishes important parts of that person's experience. Thus, when the more powerful psychologist reduces, distorts, and impoverishes the humanness of the less powerful client through the preemptive use of DSM categories, violence—even if subtle (Leitner & Faidley, 1995)—is done to the client in at least three ways.

First, the client is conceptualized in terms of flaws, weaknesses, or "sickness." John probably would not want to walk down Main Street waving a banner describing him as a generalized anxiety disorder in a dependent personality disorder. It is not a source of pride and respect for most people. We are aware that many people would argue that, because it is the therapist's job to treat disorder, a diagnostic system must focus on describing the disorders of the client. However, even if you believe that the role of the therapist is to fix problems (a theoretical assumption also), there is an extensive literature suggesting that therapists who are skilled at helping people overcome problems also are therapists who can grasp clients' strengths, not just their pathology. Reducing people to pathology is counter-therapeutic.

Second, a DSM-like diagnostic system, by minimizing or distorting client strengths, makes it more difficult for a therapist to empathize with aspects of the client's lived experience. If a goal of psychotherapy is to make the therapy relationship a place where the client feels safely understood so that creative reconstruing of life may occur (Leitner & Faidley, 1999), such empathic failures damage the client's continued evolution. Many therapists intuitively know this and attempt to "talk" DSM to fellow professionals and insurance companies while thinking more respectfully about their clients. While we can respect the dilemmas that lead therapists to this position, we also are aware of R. D. Laing's (1969) famous comment that it is self-deceptive to believe we can think one way while speaking another.

104

At the very least, the reduction of the person to a disorder within the DSM makes empathizing more difficult.

However, perhaps the greatest damage occurs when the therapist convinces the client to think of the client's experience in reductionistic terms. When I believe such descriptions of me, I wind up in the position of no longer trusting my experience in the world. After all, my experience is pathological, problematic, and diseased. When my experience is discounted, I am disempowered. For example, rather than being a "sickness," perhaps John's anxiety can be better understood as a creative way of engaging a world that has been dangerous and threatening to him in ways the therapist does not yet understand. Being able to trust our experience as revealing certain "truths" about our lives is an important component of psychological health. (Note: nothing in these statements implies that the client also should not step back and reflect on experience to determine the extent to which old "truths" are still being experienced as current, unquestioning "realities.")

In summary, reducing the client's struggles of humanness to a disorder leaves the client injured in many ways; fundamental aspects of the client's lived experience are distorted through this reductionism. Interestingly, qualitative approaches to psychological research have been gaining popularity precisely because researchers are realizing the distortions inherent in reductionistic approaches to human experience. Unfortunately, the field has been able to critique methodological reductionism, yet continues to ignore nosological reductionism. Approaches to understanding psychological distress that are less reductionistic are desperately needed.

AN EXPERIENTIAL PERSONAL CONSTRUCT ALTERNATIVE

Rather than naming a disorder, a transitive diagnosis describes a struggle of humanness. The description is set within a theoretical perspective, which gives it a structure that focuses treatment. The description endeavors to capture an understanding of the person's experience, reality, and meaning-making process. We have attempted to honor these points by creating an experiential personal construct diagnostic description. Experiential personal constructivism is a conceptualization of human experience (including psychopathology) in terms of persons' struggles around profoundly connecting with versus retreating from others. In this regard, experiential personal constructivism assumes that people need close, intimate, relationships in which the very meaning making process of the other is grasped (termed "ROLE relationships") in order to have a

105

rich, vibrant, and meaningful experience of life. On the other hand, such relationships also are potentially terrifying as they contain within them the possibility of profound interpersonal betrayal and devastation.

Psychological distress occurs when someone retreats too fully and completely from ROLE relationships, opting for the safe yet meaningless experience of a life without profound interpersonal connection. Many people retreat from ROLE relationships by distancing themselves such that the experience of interconnection is minimized or ignored (Leitner, in press; Leitner et al, 2000). Others, however, retreat from ROLE relationships by attempting to deny the separateness inherent in relational life (e.g., trying to fuse with another such that one does not have to experience aloneness).

The diagnostic system uses three axes, with hypotheses in regard to therapist-client relational interactions considered in all three areas (see Figure 1). The first axis, *Developmental-Structural Issues*, looks at how the person has constructed self, other, and the boundaries between self and other. (See Figure 2.) It assumes that, in childhood, traumas can occur that may arrest the continued evolution of the construction of self and other; the person's growth is blocked or distorted by restricted constructions.

Self-other permanence refers to the person's capacity to experience the other as psychologically present even when out of the person's awareness. Obviously, if a person loses the felt sense that the other is "out there," still invested and caring for him or her whenever they are separated, the resulting fear, confusion, and disorganization makes ROLE relationships extremely limited, if not impossible. Likewise, self-other constancy (the ability to integrate various components of self and other into a coherent picture) is a necessary prerequisite to a rich and deep ROLE relationship. Absent self-other constancy, any change in the other implies that he or she has become a totally different person, with the renewed potential for betrayal and invalidation in the relationship. Because people are, by definition, evolving processes of meaning making, the other is constantly growing and threatening the person who lacks self-other constancy.

John seems to be struggling with self-other constancy. If so, he may find it difficult to see aspects of Rachel's personality other than those of the "wonderful, loving" wife. She would be experienced as totally negative if John found reason to believe she was ever self-centered or unfaithful. Further, John feels totally humiliated when his needs for Rachel become so strong that he acts in ways he

106

believes are less than "honorable," such as acquiescing to her willingness to engage in quick and meaningless sex. He cannot integrate such needs into a construction of self that also is capable of acting with integrity and honor.

John's struggles with self-other constancy also have implications for the therapy relationship. For example, he may find it difficult to experience the therapist as competent if she makes mistakes or is unempathic at times. He also may be quite insecure at the beginning of the therapy hour, as he may need to determine whether the therapist still cares for him in the ways she did during the previous hour. (After all, because she could have changed during the week, she may no longer care for him.) The therapist should have many opportunities to help John in this area as their relationship evolves. For example, after he recounts giving in to having meaningless sex with Rachel, the therapist's acceptance and respect can provide an experience in contrast to the ways John experiences himself.

FIGURE 1. Diagnostic Axes

Developmental/ Structural Issues	Interpersonal Components	Experiential Components
Construct of self versus other	Undispersed Dependency	Discrimination
Self-Other Permanence	Excessively Dispersed Dependency	Flexibility
Self-Other Constancy	Dependency Avoidance	Creativity
Attachments	Physically Distancing Self	Responsibility
	Psychologically Distancing Self	Openness
		Commitment
		Courage
		Forgiveness
		Reverence

Note: The system assumes that, in cases where developmental/structural arrests have occurred, many of the interpersonal and experiential struggles over ROLE relationships are linked to the arrest. The traumas associated with the arrest would need to be reconstrued before any meaningful change could occur on the interpersonal and experiential axes. In cases where the developmental/structural arrests have not occurred, therapy can be more time limited and address the interpersonal and experiential issues more directly.

FIGURE 2. STRUCTURAL ARRESTS
DIAGNOSTIC IMPRESSION WORKSHEET

I. Presenting Problems

GENERAL ISSUES   HYPOTHESES ABOUT
AROUND/EVIDENCE FOR   THERAPY
RELATIONSHIP

II. Structural Arrests
Axis

A. Self-Other Permanence

B. Self-Other Constancy

C. Structural Arrests Axis Treatment Goals

The second axis looks at *interpersonal components* associated with human meaning making in intimate relationships (Figure 3). As with the first axis, all of these components may be tied to limiting the development of a ROLE relationship. For example, *undispersed dependency* struggles (Walker, 1993) lead the person to rely on one person to meet the overwhelming majority of one's dependency needs. (Note: for Kelly, we all are dependent; the issue is what we do with our dependencies.) A person who relies on one other person for so many dependencies would have great difficulty embracing certain changes in the growth of the other (e.g., the other changing in such a way that one could not be as dependent). Thus, the person who under disperses dependencies may need to desperately insist the other continue to be there. Such hostility has been associated with limiting the depth of the ROLE relationship (Leitner, 1985).

John very well may struggle with undispersed dependency. He relies on Rachel to meet the overwhelming majority of his dependency needs and does not allow others access to such central constructions. If so, he may be quite terrified of the possibility of a life with no one on whom to rely for his most central meanings. John also may tend to psychologically distance himself from everyone other than his wife. He can be friendly and outgoing with others, as long as he does not have to tell them about his inner life.

These issues provide both problems and opportunities for the therapy. John could transfer these dependencies totally onto the therapist if his relationship with Rachel continues to deteriorate. Alternatively, he might become phobic of dependency and desperately avoid anything resembling a dependent caring. The therapist can use these processes to work with John on dispersing his dependencies more broadly in the world. Such dispersion would help ameliorate his tendency to distance himself psychologically from others.

FIGURE 3.   Interpersonal Axis

GENERAL ISSUES AROUND/EVIDENCE FOR RELATIONSHIP	HYPOTHESES ABOUT THERAPY

III.   Interpersonal *Axis*

A. Physically Distancing Self

B. Psychologically Distancing Self

C. Dependency Struggles

D. Treatment Goals of the
Interpersonal Axis

The final axis (Figure 4) explores nine aspects of experiential empathy associated with being able to form rich relationships in the world (Leitner & Pfenninger, 1994). In addition to a basic description, Leitner and Pfenninger (1994) discuss the ways these aspects are associated with deep ROLE relating. John brought up concerns and fears associated with discrimination early in his therapy. Essentially, he wondered whether there were ways he could have been more aware of Rachel's potential to injure him as badly as she did. For example, she broke up with him once during their courtship; could this have been a signal that she might choose to leave him yet again? Alternatively, should Rachel leave him and he have to start his relational life anew, how will he come to trust other women? After all, he had trusted Rachel and she abandoned him. Questions like these, all associated with interpersonal richness, involve wrestling with understanding both the similarities and the differences between self and other as well as making tentative, sometimes terrifying, guesses as to how those differences may affirm or injure one.

John is using his present relational crisis to explore issues of flexibility (the ability to construe alternative constructions) also. As Leitner and Pfenninger (1994) point out, absent flexibility, "a relationship risks being frozen in the interpersonal understandings developed earlier in time" (p. 122). Interestingly enough, while quite flexible in his approach to most people, John decided that he had allowed his relationship with Rachel to remain static over the years. They had settled into a mutual construction of one another and did not recognize the ways that each of them continued to grow until the relational crisis occurred.

John's heightened awareness of the importance of flexibility, when combined with his struggles with self-other constancy, created many emotionally intense moments in the therapy. Becoming more aware that he needed to see the other as growing and changing left John wondering whether his therapist would change to the point that she would no longer desire to be present for him. While quite distressing emotionally, these incidents helped John and his therapist struggle over the chaos and complexity of a ROLE relationship in the here-and-now relationship of the therapy room.

As John anticipates the possibility of life without Rachel, he obviously is faced with the challenge of reconstruing self, other, and relationship in new and unforeseen ways. In other words, one aspect of his current crisis is the challenge of creative reconstruction of life. Interestingly enough, while John is not at all certain how his reconstruction of life will turn out, he is quite confident that he can "land on his feet" and go on with life. A constructivist therapist may view such confidence as a good sign. John's confidence is telling him and his therapist that, at some level, he recognizes that he is up to the challenge of creatively reconstruing his life (McCoy, 1977).

John is actively dealing with issues associated with responsibility (the willingness to examine his construct system and its implications for others) in his therapy. For example, he is wondering to what extent her complete withdrawal from the relationship is his fault (i.e., a reaction to some aspect of how he has structured life and their relationship). At times, he experiences himself as totally responsible for the deterioration of the relationship; at other times, he blames it completely on Rachel. Both of these positions (besides indicating possible self-other constancy struggles) suggest that John needs to delve into the matter of responsibility in more depth. Each position implicitly denies the ways that, within experiential personal construct psychology, relationships always are co-created journeys. It also may be useful to do further work on sorting out the confusion between responsibility and blame as well as the ways that, because each person is an evolving process, one can never be certain that a relationship can be made to last.

John seems to be doing quite well with issues of openness (the willingness to reconstrue when invalidated). For example, he continually attempts to have conversations with Rachel about their relationship and is ready to either work on improving the marriage (if she is open to this option) or deal with its ending. Early in his therapy, he began to experiment with telling friends about the relational crisis and was able to see himself in the new role of someone being supported by others. He also would thoughtfully consider ideas raised by his therapist, as opposed to either rejecting them out of hand (too closed) or believing that the therapist's hunches were objective truth (excessive openness).

Issues of commitment can easily be seen when a long-term relationship is in a crisis. Experientially, commitment struggles can be inferred from one of the more pressing concerns in John's current life: Should he continue to wait for Rachel to "come around" or should he leave the relationship. On the one hand, waiting patiently for Rachel to re-commit to him left John "stuck" in the present crisis. It also negated a commitment to himself, in terms of affirming constructions of him as capable of having a woman be open with him and love him in ways Rachel could not. He also wondered about the ways waiting for Rachel to solely determine the future of their relationship negated his commitment to their children, in terms of what it implied about responsibility and control in intimate relationships. On the other hand, ending the relationship raised issues around prematurely deciding and possibly depriving his children of an intact family as they grew up. Finally, ending the relationship raised concerns about how (and whether) he could commit to another woman in the future.

John is courageously engaging life along many fronts. The possible dissolution of his marriage is among the most threatening events in his life. Despite the great fear associated with this possibility, he is thoughtfully and creatively exploring ways to reconstrue life. He openly wrestles with issues in the therapy room, including his relationship to his therapist. His willingness to continue to risk, in the face of uncertainty and potential pain, will continue to serve him well in life.

Forgiveness (reconstruing self and other such that major injuries do not hinder future ROLE relationships) will continue to be a major struggle for John. For example, it plays itself out with concerns around whether he and Rachel can be caring friends if she abandons him. If they cannot, John believes that it will be because one or both of them harbors too much pain and resentment over the injuries experienced in their relationship. Such resentments can complicate future ROLE relationships as old fears raise their heads in the ambiguity of a newly forming relationship. John also worries that, absent satisfactory work on forgiving one another, the children may suffer due to unresolved acrimony in the parental relationship. Finally, John needs to be able to forgive himself for being a part of a relationship that, for whatever reason, got itself into such serious trouble.

At the present time, John's lack of reverence is quite understandable. His primary relationship, the mainstay of his psychological life, is in disarray. As he narrows his experiential field to deal with this crisis, he lacks the awareness that he can and does affirm the core processes of others (e.g., his children). He also loses touch with the awareness that he is capable of being centrally affirmed by others. However, John's therapist can use this struggle experiencing reverence to monitor John's growth in therapy. As he gains newer ways of construing himself, others, and relationships, the experience of reverence for life will return. In so doing, it will be an indication that John has overcome some of the most difficult problems a person can face.

FIGURE 4. Experiential Axis

GENERAL ISSUES AROUND/EVIDENCE FOR RELATIONSHIP	HYPOTHESES ABOUT THERAPY

IV. Experiential Axis

A. Discrimination

B. Flexibility

C. Creativity

D. Responsibility

E. Openness

F. Commitment

G. Courage

H. Forgiveness

I. Reverence

I. Treatment Goals of Interpersonal
Richness Axis

SOME FINAL THOUGHTS

The experiential personal construct diagnostic system goes beyond a simple constructivist critique of the DSM. The system, like all of experiential personal constructivism, is more concerned with the process of meaning making than the specific content of the constructs being created. Because the system is based upon the same struggles over ROLE relationships with which experiential personal construct psychotherapy is most centrally concerned, it is a system filled with treatment possibilities. Further, the system attempts to be true both to the client's experience and to the realities that may impinge on the client's attempts to creatively engage life. In this way, the system hopefully respectfully engages the client around vital personal issues. Finally, the system allows the therapist to be present in the client's life in at least two ways. First, the conceptualization of the client's process of meaning making in ways that open treatment implications allows the therapist to actively explore avenues of potential growth. Even more fundamentally, each component of the diagnostic system can be looked at in terms of its implications for the therapy relationship. In other words, the diagnostic system seems to meet the requirements of a transitive diagnostic system.

We have two caveats with regard to the experiential constructivist diagnostic system. First, note that we have referred to it as "a transitive diagnostic system," not "the transitive diagnostic system." Kelly's basic philosophy of constructive alternativism implies that the universe is open to an infinite number of constructions. Therefore, there is no doubt that many transitive diagnostic systems are available to therapists, if we are creative enough to develop them. As a matter of fact, the experiential constructivist system differs in many ways from Kelly's original approach to diagnosis (and, as we stated earlier, therapists from different theoretical perspectives will need systems relevant to their perspective). In other words, we will have failed in our work here if the experiential personal construct diagnostic system becomes in some ways reified as the truth, rather than a potentially useful way of understanding human distress.

Second, the system is a conceptualization of the process of human struggles. The issues raised are issues of complexity and ambiguity, not health or disease. In other words, the therapist, like the client, struggles with these issues as the therapist, like the client, is a human being engaged in the complex, frightening, unclear world of interpersonal connection and separation inherent in relationships. If the issues are understood in this way, there is less risk of

119

the therapist using the system in demeaning ways (e.g., focusing on all the things "wrong" with the client rather than on how this client is dealing with these universally difficult issues).

Without doubt, a diagnosis consisting of many pages differs from a phrase of a few words. We believe these pages are a manageable format for creating an outline conceptualization of the client and a set of hypotheses that anticipate the treatment. The diagnosis can be enriched by new material as it arises in the therapy and evolve as the client evolves. The depth and scope of the diagnosis acts as a continual reminder to the therapist and the client that the struggles of humanness are deep, broad, complex, and significant. As such, hopefully, it will continuously remind the therapist to approach every client with respect, reverence, and humility.

REFERENCES

American Psychiatric Association (2000). *Diagnostic and statistical manual for mental disorders* (4th ed., Text Revision). Washington, DC.

Kelly, G. A. (1991). *The psychology of personal constructs. Vol. 2: Clinical diagnosis and psychotherapy.* London: Routledge. (Original work published 1955)

Laing, R. D. (1969). *The divided self.* New York: Pantheon.

Landfield, A. W. (1977). Interpretive man: The enlarged self-image. In J. K. Cole & A. W. Landfield (Eds.), *Nebraska symposium on motivation* (Vol. 24, pp. 127-177). Lincoln, NE: University of Nebraska.

Leitner, L. M. (1985). The terrors of cognition: On the experiential validity of personal construct theory. In D. Bannister (Ed.), *Issues and approaches in personal construct theory* (pp. 83-103). London: Academic.

Leitner, L. M. & Faidley, A. J. (1995). The awful, aweful nature of ROLE relationships. In R. A. Neimeyer & G. J. Neimeyer (Eds.), *Advances in personal construct psychology* (Vol. 3, pp. 291-314). Greenwich, CT: JAI.

Leitner, L. M. & Faidley, A. J. (1999). Creativity in experiential personal construct psychotherapy. *Journal of Constructivist Psychology, 12,* 273-286.

Leitner, L. M., Faidley, A. J. & Celentana, M. A. (2000). Diagnosing human meaning making: An experiential constructivist approach. In R. A. Neimeyer & J. D. Raskin (Eds.) *Constructions of disorder: Meaning-making frameworks for psychotherapy* (pp. 175-203). Washington, DC: American Psychological Association.

Leitner, L. M. & Pfenninger, D. T. (1994). Sociality and optimal functioning. *Journal of Constructivist Psychology, 7,* 119-135.

McCoy, M. M. (1977). A reconstruction of emotion. In D. Bannister (Ed.), *New perspectives on personal construct theory* (pp. 93-124). London: Academic.

Rychlak, J. F. (1968). *A philosophy of science for personality theory.* Boston: Houghton-Mifflin.

Walker, B. M. (1993). Looking for a whole "Mama:" Personal construct theory and dependency. In L. M. Leitner & N. G. M. Dunnett (Eds.), *Critical issues in personal construct psychotherapy* (pp. 61- 81). Malabar, FL: Krieger.

CHAPTER 6

Abnormality:
Does It Define Us or Do We Define It?[1]

Caroline M. Stanley and Jonathan D. Raskin

Among the many types of abnormality described in the *Handbook of Immigrant Health* (Loue, 1998), there exists the disorder of "Ghost Sickness." Ghost Sickness describes the condition where one is preoccupied with phenomena such as ghosts, death, and the deceased. This disorder, often found in Native Americans of the Southwest, differs from Western disorders in that a person's experience with the supernatural is considered an actual occurrence rather than a delusion or hallucination (Gaines, 1998).

There is also the disorder of "Evil Eye." Diagnosed through symptoms of rash, nervousness, headache, weeping, and disturbed sleep, Evil Eye is caused by the envious stare of an evil person or magical force (Baer, Clark, & Peterson, 1998). Although some may question the symptoms and causes of this disorder, Evil Eye nonetheless describes a state of physical and psychological suffering experienced by individuals in Mediterranean and Latin American cultures (Loue, 1998).

Neither Ghost Sickness nor Evil Eye exists within American culture. When considering these examples, it seems clear that different cultures assign different meanings to abnormality and that these meanings are reflected in the different types of disorder that a culture will recognize. In some countries, behaviors known as "pedophilia" constitute a mental disorder. In others, such behavior depicts nothing other than a crime. And, still for some, pedophilia is seen as neither a crime nor a disorder (Bleibtreu-Ehrenberhg, 1990). In fact, even conditions perceived as universal, such as depression and schizophrenia, may be completely absent or nonexistent in some cultures (Gaines, 1998).

[1] This chapter is based on the first author's master's thesis, for which the second author served as advisor. The authors thank committee members Glenn Geher and Tove Finnestad for their feedback.

In this chapter we address some of the cultural, social, and philosophical issues related to the many definitions of abnormality.[2] We challenge the idea that psychological abnormality, as portrayed through definitions and diagnoses of disorder, pertains to some inherently real or abnormal condition existing within the human being. Rather, we consider the question of what constitutes abnormality by examining abnormality from a social constructionist perspective. Social constructionism is used to analyze the implicit operations in society that help create meaningful conceptions of the abnormal. While the very process of defining the term "abnormal" suggests that there "exist" certain properties common to all cases of abnormality (or specific criteria that make it distinctly different from normality), this chapter entertains the possibility that the only "common" attribute of all such theories is that they are constructed through social networks. The advantages of using social constructionism as an approach to understanding abnormality are also explored.

ABNORMALITY: THE LACK OF A SINGLE DEFINITION

Psychological abnormality—synonymous nowadays with the terms "mental illness" and "mental disorder"—has been an area of study throughout history and across cultures (Parker, Georgaca, Harper, McLaughlin, & Stowell-Smith, 1995). In Western civilization, "abnormality" was once synonymous with the term "madness," where physical, animistic, or supernatural forces were considered the causes of abnormal behavior (Gillman, 1988; Parker et al., 1995;

---

[2] In this paper, the term "abnormality" (unless otherwise noted) refers to the behaviors, symptoms, traits, and conditions typically considered *psychologically* abnormal. The term "psychological," however, is also used quite loosely: the paper makes little attempt to consider which conditions specifically "belong" to psychology and which ones cross over into other fields. Thus, although somewhat elusive, the term "abnormality" (as opposed to the limiting psychological/mental health terms of "mental illness" or "mental disorder") is preferred for several reasons. First, "abnormality" is used to depict the difficulty in separating psychology from its related disciplines. Psychological abnormality has yet to be clearly distinguished from sociological "deviance" or from the genetic/biological abnormalities often deemed to be the cause of abnormal behaviors. The term "abnormality" is also used in an attempt to argue that abnormality may only be understood within a framework, an area of study, and, thus, within a particular point of view. In other words, through promoting the term "abnormality", it is argued that the concept of the abnormal (1) is cast into various disciplines and various frameworks, (2) is exhibited in a multitude of conflicting theories and definitions, and (3) bridges boundaries between disciplines, with the very definitions of abnormality changing as a function of time, culture, and as a result of sociopolitical trends.

124

Wallace, 1994). Over time, these theories were replaced with other definitions of abnormality. Modern frameworks for understanding abnormality include, but are not limited to, the psychodynamic, behavioral, cognitive, biological, social, genetic, and neuropsychological approaches, as well as their various combinations (e.g., sociobiological, cognitive-neuropsychological). Together, these models define abnormality as an illness of the body, as hidden conflicts of the psyche, as disordered modes of thought, as maladaptive behaviors, or as physical and genetic anomalies (Andreasen, 1984; Parker et al., 1995; Wright & Treacher, 1982).

Yet, rejections of these theories may be as numerous as the theories themselves. Some argue that psychological abnormality cannot be explained as physical illness (Szasz, 1974; see also Aneshensel & Phelan, 1999; Ingleby, 1982) or genetic aberration (Rowe & Elam, 1987; Valenstein, 1998; Yoxen, 1982). Others contend that the description of abnormality cannot be reduced to a dysfunction of the psyche (Gergen, 1994; Gergen, Hoffman, & Anderson, 1996), nor should it be understood as a distinct biochemical or anatomical irregularity (Simon, 1994; Valenstein, 1998). Another perspective—one that can be found in sources ranging from abnormal psychology textbooks (Seligman & Rosenhan, 1998) to sociological works (Aneshensel & Phelan, 1999) to the Handbook of Immigrant Health (Loue, 1998)—is that conceptions of abnormality vary so greatly that there may not be a single cause nor a single model sufficient for explaining them all (Rosenhan, 1975, 1973/1992).

The various explanations of abnormality (both past and present) and the radical changes that these explanations have undergone, seem indicative of society's uncertainty in defining what abnormality is (Parker et al., 1995). In fact, despite "the development of psychiatry as a scientific discipline over the past 100 years, the fundamental question of what mental illness is, [sic] still haunts the profession" (Sadowsky, 1996, p. 92).

It may be best argued that, at the present time, there is no known quality that all instances of abnormality share, nor a precise definition distinguishing the normal from the abnormal (Rosenhan, 1973/1992; Watzlawick, 1992). Some speculate that there will never be a definitive explanation of abnormality (Parker et al., 1995). As such, conceptions may be viewed as perpetually changing affairs (Gaines, 1992; Raskin & Lewandowski, 2000). While there is considerable acknowledgment that definitions of abnormality will vary as a function of time and culture (Gaines, 1992, 1998; Macklin,

1972; Parker et al., 1995), there remains the vital question of whether a single definition—the "reality" of abnormality—can be conclusively discovered. That is, while some (such as the authors of the DSM-IV-TR) claim that the concept of abnormality relates to a real, discoverable phenomenon that can be objectively defined, social constructionists contend that such phenomena can only be inter-subjectively defined. Thus, the greater philosophical issues of reality and knowing do play a crucial role in the quest to define abnormality.

PHILOSOPHICAL ISSUES OF REALITY AND KNOWING

Common to the field of psychology is the belief that our frameworks for understanding psychopathology are based on objective, scientific, and stable knowledge about reality, or the true ways in which things work. There is great disagreement, however, as to whether this is the case (Gaines, 1992; Kutchins & Kirk, 1997; Newman & Holzman, 1996; Simon, 1994; Watzlawick, 1992). While it is generally agreed that philosophical considerations encompass the field of psychology (Mahoney & Lyddon, 1988; Sadler, Wiggins, & Schwartz 1994; Warren, 1998), Watzlawick (1992) argues that some issues are *as much* related to the epistemological and metaphysical frameworks of philosophy as they are to the discipline of science. He addresses a pivotal, yet binding, ontological issue that relates to all systems of knowledge; namely, whether there exists a reality to which such systems apply. Thus, when attempting to decipher the truth of what abnormality is, the vital questions involve whether abnormality "exists" in the ontological sense, and whether it can be known.

Modernist and postmodernist philosophers debate the possibilities of what can be known to the thinking being. That reality exists as a set of empirically knowable or objective truths is often regarded as a "modernist" position. The rejection of this idea is often termed "postmodernist" (Flaskas, 1994). The dominant framework for defining abnormality, the *Diagnostic and Statistical Manual of Mental Disorders* ([DSM-IV-TR]; American Psychiatric Association, 2000), advocates the modernist approach through promoting the idea that a diagnosis clearly names and describes the "ontologically-evident" (Gergen et al., 1996) abnormality existing within a human being.

There are several assumptions in the DSM-IV-TR and the modernist approach that need to be addressed. The first is that there exists a real, ontological abnormality and that it can be found inside the individual. The second assumption is that this reality, should it exist, not only needs naming and describing, but that (and in clear opposition with postmodern philosophy) our diagnostic system is capable of describing this truth as it "really" is (Gergen et al. 1996). This paper, drawing upon a postmodern framework, argues that conceptions of reality cannot be distinguished from subjective *impressions* of reality (and thus may not be considered reality itself). Specifically, this paper rests on the postmodern premise that the foundation of our diagnostic system, like all systems, relies on certain values and certain assumptions that cannot be known beyond all doubt (Gergen, 1994; Sadler et al. 1994; Sosa, 1986). The criticisms often used against the latter assumption (the postmodern assumption that no assumption can be known) will be addressed as they relate to the treatment of individuals.

THE BASICS OF SOCIAL CONSTRUCTIONISM

Despite the position that no model can assert, with complete certainty, what abnormality is or how it can be known, and while no conceptual framework can be certain of "its own grounding ontology" (Gergen, 1994, p. 75), most perspectives remain nonetheless stringent in addressing abnormality in a manner that asks "how can we know?" or "how can we discover the truth?" The social constructionist perspective, however, representing a postmodern approach, focuses not on how we can know, but on the social practices we rely on to make us *believe* that we know. This is a unique approach for studying abnormality as it "challenge[s] traditional concepts of reality, knowing, and rationality, as well as disorder and disease" (Mahoney & Lyddon, 1988, p. 212). It questions, in other words, the notion of certainty in a world where most are concerned with the uncertain (Gergen et al. 1996). As we shall later see, such questioning is crucial, as it is the very notion of certainty that may be more harmful to individuals than the lack of it.

SOCIAL CONSTRUCTIONISM:
THE FUNDAMENTAL PRINCIPLES

Social constructionism is an approach to psychology that "invites us to be critical of the idea that our observations of the world unproblematically yield its nature to us" (Burr, 1995, p. 3). It differs from modern approaches in that it does not assume that knowledge is an objective, unbiased assessment of the world. Rather, knowledge is created through social processes of people interacting and negotiating understandings within specific contexts. What we regard as "truth" can only be seen as *conceptions* of truth, or as one, amongst many, of the possible interpretations of the world. Our realities consist of "negotiated" meanings, where cultural and social interactions between people determine how individuals will construe the "reality" that works best for them (Burr, 1995).

A social constructionist approach to abnormality, then, would subscribe to the idea that there are no "essences" or inherent qualities in an individual that would determine the truth of his or her abnormality. Additionally, because social constructionism views knowledge as socially and culturally specific, constructionism may also be viewed as an approach to understanding knowledge itself. On a specific level, constructionism might be used to reject the idea of an abnormal "essence" residing in the individual. On a broader level, constructionism might be used to reject the "essence" or inherent truth of psychological theories in general:

> The theories and explanations of psychology…become time- and culture-bound and cannot be taken as once-and-for-all descriptions of human nature. The disciplines of psychology…can therefore no longer be aimed at discovering the "true" nature of people and social life. (Burr, 1995, p. 6)

It becomes clear how the constructionist approach can be applied to the question, "what is abnormality?" It asserts what abnormality is not (a human essence), and what its definitions might be (social creations).

SOCIAL CONSTRUCTIONISM: THE ROLE OF DISCOURSE

In social constructionism, the role of discourse is seen as a powerful tool in assigning meaning to our conceptions. A discourse refers to "a set of meanings, metaphors, representations, images, stories, statements…that in some way together produce a particular version of events" (Burr, 1995, p.18). Personal constructivists, using George Kelly's individuality corollary, reason that an individual's meaning or understanding of a discourse—of such a vast set of symbols, stories, and images—is unique and never identical to another's (Kelly,1955/1991).[3] On a similar note, social constructionism maintains that there may be many discourses within a single language.

---

[3] In exploring the social constructionist approach to abnormality, it is important to address its similarity with approaches labeled "constructivist." Though there are specific differences between the social constructionist and constructivist perspectives (Franklin, 1995), Speed (1991) argues that the main distinction "is reflected

Thus, in a given society, where there are multiple ways of conversing, there will be multiple ways of bringing meaning to a single issue (Burr, 1995). For this reason, social constructionists tend to favor the idea of including all "voices" in the process of creating meaning. Restricting this process to, say, professional voices and professional discourse alone, is seen as limiting (Gergen, 1994).

The constructionist approach strongly emphasizes language as a necessary tool for creating meaningful concepts, on the grounds that it serves as the basis for all systems of human thought and understanding: "The way people think, the very categories and concepts that provide a framework of meaning for them, are provided by the language that they use" (Burr, 1995, p. 7). Because language is seen as a social creation, even the processes of thinking, understanding, and inferring meaning are examples of socially constructed phenomena. If language is a shared discourse used between people of the same culture, and if language is present at even one's most subjective experiences, it seems impossible to eliminate the social when attempting to create meaning (Burr, 1995). Thus, when trying to objectively define the meaning of abnormality, people cannot contend that they are acting beyond the constraints of both social and subjective ideologies. When attempting to understand psychological abnormality, then, it seems essential to examine how psychological language is created and the manner in which it is used.

THE CONSTRUCTION OF REALITIES

In his analysis of social epistemology, Searle (1995) contends that certain social facts "exist" or are "real" only by virtue of human agreement. Gergen (1994) explains that conceptions of the abnormal are created through discourse and that these meanings then become transformed into agreed-upon systems of knowledge. He argues that "the discourses of psychology...spring from the natural or everyday languages of the culture....[and] are inherited from commonplace cultural traditions. As a result, the referential or realistic quality of such languages is already consensually validated" (p.

more...on [the word] 'social' rather than in what ending the word 'construct' has" (p. 400). Without disregarding the important differences between the two perspectives, and, while acknowledging that, in certain contexts, these differences would be important to address, this paper draws solely on the similarities found within constructivist and constructionist positions. That is, both approaches focus on the *creation* of knowledge rather than its discovery (Mahoney & Lyddon, 1998). Thus, constructivist and constructionist works will be used simultaneously to explore what may be considered the *construction* of abnormality.

151). In this view, concepts such as "mental disorder" become "real" because "their presence within persons is already transparent within the cultural milieu" (p. 151).

Newman and Holzman (1996) contend that the role of discourse in creating meaning is so powerful that not just specific terms, but entire frameworks change as a result of changing discourses. Gergen (1994) demonstrates how this process occurs in the discourse of mental health, where a language becomes "technologized" by the people who use it. Here, certain terms are removed from their everyday usage and turned into technical terms used and owned by professionals. The word "fear," for instance, might be transformed into the psychological term "phobia." A child's "fervor" might be transformed into "hyperactivity." Through this process of owning, changing, and shaping language, the mental health profession—a system consisting of shared knowledge, values, and justifications—creates its own realities:

> There is no *pattern of illness* to which the professionals are responding; rather, the conception of illness functions in ways that link the professional and the culture in an array of mutually supportive activities... Mental health professionals... [respond] not to the world as it is, but to a world that is constructed. (Gergen, 1994, p. 155)

One of the dangers that occur when these "clinical realities" (Watzlawick, 1992) are constructed is that they are granted a sort of "ontological status" (Gergen, 1994) where they are treated as objective truths free from social influence. The latter point, once again, illustrates the tremendous role that discourse exerts in the construction of realities. Particularly, the field of clinical psychology "has never stopped assuming that the existence of a name is proof of the 'real' existence of the thing named" (Watzlawick, 1992, p. 59). In other words, while social constructionism argues that there are many different ways to view abnormality and that such views are contingent upon agreement between people, language, and society, it warns that some may be misled into believing that the agreed-upon conception is one that is ontologically accurate (Gergen et al., 1996).

Watzlawick (1992) criticizes current psychological practices for this very reason. Burr (1995) describes how certain constructed ideas only have moral/political status, but "are treated as if they had the same kind of 'reality' as ontological things" (p. 87). Watzlawick (1992) sees the latter as a frequent occurrence in the field of psychology. He refers to this notion as "reality adaptation."

130

Reality adaptation is a definition of normalcy that assumes that normal people see reality in the "right" way (the way it really is), while people suffering emotional or mental disorder interpret things in a distorted way (they perceive reality "incorrectly"). This view assumes: (a) that there is a reality, (b) that certain people have access to it, and (c) that certain people do not. This modernist perspective seems to govern the professional world and thus our current understanding of what it means to be abnormal (Watzlawick, 1992).

Strauss (1992) questions the criteria used to diagnose schizophrenia in a manner that coincides with Watzlawick's (1992) criticisms of reality adaptation. Strauss claims that one of the difficulties in assessing a schizophrenic symptom is that it is difficult to determine whether a pattern of thought is normal, or "in tune" with reality, and whether it is delusional, or an "impaired" view of reality:

> [A] number of patients…described intermediate experiences between a thought and a voice, or between a delusion and a hallucination. And yet supposedly, these phenomena were discretely different symptoms….it was not possible at times to tell whether a thought was really a delusion, a normal thought, or some exaggeration of a normal thought not quite delusional. (Strauss, 1992, p. 20)

He continues to question whether "these 'reliable,' 'clear-cut' symptom concepts [are] really points on continua as experienced by real people," (p. 20) and whether there are indeed any "continua between delusions and hallucinations, between normal and abnormal" (p. 20).

This critique leads to some questions concerning the many gray areas of abnormality. How do we deal with behaviors that seem to fall "on the border" between normal and abnormal? If there is no clear way of identifying what normal behavior is, how do we distinguish a *deviation from* the norm (Watzlawick, 1992)? In other words, if abnormal behavior is viewed as occurring on a spectrum—a continuous realm where there are no clear distinctions between what is normal and abnormal (Strauss, 1992)—how do distinctions get made? How do we draw the line between what is normal and abnormal?

DRAWING THE LINE: DEFINING ABNORMALITY

DEFINING THROUGH DISCOURSE: A DIAGNOSIS

In the social constructionist framework, the diagnosis of a mental disorder is a clear example of where "the line" has been drawn between the normal and abnormal. A diagnostic label is considered an agreement in discourse where social interactions create specific terms used to make sense of behavior (Gergen et al., 1996). There exists, of course, cultural variation as to what constitutes a mental disorder (Gaines, 1992, 1998; Macklin, 1972). Different societies will engage in different practices, leading to different terminology describing contextually different conditions. The latter may explain why conditions such as "Ghost Sickness," "Evil Eye," or "Fright Illness," are devised in some cultures and why "schizophrenia," "anorexia," or "depression" manifest in others (Gaines, 1998). Namely, a group's social and cultural consensus, negotiated through discourse, defines what a disorder is and what it will generally mean to a group of people.

Problems of defining through diagnosis. Many, however, point out that the process of diagnosis risks the possibility of being injurious to both clients and professionals (Bindeman, 1996; Gergen & McNamee, 2000; Kottler, 1991; Raskin & Lewandowski, 2000; Shackle, 1985). Because of the relationship between discourse, the meaningful conceptions that it creates, and the manner in which it is used, the system of labeling may establish meanings that restrict clients and clinicians to particular and binding conceptions of the person. Not only may implicit meanings behind a system stigmatize the individual (Rosenhan, 1975, 1973/1992; Shackle, 1985), but practitioners' failure to acknowledge such connotations (through contending that diagnoses are objective and neutral facts) may lead a person to become "stuck" in a system where there is only one way of "seeing" reality: "Once...[one] construes himself as a schizophrenic, other meaningful ways of constructing his circumstances are eliminated. Constructivism discourages foreclosing meaning making through preemptive adoption of only one construction of disorder" (Raskin & Lewandowski, 2000, p. 19).

Gergen (1994) explains that when a language and the realities that it creates are shaped by a profession—as in the case when everyday terms such as "abnormal" become "technologized" into diagnostic terms such as "schizophrenia"—it often suppresses the "voices" of the very people who receive such labels. Bindeman (1996) adds to this critique of diagnosis, arguing that a label transforms a person's struggles into a "fact" where individual experience becomes owned and controlled by a profession rather than by a person. With this in mind, it becomes interesting to contemplate what occurs if a person diagnosed with schizophrenia disagrees with her diagnosis. It is likely that, in many cases, her ideas are disrespected and she is treated as one who harbors even greater pathology: not only is she disordered, but she also *denies the reality* of her disordered condition. Although she is treated as one who is inherently wrong, it is not clear that she is. One must assess whether she is indeed denying a condition that is factually true, or whether she is denying the widespread, *socially constructed idea* that this disorder is true (and that she is currently afflicted by it). The professional, in having the authority to identify and diagnose the client's "denial," becomes "the arbiter of what is rational or irrational, intelligent or ignorant, natural or unnatural" (Gergen, 1994, p. 152). He becomes, in other words, *the arbiter of reality.* The patient, rendered voiceless as the "realities" of her condition are determined by others (Gergen, 1994), becomes "shorn of credibility by virtue of...[her] psychiatric label" (Rosenhan, 1973/1992, p. 217).

DEFINING WITH SOCIAL VALUE

Gergen et al. (1996) contend that diagnostic terms may be more reflective of the personal, cultural, and political values incorporated in assessment than they are descriptive of behavior alone. Simon (1994) supports this view, interpreting a disorder as a judgment-call made "in the opinion of some authority doing the judging" (p. 131). He claims that the "term *disorder* does not even refer to a description of behavior but rather a series of judgments about...behavior" (p. 131).

While it seems clear that every society places value on certain traits or behaviors, sociological studies of mental illness (e.g., Horwitz, 1999; Rose, 1962) suggest that abnormal behaviors can be understood entirely in terms of how society reacts to them. That is, symptoms of mental disorder must, in some way, be socially, culturally, contextually, or individually inferred. An illustration of this process can be seen in the assessment of dysfunctional behavior. Gergen et al. (1996) reason that the *dysfunction* of a behavior cannot be directly observed. Rather, one can observe only a behavior that one has chosen to label, or to judge, as being dysfunctional. Furthermore, the very act of observing behavior, or of making statements about observed behavior, draws upon vocabulary, theory, value, and, in particular, an observer—one who perceives events in a particular, personal, and subjective way (Sadler et al., 1994).

The social values necessarily inferred in the assessment of "dysfunctional" or "abnormal" can been seen in the multiple meanings of these terms. In a literal sense, "abnormal" refers to that which deviates from the norm. It describes behaviors that are statistically uncommon or infrequent. On the other hand, the term "abnormal" is generally used in reference to that which deviates from the norm in a socially unacceptable or undesirable way (Macklin, 1972). A child genius, for instance—just as atypical as the child with Autism—is considered "exceptional" rather than abnormal. While both conditions deviate from the norm, only the Autistic child is rendered "abnormal" through means of a diagnostic label. Why is this so? Statistically, the two are equivalent. Culturally, they are not. "Abnormal," as decided through social definition, also refers to that which is "unhealthy," "unwanted," or "undesirable" (Burr & Butt, 2000). Normality, then, may be interpreted in several contradictory ways: "sometimes construed as a normative concept....of how people ought to act....and sometimes as a statistical one" (Macklin, 1972, p. 349).

Social value is also employed in deciding the particular framework in which a behavior will be understood. Sexual behavior, for instance, is an area where distinctions between what is normal and abnormal are consistently being made (Kutchins & Kirk, 1997) and where one might find similar behaviors being cast into very different frameworks. One may question why certain sexual behaviors (such as homosexual behavior) are considered relevant to issues of abnormality and, sometimes, even to morality, while other sexual behaviors (such as heterosexual behavior) remain free from such scrutiny (Epting, Raskin, & Burke, 1994). Similarly, one may question why transsexual or voyeuristic behaviors are pertinent enough to psychology that they receive diagnostic labels, while prostitution (seemingly more sociological, perhaps?), does not. In these instances, a behavior is comprehended through the social values used to judge it, and becomes real only within the framework in which it develops.

Problems of defining with social value. A matter of concern, as illustrated by Gergen and McNamee (2000), is that people treat discourses as neutral assessments while ignoring their relation to social value systems. The relationship between a discourse and its socially inferred realities may hurt or stigmatize an individual:

> [There are] implicit value systems underlying the concept of mental health....Images of the "fully functioning," "well adjusted," or "normal" person are burdened with values and ideals....Diagnosis does not function neutrally, to merely describe. It renders a moral judgment. It communicates a deficit in worth. (Gergen & McNamee, 2000, p. 337)

The values and ideals intermeshed within discourse become apparent when conceptions of abnormality evolve as a result of other changing norms. It has been argued that many DSM-IV –TR disorders are based primarily on "evaluative" judgments (i.e., subjective or intuitive; Fulford, 1994) or moral and political considerations, rather than scientific or statistical ones (Kutchins & Kirk, 1997). The decision to include, and then to exclude, homosexuality from the DSM is often given as an example of this (Bayer, 1987; Kutchins & Kirk, 1997; Raskin & Lewandowski, 2000). The criteria for diagnosing the aggression or social deviance in Antisocial Personality Disorder are another example (Agich, 1994). The social, political, or moral judgment used to define abnormality seems to reflect societies' *deciding* what it would like abnormality to be. Burr and Butt (2000) consider the current "pathologization of everyday life" as an example. Here, underlying social orders organize or select which individual difficulties will be turned into specific psychological problems. A danger, however, is that society may use its power to "explain" undesirable or unacceptable behaviors through labeling them as symptoms of disorder (Burr & Butt, 2000; Sadler et al., 1994).

THE NATURE OF SOCIAL CONSTRUCTIONS

Social constructionism, thus far, may be used to argue that abnormality rests not within an individual, her biology, or her behavior, but within the language we use to describe such phenomena, the values we impose on it, and the frameworks in which we evaluate it. Although often taking the position of "ontological muteness" (Gergen, 1994), social constructionism asserts that there are many ways for a society to "draw the line" or to interpret what abnormality is, and many ways for society to change these meanings in response to changing norms. Through the analysis of how social relationships, cultural values, and discourses are used to construe meaningful representations of the abnormal, social constructionism seems to suggest that abnormality is a social phenomenon: it is, or will be, what society *decides* it ought to be. "Abnormality," in this view, "exists" as a word, as a discourse, and thus as an ideology of shared ideas, definitions, and meanings. Though abnormality, as we know it, may not exist as an objective truth, it does, in the end, seem to "exist" as a social construction that impacts human experience.

Yet, if constructionists are to be consistent with postmodern assumptions of reality, on what grounds can they claim that a phenomenon is a social construction? If the very premise on which social construction rests asserts that all constructions are creations, then the social constructionist claim itself must not only be considered a construction, but one that is no more real or superior to others (Gergen, 1994). How, then, can constructionism assert what something is, while doubting, simultaneously, the truth of such an ontological assertion? If the conception of abnormality as a social construction is itself a social construction, how can this approach to abnormality be validated?

In defense of the social constructionist framework, Gergen (1999) argues that "constructionism does not ask to be accepted because it is true. Rather, constructionism invites collaboration among people in giving sense and significance to their world" (Gergen, 1999, p. 228). Though social constructionism may be criticized because it denies the existence of a single "truth" or reality through which we can live (Held 1995a, 1995b), it questions whether such a reality is as vital as it seems. Modernist approaches imply that, in order to understand or make sense of the world, people must posses the means for identifying the correspondence between their theories and reality. Constructionism, however, differs from such approaches in that it not only questions whether this correspondence to reality is possible, but whether it is *needed* (Butt, 2000; Gergen 1994, 1999; Raskin, 2001).

Potter (as cited in Burr, 1998) suggests that questioning the reality beyond our constructs is irrelevant: "He maintains that we do not need to believe in a reality lying outside social phenomena in order to see that certain social relationships and accounts have ideological functions" (Burr, 1998, p. 19). As such, the focus remains on the realities that we inter-subjectively "know"—our personal and socially meaningful realities—rather than on reality itself. Through this approach, what matters most is not whether a disorder (such as Ghost Disorder or Evil Eye) is objectively right, but whether it is subjectively meaningful. The more pressing issue becomes whether a particular way of understanding hurts or benefits a group of individuals. The latter suggests that, rather than deciphering what abnormality *is*, society might benefit from considering and negotiating what abnormality *ought* to be. Individuals should be concerned with how we think about abnormality, how we experience abnormality, and how we live as a result of these beliefs. Because constructionism "makes no claim to be 'true'—a position beyond question—it...prompts one to ask, What are the gains and losses to our way of life that follow from each view?" (Gergen, 1994, p. 79). In other words, as a framework, espousing its own beliefs, values, and assumptions, constructionism discourages the claim that abnormality is "really" a social construction. It calls, however, for discussion as to why it may be useful to view it as such.

ADVANTAGES OF VIEWING ABNORMALITY AS A SOCIAL CONSTRUCTION

David Rosenhan's classic study of pseudopatients on a hospital ward, "On Being Sane in Insane Places" (Rosenhan, 1973/1992; see also Rosenhan, 1975), may be used to illustrate the many reasons why it is crucial to evaluate our psychological "truths." While his study may be best known for the challenges that it poses to diagnostic reliability, it may also be seen as a challenge to the claim that our theories necessarily reflect reality. Rosenhan (1973/1992) contends that, despite the assumptions guiding clinicians and mental health systems, we simply cannot distinguish the normal from the abnormal. This is observed in his study as "normal" individuals, once given a diagnosis and placed in a psychiatric setting, have their otherwise typical behaviors viewed as symptoms of pathology. Nurses observing a pseudopatient, for instance, assessed his "writing behavior" as pathological. A psychiatrist, furthermore, observed the "oral-acquisitive nature" of patients' syndromes when several patients arrived to lunch half an hour early. The fact that patients resided in the context of a psychiatric hospital—where freedom was limited, interactions were scarce, and where dining and writing may have been among the few indulging activities—bore little significance when assessing their "abnormality" (Rosenhan, 1973/1992).

While Rosenhan (1975, 1973/1992) cites many examples where clinicians misunderstood patient behavior, his studies unravel the potential harm that results from viewing clients through a single and narrow perspective. Not only may clinicians act on unstable assumptions about their clients, but also they may fail to consider the various contextual, relational, or social factors contributing to a person's difficulties. When the aim of psychiatry, as argued by Rosenhan (1973/1992), is to "locate the source of aberration within the individual" (p. 210), clinicians may view their clients in a manner that ignores their often "normal" behavior or denies them many of their freedoms and civil rights (Rosenhan, 1975, 1973/1992; Szasz, 1974). Consequently, individuals may be trapped in a system where their difficulties are ignored, disrespected, or misunderstood

(Bindeman, 1996; Rosenhan, 1975, 1973/1992; Shackle, 1985). This seems not only countertherapeutic, but also oppressive, unethical, and unjust.

Of the many problems addressed thus far, most seem to arise when socially, culturally, or politically influenced ideas are treated as objective truths free from human involvement. This process has been seen in discourses where value-laden terms are treated as neutral descriptions of reality. As occurs with diagnostic labels in particular, individuals are frequently hurt or stigmatized through the uncontestable "truths" that these meanings hold. Those who challenge or disagree with these "facts" (as might occur when a person disagrees with her diagnosis) may find their voices suppressed and are excluded from participation in what their experience means.

Rosenhan (1973/1992) hints that the origins of these problems lie in our attitudes towards knowing: "we [clinicians] tend to invent 'knowledge' and assume that we understand more than we actually do" (p. 220). He implies that many of the injustices observed by his pseudopatients arose from the ways in which practitioners dealt with their knowledge, particularly their failures "to acknowledge that...[they] simply don't know" (p. 220). Rosenhan (1973/1992) suspects that, had the context been different—had professionals not held the power to diagnose what they did not know, or had patients been allowed to offer something other than the "truth" of their labels—the perceptions, attitudes, and, therefore, the behavior of the staff may have been different: "In a more benign environment, one that was less attached to global diagnosis, their behaviors and judgments [clinicians and staff] might have been more benign and effective" (Rosenhan, 1973/1992, p. 222).

It is here where the advantages of social constructionism as an epistemological approach come into play. While the modernist approach may result in a notion of universal knowledge, it may also be oppressive in that society's "less desirables" are "explained" by those claiming to know truth (as in "reality adaptations" [Watzlawick, 1992]). The practitioner, with her authority to diagnose abnormality and her profession's control of such knowledge, seems to posses a certain authority in defining the "reality" of individual experience. In such cases, practitioners may be unwilling to reevaluate their beliefs or to treat them as anything other than facts. As seen in Rosenhan's studies (1975, 1973/1992), the harm occurs when unchallenged assumptions become transformed into "facts" through a certain confidence in knowing "what is." In other words, it is not the definitions, the theories, or the constructions of disorder themselves that are harmful. It is how they are used. It is the attitudes toward definitions of abnormality that yield the most damage. The manner in which we employ our theories and how we teat people as a result of them, are what matter more to individuals than the notions of "truth" or "reality." Precisely, it is the latter concern with "the real" that may divert us from what is important: how we experience the "real." The risk is not that, through social agreement, we might define abnormality ourselves, but that, through contending that it is real, it—our theories, our constructions—will define us. People become limited when they treat their constructions as absolute truths, thereby making themselves more resistant to change and less amenable to alternatives. Similar to Rosenhan's pseudopatients trapped in a system where there is only one way of "seeing" reality, clinicians may imprison both their clients and themselves when they are limited to a single or narrow frame of understanding (Kelly, 1955/1991). In essence, what we "know" will limit, control, and potentially harm us if we continue to treat it as the "final word" (Gergen, 1999).

If many difficulties arise when we view individuals through a single system, entertaining our "facts" as relationally based social creations may help prevent the dangers associated with ontological certainty. Social constructionism, with its emphasis on multiple voices, allows for greater flexibility in viewing abnormality through different frameworks, evaluating it with different criteria, or understanding it through the eyes of different people. Specifically, social constructionism "invites us to be critical" (Burr, 1995, p. 3) of our ideas and the potentially harmful view that "our observations of the world unproblematically yield its nature to us" (Burr, 1995, p. 3). Through being critical in this way, clients, clinicians, staff, and society at large may be more flexible in employing various modes of meaning. It invites us to pause, to reflect, and thus to evaluate our theories, our knowledge, and ourselves. In essence, when leaving room to relationally construct abnormality in radically new and different ways, we create possibilities for behaving in perpetually more useful and more effective ways. Not only may we become more aware of the constructions that hurt us, but we may realize our collective potential to judge, evaluate, and change them as needed.

REFERENCES

Agich, G. J. (1994). Evaluative judgment and personality disorder. In J. Z. Sadler, O. P. Wiggins & M. A. Schwartz (Eds.), *Philosophical perspectives on psychiatric diagnostic classification* (pp. 233-245). Baltimore: John Hopkins University Press.

American Psychiatric Association. (2000). *Diagnostic and statistical manual of mental disorders* (4th ed., Text Revision). Washington, DC: Author.

Andreasen, N. C. (1984). *The broken brain.* New York: Harper & Row.

Aneshensel, C. S., & Phelan, J. E. (Eds.). (1999). *Handbook of the sociology of mental health.* New York: Plenum Press.

Baer, R. D., Clark, L. & Peterson, C. (1998). Folk illnesses. In S. Loue (Ed.), *Handbook of immigrant health* (pp. 183-202). New York: Plenum Press.

Bayer, R. (1987). *Homosexuality and American psychiatry: The politics of diagnosis.* Princeton, NJ: Princeton University Press.

Bindeman, S. (1996). Schizophrenia and postmodern philosophy. *The Humanistic Psychologist, 24,* 262-282.

Bleibtreu-Ehrenberhg, G. (1990). Pederasty among primitives: Institutionalized initiation and cultic prostitution. *Journal of Homosexuality, 20*(1-2), 13-30.

Burr, V. (1995). *An introduction to social constructionism.* London: Routledge.

Burr, V. (1998). Overview: Realism, relativism, social constructionism and discourse. In I. Parker (Ed.), *Social constructionism, discourse and realism* (pp. 13-25). London: Sage.

Burr, V., & Butt, T. W. (2000). Psychological distress and postmodern thought. In D. Fee (Ed.) *Pathology and the postmodern* (pp. 186-206). London: Sage.

Butt, T. (2000). Pragmatism, constructivism, and ethics. *Journal of Constructivist Psychology, 13,* 85-101.

Epting, F. R., Raskin, J. D., & Burke, T. B. (1994). Who is a homosexual? A critique of the heterosexual-homosexual dimension. *The Humanistic Psychologist, 22,* 353-370.

Flaskas, C. (1994). Postmodernism, constructionism and the idea of reality: A contribution to the "ism" discussions. *The Australian and New Zealand Journal of Family Therapy, 16*(3), 143-146.

Franklin, C. (1995). Expanding the vision of the social constructionist debates: Creating relevance for practitioners. *Families in Society: The Journal of Contemporary Human Services, 76*(7), 395- 407.

Fulford, K. W. M. (1994). Closet logics: Hidden conceptual elements in the DSM and ICD classifications of mental disorders. In J. Z. Sadler, O. P. Wiggins & M. A. Schwartz (Eds.), *Philosophical perspectives on psychiatric diagnostic classification* (pp. 211-232). Baltimore: John Hopkins University Press.

Gaines, A. D. (1992). From DSM-I to III-R; voices of self, mastery and the other: A cultural constructivist reading of U.S. psychiatric classification. *Social Science and Medicine, 35,* 3-24.

Gaines, A. D. (1998). Mental illness and immigration. In S. Loue (Ed.), *Handbook of* immigrant health (pp. 407-421). New York: Plenum Press.

Gilman, S. L. (1988). *Disease and representation.* New York: Cornell University Press.

Gergen, K. J. (1994). *Realities and relationships: Soundings in social construction.* Cambridge, MA: Harvard University Press.

Gergen, K. J. (1999). *An invitation to social construction.* London: Sage.

Gergen, K. J., Hoffman, L., & Anderson, H. (1996). Is diagnosis a disaster? A constructionist trialogue. Retrieved July 9, 2001, from the World Wide Web: http://www.swarthmore.edu/socsci/kgergen1/text5.html

Gergen, K. J., & McNamee, S. (2000). From disordering discourse to transformative dialogue. In R. A. Neimeyer & J. D. Raskin (Eds.), *Constructions of disorder: Meaning-making frameworks for psychotherapy* (pp. 333-349). Washington, DC: American Psychological Association.

Held, B. (1995a). *Back to reality: A critique of postmodern theory in psychotherapy.* New York: Norton.

Held, B. (1995b). The real meaning of constructivism. *Journal of Constructivist Psychology, 8,* 305-315.

Horwitz, A. V. (1999). The sociological study of mental illness: A critique and synthesis of four perspectives. In C. S. Aneshensel & J. E. Phelan (Eds.), *Handbook of the sociology of mental health.* (pp. 57-78) New York: Plenum Press.

Ingleby, D. (1982). The social construction of mental illness. In P. Wright & A. Treacher (Eds.), *The problem of medical knowledge: Examining the social construction of medicine* (pp. 123-143). Edinburgh: Edinburgh University Press.

Kelly, G. A. (1991). *The psychology of personal constructs. Vol. 1: A theory of personality.* London: Routledge. (Original work published 1955)

Kottler, J. A. (1991). On the dangers of traditional diagnoses. *The Humanistic Psychologist, 18,* 347-349.

Kutchins, H., & Kirk, S. A. (1997). *Making us crazy. DSM: The psychiatric bible and the creation of mental disorders.* New York: Free Press.

Loue, S. (Ed.). (1998). *Handbook of immigrant health.* New York: Plenum Press.

Macklin, R. (1972). Mental health and mental illness: Some problems of definition and concept formation. *Philosophy of Science, 39,* 341-364.

Mahoney, M. J., & Lyddon, W. J. (1988). Recent developments in cognitive approaches to counseling and psychotherapy. *The Counseling Psychologist, 16,* 190-234.

Newman, F., & Holzman, L. (1996). *Unscientific psychology.* Westport, CT: Praeger.

Parker, I., Georgaca, E., Harper, D., McLaughlin, T., & Stowell-Smith, M. (1995). *Deconstructing psychopathology.* London: Sage.

Raskin, J. D. (2001). On relativism in constructivist psychology. *Journal of Constructivist Psychology, 14,* 285-313.

Raskin, J. D., & Lewandowski, A. M. (2000). The construction of disorder as human enterprise. In R. A. Neimeyer & J. D. Raskin (Eds.), *Constructions of disorder: Meaning-making frameworks for psychotherapy* (pp. 15-40). Washington, DC: American Psychological Association.

141

Rose, A. M. (Ed.). (1962). *Human behavior and social processes.* Boston: Houghton Mifflin.

Rosenhan, D. L. (1975). The contextual nature of psychiatric diagnosis. *Journal of Abnormal Psychology, 84,* 462-474.

Rosenhan, D. L. (1992). On being sane in insane places. In J. M. Morse (Ed.), *Qualitative health research* (pp. 202-224). Baltimore: John Hopkins University Press. (Reprinted from *Science, 179,* 250-258, 1973)

Rowe, D. C., & Elam, P. E. (1987). Siblings and mental illness: Heredity vs. environment. *Journal of Children in Contemporary Society, 19*(3-4), 115-130.

Sadler, J. Z., Wiggins, O. P., & Schwartz, M. A. (Eds.). (1994). *Philosophical perspectives on psychiatric diagnostic classification.* Baltimore: John Hopkins University Press.

Sadowsky, J. (1996). The confinements of Isaac O.: A case of 'acute mania' in colonial Nigeria. *History of Psychiatry, 7*(25), 91-112.

Searle, J. R. (1995). *The construction of social reality.* New York: Free Press.

Seligman, M. E. P., & Rosenhan, D. L. (1998). *Abnormality.* New York: Norton.

Shackle, E.M. (1985). Psychiatric diagnosis as an ethical problem. *Journal of Medical Ethics, 11,* 132-134.

Simon, L. (1994). *Psycho"therapy": Theory, practice, modern and postmodern influences.* Westport, CT: Praeger.

Sosa, E. (1986). Presuppositions of empirical knowledge. *Philosophical Papers, 15*(2-3), 75-78.

Speed, B. (1991). Reality exists o.k.? An argument against constructivism and social constructionism. *Family Therapy, 13,* 395-409.

Strauss, J. S. (1992). The person key to understanding mental illness: Towards a new dynamic psychiatry, III. *British Journal of Psychiatry, 161*(18), 19-26.

Szasz, T. S. (1974). *The myth of mental illness: Foundations of a theory of personal conduct* (rev. ed.). New York: Harper & Row.

Valenstein, E. S. (1998). *Blaming the brain: The truth about drugs and mental health.* New York: Free Press.

Wallace, E. R., IV. (1994). Psychiatry and its nosology: A historico-philosophical overview. In J. Z. Sadler, O. P. Wiggins & M. A. Schwartz (Eds.), *Philosophical perspectives on psychiatric diagnostic classification* (pp. 16-86). Baltimore: John Hopkins University Press.

Warren, B. (1998). *Philosophical dimensions of personal construct psychology.* London: Routledge.

Watzlawick, P. (1992). The construction of clinical "realities." In J. K. Zeig (Ed.), *The evolution of psychotherapy: The second conference* (pp. 55-62). New York: Brunner/Mazel.

Wright, P., & Treacher, A. (Eds.). (1982). *The problem of medical knowledge: Examining the social construction of medicine.* Edinburgh: Edinburgh University Press.

Yoxen, E. J. (1982). Constructing genetic diseases. In P. Wright & A. Treacher (Eds.), *The problem of medical knowledge: Examining the social construction of medicine* (pp. 144-161). Edinburgh: Edinburgh University Press.

Chapter 7

The Social Construction of Disorder: From Pathology to Potential

Sheila McNamee

As I rushed down the highway at nearly 80 miles an hour, late to give a talk to a nearby group of colleagues (because I had taken the time to check my morning e-mail), I heard a report that declared the *discovery* of a new mental disorder, *Internet addiction*. Alarmed, I realized that I must be suffering from this addiction if, indeed, my burning need to check my e-mail had put me in a situation where I would surely be late to give my talk and might, in fact, be endangering myself physically by driving so fast. Because the talk I was rushing to give was focused on the pathologizing effects of psychological diagnosis, I found my present situation prophetic. The challenge was before me. Do I accept the radio's report and chuck my own arguments out the window? Or do I follow my position, thereby locating alternative narrative descriptions that are focused on generating possibilities rather than pathologies? Clearly, my own well being was best preserved in the latter choice.

My story could seem fabricated if we were not already accustomed to the profusion of labels, categories, and diagnoses of deficit within our culture. Everywhere we turn it seems we are confronted with yet another problem of which to beware, another danger that we might impose upon ourselves (or others), or another assessment that might contaminate our futures. The chief metaphor today seems to be that of an organism under attack. There is danger lurking in the streets, in our social institutions, in our relations, and in our bodies. If we are not able to confront that danger—to manage it and control it—our teachers, therapists, doctors, judges, employers, family members, and friends identify us (label us) as deficient.

Gergen (1994) and Kutchins and Kirk (1997) discuss the proliferation of deficit discourse within the field of mental health. In her book, *The Argument Culture: Moving from Debate to Dialogue*, Deborah

Tannen (1998) addresses a broader, popularly appealing view of the cultural impulse to critique and thereby ultimately highlight the deficiencies in the other. She argues that we have become a culture of argument where the unquestioned impulse is to negatively evaluate another rather than search for the potential in the other's viewpoint, and thus in the other's actions. This broader issue of a dominant cultural discourse is important for our purposes because it helps us to understand the accelerated creation and use of diagnostic categories and labels.

We are hard pressed to locate any institutional or general cultural context within which evaluation is not dominant. We see it not only in mental health but in education, healthcare, business, government, as well as in our intimate relations with family, with friends, with co-workers and neighbors. Why is there such a profusion of evaluation in general and an urgency to *uncover* problems, pathologies, deficits, inadequacies in general? One might argue (as have many already) that such a proclivity emerges from the rampant cynicism that has infused itself in our everyday lives. Yet cynicism alone is not the problem. Rather, cynicism is a symptom of a greater concern: individualism. Cynicism is born of the individualist ideology that dominates Western tradition. A host of scholars have argued powerfully of the dangers of privileging individuals over community. Christopher Lasch (1979), in his powerful book *The Culture of Narcissism*, describes how our focus on the individual produces self-interest at the cost of communal betterment. Bellah, Madson, Sullivan, Swindler, and Tipton (1985) argue that the individualist tradition stands as a threat to any form of relational engagement, with all efforts focused on self-preservation. If each of us is centrally concerned with our own well being, and yet we are dependent upon each other and our cultural institutions to "get ahead" or "be effective," then cynicism becomes a *naturalized* response. Individualism, as an ideology, invites us to approach the world as if we, alone, can tame it. It is the individual who can solve problems, make decisions, think rationally and act effectively. Thus, in those instances when such activities are not possible, when the results of one's actions do not move one further along in successful ways, we are left with the choice of blaming the individual for his or her under-developed capabilities or blaming the broader cultural institutions for presenting the unsolvable problems in the first place. Because the first choice requires us to pathologize ourselves, it is often the second option that we engage. It is far easier to blame our apparent inadequacies on "the system" or on another rather than on ourselves. Under such circumstances, it is easy to see how cynicism becomes the likely response. In the face of failure or ineptitude, we begin to ask ourselves why we ever thought "the system" or another person could be counted on to help us achieve, succeed, thrive. Because cynicism is a symptom of our individualist discourse, let us explore in more depth the domain of individualism and its implications.

LIMITS OF INDIVIDUALISM

Individualism, as a mode of practice, is largely unquestioned. Most discussions in the development and implementation of new institutional activities and social policies take this form. In our culture, we are hard pressed to find an institutional context where attention is placed on anything but the individual. Others' actions are of concern to us only to the extent that they affect our own well being. To that end, the dominant discourse of individualism focuses our attention on techniques and procedures for insuring that we develop the kinds of individuals we desire in our culture. Attention is placed often on transmission of information as opposed to the building of communities and relationships within which people can live and coordinate their activities.

The individualist tradition champions the self as an originary source of thought and action. Consequently, we conduct psychotherapy, we educate individual minds, reward and punish individuals at work, and hold individuals responsible for all their actions, thoughts, beliefs, and more. In sum, the individual is the unquestioned, natural entity of concern in our attempts to understand social life. In order to know anything about the complexity of social interchange, we must begin with the individual—most obviously the basic unit of examination.

One of the reasons the individual appears to be such a natural starting place for our examination of social relationships and social processes is because our bodies offer obvious boundaries that separate us from each other. It seems ludicrous to challenge the notion that my body contains my intellect, my beliefs, my values, my traits, my abilities and more. This belief is so ingrained in our Western way of living that when there are problems, it seems logical and necessary to focus on the individual.

Yet, if we were to draw on the language of other professions, such as physics and engineering, we might literally see that the skin

145

does not bound one's body. David Watt describes how the molecules in any material or object (such as a body) vibrate and as they vibrate they "excite electro-magnetic waves that propagate through space and transfer energy between objects" (personal communication). The image that is seen with the help of specialized equipment is the blending of bodies or objects. To scientists interested in heat transfer, our bodies are not naturally bounded containers. And at the same time, to scientists interested in medical disease, the body does, indeed, serve as a container. Could we draw analogies from these opposing ways of viewing the body in science to construct some alternative discourses for talking about personhood in the social world?

There are already several moves in just this direction. In a variety of ways, social theorists and philosophers have challenged the idea of the self-contained individual. Rather than assume that intellect, knowledge, beliefs, values, and so forth are contained within persons, the move is to recognize each as constructed within communities. In fact, the very idea of private mental functioning, of a separate, "mindful" individual is, itself, the byproduct of communal construction. In his book, *Constructing the Self, Constructing America*, Philip Cushman (1995) tells us:

> Individualism wasn't simply a coincidence, a mutation that popped out of the Zeusian forehead of some late medieval poet. It is a slow-building, centuries-old phenomenon that has developed in part because of the oppressiveness of certain traditions, the stifling inertia of life in small communities, and the compelling decision to resist the old, the given, the unjust, and to be creative, unique, and unusual. Viewed in this way, individualism is itself a Western tradition, a response to the economic arrangements, moral understandings, and political constrictions of feudal life. (p. 10)

Cushman suggests that the fall of the feudal system, marked as it was by "the beginnings of capitalism, and the growth of larger cities, the beginnings of the concept of romantic love . . . " (p. 364) all coincided with the beginnings of individualism. He says:

> We can see the beginnings of individualism in a myriad of small changes, such as portraits that began to reflect personal idiosyncracies as well as one's place in the social hierarchy; the concept of personal friendship rather than corporate feudal bonds; the philosophical growth of mysticism that emphasized personal communion, rather than a solely institutional, mediated relationship with God; the shift in art from a fixed to a moveable perspective; and literary forms such as the biography and auto-

146

> biography. Peter Abelard, in an unusual individualistic move that would become important to the field of psychology hundreds of years later, maintained that it was not the act, but the individual's internal *intention* behind the act that constituted sin. (p. 364)

Thus, individualism as an ideology *emerged* in a particular historical moment. It was not *naturally* evident. And it emerged through collective coordination among citizens.

Philosophers such as Rorty (1979) have argued that the idea of an interior mind reflecting an exterior nature is not a simple reflection of human existence but a historically situated *convention*. Historical studies document the shifting conceptions of mind. We no longer, for example, talk of "hysteria" or "soul" as manifestations of mind and we continually add new mental realities to the ledger (Kutchins & Kirk, 1997; Harre, 1979; Graumann & Gergen, 1996). Anthropological work demonstrates different conceptions of mind in different cultures (Lutz & Abu-Lughod, 1990; Heelas & Lock, 1981; Shweder, 1991). To the Buddist unity is significant, but selfhood is not. Literary theorists call into question the long accepted belief that the task of the reader is to locate the author behind the text—to ferret out the true meaning of a text. In contrast, deconstructionists such as Derrida (1976) and Fish (1980) illustrate how writing is not a manifestation of the author's mind but of systems of language that entail genres and traditions of writing. To them, writing is a culturally and historically contingent practice of effective language use. Thus, to read is to *participate* in culturally embedded practices of interpretation.

The implications of these critiques are significant for our discussion. One cannot constitute meaning alone, nor engage in a rational choice among competing goods, without having absorbed the intelligibilies of a community. Yet, individualist discourse is our dominating tradition (convention). It affects cultural life by valorizing the self as the origin of action. The result is that the self is prioritized. We value our own goals, needs, wants, and rights. Our chief concern is how we win or lose. We only examine other's actions as they affect our own.

Individualist discourse generates a sense of fundamental independence or isolation. I am never certain if I am being understood or not. Why should I pursue investments that might curtail my individual freedom? The byproduct of this way of talking is that relationships become artificial. Relationships "need to be worked on."

147

When working on a relationship becomes burdensome, we simply retreat to the self (what is best for *me*?).

There are also deleterious effects on society. If everyone is self-absorbed, who cares about the environment? In this realm, individual gain is impoverishment for the community. Little attention is given in higher education to cooperative modes of learning. Business training emphasizes individual performance and workshops abound in leadership and management training. Courts seek to allocate individual blame and remain blind to the broader social processes in which crime is embedded. On both local and global levels, individualism promotes interminable conflict among incommensurate moral or ideological commitments. *Is this a useful path for the future?*[1]

INDIVIDUALISM AND PSYCHOLOGICAL PATHOLOGY

Let us consider for just a moment the specific ramifications of individualist discourse in the context of psychotherapy. At stake here is the dominating factor that psychotherapy, as a profession, provides diagnosis for a person's psychological distress. While there are many modes of psychotherapy where emphasis is placed on moving beyond personal or psychological distress, the profession requires first and foremost that a diagnosis be identified before moving toward problem resolution or treatment. In fact, because psychotherapy is tightly linked to the medical profession, the overwhelming belief is that psychotherapy, in order to proceed, demands diagnosis. How can a therapist know how to treat a client if that therapist is operating without a clear idea of what the client's problem is in the first place? To treat a problem then requires diagnosis. Two issues are relevant here: (1) the issue of diagnosis as it relates to individualism and therefore the implication that deficiency resides within the person requiring individual diagnosis and (2) the issue of diagnosis as a necessary conversation (particularly in psychotherapy) that revolves around identification of problems, the causes of the problems, and the resolution of problems. These issues are not necessarily separable. Let me expand on each to set the context for a relational alternative to diagnosis.

---

[1] For a more detailed discussion of individualism and its limits see McNamee and Gergen (1999) and Gergen (1999).

Diagnosis of Individuals

Central to our discussion here is the observation that diagnosis in psychotherapy means diagnosis of an individual. If one's identity is located within the person, as individualism tells us, then all that is problematic must emanate from the internal mind or psyche of that person. Thus the diagnosis must be of the person, of the individual. There are certainly situations where such diagnosis can be useful. I think of the varying responses different people might have to the diagnosis of chronic depression. For some, learning from the "expert" (i.e., psychotherapist) that they are suffering from chronic depression can be helpful. The diagnosis gives them the sense that now that the problem has been identified, a treatment program can begin. There is hope in sight. Yet, we must not forget all those others for whom the diagnosis of chronic depression (or any other diagnosis) initiates a tailspin into further malaise. Armed with the diagnosis, these people lose hope by virtue of being identified as flawed, inferior, unhealthy, and anything but "normal."

Diagnosis Requires Problem Talk

Psychotherapy, diagnosis, and problems are terms that naturally go together. We seek psychotherapy when we feel uneasy, unsettled, or disturbed. Things are not going well in our lives and psychotherapy is one of the central places we turn for help. Given this assumption, it is difficult to imagine the utility of a psychotherapeutic conversation where the central topic of discussion is not problem oriented. Several forms of therapy already attempt to move beyond problem discussion. Solution focused therapy (deShazer, 1994; O'Hanlon & Weiner-Davis, 1989) and the narrative therapy of White and Epston (1990) are popular illustrations of therapeutic models where emphasis is placed on the imagination of alternative constructions of the situation at hand, as well as of the future. These methods shift the conversation away from problems and diagnosis, refocusing therapy on conversations about possibilities. Yet, talking about solutions implies problems and constructing new narratives in therapy suggests that the client's story is defective. While these models are seen as significant moves in the development of alternatives to individualist diagnostic models of therapy, to the constructionist they do not go far enough.

To view therapy as social construction is to press the therapeutic conversation in entirely different directions. Might both client and therapist gain by initiating conversation on what are valued and reliable resources for action that the client harbors? What stories can be told that illustrate these valued resources? If the client were to imagine that she or he was able to draw on those resources at will, what would be the activities in which she or he might no longer be engaged? What new activities might she or he be inviting others to co-construct? In these conversations about resources, diagnosis is stripped of its power. If I can talk with you and others about these potentials, I might no longer need to focus my attention on my deficits. Or, more likely, conversation about the relational resources I already have successfully constructed with others might suggest to me that these could be usefully recruited into the relationships where problems have become the byproduct of coordinations with others.

To engage in what I refer to as "resource-oriented" conversations in therapy, it is useful to draw on a multiplicity of voices (see McNamee & Gergen, 1998). These voices could be others who might not seem associated with the situation at hand. They could also be the host of *internalized others* (Tomm, 1998). Here the notion is that we each harbor many feelings and views from other relationships (real or imagined). When we speak or act, even with the intent of voicing our *own* beliefs, we are giving voice to the constructions that emerge within other coordinated relationships. My beliefs are not mine alone. They are not my private possession. They are already populated by myriad *others*. Gergen (1999) refers to this as polyvocality. He explains the utility of this term, "when individuals begin to talk about their problems, the therapist might ask them if they can locate another voice within, a voice that would construct the world in a different light or with different possibilities" (p. 174).

Without claiming that diagnosis is wrong or bad, let me shift my focus now to the ways in which diagnosis invites us into debilitating patterns of relationship. Kenneth Gergen and I have discussed some of the deleterious byproducts of diagnosis elsewhere (Gergen & McNamee, 2000). Let me quickly review these detrimental patterns here. These limitations of diagnosis illustrate both individualism and problem talk as potential barriers to the generation of potentials for social transformation.

The Downside of Diagnosis

First, there are ways in which diagnosis becomes stigmatizing for the individual. The field of psychology in general, and psychotherapy in particular, carries with it an implicit set of values.

There are ways of being in the world that are preferred over others. So, for example, we value a person who is responsive to us when we are in conversation. Such a person is generally labeled as "normal" and "fully functioning." On the other hand, a person who systematically introduces an irrelevant topic into any conversation is seen as being "odd," perhaps "schizophrenic." Arthur Kleinman (1988) talks about cultural differences in diagnosis and illustrates how forms of action that are deemed significantly problematic in one culture might go completely unacknowledged in another. Thus, what is labeled a severe case of schizophrenia in Western culture is noted as only a minor oddity in South Asian culture. Explaining this difference is not a matter of which culture *understands* science more fully, but rather it is a matter of communal relations. The person in South Asian culture is cared for within a tightly connected community and thus there is no reason to fear that person or label his or her behaviors as severely problematic.

Most important in terms of the ways diagnosis stigmatizes people is the observation that, in so doing, diagnosis is rendered a valuational process. It is not, as scientific discourse would claim, value neutral. Diagnosis does not simply describe what is *there*. Rather, diagnosis functions as a moral judgment. It conveys the deficit of one to others. Consider the case of Attention Deficit Hyperactivity Disorder (ADHD). The unquestioned value within this diagnosis is a quiet, calm, and orderly classroom. There is an assumption that moving at rapid pace from one thing to another—depending on what captures your attention—is bad or wrong. Yet, children being raised in today's global economy have a difficult time avoiding the multiplicity of activities surrounding them. Rather than pathologize them for patterns of relating to which they have become accustomed, what potential could there be in schools and parents initiating inquiry into how the classroom might integrate or simulate the stimulation provided by the infusion of technology into the lives of these children and the quick pace of contemporary life?

Peter Hoeg, a Danish novelist, has written about the stigmatizing aspects of diagnosis. He writes:

> They believed that it was of great help to children to be assessed. I suppose they still believe that. In our society it is a pretty widespread belief. That assessment is a good thing. . . . I was at the playground with the child . . . she had climbed up on to some railway sleepers. She was about one metre (sic) off the ground. She called to me from there. "Look!" I did not get the answer out. I had no time. It came from a stranger - she was

also there with her child. "What a clever girl!" she said. I had
no time to think. I was on my feet and on my way over to bite
her head off. Then I remembered that she was the mother of a
small child and that she was a woman. . . . I sat down, but it was
a long time before I stopped shaking.

The child had wanted attention. She had just asked to be
noticed. But she was given an assessment. "What a clever girl!"
(Hoeg, 1995, p. 99)

Once stigmatized, assessed, diagnosed, there is little way for
a client to escape. The "illness" or "deficit" hides under the thin
veneer of treatment.

Added to the problem of stigmatization is the impulse to
blame the person for his or her failings. Elsewhere I have talked
about the ways in which individualism invites us into patterns of
blame and evaluation (McNamee & Gergen, 1998). If my actions are
motivated by my internal, individual beliefs, values, and commitments, then any flaw or deficit must also be seen as residing within
and thus I am held responsible for my actions. If I am responsible
for my actions and they are deemed wrong or bad or inappropriate,
then I am the only one to blame. My dysfunction is located within
me. My failing is my inability. Within this logic, I am likely to withdraw from others so as not to inflict my problems on them. Others
then become evaluators ("She's at it again") and thus engage in conversations of blame as well. There is little room here for exploration
into external factors that might contribute to the deficiency.

Thus, as diagnosis proceeds, relationships are torn apart. If I
have a problem (particularly one that has been diagnosed), then I
must work it out myself. Those closest to me are probably those who
I am most likely to protect from my problem. Why burden my loved
ones with my deficiencies? And, if it is my loved ones who are constructed as the "cause" of my problem, then all the more reason to
avoid them. As I seek help from mental health professionals, my
dearest family and friends are advised to stay away and let the "professional do his or her job." If I believe my problem stems from my
marriage, I seek council from my therapist rather than my spouse. If
my problem seems to be a product of a stressful workplace, I again
seek help from my therapist rather than co-workers or supervisors.
In this way, the mental health profession at large and the process of
diagnosis and treatment actually inhibits the growth and evolution of
relationships, ranging from intimate to community to organization-
al.

With the deterioration of relationships we begin to see how our sense of community is depleted. The lack of community naturally limits our attention to traditions, rituals, and folkways that previously bound us together. When in need, I am more likely to turn to the mental health professional for help than to a person or group of people with whom I share religious beliefs, professional interests, or leisure activities. The more I depend on the psychology professional to help me, the more I contribute to placing community and relationships at the boundary. Consequently, if community becomes "other," why should I care that my desires might threaten your family, your life, and your property?

Finally, the discourse of diagnosis, the profession of mental health, provides the individual with little in the way of resources for moving on in life. Think of how managed care, for example, controls how much help we can receive and how we will receive it. Managed care also identifies those issues for which we need professional help, thereby categorizing some as more seriously troubled than others. We now have an enormous array of professionals making decisions about a person's life, thereby disempowering the person him or herself. As Foucault (1979) points out, when we offer ourselves for professional examination, we are giving ourselves over to the disciplinary regimes (in this case the mental health professionals and administrators) to be labeled and explained in their terms. As we do so, we carry these terms into other realms of our daily life (for example, when someone is acting in ways that you do not like, you might say with rolling eyes, "She must be off her medication today."). We speak to others now of our depression, our anxiety, our stress, and our attention deficit; each one a technical term constructed by professionals. As we use these terms in our common parlance, we engage in relationships wherein we extend control to those professionals to circumscribe the ways we talk about ourselves. Professionals then begin to influence policy and practice amongst the general public and we become further controlled in their terms.

Hoeg (1995), in his novel exploring the lives of three children living at an experimental, residential school where they were constantly being assessed by the "authorities" for purposes of determining their futures, summarizes the problems we face with diagnosis (assessment):

> When you assess something, you are forced to assume that a linear scale of values can be applied to it. Otherwise no assessment is possible. Every person who says of something that it is good or bad or a bit better than yesterday is declaring that a points

system exists; that one can, in a reasonably clear and obvious
fashion, set some sort of a number against an achievement. . . .
But never at any time has a code of practice been laid down for
the awarding of points. No offence intended to anyone. Never
at any time in the history of the world has anyone . . . been able
to come up with a code of practice that could be learned and
followed by several different people, in such a way that they
would all arrive at the same mark. Never at any time have they
been able to agree on a method for determining when one
drawing, one meal, one sentence, one insult, the picking of one
lock, one blow, one patriotic song, one Danish essay, one play-
ground, one frog or one interview is good or bad or better or
worse than another . . . But a code of practice is essential. To
ensure that things can be spoken of, fully and frankly. A code of
practice is something that could be passed on . . . (pp. 78-79)

Hoeg's position gives us reason to consider alternatives to
diagnosis.

Is There Any Hope?

In today's global world, cultures are thrown into ever increasing contact. There is both pragmatic and theoretical demand for
communal forms of practice. Individualist ideology can often be a
disaster. In what follows I outline relational alternatives that might
supplement our individualist traditions. Are there ways of relating—
of talking and doing—that privilege relations over individuals and in
so doing provide opportunities for transformative dialogue? After
all, psychotherapy is focused on transformation. How can a relational sensitivity provide resources for acting in the psychotherapeutic context—resources that are generative and transformative?
Simultaneously, it is significant to recognize psychotherapy's role in
perpetuating and/or transforming more global social practices.
Social construction offers us, I think, a useful alternative. It is an
alternative that centers on relational constructions of meaning and in
so doing provides sustainable resources for constructing relational
realities of potential and possibility. These resources help move us
beyond diagnosis toward social transformation.

INDIVIDUALS AS A DISCURSIVE OPTION

To the constructionist, placing our focus on individuals, as
described above, is a "way of talking" or a discursive option. To consider individualism as a conversational resource rather than as an
essential or fundamental reality is to shift the terrain of our discussion. Rather than simply reflect reality, our discursive tradition has

154

created a particular kind of reality. This reality includes features such as objectivity, individuality, uniform rationality, and progress. To put it this way is to say that this way of orienting ourselves to the world provides a distinctive discursive repertoire. It is to see these views as byproducts of a particular approach to language rather than as descriptions of the essential nature of reality. This orientation provides us with some means for employing alternative resources. It allows us to question the utility of seeing our words as reflections of our interiors and recognize that this is not necessarily the case but is, rather, a discursive tradition.

Individualism, while enduring and valuable, is only one way of talking and thus only one way of being. Fully armed with the discourse of individualism we are able to locate a broad array of qualities within persons ranging from intellect, leadership, sociability, and agency, as well as mental illness, insecurity, deviance, and perversion. It is individuals who reason, who lead, who relate, and who act intentionally. Thus, it is only reasonable to conclude that it is individuals who should become the focus of diagnosis and treatment when actions or meanings do not fit with culturally preferred norms.

TOWARD POTENTIALS

Of course, not all diagnosis of mental disorder is damaging. As I mentioned earlier, for some the diagnosis serves as an aid in moving on in one's life. My argument here is not to abandon diagnosis but to augment this (largely) unquestioned cultural practice with an alternative. The alternative that I would like to suggest is that of relational engagement. With emphasis on *what people do together*, the negative effects of diagnosis can be lessened. I am not proposing a focus on relational engagement as a *more correct* approach to dealing with problems. The relational alternative I propose should be seen as simply another resource for action; one that I believe offers us many generative ways of going on together.

At this point, it is useful to draw on the practical resources offered within a social constructionist discourse. Constructionism (Gergen, 1999; McNamee & Gergen, 1998) proposes that meaning is always an emergent process of persons in relation. This suggests that meaning is not fixed. It is not stable. It is, rather, in constant flux, always open to new possibilities. Any sense we have of permanence arises from the skill we have in ritualizing our forms of interaction. I find it useful to think of our social activities as *invitations to* others. Thus, when I say I love you, I invite you into the game (as Wittgenstein, 1953, would say) or the ritual we commonly know as romance. To a realist, saying "I love you" is taken as a statement of fact, an expression perhaps of one's true, inner feelings. It is in the contrast between the social constructionist notion of words and gestures as invitations and the realist's notion of words and gestures as representations that the entry to relational practices is located. If my words and actions invite you to engage with me in particular cultural performances (rituals), I *need you* to accomplish that performance. Your responses to my actions are required in order for me to realize (literally, *make real*) my efforts. Does this make a statement like, "I love you" meaningless? It absolutely does not. The shift that social construction offers is important. It is a shift to recognizing how, in this illustration, a relationship is *required* to engage in the performance of romance in order for it to be *real*. As Edward Sampson says, "the *most important thing about people is not what is contained within them, but what transpires between them*" (1993, p. 20). The significance of placing meaning in the joint activities of participants, as opposed to in the heads of persons, is precisely the aspect of social construction that offers us alternatives to diagnosis.

Within social constructionism, meaning emerges as communities of people coordinate their activities with one another. The continual coordination required in any relationship or community eventually generates a sense of common practices, a vocabulary if you will. So, for example, as those closest to me both personally and professionally rely more and more on e-mail, it has become a well coordinated part of our relationships. It is no longer "impersonal" or "unfriendly" to send e-mail messages instead of phoning or writing a letter. There are entire patterns of communication (patterns of relating) that are now expected among my colleagues and friends and we have even constructed terms and activities that are unique to these relationships. As an illustration, I have noticed that when someone describes an e-mail "conversation," the narration is frequently accompanied by an intriguing gesture: the movement of fingers in the air as if the person is typing. The words that accompany this gesture are usually, "and then she said," or "he explained," or "I said." This is an illustration of not only coordinating activities, but also generating a vocabulary (words and actions) specific to a ritualized performance.

The patterns or rituals that emerge within relationships or communities generate standards over time. There are standards of expectation and standards of value. We come to expect the enact-ment of given patterns (e.g., for friends who have constructed a pat-tern of daily email exchanges, an absent message is likely to raise concern). We also implicitly construct a set of values associated with the performance (e.g., daily e-mail is a good thing). As these stan-dards emerge and the coordinated activities become more and more entrenched within the relationship or community, a way of life is established—actually appearing as if "natural" and "normal" and transcendent of time or place or persons. This is a socially achieved reality, but we must be clear: this is "as real as it gets."

Important to note here is that within communities all over the globe, this process is occurring. Thus, the potential for incom-mensurate life-worlds is enormous. Further, because each of us is immersed in multiple communities simultaneously, the potential for difference is great. It is even possible that we each harbor opposing positions on a topic by virtue of the very different communities within which we participate.

To the social constructionist then, meaning is always fluid and supple. Meaning is always in motion. The extent to which we encounter consistency in meaning and patterns of relationship is attributable to the coordinated achievement of participants. In effect, we could say that any sense we have of stability can be credited to the participants' abilities to "play the language game."

To understand meaning, and thus reality, in these terms is to embrace the discourse of social construction. We can put aside (and I think we must) the popular critiques of social construction—cri-tiques that claim social construction is amoral and unethical. Such critiques are grounded on claims of rampant relativism. Yet, to the constructionist, it is not an *anything goes* world. Because all meaning is dependent upon the coordination of people in relation, and because any configuration of persons is likely to yield a unique or different meaning from any other group, social construction is sure-ly relativistic, but is surely not rampant. One is not free to simply construct the world at will.[2] We are ultimately dependent on each

[2] We have an extensive history of distinguishing constructivism from social con-structionism and it seems useful at this point to both recap that distinction and point to recent movements that go far to erase the differences. First, construc-tivism, as influenced by George Kelly (1955) and Jean Piaget (1954), claims that the world is constructed and also places significance on the social relationships within which persons operate. However, it is still the mind of the individual that constructs reality. The mind is influenced by the social world and to that extent, the constructions of one person carry vestiges of the social world. Here, the indi-vidual is still the basic unit of analysis, although social relations certainly are sig-

other to (literally) *make* our worlds. Once we dismiss the "anything goes" critique, we can focus directly on the *potential* offered by social constructionist discourse. We might not be able to simply claim that X is the case. However, we can *invite* others and ourselves into different patterns of coordination. In the remainder of this chapter I explore some resources that move us beyond the negative consequences of diagnosis and toward potentials for action in the realm of psychotherapy. These resources, I should add, all center on embracing *what people do together* as the focal point. Once more I refer to the novelist Hoeg. The narrator of his story, Peter, devotes most of his time to articulating how standardized tests and evaluations can never really get at what is *really* there. He argues that even in the laboratory, scientists are not really measuring the essence of something. He advises, ". . . it is important that people enter the laboratory every now and then, and *ask questions of a different kind to those that are otherwise asked*" (p. 215, italics added). Social construction, by placing our attention on what people do together, allows us to ask different questions. Let us explore some.

Can participation in diagnosis be extended such that a wide range of relationships are recognized as potential contributors to generative realities?

How do we confront Foucault's (1979) critique of the ways in which disciplinary regimes disempower us? When we confront daunting difficulties, we are likely to find ourselves in the hands of professional psychotherapists. These professionals are charged with the process of diagnosing those who come to them seeking help because, as we have mentioned, the traditional discourse of individualism tells us that once we *know* what is *wrong* with a person, we can focus attention on treatment methods. The deleterious effects of this process have been articulated elsewhere (Gergen & McNamee, 2000; Kutchins & Kirk, 1997). How might we open this process to the

---

nificant. In contrast, social constructionism emphasizes discourse—or what people do together. Self and the world are created in relationships. There is no need to return, in social constructionism, to the private mind of the individual. Neimeyer (1996) has proposed a range of arguments that draw constructivism and social constructionism more closely together. Pertinent to this chapter, Neimeyer talks of a "therapy of engagement," which "highlights the delicate interplay of therapist and client construing, in the service of restructuring, the personal realities of one (or both) participant(s)" (p. 406). My own interests are less focused on which "camp" one chooses to inhabit and more on how to use constructionist discourse to envision therapeutic process as potentiating rather than pathologizing.

realm of relational coordination? Can we replace the coordination of therapist and client with a multiplicity of voices? Are there ways in which to invite others into the process of constructing possibilities for the client?

Note that the focus shifts as we consider how to include other voices, including alternative voices of the client and therapist, as well as voices of others not readily imagined as "participants" in the situation. The shift is significant. Not only are social constructionists proposing an expansion of participants in the therapeutic conversation, but also that the therapeutic conversation itself entertain domains of possibility and hope rather than focus on problems and their history. Social constructionists find this useful because, in the stories of others, there are likely to be very different understandings of the situation at hand.

There are many illustrations of such work being effectively conducted within a variety of communities. Jakko Seikkula and his colleagues offer one illustration (Seikkula, Aaltonen, Alkara, Haarakangasm Keranen, & Sutela, 1995). In the Lapland of Finland, his team of psychiatrists invites a wide range of professionals, friends, family, and neighbors into what would generally be called the crisis intervention process. The person in psychiatric crisis is also included in the conversation and thus, development of a treatment plan necessarily draws on the resources for action that are readily available to not only the client but his or her network of relations. Because this project is discussed in detail elsewhere (Seikkula et al., 1995; Gergen & McNamee, 2000), let me offer one additional illustration from a work in progress.

Stub (1999) is currently conducting research on the quality of life for brain-injured patients. These patients are frequently given psychiatric assessments, as well as evaluations geared toward day-to-day functioning in a wide range of areas, including social, psychological, physical, and neurological. On-going diagnosis is a large part of assessing this population. Diagnosis typically involves a neuropsychologist delivering a battery of tests to the patient. Frequently, spouses or other close family members' assessments are also given serious consideration after extensive interviewing by the professionals. Stub is interested in how we might extend the range of relationships participating in this process and simultaneously broaden our "assessment" or understanding of what counts as quality of life? Quality of life currently is evaluated by tallying check marks on a list

159

of activities that can or cannot be performed by the patient. Does this standardized measure *really* get at quality of life?

To address these provocative issues, Stub is engaged in interviewing patients and their families to understand *from within their significant relationships* what it means to have "quality of life." Because the tendency for most of us would be to refer to abstract, cultural standards (e.g., quality of life requires independence in daily activities such as ability to bathe, dress, and feed oneself), Stub begins her interviews by asking the patients to tell a story that captures what they most value about themselves in their relationships with others (specifically family members) and from that story to identify what they see as their biggest contributions to those relationships. This question opens the possibility for a very different conversation. With significant family members present to hear this story, dialogue on resources, rather than deficiencies, is enabled. Stub goes on to explore the resources that family members have noted in the patient. The inclusion of many voices—all significant within the patient's day to day life—engaging in dialogue about potentials, possibilities, and resources helps to affirm the *local* understanding of quality of life. To these patients and their families, quality of life is no longer assessed by applying a set of abstract categories, but is *situated* in the very parochial arena of their lives. Furthermore, by including family members in these "assessment" interviews, participants are equipped to extend the dialogue that they have at home, as well as continue the conversation of possibility that is generated in the assessment interview.

What potential is there for clients and communities if we replace abstract labels and categories with focused attention on lived narratives?

We can see from the illustration above that there might be great potential in giving voice to the lived stories of participants. In so doing, Stub's research is similar to the work of the Public Conversation Project (Roth et al, 1992). In their attempts to engage people in dialogue (as opposed to debate) on difficult topics such as abortion, Roth and her colleagues recognize that all strongly held beliefs and positions are located in visceral, lived conversations with others. Thus, for the pro-choice advocate, there is always a personal story that gives significance to the abstract position. Yet, in public or professional contexts where difficult issues are discussed, we have fostered a value (i.e., constructed a value) that personal stories in some way detract our attention from the "heart of the matter." What Roth and her colleagues have found, however, is that initiating conversation on difficult issues with a question that invites participants to voice their "personal" relationship to the topic provides the resources for incommensurate groups to engage in dialogue as opposed to debate. What this means is that rather than engage with another for purposes of proving one's point or "winning the argument," participants harboring oppositional orientations take the time to consider the very local rationale or reality of the opposition's stance. This does not mean that these extremely different orientations are embraced and accepted. There is no attempt here to persuade or convince. Rather, the purpose is to expand the resources for (in Wittgenstein's terms) *going on together.* I can disagree strongly with your opinion on a given issue but my disagreement will take a very different form if I first and foremost grant you the local coherence and rationality of your opinion within (at the very least) your own significant community. Recognizing that there are multiple and diverse rationalities that gain coherence within communities is the first step toward transformation of social practice. In relation to diagnosis, can we imagine listening to the stories of our clients in therapy *not* for purposes of locating those stories within some diagnostic category but rather for purposes of granting coherence to the difficulty that has brought the client to therapy? In other words, how does the client's story grant a situational coherence to activities that, placed in broader social context, are negatively valued? Discussions that invite these stories give voice to the complexity and locality of social life and thereby open new resources for engaging in that life.

What might be the benefit of suspending certainty in the process of diagnosis?

As Hoeg (1995) so aptly points out in his novel, *Borderliners,* the certainty with which diagnosis proceeds can be extremely debilitating to clients and their significant relations. The challenge for professionals centers on how to be a professional and simultaneously suspend what Sampson refers to as the "God's eye view from nowhere" (1993, p. 8). Unfortunately, professionalization (which can be seen as a byproduct of modernist attempts to train individuals in the proper methods and techniques required to work in specific fields) has created a bifurcated culture where there are those who "know" and those who are in need of "knowledge." Given this context, the expectations of professionals for themselves—as well as of "clients" for professionals—are daunting. To be, for example, a competent and successful psychotherapist *requires* the intuitive or skilled ability to quickly diagnose those in treatment and generate effective treatment plans. Add to the therapist's own expectations for self and the client's expectations for the therapist the expectations of the insurance companies and managed care authorities. Effective psychotherapy must be effective *and brief*. It must be cost efficient. At the same time, the pressure to make ends meet for the therapist means developing the ability to move through clients at a rapid pace. Thus, certainty in the professional diagnosis of a client is paramount. There is no room for doubt, uncertainty, or entertaining a myriad of alternatives.

But what would happen if the psychotherapist did entertain alternatives? In order to do so, he or she would need to engage in self reflexive critique where there is freedom to suspend the certainty that one diagnosis, one way of working, one understanding could be the best (or correct). While we have a professional responsibility to act in ways that are focused, meaningful, and ethical, we must realize that too much certainty or understanding negates the argument for a relational alternative to diagnosis. When we are too certain about our approach, our answers, our analysis, we close out the voices of others and our own multiplicity. In addition, we must respect that what constitutes generative dialogue in one community might not secure the same position in another (e.g., within one form of therapy over another, for people confronting similar difficulties that bring them to therapy, and so forth). The rhetorical force of a particular discursive argument can vary dramatically from community to community.

In other words, we must be constantly asking ourselves which discursive tradition warrants these particular questions, observations, and conclusions? Why this discourse and not another? Which community is being represented here and by virtue of its representation, which communities are being erased? This sort of reflexive critique is relational engagement. Here we recognize the possibility of other discursive communities and traditions and through such recognition might grant them voice. At the same time, the willingness to entertain doubt (spawned by self reflexive critique) does not imply that there can never be a decision or a selection of how things "should be." Rather, how things "should be" is accepted as a stance that is generative in the *situated moment*. This does not imply that any reality constructed in the therapeutic conversation is the "right" one or the only one. A central aspect of self-reflexive critique is not only the willingness to entertain doubt about our own positions, but also to give voice to the stories that provide coherence to radically different positions. To that extent, providing conversational arenas where personal narratives can be told and heard with reference to the relational communities within which they are valued helps tremendously in avoiding continual referral to abstract positions and policies. Can therapy provide this conversational arena?

This question raises another provocative suggestion. How is it that psychological professionals can be certain that the context within which they conduct psychotherapy is the most generative? How can they be certain that those seeking therapy are actually those in need? Granted, these sound like silly questions. Many psychological professionals would agree that those "in" therapy are not always the ones in "need" of therapy. Also, many psychotherapists believe strongly in practices that take them into the homes of families, into the communities, into the schools, and so forth. Yet, despite all of these variations (and many more that I have not mentioned here), the dominant approaches to therapy do not reflect on whether therapy is taking place in the contexts where it could be most useful or with the people who might gain most from it. As an illustration, I think of the work of Saul Cruz-Ramos in Mexico City (personal communication). He works with poor families in the ghettos of the city. These families rarely seek therapy. In an attempt to engage these families, Saul moved his family into the ghetto. He quickly found that just being in the same community, in the same context, was not enough. Still, despite all the problems and difficulties families faced day in and day out (drugs, alcohol, violence, death), and despite his constant presence and availability, the families did not rely on his services. His attempts to call open meetings were acknowledged with a resounding silence and lack of active engagement.

One consistent aspect of this community that Saul quickly recognized is, unfortunately, the ritual of the wake after a person's death. Almost all the youth in the community are associated with gangs and these gangs are constantly "at war" with one another over turf and drugs. Consequently, shootings, deaths, and (inevitably) wakes are almost weekly events. The wakes are community-wide events. As Saul describes them, members of the community come and sit for hours at a time in a large circle around the casket of the

163

dead youth, often chatting with each other. Despite day-to-day differences, there is a sense of community that emerges through death in this ghetto. Because the wake is the place where families and community members gather, during one Saul asked if they could have a conversation about life in the community and the problems everyone faces. The participants happily agreed to talk about the issues confronting them. This spawned a series of transformative projects throughout the community—all addressing issues that would likely, in another community, bring individuals, couples, and families to psychotherapy. Saul's lesson to us is that working for generative futures often requires going to those you want to help rather than expecting them to come to you. Additionally, focusing on potentials within the community rather than individual pathology allows for constructions of new futures. Metaphorically, in this ghetto, death is transformed into new life potentials.

Saul's story illustrates the benefit of suspending our certainty as professionals. By questioning the utility of meeting clients in the psychotherapy context, as well as questioning the utility of identifying individuals or families as the treatment unit, Saul has been able to join in a fully participatory mode of social transformation. He is probably less likely than most to identify himself as the professional "helping" people of this community change. I am sure he is more inclined to talk about the mutual transformations for himself, his family, members of this community, and the "therapeutic" process.

How might a focus on images of the future transform pathology into potential?

Psychotherapy, in general, has a reputation for focusing on problems. This much we have discussed at length. Additionally, as a professional form of practice, attention is largely focused on the past causes of problems and the present ways that clients deal with or cope with the problems. Full assessment of these stories becomes the basis of diagnosis.

What might happen if therapists were to shift the psychotherapeutic conversation from the realm of charting the history of a problem to the realm of future images? An immediate objection many have is that such a move appears to "ignore" the "very real" problems of persons seeking help. Yet, the idea is not to either ignore or elevate a person's problems as if they were essential entities. After all, social constructionism argues that our ways of relating together construct the worlds we inhabit. To that extent, when we focus our interactions on problems, we live within a "problemed" reality. There are many alternative resources available that, once invited into the conversational "space," have potential for integration into the "problemed" relational reality.

Here I think of Harlene Anderson's (1997) work. When working in a training or supervision context, Harlene invites participants into an "as if" posture. After a case has been presented, the group participants take turns speaking "as if" they are different members of the client system. Anderson says that by inviting participants to speak "as if" they were the mother or the therapist, for example, they engage in a "problem dissolving" process. Here, they are free to voice alternative interpretations of the "problem" and also to imagine how else the situation might be. What other possible narrations are there? The co-mingling of multiple voices provides the person presenting the case with a symphony of possibilities. Rather than returning to therapeutic conversations entrenched in problem talk, the psychotherapist enters the conversation with stories that offer images of potential and hope.

Similarly, there are processes where the focus is on imagining an ideal future and talking through the various ways in which a client might real/ize (literally make real) that ideal. What sorts of activities and relationships might the client need to continue? What might be terminated? What could the client begin to develop as possible actions and/or relations? All help construct the future by acting into it as opposed to acting within what appears to be an already constructed reality.

CONTINUING THE CONVERSATION

In offering a new set of questions, I have attempted to provoke a broader conversation in the psychotherapeutic realm. Must diagnosis be the focal point of therapy? Who benefits from such a focus? Clearly, the psychological professionals, who are responsible for developing the diagnostic criteria, benefit in terms of professional advancement. Additionally, for those diagnoses requiring or suggesting medical treatment, the large pharmaceutical companies stand to gain enormously. Some who seek psychotherapy benefit from diagnosis, as well. Yet, as our culture becomes more and more immersed in practices of assessment and evaluation (diagnosis) – all offspring of modernist social science – we find ourselves hard pressed to find forms of practice that inspire potential and possibility by drawing on resources for action already available in relationships. Psychotherapy, of course, is not alone. Education is another of our cultural institutions that is now confronting daunting difficulties as the culture of deficit takes control. Illustrations abound in all sectors of life.

New efforts are emerging in small pockets, each attempting in their own ways to revitalize the positive potential of social life. For example, Martin Seligman's positive psychology (Seligman & Csikszentmihalyi, 2000), the appreciative inquiry method developed by David Cooperrider (1990), the work of Cooperrider and Dutton (1998) on cooperation and global change, performative approaches to psychology (Holzman, 1999), articulations of collaborative education (Bruffee, 1999), and a host of other projects all move to embrace human potential, to focus on what is working as opposed to what is not working. These approaches, which focus on the future as opposed to the past, are exciting new trends.

The significance of talking about diagnosis as a social construction is that it allows us to "de-essentialize" psychological problems. By locating meaning in the activities of persons rather than in their heads, social construction provides us with the resources for deconstructing pathology. If pathology emerges only in particular forms of practice, what might be the generative practices we can suggest to move beyond pathology toward potential? This form of reconstruction draws heavily on the idea of polyvocality. We each harbor the voice of possibility and yet it is the voice of deficit, of assessment, of diagnosis, that gains our attention. It is time to reconsider forms of practice and relational communities where multiple participants, personal stories, self-reflexive inquiry, and images of the future are given voice.

REFERENCES

Anderson, H. (1997). *Conversation, language, and possibilities*. New York: Basic Books.

Bellah, R. N., Madsen, R., Sullivan, W. M., Swidler, A., & Tipton, S. M. (1985). *Habits of the heart*. Berkeley: University of California Press.

Bruffee, K. (1999). *Collaborative learning* (2nd ed.). Baltimore: Johns Hopkins University Press.

Cooperrider, D. L. (1990). Positive image, positive action: The affirmative basis of organizing. In S. Srivastva & D. L. Cooperrider (Eds.), *Appreciative management and leadership: The power of positive thought and action in organizations* (pp. 91-125). San Francisco: Jossey-Bass.

Cooperrider, D. L., & Dutton, J. (Eds.). (1998). *No limits to cooperation: The organization dimensions of global change*. Newbury Park, CA: Sage.

Cushman, P. (1995). *Constructing the self, constructing America.* Reading, MA: Addison Wesley.

Derrida, J. (1976). *Of grammatology.* Baltimore: Johns Hopkins University Press.

deShazer, S. (1994). *Words were originally magic.* New York: Norton.

Fish, S. (1980). *Is there a text in this class? The authority of interpretive communities.* Cambridge, MA: Harvard University Press.

Foucault, M. (1979). *Discipline and punish.* New York: Vintage.

Gergen, K. J. (1999). *An invitation to social construction.* London: Sage.

Gergen, K. J. (1994). *Realities and relationships: Soundings in social construction.* Cambridge, MA: Harvard University Press.

Gergen, K. J., & McNamee, S. (2000). From disordering discourse to transformative dialogue. In R. A. Neimeyer & J. D. Raskin (Eds.), *Constructions of disorder: Meaning-making frameworks for psychotherapy* (pp. 333-349). Washington, DC: American Psychological Association Press.

Graumann, C. F., & Gergen, K. J. (1996). *Historical dimensions of psychological discourse.* New York: Cambridge University Press.

Harre, R. (1979). *Social being.* Oxford: Blackwell.

Heelas, P., & Lock, A. (Eds.). (1981). *Indigenous psychologies.* New York: Academic Press.

Hoeg, P. (1995). *Borderliners.* London: The Harvill Press.

Holzman, L. (Ed.). (1999). *Performing psychology.* New York: Routledge.

Kelly, G. A. (1955) *The psychology of personal constructs* (2 vols.). New York: Norton.

Kleinman, A. (1988). *The illness narratives.* New York: Basic Books.

Kutchins, H., & Kirk, S. A. (1997). *Making us crazy. DSM: The psychiatric bible and the creation of mental disorders.* New York: The Free Press.

Lasch, C. (1979). *The culture of narcissism.* New York: Norton.

Lutz, C., & Abu-Lughod, L. (Eds.). (1990). *Language and the politics of emotion.* Cambridge, UK: Cambridge University Press.

McNamee, S., & Gergen, K. J. (1998). *Relational responsibility: Resources for sustainable dialogue.* Thousand Oaks, CA: Sage.

Neimeyer, R. A. (1996). Process interventions for the constructivist psychotherapist. In H. Rosen & K. T. Kuehlwein (Eds.), *Constructing realities: Meaning-making perspectives for psychotherapists* (pp. 371-411). San Francisco: Jossey-Bass.

O'Hanlon, W. H., & Weiner-Davis, M. (1989). *In search of solutions: A new direction in psychotherapy.* New York: Norton.

Piaget, J. (1954). *The construction of reality in the child.* New York: Basic Books.

Rorty, R. (1979). *Philosophy and the mirror of nature.* Princeton, NJ: Princeton University Press.

Roth, S., Chasin, L., Chasin, R., Becker, C., & Herzig, M. (1992). From debate to dialogue: A facilitating role for family therapists in the public forum. *Dulwich Centre Newsletter, 2,* 41-48.

Sampson, E. E. (1993). *Celebrating the other.* Boulder: Westview Press.

Seikkula, J. Aaltonen, J., Alakara, B., Haarakangas, K., Keranen, J., & Sutela, M. (1995).   Treating psychosis by means of open dialogue. In S. Friedman (Ed.), *The reflecting team in action* (pp. 62-80). New York: Guilford Press.

Seligman, M. E. P., & Csikszentmihalyi, M. (Eds.). (2000).   Positive psychology [Special issue]. *American Psychologist, 55*(1).

Shweder, R.A. (1991). *Thinking through cultures.* Cambridge, MA: Harvard University Press.

Stub, S. (1999). Quality of life after brain injury: A postmodernist research. Unpublished doctoral dissertation proposal, University of Copenhagen, Denmark.

Tannen, D. (1998). *The argument culture: Moving from debate to dialogue.* New York: Random House.

Tomm, K. (1998). Co-constructing responsibility. In S. McNamee & K. J. Gergen (Eds.), *Relational responsibility* (pp. 129-137). Thousand Oaks, CA: Sage.

White, M., & Epston, D. (1990). *Narrative means to therapeutic ends.* New York: Norton.

Wittgenstein, L. (1953). *Philosophical investigations* (G. Anscombe, Trans.). New York: Macmillan.

CHAPTER 8

"Diagnosing" Behavior: Cui Bono?

Thomas Szasz

The Poets pass the Gate of Hell and are immediately assailed by cries
of anguish. Dante sees the first of the souls in torment. . . the souls
of those who in life were neither for good nor evil but only for themselves. Mixed with them are those outcasts who took no sides in the
Rebellion of the Angels. They are neither in Hell nor out of it. . . . The
law of Dante's Hell is the law of symbolic retribution. . . . They took
no sides, therefore they are given no place.

John   Ciardi   (1954, p.   41),
Introduction to Canto III in Dante
Alighieri's (1265-1321) The Inferno

I must begin with a disclaimer: I consider myself neither a
constructivist nor deconstructivist. In my view, the mind cannot be
diseased and depriving an innocent person of liberty under allegedly medical auspices is an act of tyranny, not a therapy. Accordingly, I
have sought to free mental patients and mental health professionals
alike from having to play the roles of afflicted and deliverer, diagnosed and diagnoser, oppressed and oppressor—that is, from the
shackles of psychiatric slavery imposed on them by a long tradition
in law and psychiatry.

II

The *Oxford English Dictionary* (OED), defines diagnosis as the
"determination of the nature of a diseased condition; ... also, the
opinion (formally stated) resulting from such investigation." The
concept of diagnosis is contingent on the concept of disease.
Diagnosis is the *name of a disease*, just as, say, violet is the name of a
flower. For example, the term "diabetes" names a type of abnormal
glucose metabolism. The abnormal metabolism is the disease; the
diagnosis, "diabetes," is its name. Disease as somatic pathology is
diagnosed by finding abnormalities (lesions) in bodies or body

169

parts; the disease may be asymptomatic and changing the classification of diseases changes its name but not its reality as somatic pathology. If we fail to distinguish between diagnoses as human artefacts
and diseases as facts of nature, we forfeit the possibility of understanding the uses and abuses of the term "diagnosis."

Manipulating things is difficult, sometimes impossible.
Manipulating names is easy. Violet may be the name of a flower, or a
color, or a woman, or a street. Similarly, a disease-sounding term
may be the name of a bodily malfunction, or the malfunction of a
car, a computer, an economic system, or the behavior of an individual or group. We cannot distinguish between the literal and
metaphorical uses of the term "disease" unless we identify its root
meaning, agree that it is the literal meaning of the word, and treat all
other uses of it as figures of speech. In conformity with traditional
medical practice, I take the root meaning of disease to be a *bodily
lesion*, understood to include not only structural malfunctions but also
deviations from normal physiology, such as elevated blood pressure
or depressed red cell count. If we accept this definition, then the
term "diagnosis," used *literally*, refers to and is the name of a disease,
and used *metaphorically*, refers to and is the name of a non-disease
(Szasz, 1987/1997, 1991).

By identifying diagnosis as an *opinion*, the OED recognizes that
it refers to a judgment. Typically, the process of diagnosing disease
begins with patients who have aches or pains, feel feverish or
fatigued, and judge that they are ill. Their complaints are called
"symptoms," a term that implies that they are the manifestations of
a disease. *Webster's* defines symptom as "subjective evidence of disease
or physical disturbance *observed by the patient*..." (italics added). Whether
a symptom is or is not a manifestation of disease depends on its confirmation or non-confirmation by objective data based, for example,
on laboratory tests or the examination of a biopsy specimen. So-
called "clinical diagnoses" may be based only on history and symptoms, while the "pathological diagnosis" is based entirely on objective evidence—that is, on histological, morphological, chemical,
serological, radiological, and other physical-chemical data.
Traditionally, scientific medicine is based on the post-mortem examination of the body; today, it is also based on ante-mortem scientific
measures of abnormal bodily functionings.

The use of diagnostic terms becomes problematic when the
conditions they name are not diseases but merely complaints refer-
able to the subject's body or behavior or mind. Psychopathology is

diagnosed by finding unwanted behaviors in persons or by attributing such behaviors to them. For example, the term "kleptomania" is both a phenomenon and its name; diagnosis and disease are one and the same. Disease as psychopathology cannot be asymptomatic and changing the classification of diseases can change disease into non-disease and vice versa (for example, homosexuality into civil right and smoking into nicotine dependence). By *professional and legal definition*, psychiatric diagnoses are diseases (or "disorders," to use the mental health professionals' preferred weasel word).

To understand the tactical rather than descriptive *uses* of terms such as "disease" and "patient," we must ask: Cui *bono?* Cicero (106-43 B.C.) explained the importance of posing this question as follows: "When trying a case [the famous judge] L. Cassius never failed to inquire, 'Who gained by it?' Man's character is such that no man undertakes crimes without hope of gain" (Guterman, 1966, p. 52-53). Similarly, people do not assert that they or someone else has an illness without hope of gain. The goods that a person gains from asserting such a claim range from securing medical help and monetary compensation to excusing crime and depriving innocent persons of liberty. The potential gains from claiming the sick role—for oneself or others—are virtually endless, because they depend on the claimants' character and motives, the social context in which the claim is advanced, and the ever-changing legal and social milieu in which so-called health care services are delivered.

In short, I object to constructing *any* type of classificatory system in which the term "diagnosis" is attached to a person's feelings, thoughts, or behavior or to a person himself, for the same reasons that I object to calling unwanted feelings, thoughts, and behaviors "diseases" and unwanted persons "ill" or "mentally ill." This objection is rooted in the semantic connections between the words "diagnosis" and "disease," and in the political implications of classifying a person to justify restraining him, existentially or physically.

III

Edmund Burke once defined freedom as "that state of things in which liberty is secured by the equality of restraint" (Burke, 1789/1994). I have tried to articulate the case for helping individuals with personal problems in a relationship in which the liberty and responsibility of both therapist and patient is regulated by an equality of self-restraint. This is not to say that the therapist does not have more authority than the patient; if not, why would the patient seek the therapist's help? But having more authority than another person is not the same as having power over the other person or being responsible for his or her behavior or welfare. The priest has more religious authority than the parishioner; the accountant, the architect, and the attorney have more professional authority than the client. But none has power over their clients and none are held responsible for their clients' criminal or self-destructive acts. Physicians have more medical authority than their patients, but no power over them and they are not responsible for controlling their misbehavior—except in psychiatry. Derivatively, mental health professionals have power over their clients and may be held responsible for their misbehavior. Let us be clear about the contours of this power and responsibility.

Mental health professionals possess the legal right and indeed the professional obligation to attach stigmatizing labels, with far-reaching legal and social implications, to people and call them "diagnoses;" to cause innocent individuals to be imprisoned and call this deprivation of liberty "hospitalization;" and to intervene in the patient's life against his will in countless ways (for example, by forcibly drugging him) and call it "treatment" (Szasz, 1966, 1987/1997). I reject the moral, political, and professional justifications for, and legitimacy of, these privileges, powers, and obligations.

Why do mental health professionals classify people (whether they seek their services or not) as mentally disordered or sick? Why don't they acknowledge, as for examples lawyers acknowledge, that they are the subject's allies or adversaries? The short answer is, because *it is the mental health professionals' task to conceal conflict as disease.* Ever since the 1950s, I have argued that mental health professionals do not deal with sick people; they deal with individuals in conflict with others or with themselves (typically, the two go together) (Szasz, 1960a-d, 1961a-b, 1963). "Classification always serves some practical, strategic purpose. ... [such as] to degrade and socially segregate the individual identified as a mental patient" (Szasz, 1970/1991, p. 239). It may also serve to bestow special advantages on him, for example, by authenticating him as disabled by a *bona fide* disease. The argument I advanced more than thirty years ago explains why I am unable to endorse efforts, however well-intentioned, to reformulate "diagnosis"—along constructivist or any other lines. I wrote:

> [If] so-called mental patients are considered responsible individuals and the agents of their own destinies, then people who consult psychiatrists need not be classified psychiatrically. . . . [T]o provide for the psychological needs of the responsible

adult, we require a classification not of mental illnesses, but of expert services. Indeed, with the singular—and significant— exception of the mental health field, this type of classification prevails in all situations where clients must seek and purchase expert services. . . . Organized psychiatry is amazingly hostile to a similar division of labor among psychiatrists: the psychotherapist unwilling to use drugs or to commit patients is regarded not as a professional person exercising judgment over his own interests and competence, but as one who refuses to shoulder the onerous responsibilities of a messianic healing art. (Szasz, 1970/1991, pp. 243-244, italics added)

I suggested that we distinguish between the two mutually exclusive functions of the therapist, namely, helping the patient, in patients' own interests, as they see them, and harming patients, in the interests of their families or society, as they and psychiatrists see fit. Today we are farther from acknowledging this situation than we have ever been. The pretense that the mental health professional can simultaneously protect the best interests of both mental patient and society is more insistently legitimized by law and public opinion than ever: the role of the court-appointed (ostensibly "neutral" and "objective") expert—examining, diagnosing, and testifying under oath—is growing by the day.

If we wish to separate the two diametrically opposed aspects of mental health practice we must not only transcend the limitations imposed on us by the established vocabulary of our profession; we must also reject the accepted ethical principles of our own profession—much as the slave-owner turned abolitionist, in the antebellum South, would have had to reject the accepted ethical principles of his own society. In short, we must repudiate the institution of psychiatric slavery.

I stated earlier that *the mental health professional's job is to conceal conflict as disease.* Now I want to add that the mental health professional receives powerful support for doing so by individuals who eagerly assume the role of mental patient. Many prominent persons—for example, Betty Ford, Tipper Gore, Cindy McCain, William Styron, Mike Wallace, to mention only a few—eagerly and publicly diagnose themselves as having suffered from a "mental illness" or being "in recovery" from it. Individuals ought to have that right, just as they have the right to define themselves as, say, born-again Christians or followers of any other faith. The problem is that members of the Religious Right identify themselves by their religion and want the state to impose a similar identification on the rest of the population. Similarly, members of what I call the Psychiatric Left identify them-

selves by their diagnosis and want the state to impose a similar identification on the rest of the population.

The French political writer Jean-Francois Revel cogently
remarked:

> The totalitarian phenomenon is not to be understood without
> making allowance for the thesis that some part of every society
> consists of people who actively want tyranny: either to exercise
> it themselves or—much more mysteriously—to submit to it. ...
> If tyranny had never enjoyed the complicity of its victims, the
> history of our times—and many other times—would have been
> quite different. (Revel, 2000, p. 25)

Therein, precisely, lies a perpetual threat to individual liberty and responsibility. Believers in religion are often not satisfied with
identifying themselves in religious terms; they want to impose a religious identification on others, by coercion if necessary. Similarly,
believers in mental health are often not satisfied with identifying
themselves in psychiatric terms; they want to impose a psychiatric
identification on others, by coercion if necessary. The Constitution
protects Americans from the denial of rights based on involuntary
religious labeling, but does not protect them from the denial of
rights based on involuntary psychiatric labeling.

IV

Ever since psychiatry came into being, we have lived in societies that have recognized psychiatric slavery as a morally praisewor-
thy institution and social arrangement. For three hundred years,
coercion and the threat of coercion have framed the context of the
psychiatrist's daily work. The two paradigmatic psychiatric acts have
always been and still are depriving innocent persons of liberty (civil
commitment) and excusing guilty persons of responsibility for their
crimes (the insanity defense). Both interventions entail the use of
state-sanctioned force against patients and both result in their incar-
ceration in prisons called "hospitals."

Terms such as "psychiatrist," "psychologist," and "therapist"
imply that the mental health professional's legal, moral, and professional duty entails protecting the patient from the dangers of his
own mental illness and protecting society from the dangers mental
patients pose to themselves, their families, and society. The professional, legal, and social legitimation of this double agency validates
the mental health profession's Big Lie, namely, that regardless of
whether therapists' clients are voluntary or involuntary subjects, they

are *always the patients' agents.* A similar Big Lie legitimated the inquisitor's role as the heretic's liberator from error (Szasz, 1970/1997).

Because we recognize that the interests of a defendant charged with a crime and those of a district attorney charging him with it *conflict,* the law permits, indeed requires, separating the roles of defense attorney and district attorney. In contrast, because we do not recognize that the interests of the involuntary mental patient and those of the institutional psychiatrist conflict, the law prohibits separating the roles of "defense psychiatrist" and "prosecuting psychiatrist." Even in insanity trials with psychiatrists testifying for both sides, the experts steadfastly *deny that they are parties to a conflict;* instead, they *maintain that they are impartial scientists,* testifying about *matters of fact.*

Unless people seek psychiatric help on their own, they can become mental patients only if *someone else complains about them and compels them*—by threats or coercion—to come into contact with a psychiatrist. The parents who seek therapy for their child do not do so if they are satisfied with the child's behavior. The teacher or school official who seeks psychological counseling or psychiatric drugs for a student; the family court judge who seeks the opinion of a mental health professional to decide a problem of custody; the lawyer or judge who seeks a psychiatric evaluation of a criminal defendant— none of these persons calls in a psychiatrist if they are satisfied with the subject's behavior.

We live in a world in which the division of labor that makes a complex civilization possible is steadily increasing. In such a world, many specialists—for example, architects and chemists—can credibly claim to be indifferent to conflicts in other people's family or between other people and society. Mental health professionals do not have that luxury. I maintain that they deal with conflict—between individuals, between individuals and institutions, and between the warring interests and impulses within individuals; and that, as mental health professionals, *they choose* to be involved in such conflicts. Hence, they cannot avoid *choosing* sides. If they claim to be neutral— to serve Health, Medicine, or Science—they perjure themselves. The truth is that, to paraphrase Dante, they are not for Health, Medicine, or Science. They are for themselves. We do not accept priests as impartial experts in religious disputes. Yet we accept—indeed, embrace—mental health professionals as impartial experts in interpersonal and social disputes, defined as psychiatric/psychological problems.

Separating the roles of defense and prosecution in mental health would compel the contending parties to recognize that the problem they face is one of conflict and power (ethics, politics), not a problem of illness and healing (medicine, science). Nothing short of such a separation would protect the self-defined interests of both parties—that is, the defendant-patient's interest in dignity, liberty, and rights as a citizen, and the plaintiff-person's or society's interest in protecting himself or itself from troublesome relatives and lawless citizens.

V

The American government provides no religious services for its civilian citizens (Congress excepted). Clergymen provide no involuntary religious services for atheists or others who do not voluntarily seek their ministrations. They have no power to detain and imprison persons because they may be dangerous to themselves or others. Were an educated American to interpret such limitations on the powers of priests as "withholding religious services" from people who need and would benefit from them, he would be dismissed as a person ignorant not only of the relationship between church and state but also of the constitutionally imposed prohibitions against coercion in the name of God.

In contrast, coercion in the name of mental health is not merely permitted, it is mandated by law. Most contemporary therapists—even those who reject or say they reject the concept of mental illness—recoil from eschewing the use of force regardless of the dangers the subject allegedly poses (for example, suicide [Szasz, 1999]). Such refusal negates what I regard as a precondition for maintaining the therapist's role integrity. The therapist who professes to be the patient's agent cannot, under any circumstances, interfere with the patient's life against the patient's wishes. Today, this kind of therapeutic self-restraint is professionally censured as "withholding essential treatment" from the patient and is rendered de facto illegal by tort law.

A relationship between patients and therapists based on mutual respect and consent requires that therapists relinquish their tools of legalized control and coercion, such as the pretense of possessing scientific "techniques" and "tests" that enable them to know patients and their "best interests" better than the patients know themselves and their best interests. This pretense is socially validated by the legal recognition of mental health professionals as "impartial experts" on other people's "mental functioning."

In our present collectivized medical-economic climate, mental health professionals and their allies in the media and government have grown estranged from, and hostile to, reciprocity, responsibility, and voluntariness in human relations involving "aid." As a result, ostensibly in the best interests of their beneficiaries, the helpers feel justified to use force against patients who resist their ministrations, and to use fraud against third parties—especially employers and insurance companies—who frustrate their benevolence. A prominent American psychotherapist cites the case of one of his patients, "Jill" —whom he describes as "dour, deeply and chronically depressed, consider[ing] suicide every day of her adult life, gruff, and lack[ing] drive" —as an example of the kind of mental patient who "deserve[s] job protection." Were Jill's employer, "Jane," to display similar behaviors toward Jill, psychiatrists would rush to help her extort compensation from Jane and her company on the ground that Jane is the cause of Jill's "mental illness." However, when Jill displays such behavior, psychiatrists rush to enlist the formidable powers of the government's criminal law enforcement apparatus to prevent Jane from firing her as an unsatisfactory employee.

Burke (1796/1994) warned:

> It requires a deep courage to be temperate when the voice of multitudes (the specious mimic of fame and reputation) passes judgment against you. The impetuous desire of an unthinking public will endure no course, but what conduces to splendid and perilous extremes. Then, dare to be fearful, when all about you are full of confidence" (p. 16)

We live in a therapeutic state—that is, in a polity in which pharmacratic controls unconstrained by countervailing powers are increasingly replacing judicial controls restrained by the rule of law and the Constitution (Szasz, 2001). Under these circumstances, I am fearful of any scheme of classifying human behavior formulated and used by mental health professionals.

VI

I began by quoting John Ciardi's comments about the fate of "neutrals" in Dante's *Inferno*. I end by quoting Dante himself. In Canto III, Dante introduces the reader to "The Vestibule of Hell," the place where the souls of "the Opportunists" reside:

177

I, holding my head in horror, cried: "Sweet Spirit, what souls are these who run through this black haze?" And he [Virgil] to me: "These are the nearly soulless whose lives concluded neither blame nor praise. They are mixed here with that despicable corps of angels who were neither for God nor Satan, but only for themselves. The High Creator scourged them from Heaven and Hell will not receive them since the wicked might feel glory over them ... No word of them survives their living season. Mercy and Justice deny them even a name." (Dante, 1954, pp. 42-43)

By becoming mental health professionals rather than, say, mathematicians or veterinarians, mental health professionals choose to be parties to conflicts between people: it is their moral duty to honestly acknowledge whose interests they support and whose interests they oppose. If they do not, they deserve the fate that Dante believed awaits those who, faced with a conflict between Good and Evil, choose to remain "neutral."

In summary, I hope this chapter will help psychotherapists of many orientations reach toward fresh understandings of human distress, and envision fresh forms of intervention. Ultimately, being a constructivist, constructionist, or narrative therapist does not imply theoretically abstracting oneself from the concrete world of human suffering, and we trust that this volume will convey some of the practical and conceptual vigor of this perspective.

REFERENCES

Burke, E. (1994). Letter to Charles-Jean-Francois Depont [1789]. In D. E. Ritchie (Ed.), Further reflections on the revolution in France (p. 16). Indianapolis: Liberty Fund.

Ciardi, J. (1954). Introduction to Canto III. In Dante Alighieri, The Inferno: A verse rendering for the modern reader (pp. xiii-xxvi, J. Ciardi, Trans.). New York: Mentor.

Dante Alighieri. (1954). The Inferno: A verse rendering for the modern reader (J. Ciardi, Trans.) New York: Mentor.

Guterman, N. (1966). The anchor book of Latin quotations. New York: Doubleday.

Revel, J. F. (2000, January 24). Democracy. . . if you can keep it. National Review, 24-25.

Szasz, T. S. (1960a). The myth of mental illness. American Psychologist, 16, 113-118.

Szasz, T. S. (1960b). Moral conflict and psychiatry. Yale Review, 49, 555-556.

Szasz, T. S. (1960c). Civil liberties and mental illness: Some observations on the case of Miss Edith L. Hough. Journal of Nervous and Mental Disease, 131, 58-63.

Szasz, T. S. (1960d). Civil liberties and the mentally ill. Cleveland-Marshall Law Review, 9, 399-416.

Szasz, T. S. (1961a). The uses of naming and the origin of the myth of mental illness. *American Psychologist, 16,* 59-65.

Szasz, T. S. (1961b). Hospital-patient relationships in medicine and psychiatry. *Mental Hygiene, 45,* 171-179.

Szasz, T. S. (1963). *Law, liberty, and psychiatry: An inquiry into the social uses of mental health practices.* New York: Macmillan.

Szasz, T. S. (1966). The psychiatric classification of behavior: A strategy of personal constraint. In L. D. Eron (Ed.), *The classification of behavior disorders* (pp. 123-170). Chicago: Aldine Publishing Company.

Szasz, T. S. (1991). Diagnoses are not diseases. *The Lancet, 338,* 1574-1576.

Szasz, T. S. (1991). *Ideology and insanity: Essays on the psychiatric dehumanization of man.* Syracuse, NY: Syracuse University Press. (Original work published 1970)

Szasz, T. S. (1997). *The manufacture of madness: A comparative study of the Inquisition and the mental health movement.* Syracuse, NY: Syracuse University Press. (Original work published 1970)

Szasz, T. S. (1997). *Insanity: The idea and its consequences.* New York: Syracuse University Press. (Original work published 1987)

Szasz, T. S. (1998). *Psychiatric slavery: When confinement and coercion masquerade as cure.* Syracuse, NY: Syracuse University Press. (Original work published 1977)

Szasz, T. S. (1999). *Fatal Freedom: The Ethics and Politics of Suicide.* Westport, CT: Praeger.

Szasz, T. S. (2001). *Pharmacracy: Medicine and Politics in America.* Westport, CT: Praeger.

PART III

EXPLORATIONS IN CONSTRUCTIVIST RESEARCH

CHAPTER 9

Owning Research:
The Appropriation of Psychological Data

Mark W. Schlutsmeyer and Nancy E. Pike[1]

George Kelly's psychology of personal constructs (1955) has had wide influence in many areas of psychology. One aspect of this approach that may lend to its influence is its self-applicability, or the ability to apply its own language to the explanation of its own existence. Kelly argued that a strong psychological theory does not just explain the "other," but encompasses and explains the work of the theorist and the existence of the theory as well (Faidley & Leitner, 1993). For personal construct psychology, this means that all human experience, theorizing included, involves the construction and reconstruction of personal meanings. In clinical psychology, for example, personal construct psychologists understand psychopathology not only in terms of the constructs that order the client's psychic world, but also in terms of the constructs that order the therapist's understanding of psychopathology. Accordingly, much of the clinical theoretical work in the area of personal constructs focuses on how psychological disorder is construed by professional psychologists (see Neimeyer & Raskin, 2000).

Similarly, personal construct psychology can be directly applied to researchers' construal of the research process. Psychological research generally involves a complex web of interrelationships that may be construed in many different ways by researchers and participants. Therefore, constructivist researchers generally 1) endorse epistemologies and research methods that are sensitive to personal meanings, and 2) observe ways in which con-

[1] The authors contributed equally to this chapter; order of authorship was determined by coin toss. We would like to acknowledge the assistance of the following individuals in clarifying and refining the ideas in this paper: Larry M. Leitner, Beverly Walker, Teresa Schlutsmeyer, Roger M. Knudson, and the Qualitative Research Group and Social Psychology Research Interest Group at Miami University.

strual of the research process affects the research process (Viney, 1992). The latter goal is the focus of our effort here.

More specifically, we focus our discussion on one aspect of the research relationship: researchers' construal of their role as data owners. We argue that this construal is potentially damaging to participants and to the research process, and results in ethical standards that are lacking in important ways. To clarify this position, we will begin by exploring some of the assumptions supporting the view of researchers as data owners. Then we will identify some of the direct ethical consequences of construing the researcher this way. We will conclude by discussing the possible benefits of an alternative construction of this relationship that views the researcher as art appropriator, rather than data owner. In this discussion we will explore ways in which this alternative construction may address the ethical concerns raised by the preceding analysis of the data-owning researcher.

ASSUMPTIONS ABOUT DATA OWNERSHIP

At a surface level, the three-way relationship between investigators, data, and participants in psychological research is very straightforward: investigators find participants who consent to give something of themselves (a story, a self-rating, a view of their behavior), which takes on the name of data and becomes the property of the investigator. This belief in a transfer of data ownership has been reflected in the practices of the field. For example, Sieber (1989) noted that, "unless otherwise specified in some funding or employment agreement, the data that an investigator collects are the investigator's own property" (p. 6). Although the legal and professional practice standards have changed over time, the concept of private ownership pervades the U.S. scientific establishment just as it does the larger society (Fields & Price, 1993). Thus, the personal construct of oneself as data owner may persist among some researchers despite the legal and professional limitations put on researchers' data property rights, such as not destroying data for a certain number of years after its publication, or making data available to interested others.

In contrast to researchers, research participants are likely assumed to have no part in the ownership of data. In fact, participants' only commonly-accepted right after data are collected and used in publication appears to be the right to choose to never be publicly identified as the original sources. Since the right to choose to be acknowledged does not usually accompany this right to anonymity, it is less a right than a statement of fact. Anonymity eliminates any publicly recognizable basis for ownership, and as a result, there is a decreased public recognition of participants' ownership of the data they provide.

Certainly, in recent years the relationship between researchers, participants, and data has grown more complex. Ethical and legal issues such as using clinical records for archival research (Leigh, 1998; Taube & Burkhardt, 1997), data sharing (Sieber, 1989), data ownership within lab groups (Fields & Price, 1993), and electronic data storage (Gellman & Frawley, 1996) have given rise to new discussions about investigators' rights and responsibilities with regard to research participants and the data they provide. However, the concept of the data-owning researcher persists. For example, Fields and Price(1993) traced the root of "misconceptions about the ownership of publicly supported scientific research" (p. S60) to the widespread assumption, mentioned above, that researchers are always the owners of their data. This assumption is evident in the simple but frequent turn of phrase "my data."

There are many factors operative in the field of psychology that may underlie both the original development and continued power of the researcher's self-image as data owner. These possible factors include: the predominance of a science that stresses objectivity; a strong belief in the concept of individual authorship; the relatively powerful position of the academic researcher in the U.S. sociopolitical hierarchy; the assumption that participants' relationship to the data they provide ends with the termination of the data-collecting session; and, in general, a view of research participants as interchangeable objects whose human subjectivity has no place in the research process. We will discuss each of these factors individually.

OBJECTIVE SCIENCE

If within the predominant paradigm of objective empirical inquiry, achieving an approximation of objective truth is seen as both possible and desirable, and if attainment of that truth is demonstrated by precise replication of findings across varying contexts, then the unique, subjective experiences of individual participants may easily appear as a threat to the research process; a threat to be eliminated as entirely as possible. This elimination of the threat of subjectivity is achieved through the use of ingenious research methods, which are created to that measure aspects of human behavior and experience without requiring consultation with the participant. Thus, such research is conducted in spite of participants, rather than with them. And because the data is obtained in spite of the participants, the data and participants may easily be seen as not having any significant relationship more profound than the match between the participant's name and a meaningless identification number. Indeed, participants may easily be seen as separate and isolated from the data being provided. Without any meaningful perceived connection to their original source, the data are available to be claimed as the property of the researcher.

INDIVIDUAL AUTHORSHIP

An essential component of the research endeavor is the expert intellectual ability possessed by the researcher who is able to design a research protocol for mining relatively pure data from participants. Bettig (1996) explained how an analysis based on John Locke's ideas about property rights originating in an investment of labor—in this case intellectual labor—can be extended to explain the development of copyright law. This argument could also be extended to explain the perceived data ownership rights that accompany research. If researchers are perceived as investing a great deal of intellectual effort into a research design, they may be assumed to own the study and the data it yields.

The expert (or group of experts) who carries out the study is also generally considered the sole author of publications resulting from the research work. The reification of individual authorship in U.S. society is reflected in the principle that one must make a "substantial scientific contribution" (American Psychological Association, 1994, p. 294) to a research project in order to receive authorship credit, and again in the definitions of substantial contributions. (For more discussion of the construction of individual authorship, see Jaszi & Woodmansee, 1994). This belief in individual authorship further serves to identify researchers as the originators and owners of everything in their written work not set off by quotation marks or accompanied by footnotes or parenthetical citations. Although authors may generously acknowledge the efforts of those who have assisted in the research process, it is the researchers identified on the title page who are seen as the unique creators of the work that bears their names. Thus, the belief common in current Euro-American society that the creative process is inherently individualistic (Jaszi & Woodmansee, 1994) is essential to and consistent with the current popular construction of researcher as data owner.

184

This individualistic conception of the creation of scholarly work can be contrasted with attitudes toward cultural production in some societies that privilege collective over individual agency (Bettig, 1996). Rather than reifying individual authorship, written works or other cultural products may be construed as group endeavors, even when only a single person gives concrete form to those products. However, the practice of science in the U.S., including the closely connected principles of individual authorship and data ownership, remains deeply enmeshed within a larger individualistic culture.

EXPERT STATUS

The powerful social status that researchers hold in our society (Pilgrim & Rogers, 1993) further bolsters the researcher's assumed role as data owner. Privileged members of our society maintain greater rights, including ownership rights, than those less privileged in the areas of education, income, and so on. A clear power differential between researchers and participants is evident even within increasingly sensitive ethical guidelines. For example, Meara, Schmidt, & Day (1996) advocated that in situations in which two or more ethical principles conflict, the professional must assume the "responsibility to balance the principles in deciding how to resolve the specific conflict" (p. 13). They illustrated this point by describing a conflict between the individual participant's right to autonomy and the potential benefit of a deceptive research design. Given that it is the research community (the individual researcher in conjunction with overview boards) that is expected to make such a decision, it is clear that the researcher holds the weight of the decision-making power in the researcher-participant relationship.

Furthermore, the power differential between researcher and participant extends well beyond the laboratory, to the policy-making branches of government, the education provided for the next generation, and media sources. That research is usually written for an audience with considerable technical expertise contributes to this power imbalance, because participants may not be eager to see findings for themselves, or to feel confident in critically evaluating what they do read. Given such a discrepancy in power and influence, it is relatively easy for researchers to lay claim to ownership of what originally began as the participant's experience.

PARTICIPANT DISCONNECTION FROM DATA

A fourth assumption underlying the researcher's role as data owner is further supported by the assumption that the participant's relationship to the data ends with the termination of the data collecting session. Perhaps the strongest evidence for this assumption is the nature of informed consent. To begin with, central to the informed consent agreement is an emphasis on participant confidentiality and its limitations (American Psychological Association, 1992). Confidentiality is intended to protect participants from violations of their right to privacy (Shaughnessy, Zechmeister, & Zechmeister, 2000). With confidentiality in place, the danger of being publicly embarrassed or suffering other consequences as a result of being publicly connected to certain responses is minimized. But in emphasizing a protective disconnection between participants and data, the possibility of any other type of continuing connection between the two is overlooked. Thus, informed consent agreements inform participants that researchers will ensure the confidentiality of data provided by participants, but make no mention of any continuing relationship between participants and the data they provide.

In contrast to the marked attention paid to confidentiality, noticeably absent from most discussions of informed consent is any mention of the specific risks posed to participants by the future interpretation and use of the data they provide. Certainly, a mention of foreseeable research risks is generally included in informed consent forms, but when what is meant by anticipated risk is made explicit, the emphasis is almost always squarely on the risks associated with the immediate act of data collection. For example, a sample informed consent form provided in a recent undergraduate research methods text focused entirely on the participant as an isolated individual in the immediate context of the data collection (Shaughnessy et al., 2000). Risk was equated to "possible discomfort" experienced during data collection. We have found no examples of informed consent which make mention of ways that participants' data may be interpreted in a way they would find personally offensive, misguided, or downright wrong. Similarly, we have found no examples of informed consent that warn participants of ways that research findings may have real implications for public policy making and other decisions that may negatively affect participants. Instead, participants may be commonly assured, as in the sample form mentioned above, that their data will be used only for research purposes, with the implications for participants presumed to end there. Thus informed consent operates like an implicit bill of sale in which a transfer of ownership is assumed, and a waiver of both liability and even acknowledgement for the previous owner is presumed, although neither is anywhere explicitly stated.

PARTICIPANTS AS INTERCHANGEABLE OBJECTS

Finally, aspects of the previous assumptions all contribute to the final assumption supporting the construct of data ownership to be outlined here: that correct usage of data requires neither a personal connection with participants nor an understanding of the subjective context of data collection from the participant's point of view. This belief is most clearly evident in the practice of data sharing. Data sharing requires that participants be asked to provide consent for the use of their data "for research purposes" at unknown times, by unknown researchers, and for unknown research agendas at some point in the future (e.g. American Psychological Association, 1992; Taube & Burkhardt, 1997). Once participants provide this consent and the data is made available to other researchers, they have relinquished any control over the use of the data they have provided. Indeed, the idea that a person could grant "informed" consent for this sort of unspecified future use of their data highlights the extent to which informed consent traditionally focuses on the immediate risks of data collection and ignores the potential consequences to participants of interpretation and use of the data.

The practice of data sharing also illustrates how easily participants may be objectified in the traditional data-owning paradigm. If one assumes, as one would from a personal construct point of view, that each participant has a unique manner of construing the world and that his or her responses reflect these unique constructions, then one cannot understand the data obtained from the participant without attempting to understand the participant's constructions of reality within the research experience. To interpret massed data without any regard for this subjective context is to suggest not only that participants are fundamentally disconnected from the data they provide, but also that they are interchangeable objects whose human subjectivity has no place in the research process. This analysis is consistent with feminist relational ethics, as described by Fisher (2000), which require that research decisions affecting participants be made and evaluated in the context of real and ongoing relationships with individual participants. There may be subfields within psychology that are less affected by these concerns. However, we would argue that the subtle influences of the data-owning researcher construct may have negative repercussions on both scientists and science in any part of the field involving research with humans. For example, holding a utilitarian view of participants as mere interchangeable sources of data might impact the quality of participant recruitment and participant research experiences or negatively influence the public's views about the field.

SUMMARY

To summarize, the objective, empirical mode of inquiry requires has been associated with an instrumental view of data collection and data sources, which in turn shapes the assumed role of researcher as data owner. In this instrumental view, the relationship between observer and observed is a value-free interaction in which the observer gains insight from measurements of an objectified data source. Because the data source is an object and relatively powerless, the more powerful researcher is unquestionably the owner of the data produced in this process. This ownership is further validated by the perceived intellectual contribution made by the researcher in designing the study that produced the data and writing up the findings. Informed consent is intended as a means of minimizing the potential harm of participating in research and maximizing participant autonomy (American Psychological Association, 1992; Faden & Beauchamp, 1986). However, informed consent also perpetuates the researcher's role as data owner in two ways. First, by emphasizing, especially through the assurance of confidentiality, the disconnection between participant and data; and second, by avoiding mention of any potential future repercussions for the participant as a result of the use or interpretation of the data provided. Finally, the practice of data sharing provides an extreme example of the belief that participants are interchangeable objects whose human subjectivity has no place in the research process, and who, therefore, do not have any meaningful connection to the data they provide after it is secured by the researcher.

THE CONSEQUENCES OF DATA OWNERSHIP

We will discuss two major deleterious consequences of holding the popular current construction of researcher as data owner. The first is the the potential for misleading of participants who are not clearly made aware of the vagaries of research design, data analysis, and interpretation that take place both before and long after their visit to the research laboratory. In other words, researchers who think of themselves as data owners may analyze and interpret data (not just collect data) in ways that result in harm to participants. The second major deleterious consequence of the data-owner construction is the perpetuation of researcher/participant relationships that are characterized by a marked imbalance of power. Assuming the role of data owner may ultimately lead researchers to a devaluing of participants' priorities, beliefs, and personal meanings.

Regarding the first major consequence, potential harm to participants as a result of data analysis and interpretation (hereafter referred to as interpretive risk), the practical problem to be addressed is not a lack of ethical guidelines regarding the importance of informed consent. There are numerous established guidelines available from professional organizations and governmental agencies (e.g., American Psychological Association, 1992; Public Welfare: Protection of Human Subjects, 1991), and most of these bodies agree that it is essential to provide research recruits with enough information – including potential risks – to make an autonomous decision regarding participation. At issue is not a lack of guidelines, but rather the construal of existing guidelines such that consideration of interpretive risk is excluded.

Perhaps it might be argued that no such interpretive risks actually exist. In support of our argument that they do indeed exist, we offer three different general ways that participants can be harmed by the manner in which data are reported and analyzed.

The first type of harm that may occur happens when conclusions are drawn about participants based on their group membership in combination with associated research findings. Leigh (1988) has termed this damage "probability-based disclosure harm" (p. 310). The example she offered was the increased chance that African-American women would be more likely stereotyped as likely crack-cocaine users, merely because their demographic group had a higher percentage of crack cocaine users than other groups according to certain government statistical reports. As Leigh explained, it may not be the resultant stereotypes and assumptions themselves that pose the most risk to participants, but the policy decisions made as a result.

However, an increase in or development of certain stereotypes and assumptions may well be considered harmful in itself. Such strengthening of stereotypes and misleading assumptions can eventually result from psychological research among identifiable subgroups of the population, whether the researcher personally makes such gross generalizations or not. Ethnic minorities, for example, should have the right to know that when they participate in research using an IQ test presuming a Eurocentric cultural background, they face the risk of having the group they identify with labeled "intellectually inferior" when the findings are reported and spread through various media. Again, it is irrelevant whether the researcher endorses such a position: once findings are released, they are free to be (mis)reported and (mis)interpreted as others see fit. Thus overgeneralizations and unsupported conclusions are not necessarily the fault of the researcher, but are a risk of which participants should be aware.

A second, more direct type of harm may occur when research findings offend or clash with the values of participants. An example of the potential for such harm can be found in Rind, Tromovitch, and Bauserman's (1998) recent controversial meta-analysis of studies on the long-term effects of childhood sexual abuse. In their study, Rind et al. stated that childhood sexual abuse "does not typically have intensely negative psychological effects or correlates" (p. 26). The study was later cited by makers of a pro-pedophilia website who sought to justify adult-child sexual behavior. Although survivors of childhood sexual abuse and those who participated in the original studies on which the meta-analysis was based may not be publicly identifiable as part of a subgroup of "abuse survivors," they might still be personally offended by the conclusions reached. The use to which the study was put by others besides the researchers may have also seemed quite objectionable to participants. Thus, another risk related to data use is the possibility that the researcher or someone else will interpret the data in a way that participants find personally offensive or simply wrong.

Of issue to our argument is not whether or not Rind and colleagues' (1998) conclusions were accurately drawn. What is important is that taking a data-owning perspective would allow a researcher to overlook all of these potential harms when disclosing to potential participants the risks they face in a study of the type that Rind et al. analyzed. Of course, as a meta-analysis their study is also a demonstration that one must not only consider the interpretive risks specific to one's own study design, but also the general risks posed by any potential future use of the data. It may be argued that no researcher can fully anticipate all future uses and abuses of data, and we would agree. This actually strengthens our point: data-owning researchers assume the impossible task of anticipating damage

190

on behalf of participants, but without participant collaboration or even awareness of the issue.

A third type of harm, related in some ways to the first two we have discussed, may occur when research findings directly or indirectly influence policy changes that in turn directly impact the participant's life. This risk should be obvious for any explicitly evaluatory design, but also exists for any study that could eventually be applied to a policy question. For example, Cole and Cole (1996) discussed two private-sector studies that examined the efficacy of the U.S. government's Head Start preschool program for underprivileged children. While in this case no policy changes occurred, the potential clearly existed for these studies to influence Congressional decision-making.

In our discussion of the above example we are not suggesting that individual researchers always be held accountable for the ways their reports shape others' policy decisions, although it probably should be sobering to reflect on the power a well-timed study may have. Instead, we are trying to highlight aspects of the research process that may be harmful to some participants, and suggesting that anyone who is not thoroughly aware of the potential for the research findings to be used against them in tangible ways, is not a well-informed participant.

It is not necessary for the researcher to agree with the participant's evaluation of what would be an undesirable consequence of the research. For example, some analysts might suggest that if Head Start is an ineffective program, then parents are better off not enrolling their children in it. However, some parents may experience and construe Head Start as a positive influence in their children's lives, regardless of what the research says. Within this argument, and from a constructivist perspective in general, the ultimate estimation of the harm suffered as a result of research participation belongs to the participant. It is merely the researcher's role to point out the general possibilities; to make participants aware that such types of harmful things do happen from time to time, and could conceivably happen in the study being explained.

We hope these examples effectively illustrate some of the interpretive risks that participants may unknowingly face. While the risks we have discussed may seem obvious to researchers, it may not be safe to assume that participants adequately foresee such risks on their own. To begin with, participants may invest a great deal of trust that the researcher's findings will reveal a form of the truth that

191

favors and is consistent with their own perceptions of the world. Additionally, admiration of scientific research as a tool for human progress may decrease participants' awareness of possible interpretive risks. Finally, participants may feel such confidence in the authority and competence of the researcher that they give little consideration to important aspects of the research process, including harmful ways in which data might be used in the future.

As mentioned earlier, the second major deleterious consequence of the data-owner construction is the perpetuation of researcher/participant relationships that are characterized by a marked imbalance of power. Our attention therefore turns from ways in which the data owner construct affects participants, to ways in which the data owner construct affects and defines the relationship between participants and researchers. We take as a starting point the notion that the nature of the researcher/participant relationship sets participants in a position of less power than researchers (Fisher, 2000). Researchers often direct participants, request that they meet certain expectations, give them feedback on their performance, and store away the data they provide; participants in turn are limited to the power of choosing whether or not to participate. From a constructivist standpoint, taking steps to limit power differentials may have many advantages, such as providing a more meaningful research interaction, increasing participants' level of investment in the research process, and increasing researchers' investment in trying to understand the participant as an individual. From these improvements would follow an overall improvement in the quality of the data that are gathered. We argue that the data owner construct undermines such ideals by contributing to the imbalance of power between researchers and participants.

Taking a data-owning perspective allows researchers greater perceived latitude in the design, conduct, and interpretation of research projects. This provides increased opportunity for the personal investments researchers have in their research, such as continued grant support, professional esteem, or religious belief, to exert influence on the research process. Furthermore, the natural influence of researchers' own biases generally goes unchecked by participants, both because researchers tend not to share those biases directly and because participants are generally unlikely to be able to access the professional journals in which these findings are shared. Even if access were not an issue, participants may not feel they have the expertise needed to understand and critically evaluate researchers' conclusions.

Fortunately, the American Psychological Association's ethical guidelines (1992) do enjoin psychologists to consider the possible consequences to society of the research they undertake. Additionally, researchers are obligated to mention how the data may be shared, or used in unforeseeable ways. From a constructivist viewpoint, this is a positive development in ethical standards for researcher behavior; however, terms such as "used" still imply a mechanistic wringing-out of the truths in the data, and fail to fully convey the nature of the interpretation that actually takes place.

Also, the expectation for researchers to weigh the costs of their research relative to both participants and the larger society assumes that researchers accurately identify research practices that may have harmful consequences. From a constructivist perspective, it may even be argued that it is impossible for any researcher to ever completely protect the participant, because the researcher's construal of what is harmful to the participant is almost certain to be different from the participant's construal of what is harmful. Hill, Glaser, and Harden (1985), for example, suggested that researchers' views about ethical research behavior cannot be divorced from the context of the power (race, class, gender, etc.) held by the researcher. In other words, researcher/participant power differentials may prevent researchers from having a sufficient awareness of the potential harm that is perceived by research participants.

Similarly, relying on the protective power of confidentiality may also reinforce researcher/participant power differentials. Because confidentiality assures the participant's anonymity, it becomes very difficult for the participant to identify instances of misrepresentation after findings have been published. This, in conjunction with the relative unlikelihood that participants will pursue access to research findings after providing data, gives the profession interpretive carte blanche to a somewhat disturbing degree.

RECONSTRUING THE ROLE OF THE RESEARCHER

According to Kelly's psychological theory of personal constructs (1955), a construct is more likely to be maintained the more it affords some prediction of the future. As outlined above, there are many assumptions common within the psychological research community that encourage viewing research data as the property of the researcher. Therefore, a researcher who construes his or her role as that of data owner is likely to experience considerable success in anticipating the reactions of colleagues and even participants to his or her actions.

However, one might ask whether the reality so accurately predicted by the construct of data-ownership is a desirable reality in which to live. Perhaps in this case a modification of constructs is advisable not to better predict the future, but to change the future. Specifically, reconstruing the role of the researcher may allow for other positive changes in researchers' meaning-making systems, challenging the potentially-destructive assumptions supporting the old role of data owner. To reconstrue, however, requires an alternative means of viewing the three-way relationship between researcher, participants, and data.

We would like to suggest one such alternative construction that may be of use: that is, viewing the researcher as an art appropriator. Artistic "appropriation" is the use of one artist's work by another artist to create a new work of art. Many artists, especially within the last few years, have used appropriation to make powerful re-interpretations of others' artwork (Erickson & Falkowski, 1999). For example, artist Sherry Levine created gallery exhibits consisting of photographs she had taken of paintings by famous male artists. Levine's work drew the viewer's attention to the troubling history of gender in the arts. She also altered perspectives by raising the question, "Whose art is really being displayed here?" Acts of artistic appropriation such as hers blur the boundaries of creative ownership, emphasize the re-interpretive nature of artistic creation, and alter assumptions about what constitutes "originality."

To translate the construct of appropriator from the art world to the scientific community, it is first necessary to acknowledge an important distinction between appropriated art and data. Art that is appropriated has already been presented for public view, and is therefore identifiable in the finished product of appropriation. In contrast, published research contains never-before-seen participant contributions, so the reader has no way of distinguishing the appropriated from the work of the appropriator. Instead, the researcher is easily given sole credit for authorship, and the nature of the product is commonly understood more as a reproduction of reality than as an amalgamated art form.

Despite this difference, there are several reasons why it is useful to think of psychological researchers as "art appropriators" rather than "data owners." To begin with, such a vision recognizes that researchers are involved in the re-interpretation of expressions (sto-

194

ries, self-ratings, behavior) that do not belong to them. Rather, these expressions are the creative work of another's meaning-making system. No matter how carefully a data-collection tool is designed, the data and therefore the conclusions that are drawn inevitably include pieces of each participant's individually-constructed pictures of the world.

Several implications follow from the above. First, the notion of the researcher as individual author and the sole intellect behind the research findings is undermined. Instead, a research study, from the methods used to the conclusions drawn, must be seen as inherently collaborative. This is not to denigrate the contribution of researchers, with their painstakingly-acquired knowledge and skill, but to elevate the contribution of the participants. Second, since it is recognized as unethical to claim authorship of another's thoughts, the appropriating researcher would be forced to publicly acknowledge their indebtedness to participants. This indebtedness refers to much more than the participants' donation of time and effort, and may also serve to decrease the power differential between researcher and participant. Third, in addition to acknowledging the substantial intellectual, conceptual, and/or creative contribution of participants, appropriating researchers would be obligated to attempt to define for the reader the constructions of the participants (or the researcher's construal of the constructions of participants) vs. the constructions of the researcher. This may also decrease power differentials by improving participants' ability to identify instances when a researcher has misrepresented them. Fourth, given acknowledgment of the inevitability of collaboration, researchers may be more willing to purposefully search out and request input from participants during all phases of research. This could in turn lead to a higher quality body of research, with misinterpretations and the invisible influences of researcher subjectivity minimized and/or made more visible relative to the traditional approach. Fifth, the appropriating researcher may treat participants with greater respect, given the participants' new standing as true colleagues rather than objectified and incidental informants. Sixth and last, participants may be more willing to join fully in the research process if the creative and meaningful nature of their contribution is highlighted for them to appreciate as well.

Another reason why it is useful to think of psychological researchers as "art appropriators" rather than "data owners" is that this approach highlights the nature of the researcher's own contribution.   Not only are they collaborating with participants, researchers are contributing a subjective picture of the world around them. Viewing the scientific contribution of the researcher this way may prevent an escape to the construct of objective truth when trying to justify conclusions one draws or the framing of a research question. Instead, appropriating researchers would have to wrestle with questions about the nature of their motivations for pursuing certain lines of research, and what their conclusions say about both researcher and participant constructions of reality. They may also feel obligated to share some information about their perspectives and values, especially those that relate to their research, with potential participants weighing whether or not to join with them in a research project.

Finally, art appropriating researchers would be more likely to understand the nature of their work to be social commentary. There are several components to this commentary. First, appropriators would attempt to understand and fairly represent the meaning and intentions behind the original art form. This doesn't mean they must agree with that artist's opinions and views, nor is it possible that they could completely comprehend the meaning of that art form for the original artist. However, as in attempting not to quote authors out of context, appropriating researchers would not purposefully manipulate the work of another to create an impression of the original artist in clear opposition to the artist's own self-presentation and -understanding.

Another major reason why it may be useful to think of psychological researchers as "art appropriators" rather than "data owners" is that, given the limitations mentioned above on accurately representing another's view of the world, art appropriators would recognize the risks present for the original artist whose work is made the subject of another's interpretation. Therefore, when interacting with the original artist, in this case the research participant, the appropriator would be straightforward and thorough in explaining the dangers of interpretation.   In the context of psychological research, this requires an acknowledgment before the research begins of the subjective nature of data interpretation, the potential for researchers to come to conclusions which are offensive to participants or seem downright wrong, and the possibility that broader social consequences of the research findings will have a negative impact on participants or the groups to which they belong.

196

A third major reason for developing a "researcher as art appropriator" construct is that by viewing the nature of psychological research as social commentary rather than truth production, the art appropriator may be more attuned to the possible social consequences of their research designs and findings. Of course, this is not to say that appropriating researchers should only render socially desirable or inoffensive interpretations. It is, however, to say that such a view of their role better facilitates a balancing between the appropriators' motivations to draw personally-desirable conclusions and a concern for the general welfare. Hopefully, appropriators as social commentators would be better at striking a balance between those competing motivations than has previously been the case, allowing the development of a more helpful and just psychology research profession. Certainly, the appropriating researcher, as a social commentator, would feel greater personal accountability for the ripples produced by their research.

Finally, we should note that acts of appropriation might be as damaging as assumption of direct ownership. Appropriation can be used to insult, defame, and injure others. What we are stressing, however, is that whether for good or bad, appropriating psychological data is what researchers do. We have argued that recognizing and acting upon this recognition may help alleviate many of the negative consequences of the data-owner construct.

CONCLUSION

The role of data owner is easy to assume as a psychological researcher. However, researchers who assert ownership rights over data also lay claim to enormous power in the researcher-participant relationship and simultaneously cut off more meaningful communication within that relationship.

To address those concerns raised by the data-owning researcher construct, we have proposed a new way of viewing the three-way relationship between researcher, participant, and data: as the appropriation by one artist (the researcher) of another artist's (the participant's) creation (the data). This view more accurately represents the creation of scientific knowledge, as we understand it. It also addresses many of the assumptions that foster an imbalance in power and prestige between researcher and participant, which in turn make possible researchers' privileging of their personal agendas, sometimes at the expense of participants' values and well-being.

The tenets of the appropriation model include the following observations. Researchers have the responsibility to provide participants with an opportunity to meaningfully choose whether and how to contribute to the ongoing dialogue of scientific research. This requires thoroughly informing participants about the possible negative repercussions of interpretation, the potential for negative consequences of research findings for themselves or a social group to which they belong, and the nature of the researcher's own worldview as it relates to the research design. Also, researchers must do all they can to respect the unbreakable connection between participants and the information they provide. This includes interpreting data in conjunction with the context and worldview in which it was presented, involving participants in data interpretation, recognizing the impact of one's own interpretations on the lives of participants, and acknowledging the collaborative nature of the research enterprise.

Finally, as appropriators of lived art rather than owners of psychological data, researchers can enjoy the fruits of more genuinely intimate interactions with research participants, of exploring the world without as much of the weight of presuming to make decisions for others, and of continually incorporating others' life art and constructions of reality into one's own. In addition to these benefits, appropriators have a way to better keep their own biases, goals, and meaning-making systems in check, and to prevent the defacing of great works of art instead of highlighting the beauty and knowledge that is already there.

REFERENCES

Ethical principles of psychologists and code of conduct. (1992). Washington, D.C.: American Psychological Association. Retrieved June 1, 2001, from the World Wide Web: http://www.apa.org/ethics/code.html

American Psychological Association. (1994). Publication manual of the American Psychological Association (4th ed.). Washington, DC: Author.

Bettig, R.V. (1996). Copyrighting culture: The political economy of intellectual property. Boulder, CO: Westview Press.

Cole, M., & Cole, S. R. (1996). The development of children (3rd ed.). New York: Scientific American Books.

Erickson, K., & Falkowski, A. (1999, July/August). A manifesto for reconstruction. New Art Examiner, 26(10), 30-35.

Faden, R. R., & Beauchamp, T. L. (1986). A history and theory of informed consent. New York: Oxford University Press.

Faidley, A. J., & Leitner, L. M. (1993). Assessing experience in psychotherapy: Personal construct alternatives. Westport, CT: Praeger.

Fields, K. L., & Price, A. R. (1993). Problems in research integrity arising from misconceptions about the ownership of research. *Academic Medicine, 68*(Suppl. 3), S60-S64.

Fisher, C. B. (2000). Relational ethics in psychological research: One feminist's journey. In M. M. Brabeck (Ed.), *Practicing feminist ethics in psychology* (pp. 125-142). Washington, DC: American Psychological Association.

Gellman, R., & Frawley, K. A. (1996). The need to know versus the right to privacy. In M. A. Freeman (Series Ed.) & T. Trabin (Vol. Ed.), *Jossey-Bass managed behavioral healthcare library. The computerization of behavioral healthcare: How to enhance clinical practice, management, and communications* (pp. 191-212). San Francisco: Jossey-Bass.

Hill, M., Glaser, K., & Harden, J. (1995). A feminist model for ethical decision making. In E. J. Rave & C. C. Larsen (Eds.), *Ethical decision making in therapy: Feminist perspectives* (pp. 18-37). New York: The Guilford Press.

Jaszi, P., & Woodmansee, M. (1994). Introduction. In M. Woodmansee & P. Jaszi (Eds.), *The construction of authorship: Textual appropriation in law and literature* (pp. 1-13). London: Duke University Press.

Kelly, G. A. (1955). *The psychology of personal constructs* (2 vols.). New York: W.W. Norton & Co.

Leigh, W. A. (1998). Participant protection with the use of records: Ethical issues and recommendations. *Ethics & Behavior, 8,* 305-319.

Meara, N. M., Schmidt, L. D., & Day, J. D. (1996). Principles and virtues: A foundation for ethical decisions, policies, and character. *The Counseling Psychologist, 24*(1), 4-77.

Neimeyer, R. A., & Raskin, J. D. (Eds.). (2000). *Constructions of disorder: Meaning-making frameworks for psychotherapy.* Washington, DC: American Psychological Association.

Pilgrim, D., & Rogers, A. (1993). *A sociology of mental health and illness.* Buckingham, England: Open University Press.

Public Welfare: Protection of Human Subjects, 45 C.F.R. § 46. (1991, August 19). Office for Human Research Protections. Retrieved June 1, 2001, from the World Wide Web: http://ohrp.osophs.dhhs.gov/humansubjects/guidance/45cfr46.htm

Rind, B., Tromovitch, P., & Bauserman, R. (1998). A meta-analytic examination of assumed properties of child sexual abuse using college samples. *Psychological Bulletin, 124,* 22-53.

Shaughnessy, J. J., Zechmeister, E. B., & Zechmeister, J. S. (2000). *Research methods in psychology* (5th ed.). Boston: McGraw-Hill.

Sieber, J. E. (1989). Sharing scientific data I: New problems for IRBs. *IRB, 11*(6), 4-7.

Taube, D. O., & Burkhardt, S. (1997). Ethical and legal risks associated with archival research. *Ethics & Behavior, 7,* 59-67.

Viney, L. L. (1992). Social science research in the 1990s: The contribution of constructivism. *International Journal of Personal Construct Psychology, 5*, 295-305.

CHAPTER 10

Putting the Heart Back Into Constructivist Research

Marla J. Arvay

I introduce this chapter with a slam poem that hopefully serves a dual purpose: as a means to illustrate the writing of evocative research texts and as an invitation to constructivist researchers to rethink the traditional psychological frames that restrain their current writing and research practices.

My introduction to slam poetry was through my daughter's participation in the World Public Speaking and Debating Competition in Cyprus. In the construction of her persuasive speech, she argued that slam poetry (Kaufman, 1999) was the only way to rejuvenate youth's participation in the reading and writing of poetry. "Similar to the eight track stereo tape or the typewriter, traditional poetry is steadily becoming a relic of the past" (E. R. Arvay, 2000). Inspired by her speech, I began to read slam poetry and started to make connections between slam poetry and constructivist epistemology. Slam poetry provides insights into the possibilities of revamping the way in which constructivists conduct and "construct" their research.

Marc Smith, an American poet and construction worker, is the founder of slam poetry (Kaufman, 1999). His intention was to revive the public's interest in poetry by presenting it as a live, participatory performance. Usually found in coffee houses or neighborhood pubs, it is performed in a three-minute bout, like a boxing match, where the words themselves throw the punches. The word "slam" conveys the idea that words have the capacity to be so powerful that an evocative three-minute poem or "round" could physically knock someone over. Although slam poetry is competitive in nature, the true spirit of slam is to create a new awareness for both the presenter and the audience. Strangers gather together to experience things they would not normally experience, to hear things they

would not normally hear. Poets get up on the stage, take the micro-
phone, and express to a room full of strangers something from their
hearts. Emily Arvay (2000) writes:

> Slam poetry combines street-wise sensibility and tough tender-
> ness. Slam poets give form to incoherence, voice songs of ugli-
> ness and show that unbearable pain is something that can be
> overcome. Like versifying Robin Hood, "slammers" steal stories
> from their wealth of experience and feed the emptiness of our
> spirits. Transforming their lives into poetry, they stir up the
> imagination until near eruption. Slam's passionate lyrical ener-
> gy is spreading fast. From the clubs of Manhattan's East Village
> to the rock stages of Venice West, a new cultural form is riding
> the upsurge of slammer's verse. Sartre once said of poets: 'They
> are not revolutionaries but men and women in revolt.' Indeed
> slam poets are in revolt, in protest against their dehumanization
> and spurred on by their need for authenticity. If slammers share
> any common feature at all it is this unspoken objective: to get in
> your face and stay there.

Thus, I begin this chapter with a poem created by Patricia
Smith (1992), a famous African American slam poet. I use her poem
as an entry point for discussing the writing of evocative, emotional
texts as a possibility for constructivist research. It is entitled
"Skinhead":

They call me skinhead and I got my own beauty.
It is knife-scrawled across my back in sore, jagged letters,
It's in the way my eyes snap away from the obvious.
I sit in my dim matchbox,
on the edge of a bed tousled with my ragged smell,
slide razors across my hair,
count how many ways
I can bring blood closer to the surface to my skin.
These are the duties of the righteous,
the ways of the anointed.

The face that moves in my mirror is huge and pockmarked,
scraped pink and brilliant, apple-cheeked,
I am filled with my own spit.
Two years ago, a machine that slices leather
sucked in my hand and held it,
whacking off three fingers at the root.
I didn't feel nothing till I looked down
and saw one of them on the floor

next to my boot heel,
and I ain't worked since then.

I sit here and watch niggers take over my TV set,
walking like kings up and down the sidewalks in my head,
walking like their fat black Mamas *named* them freedom.
My shoulders tell me that ain't right.
So I move out into the sun
where my beauty makes them lower their heads,
or into the night
with a lead pipe up my sleeve,
a razor tucked in my boot.
I was born to make things right.

It's easy now to move my big body into shadows,
to move from a place where there was nothing
into the stark circle of a streetlight,
the pipe raised high up over my head.
It's a kick to watch their eyes get big,
round and gleaming like cartoon jungle boys,
right in that second when they know
the pipe's gonna come down, and I got this thing
I like to say, listen to this, I like to say
"Hey nigger, Abe Lincoln's been dead a long time."

I get hard listening to their skin burst.
I was born to make things right.

Then this newspaper guy comes round,
seems I was a little sloppy kicking some fag's ass
and he opened his hole and screamed about it.
This reporter finds me curled up in my bed,
those TV flashes licking my face clean
Same ol' shit.
Ain't got no job, the coloreds and spics got em' all.
Why ain't I working? Look at my hand, asshole.
No, I ain't part of no organized group.
I'm just a white boy who loves his race,
fighting for a pure country..
Sometimes it's just me. Sometimes three. Sometimes 30.
AIDS will take care of the faggots,

then it's gon be white on black in the streets.
Then there'll be three million.
I tell him that.

So he writes it up
and I come off looking like some kind of freak,
like I'm Hitler himself. I ain't that lucky,
but I got my own beauty
It is my steel-toed boots,
in the hard corners of my shaved head.

I look in the mirror and hold up my mangled hand,
only the baby finger left, sticking straight up,
I know it's the wrong goddamned finger,
but fuck you all anyway.
I'm riding the top rung of the perfect race,
my face scraped pink and brilliant.
I'm your baby, America, your boy,
drunk on my own spit, I am goddamned fuckin' beautiful.

And I was born

and raised

right here.

(Kaufman, 1999, p. 239-240,
used by permission of
Patricia Smith)

If we imagine for a moment that Patricia Smith is a constructivist researcher, and that she has been able to infiltrate the skinhead culture by being given permission to observe and interview
them over a period of time, as an investigator studying the lived
experience of being a skinhead, we are able to see, feel and hear
Smith's interpretation of her data. We are also able to see how the
evocative text works. It draws us in, it evokes imagery and emotion
and, given our own experiences with individuals who call themselves "skinheads," we can take up a position that places us either
inside or outside the skinhead experiences depicted here. We might
align ourselves with the author's viewpoint, or we might react to her
portrayal of this participant, and if we have no experience with skin-

heads at all, then we are shown a very poignant rendering. Whatever the reader's response, we are pulled into the text because it is compelling.

In writing her research findings, Smith has taken up her participant's voice. She writes her research as a first-person account. All of her biases, understandings, experiences of her participant are revealed in the writing—there is no hiding behind the research text—she becomes her interpretation. Now this is a stretch, but remember we are just imagining here, as an African American woman, she takes up the gaze of the white male racist. She turns the gaze upon itself by standing inside it, inside her interpretation, even as an outsider.

So I put it to you: Can she speak from this position? Can any of us speak from the positions of our participants when their lives are so diverse from our own? What happens when we attempt to step inside the "skin of Other?" These are ethical and political questions that address who we can study and how we study them. It is a question that begs us to deconstruct issues concerning the re-presentation of our participants' lives, the politics of voice within our research texts, the subjectivity of the researcher in conducting and writing research, the dialogical and co-constructed nature of the research act, and the art of interpretation in conducting research. Where do constructivists stand on these issues? What are we currently doing in our research practices that address these concerns? Are constructivist researchers consciously engaged in making their research practices congruent with constructivist epistemology (Hoskins & M. J. Arvay, 1999)? If constructivists believe that knowledge or "truth claims" are co-constructed, then how do we move toward interactional and dialogical forms of representation? Furthermore, why do we want to? Why is it important to the enterprise of constructivist psychology?

CONSTRUCTIVISM, SOCIAL CONSTRUCTIONISM AND NARRATIVE EPISTEMOLOGIES

Before I attempt to answer these last three questions, it is important to understand the nexus between constructivism, social constructionism and narrative as epistemologies. Although these theories have distinctive foundational tenets, they also overlap and are commensurable in complex ways with regard to human meaning making.[1] All three are products of the postmodern turn that rec-

[1] I recognize in making this claim that not all constructivists, constructionists or

ognizes no single, objectifiable "truth" or "reality" and instead promotes the idea that truth claims are based on contingent, transient, partial and situated realities. Because "reality" is socially constructed, there exists at any given time multiple versions of reality, which are individually and communally created. Individual, temporal and sociohistorical factors influence these constructed realities.

Constructivist epistemology is based upon a systems and process model of the human being. Within a constructivist framework, knowledge is created through one's intra and interpersonal engagement in the world, and people are active agents in creating the personal meanings of their lives. George Kelly, the founding father of personal construct psychology, maintained that people understand and create meaning through personal construct systems (Kelly, 1955). Decades later Michael Mahoney (1991) expanded on Kelly's work by developing a constructivist epistemology based on a systems and process model of core ordering processes, which operate mostly at the tacit level. Mahoney (2000) describes core ordering processes as "principled patterns of activity attracted to and defined by polar contrasts fundamental to life as people live it" (p. 49). He states that these "core ordering process are given special protection against change and they organize experiences and activities along the dimensions of emotional valance, reality states, personal identity and power" (Mahoney, 2000, p. 46). According to Mahoney, the self is self-organizing, relational and based in a system searching for balance (or homeostasis). Understanding, meaning making and change require novel experiences that challenge older beliefs, assumptions or predictable patterns of experience. "The tapestries of order that permeate one's daily life become apparent only when one loses them" (Mahoney, 2000, p. 48). Further, people are aware of these core ordering processes "when such embodiments are 'called' to their attention either by (a) disorder, disease, or distress or (b) symbols (spoken, written, performed) that 'remind' one of one's bodily being" (p. 48). Mahoney (2000) states:

> [People] seek explanations and assurances of order. They want to know (why, how, when, what, who). They seek a "firm" foundation for their beliefs (the origin of the verb to understand is

---

narrativists would necessarily agree with this statement and further, in making this statement I am not attempting to neglect the fact that there are many types of constructivists, social constructionists and narrativists in each of these camps. However, it is my opinion that each offers epistemological insights and possibilities when combined that expand the possibilities for creating new methodologies for researching the human condition.

206

to have the intimate knowledge that comes only from "standing under" the object of one's interest). (p. 56)

Most *social constructionists* (e.g., Burr, 1995; Efran, Lukens & Lukens, 1990; Gergen, 1994) would not necessarily argue with a constructivist epistemology but would expand it to include the social realm of people's lives as impinging on the knowledge that one can know. Neimeyer and Raskin (2000) state:

> . . . constructivists tend to focus on experiential exploration of the tacit processes of self-construction. . . . In contrast, social constructionists—who themselves constitute a complex and even contradictory camp—differ from constructivists in their emphasis on the social as opposed to individual origins of meaning and in their concentration on discursive practices as opposed to individual cognitions as the object of study, critique and transformation. (p. 6)

A social constructionist epistemology acknowledges that one comes to know through reflection on and the deconstruction of discursive practices and discourses within which one lives. Social constructionists emphasize the co-constructed nature of "reality" and the importance of language practices as a basis for multiple "reality" claims.

Narrative as an epistemology has important links to both constructivism and social constructionism.

> The narrative is present at all times, in all places, in all societies; the history of narrative begins with the history of mankind [sic]. There does not exist, and never has existed a people without narrative. (Barthes, 1966, p. 14)

Roland Barthes (1966) claims the universality of narrative, which is a central premise in narrative epistemology. Stories exist in every culture and are present in a multitude of forms: novels, nursery rhymes, folktales, myths, newspapers, commercials, popular magazines, historical, educational and scientific texts, cinema, and other forms of literature and art. We make ourselves and the lives of others known through the stories we construct (Bruner, 1986; Denzin, 1989; Mishler, 1986; Polkinghorne, 1988; Richardson, 1997; Ricoeur, 1984; Riessman, 1993; Sarbin, 1986). Our stories reveal our purposes and intentions as human beings and the meanings we make of our experiences. Clarissa Pinkola-Estes (1992) contends "stories are embedded with instructions which guide us about the complexities of life" (p.16). Narrative provides explanation of how the episodes and events in our lives are meaningfully linked.

A strong argument for using narrative methods within the human sciences is based on the premise that humans are storytelling organisms (Polkinghorne, 1988). Narrative researchers maintain that narrative form is the primary way people make sense of experience (Bruner, 1986; Mishler, 1986; Polkinghorne, 1988). Moreover, narrative functions as a means to self-construction in that storytelling or story construction is a way of coming to know oneself and one's world. Narratives are both product and process (Polkinghorne, 1988); narratives are the stories we tell ourselves about ourselves, as well as the stories we tell others about ourselves. How and what we tell in our stories becomes a means by which we make meaning. In our storytelling, we not only create a narrative, we are constructing ourselves or, as Theodore Sarbin (1986) claims, we are always involved in the activity of self-narration: the "I" construes the story in which the "me" will be shown as one of the main characters, or actors.

Mikhail Bakhtin (1986) furthers Sarbin's notion of self-narrative by conceptualizing the self as a "polyphonic novel." Bakhtin views the self as a multiplicity of voices and a person's inner world as a network of intrasubjective relationships. He claims that in every conversational situation there are three parties within the speaker: the speaker who is speaking, the recipient (or the one who hears), and the "superaddressee," a third party presumed to understand what is being spoken. In this view, there is no single author, but several authorial voices—each constructing their own stories within a dialogically internal relationship.

Barthes (1966) maintains that narratives provide two significant rhetorical functions. At the individual level, stories are produced to explain one's life in the past, present and future; at the sociocultural level stories serve to unify common cultural beliefs and values. Laurel Richardson (1990) extends Barthes' explanation of narrative function to include a process of personal organization. She writes:

> Narrative functions at the autobiographical level to mark off one's own individual existence from all others; it has its own finitude. One's life is separable from others; it has its own beginning and its own ending. But, because of that separation, one can be an integrated whole—a being with its own unique past, present, and future. Narrative thus provides the opportunity for the individual to make existential sense of mortality, and, correlatively, through the narrative, the profound experience of mortality becomes sociologically accessible. (p. 23)

I would add that this sense of mortality is also accessible educationally and psychologically.

Narrative operates at the cultural level, as well. Cultural tales are embedded with implicit instructions, values, and norms that influence the kinds of tales we tell. Story construction provides endless opportunity for the re-authoring of our lives (Richardson, 1997). In human science research, both the storyteller and the recipient of the story are involved in constructing meaning. It is a purposeful activity similar to the constructivist's idea of personal agency. Both the storyteller and the recipient of the story are situated in a larger cultural context. The multiple subjectivities of the storyteller, the recipient, and the context within which they are situated influence the construction of their stories.

The nexus between *constructivism, social constructionism* and *narrative* as epistemologies is evident. All claim that the self has agency, lives within multiple "realities," is relational and contextually bound, is a process or a life unfolding, operates within self-systems and cultural systems, and makes meaning by contrasting differences both dialogically and through human activity, often at a tacit level of awareness. The most important feature that all three share is the understanding that humans construct the meaning of their lives through language practices.

THE DIALOGICAL NATURE OF KNOWLEDGE

Only in the stream of thought and life do words have meaning.

(Wittgenstein, 1981, no. 173)

Language lives only in the dialogic interaction of those who make use of it.

(Bakhtin, 1984, p. 183)

The differences which help us locate and identify forms of understanding . . . are not to be found in static pictures, nor in fixed inner mental representations or ideas, but in the moving, momentary, dialogic living relationships that occur in the steams of life between us.

(Shotter & Katz, 1999, p. 86)

I wish to highlight the importance of understanding the dialogical nature of language and its significance in the human sciences, particularly regarding constructivist research practices. If we focus more closely on the dialogical co-constructed space between our-selves and others, a complexity unfolds that often goes unnoticed in constructivist research. Bakhtin (1993) states:

> Even if I know a person, thoroughly, and I also know myself, I still have to grasp the truth of our interrelationship, the truth of the unitary and the unique event that links us and in which we are participants. That is, my place and function and his [sic], and our interrelationship in the ongoing event of being ... It is only from within that act as my answerable deed that there can be a way out into the unity of Being, and not from its product, taken in abstraction. It is only from within my participation that the function of each participant can be understood. (pp. 17-18)

Thus, the co-constructed space created through language practices (such as speaking, nodding, smiling, laughing, pausing, crying) changes from moment to moment, allowing each to be dif-ferent from the other yet simultaneously creating a communal space, a "third space." This space manifests as a "plurality of unmerged con-sciousnesses" (Bakhtin, 1984, p. 9). John Shotter (1993, 1996, 1999) has written extensively on the nature of this dialogically, co-created space. He writes:

> The dialogical reality or space people spontaneously construct in their joint action is experienced (sensed) as a "third agency" with its own specific demands and requirements. . . . This is what is so special about dialogically structured activities: the very responsive nature of the activity between us makes it impossible to say which aspect of it is due to you and which to me. An "it" emerges between us with its own requirements, a responsive order, which we are both a part of and participate in, and which as such can make calls upon us both. . . . Although no written formulation is ever adequate to its capture, the lived experience of moments when juxtaposed thoughts meet in a dialogue ... have a kind of "fractal fullness" in that as one looks into their ordering one can see endless future orderings. (1999, pp. 7-8)

Shotter brings together convincing arguments based on the philosophical writings of Wittgenstein (1953), Bakhtin, (1984, 1986, 1993) and Volosinov (1986). At the heart of his treatise are the ideas that we "body forth" words, that our mental activity is "out there" in the world between us, not inside our heads, that under-standing or meaning making takes place in living moments, dialog-ically, and that the "third space" provides infinite opportunities to create connections and understandings in the "stream of life." Shotter (1999) states:

210

The unique nature of such spaces can, thus, only be studied from within the practices in which they are created. Thus to investigate their nature, their structure, the calls they exert on us, what is possible for us within them and what is not, we need some utterly new method of investigation, quite different from the "on looker" methods inherited from the natural science. (p. 2)

Currently in constructivist research, where can we find examples of methods based upon the dialogical nature of knowledge? If knowledge and/or personal reality are co-constructed dialogically, where is the dialogue, or "living moments" in repertory grid research, for example? Where is the sentient being in constructivist research texts? Why do we not acknowledge the gap between our epistemology and our research practices? Further, how can we revamp or create anew research methods that are congruent with our philosophical tenets? I suggest what is needed is a collaborative narrative method (M. J. Arvay, 1998), a method founded upon the nexus between three epistemologies: constructivism, social constructionism, and narrative.

THE PROMISE OF A COLLABORATIVE NARRATIVE METHOD AS A FORM OF DIALOGICALLY EMBODIED CONSTRUCTIVIST RESEARCH

How do we re-present the story as told? How do we show the multiple perspectives that have influenced the author's interpretation, and the co-constructed nature of knowledge produced through constructivist research? How do we articulate and work through our research practices in this "third space?" Doing collaborative narrative research is about entering this "third space." At some point you are between the boundaries of the known and the unknown in terms of methodology. Many questions plague the constructivist narrative researcher as s/he moves through the research process from initial interview to writing or performing the research findings. The constructivist narrative researcher has the daunting task of moving the research from a dialogical or conversational format (an activity that is alive) to a narrative format (a written or video-taped format) that may take many forms—a poem, a play, a story, a narrative summary, a biography or autobiography (to name a few possibilities). The complexity of moving through each stage of narrative research is often not articulated in human and social science research writing. Furthermore, there are very few guidelines, if any

211

at all, in constructivist literature, for keeping the story as told "alive" in the written research text.

A COLLABORATIVE NARRATIVE METHOD

The collaborative narrative method (M. J. Arvay, 1998) was developed during my doctoral research while investigating the experience of secondary traumatic stress among female trauma therapists.[2] By the late 1990s, very few traumatic stress studies had been conducted using qualitative methods. Of the handful of studies investigating secondary trauma (M. J. Arvay & Uhlemann, 1996; Follette, Polusny & Milbeck, 1994; Schauben & Frazier, 1995), none had used a narrative approach—a methodology rooted in social constructionism and poststructuralism. Narrative inquiry differs dramatically from other forms of trauma research due to its focus on the dialogical nature of knowledge and its emphasis on the social world as a site where power relations are played out. Meanings are always disputable depending upon who is speaking to whom and their relative positions or perceived status within their interactions.

The collaborative narrative method has six stages: (a) setting the stage, (b) the performance: co-constructing the research interview, (c) the transcription process, (d) four collaborative interpretive readings, (e) writing the narratives, and (f) sharing the story.

The participants for this study were six trauma therapists who were interviewed on three separate occasions for a total of 9 to 10 hours of audiotaped transcriptions per participant. These therapists were all women between the ages of 27 and 52 years. They worked in various trauma centers in the Pacific Northwest dealing with clients traumatized by sexual abuse, adult survivors of child sexual abuse, survivors of torture and war-related trauma, and spousal abuse. The participants were invited to participate through presentations at their workplace on secondary traumatic stress. Each participant who volunteered for the study was screened using the Impact of Event Scale-Revised (Weiss, 1996) and a short version of the Trauma History Questionnaire (Green, 1996)

SETTING THE STAGE

To begin the research process, it is important to meet with all the participants for the following reasons: (a) to develop rapport; (b) to begin facilitating a dialogue pertaining to the research question;

---

[2] This research methodology is applicable to any research topic that strives to understand how individuals construct meaning in their lives.

(c) to explain the research process by detailing all the stages of the research; (d) to describe the roles and responsibilities that both the participant and the researcher will have in the research; (e) to articulate one's own values regarding the research relationship and finally, (f) to explain the basic philosophical values upon which the research design rests (e.g., the storied nature of our lives; that the self is constituted through the stories we tell, that telling our stories can be a transformative experience, that stories always change with each retelling and that the researcher can never hope to recapture the lived moment of the telling in the research text). Taking time at this phase of the research to inform the participants about the nature of their participation and to lay the groundwork for the research relationship will prove to be invaluable later during the interpretive phase of the research. I usually share the reasons why I am interested in the research topic with the participants before we start the process.

THE PERFORMANCE

Understanding the research interview as "joint action" (Shotter, 1999), I am always conscious of the role that I am playing in the construction of the "script." Using the model explicated by Ellis, Kiesinger, and Tillmann-Healy (1997), my goal was to "invite stories" (Polanyi, 1985) from my participants concerning their experience with the research question. Although this "inviting" may sound simple, it is actually a very complex act because it is simultaneously easy and difficult and requires more than interviewing skills. It is about entering the "third space" by being present to it and trusting that the process will unfold—a leap of faith that meaning making activity will unfold dialogically.

I envision my participants as co-investigators and co-actors in this research performance, not as respondents answering upon request, nor as informants merely imparting information. As a performance, the conversation is complex on many levels. Both the participant and I hold multiple "I" positions in the exchange (Hermans, Rijks, & Kempen, 1993) as various possible selves of my co-investigator and myself interact within this research space wherein an invariant number of self-positionings are possible. I am also aware that inviting a participant's story is more than just opening up the conversation or asking "good" questions. It entails attending to the narrative account at both the mirco-level of the individual experience of the narrator, and at the macro-level of cultural discourse. It means being engaged at both an experiential level and a reflexive level—in other words, holding dual consciousness. I ask participants about the metaphors, the paradoxes, the silences and pauses, the body language. I ask them to respond to me in the same manner. We attempt to uncover the contradictions and to articulate tacit knowledge through metaphor, body language, and by comparing similar experiences. Self-disclosure concerning the personal experiences of the researcher often initiates authentic dialogue and opens up an opportunity for the researcher to reexamine her/his own interpretations or beliefs. There were several instances during this research project on secondary trauma that I offered an anecdote, shared my feelings about my participant's experience, or told a parallel story. We mutually explored the meanings of our shared experiences. We laughed together, cried together and struggled to understand what it all meant. An interactive interview could entail at least a three to four hour session.

THE TRANSCRIPTION PROCESS

Transcription as an interpretive practice underscores the researcher's theoretical and epistemological assumptions about research (Denzin, 1997; Kvale, 1996; Mishler, 1992; Richardson, 1997). The method of transcription for this research project was designed using models of transcription described by Susan Chase (1995), Elliot Mishler (1992), and Catherine Kohler Riessman (1993). I preface the description of my transcription procedures with two caveats. First, I recognize that the exact reproduction of the speech act is impossible. All we can do is attempt to reproduce the communicative events as closely as possible—they will never be exact (Denzin, 1997; Richardson, 1997). Second, we cannot reproduce past events. Our stories (and the record of these stories) do not mirror the world as lived because our stories are constructed retrospectively and in this case, they are co-constructed performances. We can only attempt to reconstruct life events and hope that there will be some degree of verisimilitude (Polkinghorne, 1988). As an analogy, there are qualitative and interpretive differences between writing a play, being an actor in a play, watching the play, or reading the play.

The participants' audiotapes were transcribed twice. The first transcription was produced as a rough draft. Carefully listening to the speech events, I recorded each aspect of the speech produced (e.g., laughter, pauses, silences and gaps, hedging, crying, tone of voice) and also noted any aspect of the speech act that was not audible on the audiotape, but was recorded in written form in my field notes (e.g., body language, movement, facial expressions, positioning, environmental influences, and other contextual clues).

For the second draft, I followed a listening method described in Riessman's (1993) text on narrative analysis. I re-transcribed the conversation by displaying the text of the rough draft in stanza form, where each episode of the narrative was kept together in a series of lines and the tone of speech and pace were marked. Each episode that was conceptualized as a story within the larger narrative, was marked at its beginning and ending by double-spacing. The tone of the speaker was marked by using a bold font to indicate emphasis and italics to emphasize emotional expression, followed by a bracketed word indicating my interpretation of the emotion. All hesitations were written into the text. Both speakers were included in the transcript and when speech overlapped, the researcher's speech was bracketed with " {} " to show that it had been spoken simultaneously with the participant.

The last transcription task, before entering into the analysis of the narrative, was to identify narrative episodes: places in the text where stories began and concluded or were taken up again later, that is, "listening for entrance and exit talk" (Riessman, 1993). I attempted to identify stories within stories in order to understand the temporal sequencing of the story line and to determine the unfolding of the plot. Finally, it must be noted that transcription is always partial; in any specified notation system, some aspects of speech are included while others are excluded (Mishler, 1986). The inclusion/exclusion dimension of transcription practices only points to the assumptions held by the transcriber/interpreter (Denzin, 1997; Ellis et al., 1997; Kvale, 1996; Richardson, 1990).

FOUR COLLABORATIVE INTERPRETIVE READINGS OF THE TRANSCRIPT

In this stage of the research process, the participants and I collaboratively participated in engaging the transcribed text in a meaningful way. I prepared a reading guide for participants to follow. I photocopied the transcript onto 11 by 17 inch paper and drew four columns in the right margin. The participants were given four different colored pens and asked to interpret the transcript during four separate readings. The general instructions were as follows:

> The following is a guide to assist you in interpreting the text. This process entails at least four readings of the text and perhaps more as the research process unfolds. I am asking you to be the interpreter of your own transcript. The purpose of each reading

is to approach the text from a different standpoint. . . . If there are other readings that you would like to engage in, please call me in order that I may do the same so that our interpretive processes coincide.

Reading for content.

In the first reading, I asked the participants to read for coherence concerning the content of the transcribed research interview. I asked them to make changes if they felt that the text needed be clearer or expanded upon. I also asked them to make corrections if they found errors in this first read through.

Reading for the self of the narrator.

In the second reading, I asked the participants to read for the narrator's self: "Read for the narrator's various 'I' positions. Ask: Who is telling this story? How is she situated in this story? What is she feeling? What are her struggles? How does she present herself? What meaning is she trying to convey? What parts of self does she share and what parts are kept hidden? Why? As the protagonist of her own tale, what does she want to convey to the reader?" The purpose of this reading is to bring to light the ways in which the participant constructs herself in the text.

Reading for the research question.

In the third reading, I asked the participants to read for the struggle with secondary traumatic stress. "What meaning does the narrator make of this struggle? How does she make sense out of her experiences? What is 'not-said', or implied? What are the contradictions between her words and actions and/or your interpretations as the reader? What metaphors does she use and how do they help in making meaning? Take time to reflect on this reading. Perhaps there will be places in the text that resonate with you but you may not be able to articulate what it is-make note of these places for our discussion later." In this reading, I am looking for the details of their personal experience with the research question, but I am also looking for layers of tacit knowledge. I focus on those places in the text (including my research notes from the interview) where the participants have disrupted the flow of conversation—places where they took a moment to pause or "arrest"—in which there appeared to be a shift in consciousness. Shotter (1999) refers to these as "striking," "moving," or "arresting" moments, as moments that have the possibility to "originate new forms of life in us" (p. 7).

216

Reading for relations of power and culture.

The final reading was a critical reading. "As you read the text, look for suggestions of power or gender imbalances. In what ways does the narrator struggle with issues regarding inequities? Where is she silenced? When does she lose her voice? Is the narrator conscious of the power or political influences in her life or of the influences of culture? How do you understand her history/context/social world? In what ways are her 'personal realities' challenged?" In this reading, I am attempting to articulate with the participants the cultural discourse at work in the text.

Interpreting the self of the researcher in the transcript.

As the participants did these four interpretive readings, I also interpreted their transcriptions using these four reading guidelines. However, I also applied the four readings to my own interaction in the transcript. Believing that the research interview is a co-construction, I needed to know the ways in which I, as the researcher, influenced the production of this transcript. Steier (1991) defines reflexivity as a turning-back on one's experiences upon oneself wherein the self to which this bending back refers is predicated and must also be understood as socially constructed. He states that "this folding back may unfold as a spiraling, if we allow for multiple perspectives, and acknowledge that the same self may be different as a result of its own self-pointing" (Steier, 1991, p. 3). I reread the transcript four additional times applying the reading guide to myself and made notes in the margins in a different color than the participants'. These notes were crucial to my final interpretation and writing of their narratives.

THE INTERPRETIVE INTERVIEW:
COLLABORATIVE INTERPRETATION OF THE TEXT

The third conversation with the participants, the interpretive conversation, was audio taped and lasted approximately three hours. We retrospectively, collaboratively and reflexively discussed the interpretations from the four readings, then listened and responded to each other's renderings. Our conversation was very moving and informative as we explored the meanings of the metaphors, attempted to comprehend ambiguous parts of the narrative account, and struggled to see the cultural implications of our interpretations. Some of the questions at this stage were: "What do you think this means?" "Where do you think you learned that?" "What were your feelings about that?" "There seems to be something left out here – something not said. What do you think this piece is about?" "Is there anything more here that needs to be said?" "What do you wish could have happened?" "What did you learn from this experience?" "There is something that I see in this piece, what do you think?" "How does my interpretation fit with yours?" And finally, I asked, "Is there anything more you would like to add to this interpretation?" Remembering that this was an interactive, dialogical co-construction, I also applied these questions to my own participation and interpretations. I shared these with the participants and recorded my responses in a journal to assist me in writing their stories.

WRITING THE STORY

The next task before writing my participants' narratives was to summarize our interpretive readings into one blended text. I first developed clarity on each of the readings, and then devised a plot line placing the episodes in sequential and temporal order. I wrote the stories as first person accounts as a literary device in an attempt to bring their stories back to life. These narrative accounts were my own construction, carefully crafted through a reflexive and collaborative research process. Unlike traditional psychological research where the author of the text is concealed and the lives of the participants are objectified by writing in the third person, I did not want to reduce my participants to themes or categories. Acknowledging that the academic author is always present in the text (Richardson, 1997), I wrote their stories as part of my own. My desire was to create embodied texts that value emotionality. I wanted to engage the reader and bring to life the multiple interpretations that informed the creation of their narratives. Their stories are teaching tales full of instructions about the meaning of the struggle with secondary traumatic stress and how to survive in the field of trauma. Their tales are not modernist tales with a clear plot line, building to a crisis point and ending with a resolution. Their stories are postmodern tales— issues were left unresolved, in a chaotic bombardment for the reader to disentangle. Their accounts were contradictory and ambiguous, like "real" life, life in process, a chapter not yet finished.

The reader may be overwhelmed at this point by the time constraints involved in this collaborative narrative method. However, the narrative method can also be used without the collaborative element. If time is a factor, the researcher can accomplish narrative analysis without the participation of the research participants by simply utilizing the four readings. However, the interpretive process will be compromised. The narratives without the collaborative process become the researcher's stories and rely solely on the researcher's interpretation of the meaning of the participants' lived experiences.

PUTTING THE HEART BACK INTO CONSTRUCTIVIST RESEARCH

I was recently inspired by a keynote address given by Miller Mair at the 18th International Human Science Research Conference in Sheffield, England. Miller asked the audience: "Where is the heart in human science research?" He reminds us that we need to return to the original quest in human science, where the word inquiry meant "to quest" – the quest meaning spiritual, personal, meaningful inquiry. It is about keeping taps on the heart of research; being willing to engage fully with the text and to stay alive to the life as told. It is a transformative practice as it can place both the researcher and the participants' lives into question. We write emotional research texts to compel the reader, to persuade and to move the reader into consciousness or action. Our hope is to bring the everyday life into the foreground—looking at the micro to see how the macro is at play. The inside view of the individual's struggle can tell us a great deal about how culture works. Writing-up my participants lives is a very complex process. All parties' claims to knowledge are put into question. Analysis of the data never ends. Our interpretations are infinite because our storied lives are always open to further findings.

I chose to write my participants' stories as evocative tales as an attempt to put the "heart back into the research text." Understanding that we live in linguistic habitats (Efran & Heffner, 1997) that everything we know and can communicate is delivered through language, that we are constituted in and through our language practices, we must recognize the power of our own words. Language shapes who we are. Postmodern theorists and philosophers continue to tell us so. Volosinov (1986) and other postmodern writers (Bakhtin, 1986; Ricoeur, 1984; Shotter, 1996) proclaim that expression creates being. Miller Mair (1999) claims that "words live us." Therefore, writing embodied research texts are political acts wrought with a variety of ethical dilemmas. At its best it is participatory, emancipatory and transformative. New stories, embodied stories that reflect the life world of the living, have the potential to impact on new practices. Their embodied stories, as research stories that speak from the heart, have the power to impact political systems and act as bridges between the political and the pragmatic.

Finally, writing the evocative text as a first-person research account is a way to address Derrida's (1967) dilemma of the unrecoverable act of storytelling. The evocative research text is an attempt to relive the "story as told" by fashioning a new telling—but it is paradoxical. The researcher writes the text knowing that it is an illusion to think that one can recover the story as given. But it is all that we have and if the text is taken back to the originator of the story for approval and creating consensus, then the process has integrity. The author's interpretation is front and center.

CONSTRUCTIVISTS ASK: WHY BOTHER?

Why is "embodied" research important to the enterprise of constructivist psychology? The human in constructivist research lives in a sentient body and is a complex subject. This complexity cannot easily be discerned in traditional experimental research designs or in repertory grid research. It is not enough to present the everyday life world if the living being is absent from the text.

Chief Dan George once said something to this effect:

> "When you speak from the heart, the heart of the other listens and hearts are transformed."

Writing embodied research for the constructivist researcher holds promise for transformative practices through the profound phenomenon of resonance—a human emotional response. Perhaps it is time that constructivist researchers bring to their research practices their beliefs about the importance of mind/body integration and engage in research that is congruent with these beliefs—a research that is embodied, holistic, and participatory.

REFERENCES

Arvay, E. R. (2000). *Slam poetry as a solution to teenage apathy*. Persuasive speech presented at the World Public Speaking and Debating Competition, Nicosia, Cyprus.

Arvay, M. J. (1998). *Secondary traumatic stress: Stories of struggle and hope*. Unpublished doctoral dissertation, University of Victoria, Victoria, BC, Canada

Arvay, M. J. & Uhlemann, M. R. (1996). Counsellor stress in the field of trauma: A preliminary study. *Canadian Journal of Counselling, 30*, 193-210.

Bakhtin, M. M. (1984). *Problems of Dostoevsky's poetics*. (C. Emerson, Ed. and Trans.). Minneapolis: University of Minnesota Press.

Bakhtin, M. M. (1986). *Speech genres and other late essays.* (V. W. McGee, Trans.). Austin, TX: University of Texas Press.

Bakhtin, M. M. (1993). *Toward a philosophy of the act.* (M. Holquist, Ed. and Vadim Lianpov, Trans.). Austin, TX: University of Texas Press.

Barthes, R. (1966). *Introduction to the structural analysis of the narrative.* Occasional paper, Centre for Contemporary Cultural Studies, University of Birmingham, England.

Bruner, J. (1986). *Actual minds, possible worlds.* Cambridge, MA: Harvard University Press.

Burr. V. (1995). *An introduction to social constructionism.* London: Routledge.

Chase, S. (1995). Taking narrative seriously: Consequences for method and theory in interview studies. In R. Josselson & A. Lieblich (Eds.), *Interpreting experience: The narrative study of lives* (Vol. 3, pp. 1-26). Thousand Oaks, CA: Sage.

Denzin, N. K. (1989). *Interpretive interactionism.* Newbury Park, CA: Sage.

Denzin, N. K. (1997). *Interpretive ethnography: Ethnographic practices for the 21st century.* Thousand Oaks, CA: Sage.

Derrida, J. (1967). *Of grammatology.* (G. Spivak, Trans.). Baltimore, MD: The John Hopkins University Press.

Efran, J. S., & Heffner, K. P. (1997, July). *Constructivism: An epistemological and clinical muddle?* Paper presented at the meeting of the North American Personal Construct Network, Seattle, WA.

Efran, J. S., Lukens, M. D., & Lukens, R. J. (1990). *Language, structure, and change: Frameworks of meaning in psychotherapy.* New York: Norton.

Ellis, C., Kiesinger, C. E., & Tillman-Healy, L. M. (1997). Interactive interviewing. In R. Hertz (Ed.), *Reflexivity and voice* (pp. 119-149). Thousand Oaks, CA: Sage.

Follette, V. M., Polusny, M. M., & Milbeck, K. (1994). Mental health and law enforcement professionals: Trauma history, psychological symptoms, and impact of providing services to child sexual abuse survivors. *Professional Psychology: Research and Practice, 25,* 275-282.

Gergen, K. J. (1994). *Realities and relationships.* Cambridge, MA: Harvard University Press.

Green, B. L. (1996). Psychometric review of Trauma History Questionnaire (Self-Report). In B. H. Stamm (Ed.). *Measurement of stress, trauma, and adaptation* (pp. 366-368). Lutherville, MD: Sidran Press.

Hermans, H. J. M., Rijks, T. I., & Kempen, H. J. (1993). Imaginal dialogues in the self: Theory and method. *Journal of Personality, 61,* 207-236.

Hoskins, M. & Arvay, M. J. (1999). The quagmire of researching the self: Implications for constructivism. *Constructivism in the Human Sciences 4,* 13-31

Kaufman, A. (Ed.). (1999). *The outlaw bible of American poetry.* New York: Thunder's Mouth Press.

Kelly, G. A. (1955). *The psychology of personal constructs* (2 vols.). New York: Norton.

Kvale, S. (1996). *InterViews: An introduction to qualitative research interviewing.* Thousand Oaks, CA: Sage.

Mair, M. (1999, July). *Where's the heart in human and social science research?* Paper presented at the meeting of the International Human Science Research Conference, Sheffield, England.

Mahoney, M. J. (1991). *Human change processes.* New York: Basic Books.

Mahoney, M. J. (2000). Core ordering and disordering processes: A constructive view of psychological development. In R. A. Neimeyer & J. D. Raskin (Eds.), *Constructions of disorder: Meaning-making frameworks for psychotherapy.* (pp. 43-62). Washington, DC: American Psychological Association.

Mishler, E. G. (1986). *Research interviewing: Context and narrative.* Cambridge, MA: Harvard University Press.

Neimeyer, R. A. & Raskin, J. D. (2000). On practicing postmodern therapy in modern times. In R. A. Neimeyer & J. D. Raskin (Eds.), *Constructions of disorder: Meaning-making frameworks for psychotherapy.* (pp. 3-14). Washington, DC: American Psychological Association.

Pinkola-Estes, C. (1992). *Women who run with wolves: Myths and stories of the wild woman archetype.* New York: Ballantine Books.

Polanyi, L. (1985). *Telling the American story: A structural and cultural analysis of conversational storytelling.* Norwood, NJ: Ablex.

Polkinghorne, D. E. (1988). *Narrative knowing and the human sciences.* Albany, NY: State University of New York Press.

Richardson, L. (1990). *Writing strategies: Researching diverse audiences.* Newbury Park, CA: Sage.

Richardson, L. (1997). *Fields of play: Constructing an academic life.* New Brunswick, NJ: Rutgers University Press.

Ricoeur, P. (1984). *Time and narrative.* Chicago, IL: University of Chicago Press.

Riessman, C. K. (1993). *Narrative analysis.* Newbury Park, CA: Sage.

Sarbin, T. R. (Ed.). (1986). *Narrative psychology: The storied nature of human conduct.* New York: Praeger.

Schauben, L. J. & Frazier, P. A. (1995). Vicarious trauma: The effects on female counselors working with sexual violence survivors. *Psychology of Women Quarterly, 19,* 49-64.

Shotter, J. (1993). *Conversational realities: Constructing life through language.* London: Sage.

Shotter, J. (1996). 'Now I can go on': Wittgenstein and our embodied embeddedness in the 'hurly-burly' of life. *Human Studies, 19,* 385-407.

Shotter, J. (1999, October). *Dialogue, depth, and life inside responsive orders: From external observation to participatory understanding.* Paper presented at conference on Dialogues on Performing Knowledge, Stockholm, Sweden.

Smith. P. (1992). Skinhead. *Big towns, big talk.* Cambridge, MA: Zoland Books.

Steier, F. (Ed.). (1991). *Research and reflexivity.* Newbury Park, CA: Sage.

Volosinov, V. N. (1986). *Marxism and the philosophy of language.* (By L. Matejka & I. R.

Titunik, Trans.). Cambridge, MA: Harvard University Press.

Weiss, D. (1996). Psychometric review of the Impact of Event Scale—Revised. In B. H. Stamm (Ed.). *Measurement of stress, trauma, and adaptation* (pp.186-188). Lutherville, MD: Sidran Press.

Wittgenstein, L. (1953). *Philosophical investigations*. (G. Anscombe, Trans.). New York: Macmillan.

Wittgenstein, L. (1981). *Zettel*, (2nd ed.). G. E. M. Anscombe & G. H. V. Wright, (Eds. and Trans.), Oxford: Blackwell.

CHAPTER 11

Towards New Methodologies For Constructivist Research: Synthesizing Knowledges For Relational Inquiries

Marie Hoskins

CONSTRUCTIVISM AND NEW PARADIGM RESEARCH

In the late eighties as a member of a constructivist research team, I fully embraced personal construct theory and constructivism,[1] but by the time I began my doctoral work 4 years later my enthusiasm was beginning to wane. These theories, I believed, were ethnocentric, without sensitivity to issues of gender, and void of any acknowledgment of the "real effects" of people's material lives. Just reshuffle your construct systems and everything would be fine, was my interpretation of the central thesis. At that time, there were few constructivist women (this is still a problem), and for the most part, literature about psychotherapy consisted of men describing women's experiences. Disappointed, I turned away from constructivist writing and focused instead on feminist theory, critical ethnography, and cultural studies—where issues of ethnicity, gender, and discourse were central organizing themes. While I was engrossed in these perspectives, constructivist theory expanded considerably, emphasizing the contextual, gendered, and discursive aspects of subjectivity. I have returned to this theory with not only a renewed sense of appreciation, but also with a broader sense of the parallels between constructivism and what is commonly referred to as "new paradigm research" (Denzin & Lincoln, 2000). After walking between these

---

[1] I have avoided discussion about the subtle and not so subtle distinctions between various streams of constructivism. Instead, I have borrowed heavily from texts that "represent" constructivist psychotherapy, such as Mahoney (1991) and Neimeyer and Mahoney (1995), so that I could illustrate the parallels between constructivist theory and practice, and new paradigm research.

225

two bodies of knowledge, I have synthesized my learning into an account of how each one can inform the other.

In this chapter I discuss the need for new methodologies in psychological research, the parallels between constructivist theory and interpretive research, and how constructivists are prepared to work in what I am referring to as *relational research*. The purpose in taking up these issues is to highlight possibilities for researching human experience that, for a variety of reasons, constructivist psychologists, psychotherapists, and counselors have not fully embraced. Few constructivists are working on developing new paradigm research methodologies. Despite the proliferation of qualitative methodologies in sociology, cultural studies, education, and anthropology, psychology as a whole has lagged behind. In a recent edition of the *Handbook of Qualitative Research* (Denzin & Lincoln, 2000), considered to be a state of the art treatise, the lack of adequate representation from psychology is apparent. Although psychology is beginning to call into question what a modernist version of science has counted as legitimate knowledge, several other disciplines have been engaged in this debate for decades.

NEW SCIENCES: RECONSTITUTING MODERN SCIENCE

There are many speculations about why the reluctance to wholeheartedly embrace what is referred to as "new paradigm research" (Denzin & Lincoln, 2000) exists. For the most part psychology's strong desire to gain legitimacy from the natural sciences has thwarted the development of methodologies congruent with human science research. This collusion with natural science has resulted in what some believe is a discipline that has not lived up to its full potential when it comes to understanding the complexities of human experience (Cushman, 1995). Particularly interesting from a history of science perspective is that this collusion has taken place at a time when science itself has undergone dramatic transformations. The natural science that psychology once thought it knew is no longer that character.

In many disciplines it is commonly accepted that Science, rather than being narrowly defined as a body of knowledge, has been reconstituted as the study of how knowledge is produced, reclaiming its origin, *sciere*, meaning to know. This redefinition is the result of several revisions to our understandings of reality. Advances made within the areas of relativity and the self-regulating universe have contributed to notions of the relative, as opposed to the absolute, and universal Truth has been replaced with multiple and local truths. The ability to separate the knower from the known has been repeatedly challenged (Carlsen, 1988; Capra, 1982; Efran & Fauber, 1995; Mahoney, 1991; Maturana & Varela, 1987). Knowledge is now viewed as non-reductionist, chaotic, non-linear, (Gleick, 1987), and historically contingent (Foucault, 1980).

Feminist scholarship has re-conceptualized processes of knowing, defining them as gendered, relational, contextual, and local (Belenky, Clinchy, Goldberger, & Tarule, 1986; Goldberger, Tarule, Clinchy, & Belenky, 1996). Power permeates how we come to know (Harding, 1991; Lather, 1991; Nicholson, 1990). Social constructionists have emphasized that language constitutes, but does not represent, reality (Efran & Fauber, 1995; Gergen, 1991). All of these assumptions about how we come to know, which are also the foundation for various constructivist perspectives (Efran & Fauber, 1995; Guidano, 1987; Mahoney, 1991, 1996; Neimeyer & Mahoney, 1995), call into question the ways in which knowledge is produced when practicing research. The parallels between "new science"(Capra, 1982, 1997; Harding, 1991; Maturana & Varela, 1987; Mingers, 1995; Wilbur, 1998), constructivist theory, and "new paradigm research" however, are seldom discussed. These new ways of conceptualizing knowing processes have been developing simultaneously, but often in different geographical and disciplinary locations.

There are several similarities in the foundations of qualitative research and constructivist theory, as Lincoln and Guba (2000) have clearly articulated, but when it comes to translating these similarities into psychological research these arguments seem to be left behind. Thus, the applicability to human science research remains buried in debates about what actually constitutes "rigorous" psychological research. The lack of clearly articulated discussions has meant that while all of these advancements in knowing processes are intricately connected, they do not tend to build on each other when it comes to developing psychological research. This lack of synthesis has serious implications for helping professionals. Neglecting to synthesize these domains of knowledge has done little to help with the onerous task of understanding the complexities of human experience that continue to challenge contemporary psychologists, especially those engaged in clinical practice, leaving the gap between research and practice as wide as ever.

Such a gap continues to make practitioners wary of the applicability of psychological research (Howard, 1985, 1993; Polkinghorne, 1988, 1991). Critics contend that research is decontextualized, void of subjective meanings, not applicable to individual cases, and excludes the co-creative dimension of human inquiry. Some take their criticisms further by claiming there are major errors in psychology's understanding of human experience because of the discipline's obsessive need for prediction, control, and generalizeabilty (Tolman, 2000).[2] In a recent edition of the *American Behavioral Scientist* (1998) devoted to concerns about the nature and direction of psychological research, the editors point out that through

> some great irony of history, psychology, the social science which seeks to plumb the most personal and intimate spheres of living or matters of the soul, is also one of the disciplines most passionately and ideologically committed to the canons of dispassionate and objective science. (Richardson & Fowers, 1998, p. 466)

This dispassionate and objective science has neglected to inform clinical practice to the extent many hoped, and several theorists argue that psychology has not had the impact on the human condition many dreamed was possible (Chorover, 1990; Cushman, 1995; Denzin & Lincoln, 1994; Denzin, 1997; Heshusius & Ballard, 1996; Horgan, 1996; Howard, 1985, 1986, 1993; Kvale, 1996; Lather, 1991; Polkinghorne, 1988; Richardson & Fowers, 1998; Sexton, 1997). Outcome studies on the efficacy of clinical practice are inconclusive, social problems still exist, and the overall physical, spiritual, and emotional health of the next generation—according to many—is at risk. At an international psychology conference, when research results were contradictory, ambiguous, and too abstract for practitioners to translate into practice, researchers concluded that

---

[2] Tolman argues that if it is assumed that "behavior" can be adequately understood in terms of stimulus and response, then ascertaining correlations of independent and dependent variables makes good sense. In addition, if the purpose of psychological knowledge is to better control people instead of understanding them, then statistical analysis of large sample sizes also makes sense. See Kvale (1996) and Denzin and Lincoln (2000) for futher discussions on the issue.

In constructivist theory, behavior (action) is viewed as teleological, agentic, and intentional. Generalized knowledge cannot be imposed on human action because of these self-organizing aspects of human experiencing. In this chapter I am arguing that if we want to understand how a person makes sense of his or her own experience in relation to discourse, then inter-subjectivity needs to be the primary mode of investigation.

what they needed was larger sample sizes so that margins of error could be eliminated. Questions of meaning, the relationship between culture (media) and identity, the challenges of everyday living in local contexts, and relationships between people, which are all issues that challenge practitioners in their offices, were virtually ignored. Regardless of the acknowledgment of these kinds of issues, there appears to be widespread reluctance within psychology to move beyond methodologies that are closely tied to a method originally intended to study the material world. This pervasive reluctance can be understood through exploring the politics of research and the dominant scientific discourse, by examining issues of academic identities, and by analyzing the allocation of research funds. But rather than taking up these issues in an effort to understand the source of reluctance, a focus on the possibilities for expanding the repertoire of human science methodologies is perhaps more fruitful. As mentioned earlier, constructivist theory, "new science thinking" (Capra, 1997), and qualitative research have theoretical constructs already in place. By highlighting the parallels between constructivist therapy and new paradigm research, a revitalized scientific study of human experience can be advanced not only for minimizing the gap between research and practice, but also for contributing to a science that re-presents the complexities and depths of human experiences.

Given that most, if not all, psychological inquiry involves the self in one way or another, how the self is portrayed in constructivist theory provides the background for this discussion. It is constructivists' contributions to understanding human beings as complex, relational, evolving, and self-organizing systems (Mahoney, 1991) that can expand the repertoire of human science research. Such contributions can be more fully utilized by capitalizing on the intersections between constructivist psychotherapy and human science research. Having discussed the changing character of science, psychology's reluctance to respond to this change, and constructivism's capacity to inform research methodologies, I want to clarify that I am referring to a particular kind of research, one that moves into the realm of the meanings of being human. I am referring to a methodology that explores human experience in an intersubjective way, one that ultimately renders it a *relational inquiry*.

Elsewhere, I have argued that epistemological and ontological congruence adds validity or strength to an inquiry (Hoskins & Arvay, 1999; Hoskins, 2000). Such congruence between epistemology, ontology, and method is acknowledged in clinical practice.

However, in traditional modes of research—for example positivist psychological research and some forms of constructivist research—minimal attention is paid to these kinds of issues. It appears the dominant discourse or the received view has not had to articulate the fundamental assumptions that gave rise to its methodologies. On the other hand, what is particularly significant about the new paradigm (including new sciences, qualitative research, and constructivism) is their contributions to knowing processes. How people come to know is as important as what they know. Capra (1997) argues that science has moved from being an "objective" effort to an epistemic effort where "the method of questioning [of how we come to know] becomes an integral part of scientific theories" (p. 40). If the self is a process of knowing, then it makes sense that how the self is perceived has direct links to how it is researched. As constructivist researchers, we need to get closer to the heart of the epistemological positions embodied in clinical practice. In other words, theories of the self should be congruent with methodological assumptions, whether in clinical practice in terms of interventions used, or in research, when specific research strategies are chosen. I want to state up front that I am not proposing a "one size fits all" approach to research; rather I am suggesting that there are dimensions and realms of human experience that cannot be addressed by what has been the dominant discourse for psychological research. Constructivist therapists pay particular attention to the multiple dimensions of human experience but, ironically, tend to ignore or minimize these complexities in their research. This neglect happens in a variety of ways, including how objectivity is dealt with, how holistic accounts are regarded, how the processes of research are enacted, and finally, how research is reported. All of these aspects of knowing processes and representations of knowledge need to be carefully considered when choosing methodologies for human science research. The question that needs to be asked is: If human beings are actively complex, socially embedded, and developmentally dynamic self-organizing systems, what are the most appropriate methodologies to research this kind of self?

The Subjectivity/Objectivity Dimension: A Different Relationship

We have to understand science. Scientia is knowledge. Only in the popular mind is it equated with facts. This is flattering, since facts are incontrovertible. But it is also demeaning, since facts are meaningless. Science, by contrast, is story-telling; it searches for a beginning, middle and end.

(John Polyani, Nobel Laureate, 2000, p. A15)

People actively construe their own realities, and in turn, these active interpretations constitute their lives. This interdependent relationship renders people as subjective beings who not only are socially and culturally embedded, but who engage in co-creative processes of knowing. As a consequence, the pursuit of knowledge is always a *relational inquiry.* Mahoney (1991) argues "knowledge is neither a disembodied collection of information nor a possession....knowing is inescapably open-ended, dynamic and simultaneously personal and collective" (p. 24). We cannot know in isolation, nor is it possible to observe a phenomenon in some kind of uncontaminated form free from the influence of the observer (Kelly, 1955; Mahoney, 1991; Maturana & Varela, 1987). These fundamental constructivist assumptions about the self and its processes of knowing have shaped clinical practice, but have not had the same impact on the nature and direction of psychological research. Although the purposes of therapy and research are different in some respects, in several ways they are similar, particularly when engaging in interpretive research. These similarities will become apparent in the remainder of this chapter. I have organized a description of interpretive research around the themes of intersubjectivity and embodied knowing. My purpose is twofold. First, I wish to illustrate the parallels between constructivist psychotherapy and newer methodologies. Second, I wish to demonstrate how constructivist researchers can expand the methodologies they use without compromising their theoretical integrity. As a way of explicating these ideas, the following description from a research project will be used. I recount my first meeting with a young woman who volunteered to be in one of my eating disorder studies. By presenting a descriptive rendering I hope to convey the complexity of working relationally with participants.

231

On a warm, sunny spring afternoon, while tired professors prepare to shut down their computers for the weekend, I prepare to meet the first potential participant in my doctoral research. A faint knock on my half opened office door is barely audible as I sit answering the endless onslaught of e-mails many of us cannot escape. I open the door to meet a young, attractive woman who I guess is about 25 years old, give or take a few years. She could have been one of my undergraduate students I imagine, except for her dark hollow looking eyes that showed little life or excitement, especially for a sunny Friday afternoon.

"Can I get you anything?" I ask, ushering her in. "Coffee, tea?" Gesturing to the remaining half of a chocolate bar left over from my afternoon tea break, I raise my eyebrows. "Chocolate?" With a look of disgust that was impossible to hide she politely responds, "No thanks, I'm full."

"Well," I chirp in, determined to make her feel at ease, "how about if you sit over there and tell me a bit about yourself, and then I'll tell you what I plan to do with my research project over the next few years." She sits in the only other available chair and painfully, lets out a long, endless sigh.

"I'm so sorry," she says with a shaky voice, "I'm not really feeling very well today." And as she takes a long, slow breath in, I notice that her hands are trembling and her nervousness begins to affect my own level of comfort.

"I'm not myself yet," she exhales slowly. "I know it doesn't make any sense to anyone, especially to my parents. I'm trying so hard but I just don't know what else to do."

Her voice trails off into a deep void and the silence is so deafening that I wonder if and when I should speak. I decide to sit patiently with the silence. She is visibly upset and I realize that she is about to lose the control she is trying so hard to maintain. And as her eyes fill up and the tears can no longer be contained, they begin to spill over, falling down her thin bony cheeks, past a flat chest, onto her lap where skeleton-like hands clutch a small brown package tied with string circled several times. Tears begin to land on her long flowery skirt, just narrowly missing the mysterious package. I feel my eyes finding solace in fixating on the string wrapped ever so carefully. Just as the minutes are beginning to feel like hours, she gains composure from I'm not sure where. She begins to wipe back the tears with the sleeve of a sweater that is at least two sizes too big, and stares at her lap.

"I've never shared the journals during my illness with anyone," she eventually tells me, "but when I heard about your research, I thought you might be interested."

This package, containing her most cherished and most anguished experiences, holds secrets too painful to be held back by string alone no matter how many times it circles around. Four tightly bound journals, all neatly stacked, wrapped in plain brown paper were yearning to break free.

"I want you to read them," she says softly, but firmly.

At that moment she handed over the tidy package wrapped ever so carefully that held the most horrific, messy stories of anguish, torment, and deep, heart-wrenching despair. Before any words were spoken, before any research plans were shared, or consent forms signed, we began a relationship that would last for years. With her life story in her hands, this young woman who was barely audible, almost invisible, confidently stretched trusting arms towards me with the raw materials of her innermost pain—pain that was felt in ways I could only imagine but was determined to come to know deeply, compassionately and ethically. While solemnly sitting with the reverence of a shared promise, our search for understanding began.

Two strangers meet to share volumes of layers of stories—all interconnected and, at the same time, partial and contradictory. These are the challenging experiences counselors and researchers face. Trauma and despair, whether through loss, abuse, or in this case a fourteen-year struggle with a life threatening eating disorder, are common client issues. While meeting my first participant, I felt incredibly challenged by the trust and hope she willingly instilled in our "research" relationship. I wondered how I could sort through the complexities of her life in order to make sense of her experiences and in turn, how she constituted herself. I also wondered how I could possibly understand the depth and breadth of her difficulties, not as a counselor but as a researcher. Given the complexity of her life story I struggled to find (or create) a methodology that would guide me through these challenges, particularly in light of my understanding of what it means to do psychological research within a constructivist framework.

INTERSUBJECTIVITY: WORKING IN THE SPACES BETWEEN

In counseling contexts, constructivists move between clients' constructions of realities and the ways in which those realities have constituted their lives. Therapists continuously pay attention to these individual interpretations and lived realities in relation to their own. The development of *alternating perception* makes it possible for constructivist counselors to work relationally with multiple kinds of knowledge, to pay careful attention to personal meanings, and to explore the discourses that surround them. The capacity to work in the spaces between the personal and the collective, and to hold the tensions between subjectivity and objectivity, means that constructivist practitioners are familiar working within an epistemology where objectivity is dealt with in different ways.

Constructivists are not overly concerned with "factual" knowledge, rather they are more concerned with emotional truths and how such "truths" have affected clients' lives. Whether or not certain events happened in an historical sense means less to a constructivist counselor than how interpretations of events have shaped their lives. Perceptions of experience, how people make sense of their experience, and how they create lives within networks of relationships become the primary "data" for counselors and their clients. The same is true for researchers who distinguish between emotional truth and "historical truth." How participants make sense of their worlds moves researchers away from verifying "facts," and observing and/or quantifying behaviors, towards interactions focused on meanings.

The distinction between emotional and historical truth is an important and difficult distinction to grasp when issues of truth, validity, and credibility are used to evaluate research. In order to generate knowledge that moves beyond subjective meanings, one must act "as if" there is an objective world while, at the same time, acknowledge that objectivity is merely a social construction or a consensual perspective. George Kelly would have understood this kind of psychological positioning in research where objectivity is revisited, but with a different understanding and in turn, a different ontology. Constructivists understand the difference between shared and unique realities and how interpretations constitute people's identities or self processes.

While working with the participant described above I needed to use my generalized psychological knowledge gleaned from several years of reviewing literature, and engaging in practice, in a

234

tentative and exploratory way. Much like the processes used in counseling contexts, where dialectically we make distinctions by comparing and contrasting, refining and elaborating, and in the end, synthesizing, these same meaning-making processes are used. Generalized knowledge therefore is not used as a map of the Truth, rather it is used as a temporary platform from which to construct new understandings and knowledge.

With my participant, I often introduced psychological theories of eating disorders to act as catalysts for further discussion. In response to these theories, she described how they did or did not fit with her experience. None of the theories were a perfect fit, which calls into question the ways in which generalized psychological knowledge is regarded and applied. Such theories, like the stories we shared, were partial and incomplete truths. Particularly important was that my participant was creating her own theory while interacting with the dominant discourse of psychology. Intersubjectively, we negotiated the meanings of her experiences in relation to other plausible explanations. This research process parallels constructivist processes of meaning making in practice.

In therapy, clients are provided with a context for inquiry, not a prescription for how to live their lives. As Efran and Fauber (1995) point out, therapy "provides a framework in which to note that people are truly responsible for answering their own questions and that a meaningful life existence cannot be obtained in any other way" (p. 302). Although my participant handed me concrete journals as data that could have been used for an "objective" textual analysis, how she made sense of her recorded experiences and how we could, together, piece those events into a cohesive narrative that could be useful to her, me, and others, became the focus of the inquiry. My interpretations and understandings were informed by hers and vice versa. There were times when I wondered if her descriptions of events could have actually happened (as some were almost impossible to fathom), but what refocused my attention was my commitment to understand how she made sense of her interpretations and how those interpretations affected her sense of self.

Once the effort to be objective is set aside, researchers can begin to build different kinds of relationships for their inquiries. Rather than holding onto the "detached observer role" that is so prevalent in psychological research, researchers can engage in the same participatory models of inquiry they are familiar with in practice. Despite differences in purposes, both counseling and research provide contexts for the generation of knowledge. Both of these

235

knowledge producing environments require collaboration and cannot be fully accessed by taking an "objective stance." To assume that objectivity uncovers reality, as it really exists, is to lack a full understanding of the co-creative process of the production of knowledge.

Given these different ways of relating to objectivity, it is not a matter of consciously choosing to be objective or subjective. When researchers work intersubjectively, they do so not to be collaborative, as in certain feminist methodologies, but because they realize there is no other option (McNamee & Gergen, 1999). It is only within these intersubjective spaces, or what Reason (1993) refers to as "sacred places," where the negotiation between the knower and the known creates new understandings. Once the value of these intersubjective spaces are fully appreciated there is no inclination to attempt to be either objective or subjective, rather the challenge is to fully acknowledge and reveal the intersubjective knowing processes that arise. Intimate connections with the question are the ways in which constructivists inquire in practice, paying attention to embodied knowing. The familiarity with these kinds of therapeutic relationships means that constructivist researchers are competent in traversing these terrains so that quality relational inquiries can be conducted.

EMBODIED AND PARTICIPATORY KNOWING

Constructivists understand the "primacy of the abstract," which Mahoney (1996) describes as "the most basic and important human processes of organizing our moment-to-moment experience [and which] operates at levels far beyond what we consider conscious awareness" (p. 389). Bodily knowing, mind/body connection, embodiment, and mindfulness are concepts used in constructivist theory, particularly as they pertain to processes of knowing within the counseling context. Mahoney (1996) points out that in the future, these holistic and embodied ways of working will only increase. Although constructivists acknowledge these ways of knowing in practice and everyday life, they tend to minimize such processes in their research.

In research, connected, participatory, and embodied knowing requires the researcher to engage in total immersion in the phenomenon. Profound interest, curiosity, acute attention, and complete openness are the ways that researchers proceed. Schwandt (2000) describes engagement as more than a "confession of positionality" and, instead, as the willingness to risk "one's stance and acknowledge the ongoing liminal experience of living between familiarity and strangeness" (p. 207). Also clarifying engagement in research, Heshusius (1992) describes her own process while exploring experiences of mentally challenged youth in a group home setting. It is not just a matter of acknowledging one's own values and emotions. She explains:

> I had to dissolve (rather than restrain) the emotions that stood between me (the knower) and them (the known). What was needed was an act of identification, a momentary unity, even if only an imagined possibility, that dissolved distance. It was something I (all of me, not part of me) had to do as a knower. Only then could I forget about myself (and the idea of managing distance between us) and fully attend and learn directly from them. (p. 26)

This kind of engagement or embodied knowing is holistic, not in a Batesonian sense, but consistent with Wilbur's (1998) work on emphasizing the dimensionality of human experience. While criticizing modern science for its flatland or exterior approach, Wilbur claims that most scientific research has failed to have the impact it could have had because it rejects, or at the very least, minimizes interior dimensions, or subjective experiences. Rather than focusing on unidimensional systems models, multidimensional perspectives remind researchers to focus holistically, including such aspects of human experience as spirituality, embodiment, intuitive knowing, and passion.

The tensions between subjectivity and intersubjectivity, or the intrapsychic and interpersonal self, are acknowledged by constructivists, but not resolved by any absolutes. In research, methodologies that acknowledge and work with these tensions are congruent with a constructivist framework. Understanding how people construct their lives and are also constrained by certain discourses allows for a deepened understanding of the complexities of negotiating identities in a postmodern context. The inclusion of all of these aspects of human experience means that different questions can be addressed, such as: How does a person construct his or her identity within a particular context? What meanings are made in relation to the person in his or her material and spiritual world? How does a person embody such meanings? Where and how has this person positioned him or herself within a network of relationships? These are the kinds of multidimensional questions that constructivist practitioners and researchers confront when trying to understand the narratives of people's lives.

237

One of the challenges that face researchers who think holistically and want to portray their work as embodied is that research reports, particularly in psychology, are often flat and unidimensional. To present findings as universal, complete, causal, and objective accounts of lifeworlds presents a kind of simulacra that is misleading, and perhaps one of the main contributors to the gaps between research and practice. Life and practice are full of complex, polyvocal texts (Denzin, 1994) but traditional research often presents life as cohesive, linear and contained within a singular narrative. As Efran and Fauber (1995) contend:

> The desire to give each thing (as created in language), a discrete beginning and end generates, as in the classic chicken-and-egg problem, a virtually endless supply of explanatory paradoxes. The process loops in which people live do not necessarily have identifiable, objective beginnings and ends, nor can exact, lineal cause-effect sequences be defined. (p. 289)

Psychological research reports tend to be void of emotionality and authors often refrain from using evocative texts for a variety of reasons, some personal and others political. Other social sciences, such as sociology and anthropology, have welcomed different styles of reporting research, but psychology has avoided entering these more expressive forms. Although the journal *Constructivism in the Human Sciences* is an attempt to break with traditional reporting of research, few authors seem to respond to the invitation.

COMPLIMENTARY METHODOLOGIES FOR ENGAGING IN RELATIONAL INQUIRIES

Perhaps most challenging for those not familiar with this kind of interpretive, relational research is that, like constructivist psychotherapy, there are no concrete "how to's" for proceeding. Epistemological, ontological and methodological congruence is what guides the research process. The same theoretical grounding needed to practice constructivist psychotherapy is needed to engage in interpretive research. Researchers need to be willing to revisit foundational premises about the nature of reality, how we come to know, and the nature and process of self-construction in order to cultivate congruence in their research. Cartesian thinking and the underpinnings of certain positivist modes of psychological research need to be re-examined in relation to constructivist research. What this means is that methodologies are not found (or discovered), rather they are created in relation to fundamental assumptions and in

238

relation to the phenomenon of inquiry itself. Nevertheless, the points I have raised in this chapter—including constructivism's different relationship with objectivity, its position on holistic, embodied and participatory knowing, and its attention to the self as an active process of construction within discourse—align constructivists with certain kinds of methodologies and not others. I will briefly highlight some that are particularly relevant for constructivists and ones that fall into the domain of relational inquiries.

Hermeneutic phenomenology is based on three important assumptions that have obvious similarities with constructivism. First, understanding is not a procedure or rule governed undertaking, rather it is a condition of being human, and hence, understanding is interpretation. Second, traditions (sociohistorically inherited biases or prejudices) cannot be filtered out of our interpretations because, like construct systems, they shape what we are and how we understand the world, therefore "the attempt to step outside of the process of tradition would be like trying to step outside of our own skins' (Gallagher, 1992, p. 87). Third, understanding is participatory, conversational and dialogic and is something that is *produced* in that dialogue, not something *reproduced* by an interpreter through that which he or she seeks to understand" (Schwandt, 2000, p. 195). All of these basic assumptions are congruent with how constructivists relate to objectivity, understanding and interpretation. Although some may argue that description is different from explanation (Guidano, 1995), hermeneutic phenomenology argues that in describing something, we are actually explaining its existence. What this methodology allows for is the non-linear, emergent and dialogic processes that simulate human experience.

Constructivism's different relationship with objectivity also aligns it with poststructural methodologies, where structures (or discourses) are not considered external, objective "things," but are socially constructed rules, language games, metaphors, and images that house a wide range of meanings. Therefore, a rule or discourse is objective in as much as groups of people agree it should or does exist. Certain versions of ethnographic research also rely on these same assumptions where individuals are viewed as active, meaning making agents. As Denzin (1997) argues, selves "create experience and in the process of creation constantly transform and defer that which is being described. The meanings of a subject's statements are always in motion" (p. 5). As part of the interpretive turn, Denzin's critical ethnography not only shares similar perspectives of the self

239

as an active meaning-maker, but also explores the social, political and gendered contexts or discourses in which people negotiate their lives. In simplistic terms, these kinds of ethnographers believe that if you want to know how culture works, then ask people about their everyday lives, pay attention to the meanings they ascribe to experiences, and attempt as near as possible to provide thick descriptions of their accounts. Both poststructural and critical ethnographies provide research strategies for exploring the self in context in a way that traditional psychological projects have not been able. When using these methodologies researchers engage in inquiries that illuminate the interrelationships between the active agent and the discourses that constrain life experiences. This way of exploring the self in context expands on methodologies such as Kelly's repertory grid technique so that constructs that are highly personal and meaningful can also be understood as holistic and socially constituted. The ways in which constructivists work in counseling contexts, in particular, their ability to use alternating perception, means that they are well prepared epistemologically and ontologically to conduct these kinds of inquiries.

More recent methodologies (see Gergen & Gergen, 2000) that are embodied and holistic include performance pieces, where audiences are invited into the phenomenon through emotionality, dialogue, monologues, and movement. Mary Gergen's piece on aging in North American culture allowed for an embodied portrayal of ageism, sexism, and in the end, empowerment. Audio-documentaries are also glimpses of embodied culture where sound, images, metaphors, and dialogue are woven together to portray an aspect of human experience. Autoethnographies focus on the person in context where "multiple layers of consciousness are displayed, connecting the personal to the cultural" (Ellis & Bochner, 2000, p. 739). Stories, novels, poetry, and personal essays are just a few of the ways of presenting research that, for the most part, have yet to be fully accepted by psychological researchers. The similarities between constructivist counseling and this genre of research are striking because within these kinds of texts "concrete action, dialogue, emotion, embodiment, spirituality, and self-consciousness are featured, appearing as relational and institutional stories affected by history, social structure and culture" (Ellis & Bochner, 2000. p. 739).

The capacity to work intersubjectively with others, to develop contexts of inquiry, and to engage in embodied, holistic, and mindful ways of understanding human experience means that constructivists can easily move into these kinds of methodologies. Counselor characteristics such as empathy, authentic interest in personal meanings, tolerance for ambiguity and a willingness to stay with difficulties, blended with these capacities, prepare researchers to work with deeply meaningful experiences that have the potential to move people to reflective stillness and then to action.

WHERE TO BEGIN?

If we accept what Polyani (2000) says about science, then all research projects are narratives differing only in their quality and purpose. Whether stories are told through statistical or linguistic representation depends on the inquiry and the audience. Science as a form of storytelling serves different purposes and agendas. What I have highlighted are different versions of telling stories of human experience. I am not suggesting that all research should be done this way; rather I am hoping that constructivists will become more creative in how they engage in research and how they report knowledge.

Constructivists will be challenged to continually create new methodologies that are congruent with their foundational and evolving epistemologies. By sharing knowledge of human experience with those who are engaged in new paradigm research in other disciplines, each one can inform the other. While attending sociology and cultural studies research conferences, the lack of understanding of self and human experience, particularly from a constructivist perspective, is apparent. Sociologists, anthropologists, and cultural theorists could learn much about constructivist theory's knowledge of the constitutive processes of creating a self. At the same time, constructivists can also learn from other disciplines about culture, the constitutive influence of media, and the discursive processes of language (symbols, metaphors, and images) that intersect with creating a self. Hermeneutic phenomenology, poststructural methodologies, performance pieces, narrative analyses, autoethnography, and audio-documentaries all have theoretical constructs in common with constructivism, and could enrich the repertoire of psychological research. To engage in relational inquiries with the same commitment that we engage in clinical practice settings, whether one-to-one or in communities, we need to take advantage of all the rich resources that are now available. Processes of knowing and creating a self are complex and this constructivist knowledge can be used to create more congruent methods, ones that simulate the actively complex, socially embedded and developmentally dynamic and self-organizing aspects of human experience.

Human science research is continually being reconstituted in light of what has been learned from new sciences mentioned earlier in this chapter. Being *scientific* within the landscape of constructivist theory will have different criteria for validity than those bound by an illusion of objectivity. The purpose of this kind of re-visioning is not to erase modern science but to release science from the clutches and rules of method driven inquiries, to allow new methodologies to emerge and thrive.

The participant introduced in this chapter symbolizes the work that is so important and that cannot be left to yesterday's detached, objective methods if we are going to be able to help co-create new understandings and the possibilities for new realities. Research is not just a matter of documenting what is; it can also document what could be. If scientific inquiry is a genre of storytelling, then constructivists have the capacity to tell the incredibly rich narratives of peoples' lives.

REFERENCES

Belenky, M., Clinchy, B., Goldberger, N., & Tarule, J. (1986). *Women's ways of knowing: The development of self, voice, and mind.* New York: Basic Books.

Capra, F. (1982). *The turning point.* New York: Simon & Schuster.

Capra, F. (1997). *The web of life: A new scientific understanding of living systems.* New York: Doubleday.

Carlsen, M. B. (1988). *Meaning-making: Therapeutic processes in adult development.* New York: Norton.

Chorover, Stephan, L. (1990). Paradigms lost and regained: Changing beliefs, values, and practices in neuropsychology. In G. Greenberg & E. Tobach (Eds.), *Theories of evolution of knowing: The T.C. Schneirla conference series* (Vol. 4, pp. 93-106). Hillsdale, NJ: Lawrence Erbaulm Associates.

Cushman, P. (1995). Psychology to 1992: A historically situated interpretation. In D. Freedheim (Ed.), *History of psychotherapy: A century of change* (pp. 21-64). Washington, DC: American Psychological Association.

Denzin, N., & Lincoln, Y. (Eds.). (1994). *Handbook of qualitative research.* CA: Sage.

Denzin, N. (1997). *Interpretive ethnography: Ethnographic practices for the 21st century.* Thousand Oaks, CA: Sage.

Denzin, N. K., & Lincoln, Y. S. (2000). *Handbook of qualitative research* (2nd ed.). Thousand Oaks, CA: Sage.

Efran, J., & Fauber, R. (1995). Radical constructivism: Questions and answers. In R. A. Neimeyer & M. J. Mahoney (Eds.), *Constructivism in psychotherapy* (pp. 275-304). Washington, DC: American Psychological Association.

Ellis, C., & Bochner, A. (2000). Autoethnography, personal narrative, reflexivity: Researcher as subject. In N. K. Denzin, & Y. S. Lincoln (Eds.), *Handbook of qualitative research* (2nd ed., pp. 733-768). Thousand Oaks, CA: Sage.

Foucault, M. (1980). *Power/knowledge: Selected interviews and other writings, 1972-1977.* New York: Pantheon.

Gallagher, S. (1992). *Hermeneutics and education.* Albany: State University of New York Press.

Gergen, K. (1991). *The saturated self.* New York: Basic Books.

Gergen, M., & Gergen, K. (2000). Qualitative inquiry: Tensions and transformations. In N. K. Denzin, & Y. S. Lincoln (Eds.), *Handbook of qualitative research* (2nd ed., pp. 1025-1046). Thousand Oaks, CA: Sage.

Gleick, J. (1987). *Chaos.* New York: Viking.

Goldberger, N., Tarule, J., Clinchy, B., & Belenky, M. (1996). *Knowledge, difference, and power.* New York: Basic Books.

Guidano, V. (1987). *Complexity of the self.* New York: The Guilford Press.

Guidano, V. (1995). Constructivist psychotherapy: A theoretical framework. In R. A. Neimeyer, & M. J. Mahoney (Eds.), *Constructivism in psychotherapy* (pp. 93-110). Washington, DC: American Psychological Association.

Harding, S. (1991). *Whose science? Whose knowledge? Thinking from women's lives.* New York: Cornell University Press.

Heshusius, L. (1992, May). *From objectivity to subjectivity to participatory knowing.* Paper presented at the Pedagogy Conference, Victoria, British Columbia.

Heshusius, L., & Ballard, K. (1996). How do we count the ways we know? Some background to the project. In L. Heshusius & K. Ballard (Eds.), *From positivism to interpretivism and beyond: Tales of transformation in educational and social research* (pp. 1-17). Columbia University: Teachers College Press.

Horgan, J. (1996). *The end of science.* New York: Broadway Books.

Hoskins, M. L., & Arvay, M. (1999). Researching the postmodern self: Implications for constructivism. *Constructivism and the Human Sciences, 4,* 13-35.

Hoskins, M. L. (2000). Living research: The experience of researching self, other, and discourse. *Journal of Constructivist Psychology, 13,* 47-66.

Howard, G. S. (1985). Can research in the human sciences become more relevant to practice? *Journal of Counseling and Development, 63,* 539-544.

Howard, G. S. (1986). *Dare we develop a human science?* Notre Dame, IN: Academic Publications.

Howard, G. S. (1993). I think I can! I think I can! Reconsidering the place for practice methodologies in psychological research. *Professional Psychology: Research and Practice, 24,* 237-244.

Kelly, G. A. (1955). *The psychology of personal constructs* (2 vols.). New York: Norton.

Kvale, S. (1996). *InterViews: An introduction to qualitative research interviewing.* Thousand Oaks, CA: Sage.

243

Lather, P. (1991). *Getting smart: Feminist research and pedagogy with/in the postmodern*. New York: Routledge.

Lincoln, Y. S., & Guba, E. G. (2000). Paradigmatic controversies, contradictions, and emerging confluences. In N. K. Denzin, & Y. S. Lincoln (Eds.), *Handbook of qualitative research* (2nd ed., pp. 163-188). Thousand Oaks, CA: Sage.

McNamee, S., & Gergen, K. (Eds.). (1999). *Relational responsibility: Resources for a sustainable dialogue*. Thousand Oaks, CA: Sage.

Mahoney, M. J. (1991). *Human change processes: The scientific foundations of psychotherapy*. New York: Basic Books.

Mahoney, M. J. (1996). Connected knowing in constructive psychotherapy. In N. Goldberger, J. Tarule, B Clinchy, M. Belenky (Eds.). *Knowledge, difference, and power: Essays inspired by "Women's Ways of Knowing"* (pp. 126-147). New York: Basic Books.

Maturana, H., & Varela, R. J. (1987). *The tree of knowledge*. Boston: New Science Library.

Mingers, J. (1995). *Self-producing systems. Implications and applications of autopoiesis*. New York: Plenum Press.

Neimeyer, R. A., & Mahoney, M. J. (Eds.) (1995). *Constructivism in psychotherapy*. Washington, DC: American Psychological Association.

Nicholson, L. (1990). *Feminism/postmodernism*. New York: Routledge.

Polkinghorne, D. E. (1988). *Narrative knowing and the human sciences*. Albany: State University of New York Press.

Polkinghorne, D. E. (1991). Two conflicting calls for methodological reform. *The Counseling Psychologist, 19*, 103-114.

Polyani, J. (2000, January). *Toronto globe and mail*, A15.

Reason, P. (1993). Reflections on sacred experience and sacred science. *Journal of Management Inquiry, 2*, 273-283.

Richardson, F. C., & Fowers, B. (1998). Social inquiry: A hermeneutic reconceptualization. *American Behavioral Scientist, 41*, 461-465.

Schwandt, T. A. (2000). Three epistemological stances for qualitative inquiry: Interpretivism, hermeneutics, and social constructionism. In N. K. Denzin, & Y. S. Lincoln (Eds.), *Handbook of qualitative research* (2nd ed., pp. 189-214). Thousand Oaks, CA: Sage.

Sexton, T. (1997). Constructivist thinking within the history of ideas: The challenge of a new paradigm. In T. Sexton & B. Griffin (Eds.). *Constructivist thinking in counseling practice, research, and training* (pp. 3-19). New York: Teachers College Press.

Tolman C. (2000). *On doing psychological research from the standpoint of the subject*. Unpublished manuscript. University of Victoria, Victoria, British Columbia.

Wilbur, K. (1998). *The marriage of sense and soul: Integrating science and religion*. New York: Random House.

PART IV

NEW DIRECTIONS IN CONSTRUCTIVIST PSYCHOLOGY

CHAPTER 12

How Firm a Foundation?
A Constructivist Response to Mahrer's
Archeology of Beliefs about Psychotherapy[1]

Robert A. Neimeyer

> It may be disturbing to visualize ourselves trying to make progress in a world where there are no firm points of departure immediately accessible to us, no "givens," nothing that we start out by saying we know for sure.... Yet the "known realities" keep slipping out from under us. Our senses play all kinds of tricks and prove themselves to be the most unreliable informants. And our theologies, far-seeing as they appear to be, do in time lead to such indecent practices that sensitive [people] refuse any longer to take them literally. Thus we find ourselves repeatedly cut off from what we once thought we knew for sure, and we must reluctantly abandon the very faiths from which we originally launched our most fruitful enterprises.
>
> The upshot of all this is that we can no longer rest assured that human progress may proceed step by step in an orderly fashion from the known to the unknown. Neither our senses nor our doctrines provide us with the immediate knowledge required for such a philosophy of science. What we think we know is anchored only in our assumptions, not in the bedrock of truth itself, and that world we seek to grasp remains always on the horizons of our thoughts.
>
> (George Kelly, 1977, pp. 5-6)

"What are the foundational beliefs in the field of psychotherapy?" With this question, Al Mahrer (in press) has recently inaugurated a search for the cornerstones of clinical theory, the "fundamental truths" embraced by psychotherapists seeking to construct a secure knowledge base in which to ground their practice. The advantages of this epistemological archeology, in Mahrer's view,

---

[1] Portions of this article will appear in R. A. Neimeyer (in press). Fragmented foundations: A response to Mahrer. *Psychology: Journal of the Hellenic Psychological Society.* Reprinted with permission.

would lie in permitting "psychotherapeutic scholars, theoreticians, researchers, and practitioners [to delve] into foundational beliefs, studying them carefully, analyzing them. . . refining them, even replacing them with better ones." On the face of it, this seems like a noble goal: holding a looking glass up to the field as a whole and increasing its reflexivity. For Mahrer, this aim is also buttressed by some ancillary advantages, including the identification of different "families" of psychotherapy on the basis of shared assumptions and the enhancement of critical reflection on the part of psychologists about the "goodness of fit" of their personal predilections with the theories they espouse.

My goal in this chapter is to develop a constructivist critique of this effort, while affirming those features of it that seem viable. This task—like the one that Mahrer set for himself—turns out to be an audacious one that could easily exceed the space allotted by the editors of this volume. However, I hope at least to provoke continued dialogue about this fundamental question by first chipping away at the foundational quest that Mahrer proposes, and then responding more affirmatively to Mahrer's invitational mood by attempting to analyze some foundational beliefs of my own. To foreshadow my conclusion, I am not sure that this analysis will move the field any closer to the fiduciary foundations to which Mahrer aspires, but I share his conviction that the resulting conversation will at least be interesting!

KNOWLEDGE WITHOUT FOUNDATION

Mahrer (in press) opens the search for foundational principles in his characteristically folksy and disarming way, seemingly allowing the reader access to his own stream of consciousness as he thinks through the very meaning of "foundational beliefs," and the sundry obstacles to their identification. Thus, he defines such beliefs as "the cornerstones on which the field rests, the ideas that are generally taken for granted as fundamental givens or truths." Examples, in descending order of ambition, include (1) basic definitional truths, like the axioms of Euclidean geometry, (2) empirically generated laws, such as the law of gravity, and (3) research-based generalizations, as might be illustrated by the assumption that depression involves dysfunctional thinking. Buttressed by these "friendly meanings," Mahrer then sets out on his own odyssey to discover these truths, discovering to his "surprise" that not only have lists of foundational beliefs not been compiled for the field as a whole, but also that few if any such lists exist for distinct groups of theorists or clinicians, or even individual psychotherapists.

Viewed from a constructivist, postmodern perspective, such an outcome would not be at all surprising (Neimeyer, 1998; Neimeyer & Raskin, 2000). Like the epigraph from George Kelly with which this chapter opened, postmodern epistemologists adopt a critical posture toward the knowledge claims advanced by traditional psychological theories, fostering a "deconstruction" of their historically conditioned assumptions, rhetorical moves, and internal contradictions. In contrast to the more logical-empiricistic metatheory of science (Radnitsky, 1973) conjured by Mahrer's search for foundational beliefs, postmodern philosophers and psychologists acknowledge—and sometimes celebrate—the foundationless, fragmentary, and constructed nature of all knowledge, whether accumulated in the laboratory or clinic. As Polkinghorne (1992) notes,

> The tacit assumptions of this epistemology of practice are: (a) there is no epistemological ground on which the indubitable truth of knowledge statements can be established; (b) a body of knowledge consists of fragments of understanding, not a system of logically integrated statements, [and] (c) knowledge is a construction built out of cognitive schemes and embodied interactions with the environment (p. 147).

Among the disturbing implications of this view are that no knowledge claims can command universal assent, and aside from political power, no source of legitimization exists by which one person or institution can impose its understanding on another. It follows that any foundational beliefs, to the extent they can be identified at all, are likely to provide only temporary grounding for our psychological constructions, and be of interest to only local "language communities" (Koch, 1976) of like-minded psychotherapists, rather than to the field as a whole. Stated differently, psychological "theory groups" (Mullins, 1979) might better be viewed as nomadic tribes establishing mobile "base camps" to sustain them in their wanderings, rather than settled civilizations laying the foundation stones for a timeless edifice of theory and practice.

George Kelly, the founding figure of clinical constructivism, summed up this situation as follows:

> I suppose that science can be regarded as moving ahead step by step—whatever that means. But with each step that brings into focus some new facet of the universe, something, which before we thought was all settled, begins to look questionable. It is not that each new fact displaces an old one, but that gradually,

almost imperceptibly as our ventures progress, a darkening
shadow of doubt begins to spread over the coastline behind us
(Kelly, 1977, p. 7)

Postmodern theorists, then, would hold that, for good epistemological reasons, clinical knowledge is far less grounded, coherent, and enduring than we are accustomed to assuming. From this
vantage point, one might question Mahrer's ambitious quest for apo-
dictic foundations, and suggest that the only absolute principle to
guide psychological practice is one of relativity!

SIFTING THROUGH THE RUBBLE

On first glance, acknowledging the inevitably fragmentary
nature of psychological understanding is disconcerting: the Tower of
Babel turns out to be built on shifting sand. But on closer inspec-
tion—as Mahrer himself seems to realize—this simply means that
the search for grounding devolves to more local and individual levels, and away from the pretension of establishing a foundation for
"psychological practice" considered as a monolithic entity. Thus, at
the level of his explicit *method* (how one might go about interrogat-
ing his or her own core beliefs about psychotherapy) if not his
implicit *metatheory* (what beliefs might serve as foundations for the
entire field), I find myself largely in agreement with Mahrer's pro-
posals. At this methodological level, Mahrer has clearly done his
homework: combing through a vast psychological literature, his
research team sought out "authoritative statements by leading
authorities" that conveyed the field's most robust convictions.
Although the 75 candidates for foundational beliefs that Mahrer pro-
pounds are clearly only approximations, they nonetheless serve
admirably as starting points for a personal search for which he provides some helpful heuristics.[2] Thus, he enjoins individual readers,
as well as whole theory groups to engage in a "great deal of thinking," undertaking the "slow careful work" required to sift through
these statements, affirm them, or revise them to reflect their own. As
he recognizes, this effort is "not like filling out a survey or an inventory or a questionnaire." Instead, "it calls for dedication, interest,
and a serious passion to uncover and explicate your own founda-

[2] These include, in abbreviated form: (1) acceptance of beliefs that correspond to
the reader's own, (2) modification of those that do not, (3) clarification rather
than obfuscation, (4) avoidance of stock terms and phrases, (5) replacement with
alternative statements, (6) formulation of related points, and (7) addition of
unique personal beliefs. A fuller treatment of each is provided in the original
report.

tional beliefs"—a process not unlike, perhaps, constructivist psychotherapy! Mahrer leads by example, reflecting on each of the general disciplinary beliefs, and reformulating it in terms of his own experiential approach to psychology and psychotherapy (Mahrer, 1996). For example, Mahrer first posits the broad foundational belief that "*Effective interpretations are parsimonious and close to the client's current understanding and affective experience.*" He then rejects this, and offers his own formulation: "Successful achievement of the goals of an experiential session is the consequence of four in-session steps [discovering the client's capacity for deeper experiencing, welcoming this potential, shifting to past scenes, and being a qualitatively new person in the present]. Traditional interpretation plays little or no role in these steps or in the successful achievement of the goals of an experiential session."

Rather than quibble with Mahrer's general or reformulated foundational statements, I would prefer to take up his challenge, and attempt to use his list as a prompt to articulate some foundational beliefs of my own.[3] These formulations follow in the same order as those appearing in Mahrer's original report, and like his own experiential variations, sidestep the onerous task of defending their plausibility on scholarly, empirical, or practical grounds. Because of space constraints, I am able to address only the first seven propositions under each of Mahrer's grand headings bearing on theory and research, problems and psychotherapeutic practice, and education and training, but this sampling should be substantial enough to spawn some closing reflections. In each case, I begin with Mahrer's general foundational belief in italics, and then offer my own alternative formulation in plain font.

THEORY AND RESEARCH

1. *There is a cumulative body of psychotherapeutic knowledge; research is a primary gatekeeper for what is admitted into or withdrawn out of the cumulative body of knowledge.* The quest for psychological knowledge has

---

[3] Indeed, I must confess that I have been motivated by some of the same animus shared by Mahrer, as I have attempted to distinguish empirically between the core and peripheral beliefs about psychology and psychotherapy espoused by personal construct theorists, a theory group to which I myself belong (Neimeyer, 1985; Neimeyer, Davis, & Rist, 1986; Neimeyer & Jackson, 1996). My effort used the method of Delphi polling of a large international panel of experts, but was more humble in its aspiration to characterize only the convictions of a single theory group, rather than the field of psychotherapy as a whole.

both evolutionary and revolutionary moments; and in this sense paradigmatic shifts introduce non-cumulative quantum leaps in understanding (Kuhn, 1972; Lakatos, 1974). Research within various traditions of thought contributes to, but only loosely constrains theory and practice, which are shaped to an equal or greater extent by social processes.

2. *Research is superior to theoretical or philosophical analysis in arriving at, extending, or revising the cumulative body of psychotherapeutic knowledge.* Empirical, theoretical, and philosophical analyses are ultimately types of discourse, whose form and function vary for different "language communities" of psychologists (Koch, 1976). Like all discursive positions, they vie for legitimacy, not only with one another, but also with other powerful discourses, such as those reflecting larger cultural and economic values. Equally importantly, they also support or contend against the tacit convictions of psychotherapy practitioners, whose beliefs are shaped more by their intimate encounters with their clients than by the domain of explicit theory.

3. *The cumulative body of psychotherapeutic knowledge is relevant and applicable across virtually all psychotherapeutic theories and approaches.* Bodies of psychotherapeutic knowledge cannot be presumed to have universal applicability, irrespective of client and therapist gender, ethnicity, nationality, age, and other conditions (Brown, 2000). Different schools of psychotherapy represent "fuzzy sets" defined by their (partial) adherence to similar standards of argument, forms of theory, and strategies of practice.

4. *Conceptual systems of psychotherapy are to include common foundations comprised of fundamental truths, postulates, and axioms.* The language of "fundamental truths, postulates, and axioms" serves interesting rhetorical functions in psychological theory,[4] but does not map onto the far more fluid and provisional ways in which psychologists describe and argue about what they know and what they do.

---

[4] This seems clearly to be the case in Kelly's (1955/1991) "postulate and corollary" formulation of his own theory, which teases the reader with scientific precision, while at the same time emphasizing the playful "as if" epistemology that undergirds his entire psychology.

5. There are generally accepted, rigorous criteria for judging the goodness, soundness, and worth of theories of psychotherapy. The search for a single set of criteria for judging the "goodness, soundness, and worth" of theories of psychotherapy is chimerical at best, and destructive at worst. Just as Spanish and English can differ importantly in their grammatical and syntactical structures, so too can different approaches to therapy adopt different conventions for constructing and "languaging" about their subject matter (Neimeyer, 2000b).

6. Once a theory of psychotherapy is conceived, it is subjected to research inquiry, examination, and testing. Theories are occasionally subjected to empirical research, but proponents seeking validation, rather than falsification of their core tenets, typically conduct this research. In the domain of psychotherapy, research usually suspends theory testing altogether, and instead concentrates on demonstrating the applicability of the researcher's preferred approach to the treatment of a particular problem, with the goal of competing with other approaches for scarce resources (e.g., funding, students, and clients).

7. Prediction and explanation of empirically validated facts are important criteria for judging the worth of theories of psychotherapy. Empirical validity of psychotherapy theories is less critical than their viability in offering helpful guidelines to their practitioners and change-promoting processes and rituals to their clients. Just as many keys can open a lock, many approaches can "unlock" psychotherapeutic movement, and positive results do not necessarily reflect the validity of the conceptual structure that spawned them.

PROBLEMS
1. Causal determinants of psychological problems generally lie in antecedent events, predominantly occurring in childhood. "Causality" is a human construction, whose role in human distress is subject to many interpretations. Certainly the more linear formulations of this concept (e.g., "childhood trauma causes adult suffering") are too simple to account for the subtle variations of the impact of untoward

events in our lives (Nash, Neimeyer, Hulsey, & Lambert, 1998). Likewise, more complex models (e.g., the "box and arrow" diagrams outlining relationships among thoughts, feelings and behaviors) represent fallible—and sometimes simplistic—attempts on the part of theorists to punctuate the seamless flow of experience and impose order on the resulting "parts." The utility of such constructions varies considerably, and adherents to different schools of psychotherapy prefer different explanatory styles.

2. *There are mental illnesses, diseases, and disorders.* "Mental illness" is a misplaced biological metaphor (Raskin & Lewandowski, 2000). Brains, like other body parts, might meaningfully be diagnosed as having lesions or physiological disruptions, but the majority of problems that clients present to therapists are not usefully viewed in these terms. Among other alternatives, concepts focusing on the client's attempts to construct and maintain a meaningful self-narrative, to negotiate a shared reality with (intimate) others, and to establish a workable position in broader cultural discourses of identity provide more helpful starting points for clinical intervention (Neimeyer & Raskin, 2000).

3. *The causal determinants of mental illness, diseases, and disorders are predominantly genetic and environmental.* Dividing "causes" of distress into crude categories such as environmental and genetic conceals more than it reveals. Instead, all human action and experience can be viewed as an emergent product of several nested orders, which range from the bio-genetic, through the personal-agentic, to the dyadic-relational, and finally to the cultural-linguistic levels of organismic functioning. All human problems likewise emerge from the co-action of processes operating at all of these levels (Mascolo, Craig-Bray, & Neimeyer, 1997).

4. *Interpersonal relationships, largely during infancy and childhood, are significant causal determinants of current interpersonal problems.* Interpersonal relationships represent a critical context for the construction of a relational self, and disruptions in them can stretch and break the sustaining bonds of attachment in which our identity is anchored (Neimeyer, 2001b). The exploration of impedi-

ments to meaningful intersubjectivity and the promotion of mutually validating relationships is therefore a focal aim of psychotherapy (Leitner, 1995).

5. Interruption of physical-psychological contact between infant and mother is a significant determinant of abnormal development. The mother-infant relationship is one of several affectively charged relationships that provide a context for the infant's (and mother's) construction of a "working model" of self and world (Guidano, 1991). Such relationships are infinitely variable in their nuances, but might meaningfully be characterized in a general way in terms of their security, reciprocity, responsiveness, intersubjectivity, and warmth.

6. When there are multiple causal descriptions or explanations of a psychotherapeutic event, (a) only one is superior as more true, accurate, correct, and (b) an approach that incorporates multiple causal descriptions or explanations is superior to one that does not. Psychotherapeutic events are independent of the explanatory frameworks within which they are interpreted, each of which highlights some courses of action while obscuring others. Although many alternative constructions can be placed upon any given therapeutic event (Kelly, 1955/1991), the clinician will necessarily operate (usually implicitly) on the basis of only one at a given moment. Accuracy or correctness of the explanatory framework plays little part in the process.

7. Clients seek psychotherapy for, and psychotherapy is, treatment of psychological-psychiatric problems, distress, mental disorders, personal difficulties, and problems in living. Clients seek therapy to relieve suffering engendered by the way they and others who matter to them are constructing their (mutual) experience. Therapy accordingly helps identify the tangles, dead-ends, empathic failures, anxieties, and sense of discontinuity that is implicated in this suffering, and assists clients in finding ways to transcend these limits (Ecker & Hulley, 1996; Efran & Cook, 2000).

255

PSYCHOTHERAPEUTIC PRACTICE

1. *Psychotherapy is an interpersonal relationship that provides a corrective experience for problematic interpersonal relationships.* Psychotherapies vary in their degree of explicit focus on the therapeutic relationship, with some using the relational patterns between client and therapist as a source of insight into the client's enactment of problematic scripts in other life contexts (Luborsky & Crits-Cristoph, 1998). Although this approach can be powerful, the therapist can also play many other roles, including that of consultant, guide, fellow traveler, audience, and director in relation to a client's self-exploration and development (Neimeyer, 2000a).

2. *There is an intrinsic drive toward healthy functioning; psychotherapy removes blocks to intrinsic healing and growth.* "Healthy functioning" and "intrinsic drives" are sometimes-helpful, sometimes-mischievous social fictions. People can be viewed as forms of movement, but with no pre-determined directions (Kelly, 1955/1991), instead constructing life trajectories that represent the distillation of their choices, both conscious and non-conscious. Psychotherapy can clarify such choices, and permit people to experiment with organizing their lives differently.

3. *The practitioner initially assesses and diagnoses the problem or mental disorder, and then selects and applies the appropriate treatment.* "Diagnosis" and "treatment" are awkward medical metaphors, which have as little relevance for psychotherapy as for any other form of human conversation or relationship (Szasz, 1974). As in any other dialogue, therapist and client continually modify their linguistic and physical positioning in relation to one another, based on subtle and typically tacit "readings" of what form of engagement is appropriate. Therapists are helpful to the extent that they target their engagement toward perceived openings that prompt the client toward higher levels of self-awareness and the reorganization of habitual and problematic ways of constructing self and others.

4. *Psychotherapeutic change occurs predominantly by means of effective changes in clients' ways of understanding, making sense and meaning of, and construing-construct-*

ing, their selves, lives, relationships, and worlds. The reconstruction of a world of meaning is a passionate process, one that frequently follows the "trail of affect" to identify significant issues requiring therapeutic attention. This implies that vivid, experiential work is often required in therapy in order to symbolize, articulate, and renegotiate clients' deepest understandings of themselves, others, and their lives (Neimeyer, 1995). At other times, reflective consolidation or behavioral exploration of fresh understandings is appropriate. In general, however, meaning making is not a dispassionate logical or "cognitive" process.

5. The therapist-client relationship is prerequisite to successful psychotherapy. The therapist-client relationship is an important crucible for change in many, but not all therapies. Care must be taken to establish "optimal therapeutic distance," in which the therapist is close enough to the client's experiencing to be moved by the client's pain, pride or confusion, but far enough away to realize that these experiences are the client's and not the therapist's own (Leitner, 1995). A meaningful therapeutic relationship enriches both (or in the case of family or group therapy, all) participants.

6. Therapists and clients attending to and talking to one another are prerequisite to successful psychotherapy. Linguistic and attentional processes are the primary tools by which therapists help clients sculpt their experience into new forms (Neimeyer, 1996). Virtually all forms of therapy underspecify these tools and how they might be used, although some schools of therapy are more explicit about this than others. Psychotherapy research would be more useful if it attended to the patterns of moment-by-moment engagement by which therapists and clients open up, explore, and reorganize patterns of meaning/feeling/acting (Greenberg, Elliott, & Rice, 1993), rather than concentrating on crudely defined symptomatic outcomes of gross classes of intervention.

7. Empathic listening and responding are prerequisite to successful therapy. Empathic listening and responding are prerequisite to successful therapy, and empathic failure is the primary cause of attrition and negative outcomes.

257

Sensitively grasping what the client is ready to do, now, in this moment of this session is facilitated by listening for the deeper implications of what the client is (almost) saying (Neimeyer, 2001a), and is hampered by the therapist's pursuit of his or her own agenda, whether overt or covert.

EDUCATION AND TRAINING

1. *Psychotherapeutic education is to include education in the cumulative body of psychotherapeutic knowledge.* Education of future psychotherapists should provide some respectful coverage of each of the major traditions of psychotherapy (e.g., psychodynamic, humanistic, cognitive-behavioral, and systemic), as well as issues shaping the field (e.g., concerns with diversity, accountability, and research). However, care should be taken to avoid the implication that these often-competing trends are amenable to a facile "integration" into a single "cumulative body of knowledge."

2. *Graduates of professional education and training in psychotherapy have scholarly knowledge of the field of philosophy of science.* Graduates of psychotherapy training programs rarely have any sophistication in philosophy of science, which when taught at all is characteristically (mis)represented to justify the dominant approach to quantitative research on therapy outcome. Education programs should be broadened to provide significant coverage of alternative philosophies of science as a hermeneutic enterprise (Radnitsky, 1973), which would justify an expanded conception of research and practice.

3. *Psychotherapeutic education is to include training in the common core of basic psychotherapy skills and methods.* Focus on a "common core" of skills is probably pernicious, insofar as it promotes training in the "least common denominator" of approved methods, typically as construed from the standpoint of the dominant disciplinary frameworks. Instead, larger programs should offer training in a diversity of approaches, and smaller programs should vary in their focus, one from another. This pluralism acknowledges the inevitable eclecticism of psychotherapeutic practice, and permits students to cultivate skills in those forms of psychotherapy that match their own evolving outlooks.

258

Ultimately, greater philosophic sophistication combined with pluralistic training can encourage practitioners to pursue a "theoretically progressive integrationism," in which novel, but coherent forms of practice can arise from the articulation and elaboration of prior approaches (Neimeyer, 1993).

4. *Psychotherapeutic education teaches theories and approaches that are significantly different from and more elevated than those of people outside of formal psychotherapeutic education.* At its best, graduate education encourages a deep engagement in theories, methods, and work with actual people in a way that refines and extends each trainee's understanding and facilitation of human change. At times, this may require experimentation with methods quite outside the technical province of psychotherapy theory, drawing on fields as diverse as theatre, communication, ethics, and ethnography.

5. *Training in psychotherapy should concentrate on those forms of treatment that have been empirically supported or validated.*[5] The pursuit of an approved list of "empirically validated" treatments serves a political as much as a scientific agenda, legitimizing dominant forms of intervention while disenfranchising others (Bohart, O'Hara, & Leitner, 1998). Psychotherapy training should critically deconstruct such discourse, and focus attention on human change processes irrespective of their "name brand" pedigree.

6. *In general, graduates of degree-granting programs in mental health are significantly more effective in psychotherapy than actors with a week of training in the role of psychotherapist.* Little evidence suggests that graduates of psychotherapy training programs outperform actors, college professors, or leaders of mutual support groups in providing assistance to people in distress. Training would do well to concentrate on those processes that facilitate greater self-awareness, meaning making, client empowerment, and

---

[5] This foundational belief, though widely current in the field (Ingram, Hayes, & Scott, 2000), was not among Mahrer's proposed list of fundamental assumptions. However, I am including it because it is powerfully shaping discussions about the future of psychotherapy, and calls for a clear constructivist response.

259

social activism, whatever the relational context in which they are displayed.

7. In general, significantly more years of academic training yields significantly higher levels of competence in psychotherapy. Much of the variance in a therapist's skill is accounted for by factors that precede her or his professional training. Graduate education should cultivate and refine this intrinsic responsiveness through the modeling of master therapists, reflective and experiential exercises, scientific and scholarly reading, and especially the supervisory processing of early attempts to help actual people struggling with actual problems.

SOME REFLECTIVE OBSERVATIONS

What have I learned from my attempt to take Mahrer's invitation seriously, and use his heuristics to enunciate (some of) my own foundational beliefs about psychotherapy? Reflecting on this question underscores in a more personal way some of the constructivist and postmodern themes with which this chapter opened. These include, broadly speaking, an enhanced awareness of the *personal, partial,* and *provisional* nature of foundational beliefs, about which I will say a few words by way of summary and conclusion.

First, I was struck by the personalism of my foundational beliefs, just as I was with those that Mahrer himself had articulated. Clearly, I had deviated significantly, sometimes wildly, from the "received wisdom" of the field, sometimes in directions shared by other constructivists, and sometimes in directions that were more idiosyncratic. Aside from the clear implication that I—and perhaps other constructivists—am deviant (!), what does this suggest? I suspect that it means that (a) any given set of foundational beliefs is inherently perspectival, (b) no such set can or will command universal assent, and that (c) such beliefs represent distillations of forms of disciplinary discourse in which the belief holder participates and perhaps help shape. This latter point underscores the sociology of knowledge, insofar as endorsement of similar foundational beliefs provides a kind of "club membership" for the belief holder, gaining him or her access to some loose or tight confederations of like-minded others, while barring entrance to others. This emphasis on the social dimension of our personal and professional meaning making efforts (Neimeyer, 1998; Neimeyer, 2000a; Neimeyer & Stewart,

2000) is perhaps the most pervasive difference between my own foundational beliefs and those propounded by Mahrer for the field as a whole. Indeed, I suspect that this social constructionist emphasis (Neimeyer, 1998) also differentiates me from many of the readers of this book, most of whom might feel at home with a more personal, agentic constructivism that places less inflection on broadly discursive forms of meaning making.

Second, I noticed that my own foundational beliefs were inevitably partial, in the sense that much was left unsaid. This seemed to reflect less the space constraints that prevented me from constructing a more complete inventory, than the essentially tacit level at which such beliefs are held. Although I made a "good faith effort" to explicate my own assumptive foundations, I found that in most cases the deeper ripples of conviction began where the words themselves ended. Each explicit statement served simply as a point of reference for a set of beliefs, personal experiences and feelings, implied arguments, and so on, which in principle could not be fully articulated. This observation brings to mind the insightful analysis of personal knowledge offered by the philosopher Michael Polanyi (1958), who argued that our explicit focal attention and beliefs necessarily rely on a host of implicit subsidiary assumptions. In other words, we assume our foundations as we assume a posture—automatically and prereflectively, not (usually) as a matter of conscious decision (Merleau-Ponty, 1962). This "taken for granted" grounding of experience seems to be part of its essential structure, much as a pianist must tacitly assume the arrangement of the keys while focusing on the sonata she is performing. This further implies for me that attending explicitly to our foundational assumptions is not necessarily a "good thing," as it can disrupt the tacit scaffolding on which any skilled performance relies. For example, for the therapist to begin asking him or herself in session, "What is my model of change? How do I conceptualize this problem the client is presenting?" and so on, at minimum brings about an empathic disconnection from the flow of the client's experience, and if prolonged, can instigate a paralyzing level of self-consciousness. Thus, like the exercise Mahrer and I each undertook in drafting our personal statements, analytical reflection on foundational assumptions is best reserved for more self-focused moments, when it can yield useful insights that can then permit the analyst to engage his or her work a bit differently in the future.

Finally, it occurred to me that my belief statements were thoroughly provisional. Certainly, I would have formulated them rather differently twenty years ago, five years ago, or perhaps even last week! Thus the image of a nomadic habitation evoked earlier, or perhaps the metaphor of a rambling home that is periodically remodeled or expanded (Neimeyer, 1996), seems a better "fit" for how I experience my position, than the sense of permanence and stability evoked by "cornerstones" and granite-like "foundations." This is not to say that some foundational beliefs might not be enduring (for better or worse), but it is to suggest that they, like all assumptive worlds, might be revised or abandoned outright, with all of the prospects of anxiety and exhilaration this implies.

In closing, Mahrer has, in his typically impish way, invited us to do something interesting as individuals and as a field. I hope that other constructivist readers will take up the challenge of articulating their own core convictions, and that the resulting dialogue with ourselves, with our colleagues, and with others in different theory groups will invigorate the discipline we call psychotherapy.

REFERENCES

Bohart, A. C., O'Hara, M., & Leitner, L. M. (1998). Empirically violated treatments: Disenfranchisement of humanistic and other psychotherapies. *Psychotherapy Research, 8*, 141-157.

Brown, L. S. (2000). Feminist therapy. In C. R. Snyder & R. E. Ingram (Eds.), *Handbook of psychological change* (pp. 358-380). New York: Wiley.

Ecker, B., & Hulley, L. (1996). *Depth-oriented brief therapy*. San Francisco: Jossey-Bass.

Efran, J. S., & Cook, P. F. (2000). Linguistic ambiguity as a diagnostic tool. In R. A. Neimeyer & J. D. Raskin (Eds.), *Constructions of disorder: Meaning-making frameworks for psychotherapy* (pp. 121-143). Washington, DC: American Psychological Association.

Greenberg, L., Elliott, R., & Rice, L. (1993). *Facilitating emotional change*. New York: Guilford.

Guidano, V. F. (1991). *The self in process*. New York: Guilford.

Ingram, R. E., Hayes, A., & Scott, W. (2000). Empirically supported treatments. In C. R. Snyder & R. E. Ingram (Eds.), *Handbook of psychological change* (pp. 40-60). New York: Wiley.

Kelly, G. A. (1991). *The psychology of personal constructs* (2 vols.). New York: Routledge. (Original work published 1955)

Kelly, G. A. (1977). The psychology of the unknown. In D. Bannister (Ed.), *New perspectives in personal construct theory* (pp. 1-19). San Diego, CA: Academic.

Koch, S. (1976). Language communities, search cells, and the psychological studies. In W. J. Arnold (Ed.), *Nebraska symposium on motivation* (pp. 477-559).

Lincoln: University of Nebraska Press.

Kuhn, T. (1972). *The structure of scientific revolutions.* Chicago: University of Chicago Press.

Lakatos, I. (1974). Falsification and the methodology of scientific research programs. In I. Lakatos & A. Musgrave (Eds.), *Criticism and the growth of knowledge* (pp. 91-196). London: Cambridge University Press.

Leitner, L. M. (1995). Optimal therapeutic distance. In R. A. Neimeyer & M. J. Mahoney (Eds.), *Constructivism in psychotherapy* (pp. 357-370). Washington, DC: American Psychological Association.

Luborsky, L., & Crits-Cristoph, P. (1998). *Understanding transference.* (2nd ed.). Washington, DC: American Psychological Association.

Mahrer, A. R. (1996). *The complete guide to experiential psychotherapy.* New York: Wiley.

Mahrer, A. R. (in press). What are the foundational beliefs in the field of psychotherapy? *Psychology: The Journal of the Hellenic Psychological Society.*

Mascolo, M. F., Craig-Bray, L., & Neimeyer, R. A. (1997). The construction of meaning and action in development and psychotherapy: An epigenetic systems approach. In G. J. Neimeyer & R. A. Neimeyer (Eds.), *Advances in personal construct psychology* (Vol. 4, pp. 3-38). Greenwich, CT: JAI Press.

Merleau-Ponty, M. (1962). *Phenomenology of perception.* London: Routledge.

Mullins, N. C. (1979). *Theories and theory groups in contemporary American sociology.* Chicago: University of Chicago Press.

Nash, M. R., Neimeyer, R. A., Hulsey, T. L., & Lambert, W. (1998). Psychopathology associated with sexual abuse. *Journal of Consulting and Clinical Psychology, 66,* 568-571.

Neimeyer, R. A. (1985). *The development of personal construct psychology.* Lincoln, NE: University of Nebraska Press.

Neimeyer, R. A. (1993). Constructivism and the problem of psychotherapy integration. *Journal of Psychotherapy Integration, 3,* 133-157.

Neimeyer, R. A. (1995). An invitation to constructivist psychotherapies. In R. A. Neimeyer & M. J. Mahoney (Eds.), *Constructivism in psychotherapy* (pp. 1-8). Washington: American Psychological Association.

Neimeyer, R. A. (1996). Process interventions for the constructivist psychotherapist. In H. Rosen & K. T. Kuehlwein (Eds.), *Constructing realities* (pp. 371-411). San Francisco: Jossey-Bass.

Neimeyer, R. A. (1998). Social constructionism in the counselling context. *Counselling Psychology Quarterly, 11,* 135-149.

Neimeyer, R. A. (2000a). Narrative disruptions in the construction of self. In R. A. Neimeyer & J. D. Raskin (Eds.), *Constructions of disorder: Meaning making frameworks for psychotherapy* (pp. 207-241). Washington, DC: American Psychological Association.

Neimeyer, R. A. (2000b). Research and practice as essential tensions: A construc-
    tivist confession. In L. M. Vaillant & S. Soldz (Eds.), *Empirical knowledge and
    clinical experience* (pp. 123-150). Washington, D. C.: American Psychological
    Association.
Neimeyer, R. A. (2001a). The language of loss: Grief therapy as a process of mean-
    ing reconstruction. In R. A. Neimeyer (Ed.), *Meaning reconstruction and the expe-
    rience of loss* (pp. 261-292). Washington, DC: American Psychological
    Association.
Neimeyer, R. A. (2001b). *Lessons of loss: A guide to coping.* New York: McGraw-Hill.
Neimeyer, R. A., Davis, K., & Rist, P. (1986). The future of personal construct psy-
    chology: A Delphi Poll. *British Journal of Cognitive Psychotherapy, 4,* 37-44.
Neimeyer, R. A., & Jackson, T. T. (1996). George A. Kelly and the development of
    personal construct theory. In W. G. Bringmann, R. Lueck, R. Miller, & C. E.
    Early (Eds.), *A pictorial history of psychology.* Carol Stream, IL: Quintessence.
Neimeyer, R. A., & Raskin, J. D. (Eds.). (2000). *Constructions of disorder: Meaning-making
    frameworks for psychotherapy.* Washington, DC: American Psychological
    Association.
Neimeyer, R. A., & Stewart, A. E. (2000). Constructivist and narrative psychother-
    apies. In C. R. Snyder & R. E. Ingram (Eds.), *Handbook of psychological change*
    (pp. 337-357). New York: Wiley.
Polanyi, M. (1958). *Personal knowledge.* New York: Harper.
Polkinghorne, D. E. (1992). Postmodern epistemology of practice. In S. Kvale
    (Ed.), *Psychology and postmodernism* (pp. 146-165). Newbury Park, CA: Sage.
Radnitsky, G. (1973). *Contemporary schools of metascience.* Chicago: Henry Regnery.
Raskin, J. D., & Lewandowski, A. M. (2000). The construction of disorder as human
    enterprise. In R. A. Neimeyer & J. D. Raskin (Eds.), *Constructions of disorder:
    Meaning-making frameworks for psychotherapy* (pp. 15-39). Washington, DC:
    American Psychological Association.
Szasz, T. (1974). *The myth of mental illness* (rev. ed.). New York: Harper & Row.

CHAPTER 13

The Notion of "Applied Psychology" from a Personal Construct Psychology Perspective

William George (Bill) Warren

A long and widely held view to the present day is the view that applied psychology is the application of results derived from pure and experimental psychology to practical life and problems (Drever, 1952; Bullock & Trombley, 1999). In his personal construct psychology, Kelly (1955/1991a, 1955/1991b, 1969c, 1969f) offered a quite radical rethinking of that view in his discussion of clinical psychology and therapy. He does not think that there is much merit in seeking to "apply" what is alleged to be knowledge of human beings and their behaving, and, in fact, in the quest to know something of that behaving the direction would be better reversed. That is, start with "real" people in their real-life struggles in order to illuminate something of the human psychological condition more generally. In developing this argument Kelly elaborates both a thoroughgoing psychology for psychotherapy (Mair, 1970) and a theory of personality and psychotherapy (Chiari and Nuzzo, 1996), but also a critique of the notion of "applied psychology."

There are interesting parallels between the position personal construct psychology takes in relation to applied psychology and developments in two areas of philosophy; in particular, discussions within philosophy of technology, and within philosophy of education. In relation to the first, Drever (1952) notes that in Europe the term "psychotechnics," derived from Titchner (1928), was commonly used to refer to applied psychology, but the term "psychotechnology" (Bunge & Ardila, 1987) better captures the idea of what is understood to be happening when findings from so called pure psychology are thought to be relevant to solving practical problems. Thus, in so far as applied psychology is a "doing," an "acting on," or, in the contemporary sense of the word, a "technology," there is a rich critical literature in philosophy of technology that challenges this understanding of technology and, thereby, calls for a different understanding of applied psychology. In relation to the second area of philosophy, personal construct psychology is also echoed in challenges to the idea of a body of knowledge being "transmitted" or applied to particular problems. A major critical perspective here was developed by a number of thinkers in the 1970s (Postman & Weingartner, 1971; Illich, 1972; Holly, 1974) and, in the elaboration of this radical critique of education and schooling, Paulo Freire emerged with a significant argument for changing the nature of the relationship between teacher and student as a way of breaking the grip of this last idea. In his argument he elaborated the notions of *praxis* and *conscientization* (Freire, 1970a, 1970b, 1972), which are equally of value to the present discussion.

This paper develops themes from Warren (1998) and discusses some of the resonances between these last fields of thought and personal construct psychology. It commences with a brief consideration of the philosophy of technology, moves to explore the notions of *praxis* and *conscientization*, and then reviews Kelly's (1955/1991a, 1955/1991b, 1969b, 1969e, 1969f) discussions of applied psychology and clinical psychology. This draws the connections that are in focus here and points to a suggestion that the notion of "the scientist practitioner" that orchestrates our psychological education might be challenged with that of "the practitioner scientist," inverting the common applied psychology relationship from one that envisages a move from theory to practice to one that moves from practice to theory to practice. This last perspective is as aptly captured in philosophy of technology in its critical mode, as it is by Freire in his critique of schooling and education.

A GLIMPSE INTO THE PHILOSOPHY OF TECHNOLOGY

The literature in philosophy of technology has grown apace since the early critical reflection on technology immediately after World War II (Juenger, 1946/1949)—its epistemological, metaphysical, religious, no less than its ethical and political impacts, have by now been exposed, if not yet fully worked-through. That literature can be roughly divided into the work of thinkers who were seminal thinkers for this field, such as Ellul (1954/1965, 1977/1980), Marcuse (1941, 1955/1969), and Heidegger (1927/1978, 1954/1977), and extensive commentary and development of their ideas in various directions (for example, Tesconi & Morris, 1972; Durbin, 1976; Zimmerman, 1990; Feenberg, 1991; Mitcham, 1994). From this writing, a number of themes can be identified, including themes of the pervasiveness and inescapable impacts (generally negative impacts) of technology on social life, our sense of self and our capacity to individuate. Or, the relatively unobtrusive manner in which technology has impacted on our lives, dramatic to be sure in some respects but leaving us at the same time relatively anaesthetised and needing to be "awakened" to the deeper impacts (Ellul, 1954/1965; Jones, 1982). While any of the seminal thinkers or commentators would suffice to show the deeper, critical understanding of technology that is in focus here, from a formidable array of ideas from which to select, Heidegger's work is most illuminating for present purposes. This last work is particularly challenging, focusing as it does on techne as a "way of knowing"—in contrast to technology as a way of doing—and the relation of our life in technology to our being and to our Being.

For Heidegger, techne was practical knowledge, knowledge derived from and in our encounters with the world and its objects:

> From the earliest times until Plato the word techne is linked with the word episteme. Both words are terms for knowing in the widest sense. They mean to be entirely at home in something, to understand and be expert in it. Such knowing provides an opening up. As an opening up it is a revealing. . . . techne is a mode of aletheuein [truth]. It reveals whatever does not bring itself forth and does not lie here before us, whatever can look and turn out now one way and now another. . . . Thus what is decisive in techne does not lie at all in making and manipulating nor in the using of means, but rather in the revealing. . . . It is as revealing, and not as manufacturing, that techne is a bringing-forth. (Heidegger, 1954/1977, p. 13)

Heidegger argues that life in social and cultural circumstances, governed by advanced technology, is conceived as a way of dominating and controlling nature. In this life, our capacity for meditative thinking is lost as we are drawn more and more into mere calculative thinking. His fear is that technology would so "captivate, bewitch, dazzle, and beguile man that calculative thinking may someday come to be accepted and practiced as the only way of thinking" (1959/1966; p. 56). Calculative thinking is encouraged by a corruption of the original sense of techne to an idea of working on the world rather than working with it. He indicts modern technology and our uncritical acceptance of it as the significant factor in our loss of our "at homeness" in the world, and sees in meditative thinking the hope for a re-engagement with more fundamental questions and real problems:

> Meditative thinking demands of us not to cling one-sidedly to a
> single idea, nor to run down a one-track course of ideas.
> Meditative thinking demands of us that we engage ourselves
> with what at first sight does not go together at all. (p. 53)

In the human person's interaction with the natural, material,
and social world, then, techne—with other related processes of such
interaction involving knowing and judging, like episteme, praxis, and
phronesis—was once a learning from nature and the world, learning
about our place, our limitations and potential as human beings,
learning something of the meaning of our existence, and of our
Being. Modern technology drastically shifts our attention to the
everyday trivia of life; it immerses, ensnares or traps us into what
Heidegger calls the "particulars" of life and living. It thereby distracts us from the bigger and more important questions; that is, from
"universal" questions that pose real problems. The world governed by
advanced technology poses merely puzzles, mere technical puzzles,
nowadays tied up with demands of industry and commerce. These
are to be addressed calculatively for practical solutions, and neither
puzzles nor solutions go to questions concerning the reasons for our
existence—as in Sartre (1943/1966)—for our being, but more than
this, our very Being (as a being which reflects on its Being) as in
Heidegger. In a context governed by advanced technology, techne is
stripped of its sense as a mode of knowing and understanding; it
becomes an "acting on" or a "doing to."

These ideas do not appear particularly difficult here, but two
analogies might assist in pinning them down. First, when a wood-
turner or potter works the wood or clay there is an intimate relation
between the material and the turner or potter. There is a sense of
"this stuff will let me do this or that but only this far" before it
breaks or shatters. There is a sense of not merely imposing on, but
of learning from the material and our interaction with it. Second, as
I am told, in the approach to sculpture among the indigenous peoples of far western Canada, there is an acceptance that the material to
be carved will have the subject "in it." Thus, asked to carve a seal
from a particular piece of rock the artist may well produce a bear
because, as will be said, "the seal was not in the rock." Rather than
demand of the material, the artist works with it to allow its natural
contours, physical and structural properties, age and environmental
impacts to "show forth," and in this approach, at least Heidegger
would say, is something of the nature of the stuff of Life revealed.

Heidegger's work, echoing and prefacing other thinkers, moves through different phases and his later work gives more significance to everyday life, to being, wherein we catch glimpses of the deeper and wider significance of our individual lives. As he had centered the conscious awareness of our own personal death in his early work, so in his later, with this focus more on being, our encounters with the deaths of others become equally as important. Thus, the everyday experiences of and with the terminally ill deepen their and our understandings, just as those who grieve deepen their own reflection on their own life in that experience (Leman-Stefanovic, 1987). However, life in advanced technological society distracts us from these potential insights. In place of individuation and dialogue between individuated beings, we are seduced into accepting ready-made answers. In the mass-society of modern life, as Heidegger said in his early work, the "They" have worked out all that we need know or think about death, and institutional imperatives take over the experience of illness and grief, corporatizing and "packaging" the experience:

> The 'they' has already stowed-away an interpretation for this event [death]. It talks ... as if to say 'One of these days one will die too, in the end; but right now it has nothing to do with us' ... Dying, which is essentially mine in such a way that no one can be my representative, is perverted into an event of public occurrence which the 'they' encounters. (Heidegger, 1927/1978, p. 297)

In general, then, the philosophers of technology, though more particularly Heidegger, have attempted to show how the notion of technology as action on the world is a distortion of another sense of that word; a sense of working with and in the world for an appreciation of what that might tell us about the meaning of our lives, and of Life and of Being. Different thinkers take different perspectives on these matters, providing a rich array of ideas with which to engage the impacts on our personal and social life of both the prospects and the problems generated by advanced technology. An instrumental theory stresses the neutrality of technology and its subservience to other values, substantive theory sees technology as a self-augmenting cultural force, and critical theory emphasises democratic participation in technology, which is seen as neither completely neutral nor totally autonomous (Feenberg, 1991). Across all of these perspectives, however, the call is to reflect more critically on the changes that have occurred in our understanding of just what technology is or means, what it does, and what we should or can do about it.

FREIRE'S PRAXIS AND CONSCIENTIZATION

Discussions of *praxis* quite understandably commence with reference to Aristotle who was the earliest philosopher to systematically contrast *theory* and *practice*. Theory (*theoria*) conveyed the pre-Socratic philosophers' focus on life in a manner that exposed a deeper understanding of it than was required to simply negotiate life's mundane dimensions. This focus was the reflective life or the reflective aspect of the soul, an aspect that for Aristotle was more developed in some people than in others; the outcome of its operation was *sophia* (wisdom). While previous to Aristotle the contrast pole for *theoria* was either of the lower order interests "love of honor" or "love of gain" (Burnet, 1914/1968), Aristotle developed the contrast pole as *practice*. This referred, however, particularly to political activity, but more generally to this activity and to various other activities where some sort of general intent or outcome, as opposed to a mere functional outcome, is in view. That is, an outcome that was not merely useful or got things done, but which saw a degree of "fitness" or "rightness" about that activity and outcome. His discussion turned around how a member of the leisured class should spend time; that is, whether the contemplative life of the philosopher was superior to the practical, but still reflective life of the politician. Thus he also emphasized a notion of *phronesis*, wise or prudent judgment in the sphere of practical life or action, a notion that stressed again the higher order of thinking and conducting oneself that his notion of *practice* denoted; the outcome of its best operation, the highest point of practice, was *phronesis* (practical wisdom).

Much later, Marx (1844/1975, 1845/1976) was to center the political context more forcefully and to develop Aristotle's idea of *practice* in terms of the same practice-reflective element that Aristotle had been highlighting exclusively for his privileged class at a time when "mere practice" was too insignificant to contemplate; this was the humdrum activity of the artisan, the worker. For Marx, however, action in and on the world in the form of our efforts to feed and clothe and shelter ourselves—the material conditions of life—activates our reflection. For Marx, the primary and essentially human activity was productive work—useful work, not useless toil—and this core activity of human beings was the origination of reflection. For Marx, *praxis* was a particular type of activity (productive labor, as contrasted with mere work) and a particular type of reflection (critical reflection on the relationships in production and control of the productive apparatus). Here the productive worker was centered rather than marginalized and *praxis* was practice that resulted in a transformation, a revolution, which entailed a humanization of humankind (Lobkowicz, 1968, p. 419).

This idea of a reflection on our practice (loosely, our work) that enlarged our contemplation of what was truly human is a refined sense of *praxis* that is developed well by Freire (1970a, 1970b, 1972). In addition, Freire develops a related idea of *conscientization*, which, we might say as a first approximation to the concept, is a state of mind resulting from an appreciation of how action or practice is situated, located or bound. Freire's writings had their own focus of convenience in the field of education, in particular, in criticizing "banking" or the "nutritionist" concept of education and arguing for a "dialogic" education. Banking education is the familiar notion of the teacher "filling up" the ignorant student with information. In the nutritionist or "digestive" concept, it is giving the student knowledge as "food" to eat in order that they will grow; the uneducated are conceived as "undernourished," as "hungry for knowledge." By contrast, dialogic education involves a two-way interaction between two individuals who, as Freire says, "make their Easter," each dying to habitual ways of thinking; for example that one is exclusively and naturally the teacher, the other exclusively and naturally the pupil, each "resurrected" or reborn as equally ignorant and equally curious human beings. This curiosity was exercised in a context where reality was understood "never just simply as the objective datum, the concrete fact, but . . . also [our] perception of it" (Freire, 1970a, p. 213).

Following Marx, Freire takes *praxis* as an inextricable interconnection of thought and action in a real world of sub- and superordination, and hence of power differentials. The essence of the word *dialogue* is reflection and action in fundamental interaction. Reflection without action, action without reflection is not *praxis*. Words devoid of action are mere "verbalisms;" action devoid of reflection is mere "activism" (Freire, 1972, p. 60). Praxis is a dialectical unity between practice and theory, action and reflection, subjectivity and objectivity; it is in operation when we are permanently engaged in reflection on our action. In turn, the most important form of practice is political practice—practice focused on transforming social relations, which that reflection discloses in our time as limiting or domesticating, rather than liberating.

In turn, real dialogue, *praxis*, develops critical reflection and what Freire calls *conscientization*. The concept of *conscientization* is a difficult one to convey in its fullest meaning, but it generally refers to a deepening of awareness to particular aspects of the relationships between people. In particular, it refers to the "situational" nature of all relationships: "Human beings *are* because they *are* in a situation. And they will *be more* the more they not only critically reflect upon their existence but critically act upon it" (Freire, 1970b, p. 90). When reality, that is, the reality of the situation, becomes clearer, when dimensions of exploitation and oppression are exposed, the individual emerges from ignorance and powerlessness to awareness and a sense of personal, hence collective, efficacy.

Thus emerges *conscientization*, which is possible because while social forces condition the consciousness of human beings, the human being can recognize that it is so conditioned. However, *conscientization* is more than mere overcoming of "false consciousness" and more than simply "becoming aware" of the real nature of the situation in which one is immersed. It involves a critical insertion of the conscientized individual into a reality that has now been demythologized, its common wisdom, rhetoric and "slogans" exposed. Thus, the contradictions of social, political and economic life are held up to the clear light of day with a determination to liberate one's self from them. Freire (1972) had restated the "thesis" of the Hegelian dialectic, that is the dominant idea or *Zeitgeist*, as what he called a "generative theme:" in any particular epoch, "the complex of ideas, concepts, hopes, doubts, values, and challenges in dialectical interaction with their opposites striving toward fulfillment" (p. 73). In our epoch he identifies the key theme as that of domination, while the opposing theme—or subsumed contrast pole—is liberation. Immersed in the reality of those themes, but only when prepared to be so immersed, people can act as cooperative co-investigators and grow in awareness, which will be a critical awareness that develops *conscientization*.

However, *conscientization* is not a "state" one achieves, but a manner in which one operates, a methodology or outlook or process (Freire, 1972, p. 76). It is a basic dimension of reflective action; if one reflects, truly and properly reflects, then, inevitably, certain aspects of reality are exposed, are demythologized. It arises from *praxis* in the core domain of human existence—work, history, culture,

and values—in which we experience the "dialectic between determinism and freedom" (Freire, 1970b, p. 453). It is viable "only
because men's consciousness, although conditioned, can recognize
that it is conditioned" (Freire, 1970b , p. 455). It implies a context
in which people are united by their reflection and action in the
world and they achieve a state of "perceptive clarity," a clarity
Goldman (as cited by Freire) called "the maximum of potential consciousness" (Freire, 1970b, p. 471). As Matthews (1980) has
stressed, it is not "enlightenment," which depends on private, reflective isolation, but something arising from public, social practices (p.
87). In turn, it issues as a project, a true revolutionary project in
which "people assume the role of subject in the precarious adven-
ture of transforming and recreating the world" (Freire, 1970b, p.
468).

　　To be sure, humanistically oriented psychologists have pointed to the importance of liberating the self from total control by
social forces in an exercise of self-actualization that provides a degree
of control and an ability to influence those social forces (Rogers,
1951/1965). This is forcefully argued by Spring (1975), who suggests, however, that the error of all humanistically oriented psychology is that it is superficial, more a "technique for management and
adjustment than for changing society" (p. 72). The advance that
Freire makes is to go further and see the self-actualized individual
actively seeking to change those social forces.

　　Spring (1975) outlines Freire's ideas within the context of
his discussion of Libertarian thought on education, emphasizing the
manner in which Freire resolves the contradiction between freedom
and determinism (agency and social construction) in the realm of
consciousness. Thus, a person without a consciousness of self who
is engulfed and exhausted by daily toil "is completely propelled by
social forces. But the person who is *aware* of these forces and *conscious*
of their nature is able to break with the trajectory of history and participate in the radical change of self and society" (p. 65). Matthews
(1980) develops the same point in terms of what he discusses as
Freire's "process ontology:" a "developmentalist, dialectical and
dynamic view of reality" in which we, and our social or group
efforts to derive knowledge, are understood as being fallible (p. 91).
However, this does not issue in a relativism, that is, the idea that one
idea is as good as another; some ideas lead to exploitation and ignorance, others to a critical consciousness. Our ideas can be improved
on and our understanding deepened. Ideas that deepen understand-

ing and expose dimensions of reality to which we might be blind, are "better" than those that continue our ignorance and contribute to our exploitation. Equally, he argues that Freire's process ontology and fallibilist epistemology, together, represent a significant opposition to dogmatism and a support of tolerance.

Freire, then, offered a view of education based on genuine dialogue between teacher and student, dialogue that fundamentally changed the relationship between them. In that view is a construal of human beings as able to recognize their social-cultural heritage, reflect critically on it, dialogue about it, and change their social reality if it is found wanting. In his development of this view he offered an ontology and an epistemology, as well as a reworked concept of *praxis* that centers our active life with others as a potential source of deeper understandings. He also offered a concept of *conscientization*, opening people and their circumstances to change in the direction of liberation.

KELLY ON APPLIED PSYCHOLOGY AND CLINICAL PSYCHOLOGY

Kelly (1969e, 1969g) records his critical observations about the notion of *applied* psychology, suggesting at the same time why *clinical* psychology is therefore so significant; and why psychotherapy is so valuable. He discusses how the theories espoused by psychologists so frequently falter in the "real world," how laws and principles generated in controlled situations, such as the so called laws of learning and experimental and empirical work drawing conclusions from the "mean" or "average," and on individuals who conform to those central tendencies, are so limited. Like Freud, he sees no discontinuity between so called abnormal and so called normal behavior, but rather that we will derive deeper understanding if we work with human beings in their own contexts and in terms of their own sense-making. This is especially productive of understanding when we engage those human beings when they are in any one or more of their "extraordinary moments, moments that may be illuminated in the course of psychotherapy" (1963b/1979, p. 214). The rejection of the idea of the "application" of psychological principles or laws derived in one domain to a different domain is not so much because of practical problems concerning the question of whether psychology has really yet derived such laws, or whether a particular observation might be generalizable, but is rather an "in principle" objection. Kelly is arguing that the issue is not one of whether we have anything to apply by way of knowledge, but that we cannot have anything to apply if we work from the laboratory, with "normal" subjects, to the real world of people and their struggles to make sense of their worlds.

For Kelly, psychotherapy provided a special opportunity to see human beings in critical moments when conventional responses, expected behaviors, conformity to expectations and so on, escaped the individual who was "left with no resources other than [their] own nature" (Kelly, 1969e, p. 215). Clinical psychology thus becomes a "focal and essential area and method of scientific inquiry" (Kelly, 1969g, p. 226) working from the real worlds of individuals, from practice to theory; just as in personal construct psychology itself, "theory followed practice . . . in somewhat the same way as 'form follows function'" (Adams-Weber & Mancuso, 1983, p. 2).

Kelly (1969d) asks us to consider clinical psychology as "pure science," a conception of client and therapist alike, and together, framing their interaction differently. That is, in terms of their verbs in the "invitational mood" rather than in the "indicative mood" characteristic of the applied scientist:

> An applied psychologist puts his verbs in the indicative mood, while the pure scientist uses the invitational mood. . . But clinical psychology does not have to be an applied discipline. It can, in the very best sense, be truly scientific. . . . I do not mean that the clinical psychologist uses his clients as unwitting guinea pigs in an experiment. . . . I mean that the clinical psychologist can be scientific in the therapy room, that the client can be— and indeed probably is—a colleague, and that the client and his therapist may come to talk to each other in the language of hypothesis. (Kelly, 1969d, p. 154-155)

The challenge is to regard clinical psychology "as if" it were the purest of sciences, that is, to suppose that it was (1964/1979, p. 162). What then? In this challenge there is a significant shift from the question of whether psychology has produced any knowledge that might be applied and, equally, whether the notion of "application" has any sensible meaning when therapy is understood as an elaboration, a reconstruction, or reordering of a less than optimally functioning construct system. Clinical psychology as applied psychology attempts to interpret for the individual, who is regarded and treated as being relatively ignorant of the real meaning of symptoms. It imposes a particular interpretation, rewards acceptance of that interpretation as "insight" and works to secure acceptance by undermining non-acceptance as "resistance." Both these last two terms, how-

275

ever, "grow out of objective speech and the prestigeful use of the indicative mood in talking about psychological matters" (Kelly, 1969d, p. 155). Clinical psychology as pure science, however, sees the client and therapist acting in the way of the scientist, framing hypotheses that challenge each of them. Personal construct therapy, then, is not the application of rules, laws or principles drawn from a body of knowledge, not the "exploitation of 'scientific findings," but, rather, "an application of basic scientific methodology" per se (Kelly, 1955/1991b, p. 297).

In this conception of therapy there is a particular conception of the therapist and clinician. One aspect of this is the therapist's versatility where he or she is now "parent," now "teacher," now "child" (Kelly, 1955/1991b, p. 45), avoiding being exclusively any of these things. Thus, the therapist is available to be cast in almost any role that the client needs filled in his or her experimentation with new ways of construing. In turn, the clinician must be prepared to give up the notion of a client as passive individual waiting "patiently" for guidance; indeed, the terms "therapy" and "patient" are called into question (Kelly, 1955/1991a, p. 129). Further, the clinician must be able to adopt the client's outlook and consider what he or she would do in the client's shoes. In the whole exercise of clinical intervention the clinician or therapist must be able to work from a *prepared set* of professional constructs, which are nonetheless sufficiently permeable to embrace *any* individual; approach therapy, that is, with "a rich background of experience and with broad conceptualizations, and then, within the matrix of the individual client's life" invent new constructs for the particular case (Kelly, 1955/1991a, p. 136).

HEIDEGGER, FREIRE, PERSONAL CONSTRUCT PSYCHOLOGY

The idea of *techne* as a way of knowing, an encounter with the world that potentially illuminates our understanding of matters beyond everyday awareness, would appear to express something pertinent to an understanding of personal construct psychology as an applied psychology. That is, personal construct psychology can be argued to endorse a notion of applied psychology consistent with the sense of *techne* reclaimed by Heidegger and other philosophers of technology. In this, it understands the applied dimension of psychology as something closer to the original meaning of the term *techne*. Equally, in personal construct psychotherapy the intent is closer to the idea of working with nature rather than demanding of it or imposing on it, particularly when that nature is the nature of human

being, even that of Being. Again, it also appears to be closer to thinking *meditatively* in contrast to thinking *calculatively*. Psychotherapy's task
is to "enable the client, as well as the therapist, to utilize behavior for
asking important questions," questions which go to deeper issues
than those of everyday practicalities but rather "get the human
process going again so that life may go on" (Kelly, 1969f, p. 223).

More generally, personal construct psychology offers a distinctive way of approaching human relationships because of the particular way of viewing the individual's relationship to the (social)
environment, that is, essentially one of understanding that environment rather than exploiting it; a non-instrumental approach that is
arguably the essence of *critical* as distinct from *traditional* reasoning
(Habermas, 1981/1987), and a core aspect of that outlook on the
world that is the egalitarian outlook in which people are always
ends, not means (Warren, 1996). Elsewhere (Warren, 1990) I have
discussed the significance of Lewin's (1931) distinction between an
Aristotelean and a Galilean mode of thought in psychology, and that
distinction is further illustrative here. Lewin argued that psychology
had been held back in its efforts to develop significant understandings of human behaving because it could not let go of the
Aristoteleian approach. Interestingly, he thought that one reason for
this was that psychology had developed from philosophy through
medicine and pedagogy—practical activities in which specific practical outcomes are present and historically, at least, fields where a
notion of "applying theory" is strong—thus remaining attracted to
the taxonomic and classificatory which were characteristic of the
Aristotelian mode of thought. This was to the detriment of psychology.

The Aristotelian mode of thought proceeds from an accepted
understanding of things, events or behavior, from which derives—
by a process of deduction—something about a particular case. This
accepted understanding of things is in the nature of a fixed schema
or fixed template to which particular observations are to be fitted.
The Galileian mode of thought, however, starts with observation of
factors operating in a particular behavior and seeks to explain that
behavior in terms of the dynamic interaction of those factors, with
no idea of applying or imposing fixed categories.

The focus of concern for the Galileian mode of thought is the
individual case, whereas in the Aristotelian mode of thought this is
merely an exemplar of a type. The Galileian mode of thought looks
rather to what is of more interest, that is, the individual case—or,

cases— which are taken in their own terms and their own structure searched-out. This is seen in my earlier (Warren, 1990) example of authoritarian mentality where quite different behaviors, such as those associated with doctrinaire Communism and its trenchant opposition in fundamentalist Catholicism or Fascism, share the same underlying dynamic and appear as but species of a similar underlying construct system or way of making sense of the world.

The Aristoteleian mode of thought sought to apply a set of categories to experience, to impose on the world an existing understanding and fit into it any new experience that came along. By contrast, the Galilean approach searches for the structure of the data in the data itself—be it individual or group "data." In this vein, Winter (1988) discusses how a personal construct psychotherapy approach to a sexual difficulty will not seek to explain the difficulty in terms of imposed ideas or interpretations, but will focus the "logic"—or, better, the "psychologic"—of the difficulty. That is, expressing the core principle of personal construct psychotherapy, the *credulous approach*, the meaning of the difficulty will be sought in the construct system of the sufferer. Thus, Winter's (1988) example of a client experiencing difficulty obtaining an erection might be understood in terms not of Oedipal strivings nor irrational thinking, but as a perfectly rational solution for someone for whom love (for a wife in that case) was totally incompatible with intercourse; in short, one does not have sex with women one loves (the client's other loved women were his mother and sister).

In summary, then, there do appear to be strong affinities between personal construct psychology and the understanding of technology illuminated by thinkers in the domain now identifiable as philosophy of technology. If technology is understood more in the original Greek sense that Heidegger has argued, then applied psychology understood as a technology in that sense—as working with the individual rather than doing something to him or her—is much closer to the exercise in which personal construct psychologists are engaged.

Further, the notion of *praxis*, especially as elaborated by Freire, appears equally as suggestive for personal construct psychology as an "applied psychology." Both the Experience Cycle and the Creativity Cycle describe processes of engagement, reflection, and renewed engagement that are highly analogous to the practice-theory-practice process described by Freire's *praxis*. In the Experience Cycle, the prediction that the individual makes derives from some particular event in the world (Anticipation). Then, that individual becomes thoroughly involved with the event (Investment and Encounter) and validates or fails to validate the prediction that things are thus or so (Confirmation-Disconformation). Finally, the individual revises as appropriate (Revision). The Experience Cycle is a process of action-reflection-action. In the Creativity Cycle, the individual is initially open to varying predictions (loose construing) but closes on a particular prediction (construes more tightly) to test a particular construction; it is a process that would appear to be in place in genuine dialogue (an I-Thou relationship) and absent when the dialogue is one-sided or an individual refuses to hear the constructions of another (an I-It relationship). Conceived as *praxis*, such therapy takes on an inherently liberating stance. Moreover, it requires that the therapist make what Freire calls a "political background choice" in favor of an egalitarian, rather than an authoritarian, outlook on the world (Warren, 1996). McWilliams' (1988, 1996) discussion of the "anarchistic" perspective, which he believes is championed by personal construct psychology, is equally illustrative of the essential dimension of liberation that these observations here generally address.

Moreover, an outlook akin to Freire's *conscientization* can be suggested as emerging from personal construct therapy. As Kelly (1969g) suggests of the person who has found therapy helpful, he or she often says, "In many ways things are the same as they were before, but how differently I see them!" (p. 227). A new awareness emerges that is the basis for new action in and on the world, just as *conscientization* involves a critical consciousness that is not deluded by the "givens" of situations. For Kelly (1955/1991b), the wider task of any clinical intervention is the "continuous shifting of the client's construct system' (p. 19). This might be more imperative if the person is psychologically unwell, but even if he or she is not, psychological health can only be maintained if that person is open to the possibility of continuous change. Equally, therapy does not move a person from this "state" (illness) to some other "state" (health), but rather sees the latter as a continuous process of moving through the Experience and Creativity Cycles.

Finally, the psychotherapeutic method in personal construct psychology, generally, is remarkably like Freire's use of "thematics" or "generative themes." There are two core elements of this psychotherapy, the creduluous approach on the part of the therapist, and the focus on elaboration. As to the first, as noted above, the therapist sees the client's symptoms always as being "logical" ("psychological;" Warren, 1998, p. 120) within that person's construct system. The second refers to the therapeutic goal of developing a deeper and wider understanding of the symptom in the context of that system; elaboration means to detail, to clarify, to specify, to embellish, to explain, and so forth. Now, Freire's use of thematics has the same end in view; essentially an examination of how individuals actually construe situations. His now well-cited example is the discussion that ensued among a group of slum residents in Chile who were shown a movie segment depicting a drunken man walking down a street and past a group of men talking. Contrary to an expectation of the man being construed in a critical way, the residents saw his behavior as completely understandable in terms of his likely sense of powerlessness and hopelessness with which they could well empathize. He was not criticized. Rather, he was seen as a good worker who worked hard and long for wages that were too low to support his family (the only one of the people portrayed in the segment who did work) and someone who was to be admired rather than devalued, and someone who drank because of his frustration. Thematizing, as a basis for reflection and dialogue, has the same method and the same end in view as does personal construct psychotherapy; that is, a joint inquiry into how people construe reality, and this the basis for a dialogue that assists both or all parties to develop deeper understanding and a determination not to be totally determined by circumstances.

Therapy, then, is a psychological process of learning about the client's world in its widest sense, not imposing on that world. Thus, in personal construct psychology, therapy is a "psychological process which changes one's outlook on some aspect of life" (Kelly, 1955/1991b, p. 130). To be sure, Freire had in mind that a particular understanding would emerge; that is, that which saw the reality of exploitation, of inequality, of oppression. However, certainly personal construct psychology proposes a stepping-off point for the type of change that Freire has in mind in its view of human beings as "too recalcitrant to allow" circumstances to control them, and, as history shows, "less and less disposed to accept the dictatorship of circumstances" (Kelly, 1969a, p. 27). In principle, as Neimeyer (1997) in particular notes, there is "nothing endemic to a constructivist model of therapy as conversation that requires a passive therapeutic stance" (p. 59). Thus, too, is that outcome of conscientization, which is the removing of obstacles preventing a clear perception of reality, in equally clear view within personal construct psychothera-py. Further just as Freire's *conscientization* focuses on what might be, on human potential, so Kelly (1969a) urges a focus on an "exploration of what human behavior might be, and what would happen if it were" (p. 36).

Somewhat tangential to, but interesting in, the present con-text of highlighting resonances with Freire's work, is a passing ref-erence Kelly (1969b) makes to the concept of "learning," as is some other more focused comment (Kelly, 1955/1991a). He notes that what he is describing as psychotherapy could equally as well be called "learning" as long as that term is understood as that activity which helps us get on with life (1969b, p. 64). His aversion to the term "learning" was its association—at that time—with the stimu-lus-response implications of that term (Kelly, 1955/1991a, p. 130). Nonetheless, the reconstruing that personal construct psychology envisaged as therapy is likely to be called "learning" by other psy-chologists. However, learning is understood in personal construct psychology as "not a special class of psychological processes; it is synonymous with any and all psychological processes. It is not something that happens to a person on occasion; it is what makes him a person in the first place" (Kelly, 1995/1991a, p. 53). This cen-tering of learning as a feature of our *being*, even our Being, is highly compatible with Freire's epistemological and ontological standpoint.

As Bannister and Fransella (1971, p. 193) suggest, personal construct psychology insists that we experiment not *on* but rather *with* individuals. Thus might psychology be advanced in its under-standing because "two people struggling with major personal issues might prove a scientifically more rewarding focus for psychology than the navigational problems of the rat" (Bannister & Fransella, 1971, p. 124). Just as Freire (1972, p. 78) insists that in real dia-logue and real education the parties are "co-investigators," that those who would otherwise be considered "objects" of investigation and now active and exploratory of their situation, so Kelly (1969d, p. 153) expresses similar sentiment by stating that "for a good many years I have been impressed with the similarities between psy-chotheraeutic and research activities." Psychotherapy is analogous to the relationship between supervisor and research student, a partner-ship in which each struggles for enlightenment, for an elaboration of their "data."

These observations accepted, then, a most apt way of con-ceptualizing personal construct psychology and psychotherapy is in terms of the concept of *praxis*. It is not a matter of "applying" a particular technique of therapeutic intervention, or applying some law or principle established in some experimental situation to understand a particular problem. Rather, situations in which one person seeks help from another, like those where one person seeks to get to know another or to learn from or be guided by another, involve "conversations" or dialogue that is originative of newer, deeper understanding for each (Mair, 1970). In that *conscientization*, which was for Freire the outcome of such dialogic encounters, there is a potent analogy for the image of therapeutic dialogue in personal construct psychology. As Bannister and Fransella (1971, p. 201) put it in respect of psychology generally: "The aim of the psychology of personal constructs, put at its most pious, is liberation through understanding." That observation appears equally an apt characterization of Freire's *conscientization* as of personal construct psychology and therapy.

SUMMARY AND CONCLUSION

Discussions in the field of philosophy of technology have challenged a narrow understanding of technology as a "doing to," challenged that it is the mere application of knowledge. In the most sophisticated form of these discussions, in the work of Heidegger, technology is reclaimed in terms closer to its original meaning where it signified a way of knowing, thereby contributing to an understanding of *Being* through practical encounters with the world; that is, the world of *being*. In so far as personal construct psychology repudiates a notion of working from the laboratory to the real world, from theory to practice, it finds itself aligned with this more sophisticated analysis. If personal construct psychotherapy is a psychotechnology, then an understanding of this in the older (rather than the newer, distorted and distorting) understanding of technology is appropriate.

The form of interaction with the world that has the most potential for both deepening our understanding (and thereby liberating us from oppression) is dialogue about practical activity in which the parties engage in critical reflection. That critical reflection on practice, which changes practice, is *praxis*. It generates *conscientization* as an outlook in which social realities are disclosed, particularly the reality of oppression and domination, and which makes possible action to correct these. Personal construct psychology is best characterized as a social-psychology, a psychology of social action (Butt,

1996): It invloves not a "standing back and pondering" others, but an interaction with them in joint ventures (p. 62). Commencing with what people do and the understandings they have of what they are doing, it is very much a *praxis* most particularly, but not only in its therapeutic mode. Moreover, its goal or aim, arguably, could not be better expressed than in terms of the notion of *conscientization* as an outlook that looks ever to the future, to "what might be." Indeed, Shaull's (1972) observation in introducing Freire's (1972) work literally rings with echoes of personal construct psychotherapy: "[Freire] operates on one basic assumption: that man's ontological vocation (as he calls it) is to be a subject who acts upon and transforms his world, and in so doing moves towards ever new possibilities of fuller and richer life individually and collectively" (p. 12). Compare this with Kelly's (1969f) view of psychotherapy as "the orchestration of techniques and the utilization of relationships in the on-going process of living and profiting from experience," this being what makes psychotherapy such a significant a contribution to human life (Kelly, 1969f, p. 223). Or, his stress on human potential as a move beyond a focus merely on what human beings have done in the past: "psychology's greater task is to join mankind in the exploration of what human behavior might be" (Kelly, 1969a, p. 36).

Finally, the underlying assumption of Freire's analysis is the idea of conflict, that is to say, an idea of human beings involved always in contention, controversy, dispute, and choice. This is also the basic idea of a psychology founded in constructive alternativism, in a belief that we are driven to place meanings on the environments we inhabit, to challenge and change those interpretations and the reality that they seek to represent. Because we can—indeed, must—represent the environment, so we can place alternative constructions upon it, indeed, "do something about it if it doesn't suit" us (Kelly, 1955/1991a, p. 6).

By way of conclusion, then, we might accept that at the least, the forgoing discussion has drawn attention to and described some interesting parallels. That there has emerged a strong critical tradition in the field of philosophy of technology with which personal construct psychology might be easily aligned may not be surprising. However, it does no ill to elaborate these links and highlight them. There is a now well-developed understanding of personal construct psychology as drawing on the wellsprings that irrigate alike phenomenology, especially in its hermeneutic turn, and Existentialism.

In turn, we note that among several areas that have generated discussion in philosophy of technology, phenomenology and Existentialism have been conspicuous.

At a more optimistic or ambitious level, we have possibly deepened our understanding of the location of personal construct psychology in a rich philosophical tradition, but also in a tradition that has never shied away from an active involvement, an engagement in real-life struggles of people, be they everyday problems people have with each other, as envisaged by Butt (1996), or larger-scale ones of the sort addressed by Freire (1972). For personal construct psychology and psychotherapy, this liberation starts with the individual. It is insurrectionist rather than revolutionary; that is, it is focused primarily on a change in "consciousness," the way we interpret the world, rather than primarily a change in social and political structures. Revolution involves replacing one constitution, one set of social structuring, with another; insurrection involves being "constitutionless," being critically aware of the social forces that shape one. Notwithstanding the debate surrounding that issue, it does seem that personal construct psychology has made a political background choice that is in the direction of egalitarianism rather than authoritarianism. That being so, our more optimistic conclusion might be that we have charted two discussions—those of Freire and of the philosophy of technology—to provide a clearer map of the liberation that personal construct psychology and therapy promises, whatever our courage in following it to its radical conclusions.

REFERENCES

Adams-Webber, J., & Mancuso, J. C. (Eds.). (1983). *Applications of personal construct theory.* London: Academic Press.

Bullock, A., & Trombley, S. (1999). *The new Fontana dictionary of modern thought* (3rd ed.). London: Harper Collins Publishers.

Bunge, M., & Ardila, R. (1987). *Philosophy of psychology.* New York: Springer-Verlag.

Burnet, J. (1968). *Greek philosophy: Thales to Plato.* London: Macmillan. (Original work published 1914)

Butt, T. (1996). PCP: Cognitive or social psychology? In J. W. Scheer & A. Catina (Eds.), *Empirical constructivism in Europe: The personal construct approach* (pp. 58-65). Giessen, Germany: Psychosozial Verlag.

Chiari, G., & Nuzzo, M. L. (1996). Personal construct theory within psychological constructivism: Precursor or avante-garde? In B. M. Walker, J. Costigan, L. L. Viney, & B. Warren (Eds.), *Personal construct theory: A psychology for the future* (pp. 25-45). Melbourne: Australian Psychological Society.

Drever, J. (1952). *A dictionary of psychology.* Harmondsworth: Penguin.

Durbin, P.T. (1976). Are there interesting philosophical issues in technology as distinct from science? *Proceedings of the Philosophy of Science Association, 2*, 139-171.

Ellul, J. (1965). *The technological society* (J. Wilkinson, Trans.). London: Jonathon Cape. (Original work published 1954)

Ellul, J. (1980). *The technological system* (J. Neugroschel, Trans.). New York: Continuum Publishing Corporation. (Original work published 1977)

Feenberg, A. (1991). *Critical theory of technology.* New York: Oxford University Press.

Freire, P. (1970a). The adult literacy process as cultural action for freedom. *Harvard Educational Review, 40*, 205-225.

Freire, P. (1970b). Cultural action and conscientization. *Harvard Educational Review, 40*, 452-477.

Freire, P. (1972). *Pedagogy of the oppressed.* Harmondsworth: Penguin.

Habermas, J. (1987). *The theory of communicative action: Vol. 2. Lifeworld and system: A critique of functional reason* (T. McCarthy, Trans.).   Boston: Beacon Press. (Original work published 1981)

Heidegger, M. (1966). *What is called thinking?* (F. D. Wieck & J. G. Gray, Trans). New York: Harper & Row. (Original work published 1959)

Heidegger, M. (1977). *The question concerning technology* (W. Lovitt, Trans.). New York: Harper & Row. (Original work published 1954)

Heidegger, M. (1978). *Being and time* (J. Macquarrie & E. Robinson, Trans.). Oxford: Basil Blackwell. (Original work published 1927)

Holly, D. (1974). *Beyond curriculum.* St. Albans, Herts.: Granada Publishing.

Illich, I. (1972). *Deschooling society.* Harmondsworth: Pelican.

Jones, B. (1982). *Sleepers wake! Ttechnology and the future of work.* Melbourne: Oxford University Press.

Juenger, F. (1949). *The failure of technology* (F. D. Wieck, Trans.). Hinsdale, IL: Henry Regney. (Original work published 1946)

Kelly, G. A. (1969a). Ontological acceleration. In B. Maher (Ed.), *Clinical psychology and personality: The selected papers of George Kelly* (pp. 7-45). New York: Wiley.

Kelly, G. A. (1969b). The autobiography of a theory. In B. Maher (Ed.), *Clinical psychology and personality: The selected papers of George Kelly* (pp. 46-65). New York: Wiley.

Kelly, G. A. (1969c). Man's construction of his alternatives. In B. Maher (Ed.), *Clinical psychology and personality: The selected papers of George Kelly* (pp. 66-93). New York: Wiley.

Kelly, G. A. (1969d). The language of hypothesis: Man's psychological instrument. In B. Maher (Ed.), *Clinical psychology and personality: The selected papers of George Kelly* (pp. 147-162). New York: Wiley.

Kelly, G. A. (1969e). Psychotherapy and the nature of Man. In B. Maher (Ed.), *Clinical psychology and personality: The selected papers of George Kelly* (pp. 207-215). New York: Wiley.

Kelly, G. A. (1969f). The psychotherapeutic relationship. In B. Maher (Ed.), *Clinical psychology and personality: The selected papers of George Kelly* (pp. 216-223). New York: Wiley.

Kelly, G. A. (1969g). Personal construct theory and the psychotherapeutic interview. In B. Maher (Ed.), *Clinical psychology and personality: The selected papers of George Kelly* (pp. 224-264). New York: Wiley.

Kelly, G. A. (1991a). *The psychology of personal constructs: Vol. 1. A theory of personality.* London: Routledge. (Original work published 1955)

Kelly, G. A. (1991b). *The psychology of personal constructs: Vol. 2 . Clinical diagnosis and psychotherapy.* London: Routledge. (Original work published 1955)

Leman-Stefanovic. I. (1987). *The event of death: A phenomenological enquiry.* The Hague: Martinus Nijhoff.

Lewin, K. (1931). The conflict between the Aristotelian and Galileian modes of thought in contemporary psychology. *Journal of General Psychology, 5,* 141-177.

Lobkowicz, N. (1967). *Theory and practice: History of a concept from Aristotle to Marx.* Notre Dame: University of Notre Dame Press.

McWilliams, S. A. (1988). On being a personal anarchist. In F. Fransella & L. Thomas, (Eds.), *Experimenting with personal construct psychology* (pp. 17-25). London: Routledge.

McWilliams, S. A. (1996). Accepting the invitational. In B. M. Walker, J. Costigan, L. L. Viney, & B. Warren (Eds.), *Personal construct theory: A psychology for the future* (pp. 57-78). Melbourne: Australian Psychological Society.

Mair, M. (1970). The person in psychology and psychotherapy. *British Journal of Medical Psychology, 43,* 197-205.

Marcuse, H. (1941) Some implications of modern technology. *Studies in Philosophy and Social Science, 9,* 414-439.

Marcuse, H. (1969). *Eros and civilization.* London: Sphere Books. (Original work published 1955)

Marx, K. (1975). The economic and philosophical manuscripts of 1844. In K. Marx & F. Engels, *Collected works* (Vol. 3, pp. 229-346). London: Lawrence & Wishart. (Original work published 1844)

Marx, K. (1976). The German ideology. In K. Marx & F. Engels, *Collected works* (Vol. 5, pp. 19-539). London: Lawrence & Wishart. (Original work published 1845)

Matthews, M. (1980). Knowledge, action and power. In R. Mackie (Ed.). *Literacy and revolution: The pedagogy of Paulo Freire* (pp. 82-92). London: Pluto Press.

Mitcham, C. (1994). *Thinking through technology.* Chicago: University of Chicago Press.

Neimeyer, R. A. (1997). Problems and prospects in constructivist psychology. *Journal of Constructivist Psychology, 10,* 51-74.

Postman, N., & Weingartner, C. (1971). *Teaching as a subversive activity.* Harmondsworth: Penguin

Rogers, C. R. (1965). *Client-centred therapy.* Boston: Houghton Mifflin. (Original work published 1951)

Sartre, J. P. (1966) *Being and nothingness* (H. E. Barnes, Trans.) New York: Philosophical Library. (Original work published 1943)

Shaull, R. (1972). Foreword. In P. Freire, *Pedagogy of the oppressed*. Harmondsworth: Penguin.

Spring, J. (1975). *A primer of libertarian education*. St. Urbain, Montreal: Black Rose Books.

Tesconi, C., & Morris, V. C. (1972) *The anti-man culture: Bureautechnocracy and the schools*. Urbana: University of Illinois Press.

Titchener, E. B. (1928). *A beginner's psychology*. New York: Macmillan.

Warren, W. G. (1990). Personal construct theory and the Aristotelian and Galileian modes of thought. *International Journal of Personal Construct Psychology, 3*, 263-280.

Warren, W. G. (1996). The egalitarian outlook as the underpinning of the theory of personal constructs. In D. Kalekin-Fishman and B. Walker (Eds.), *The construction of group realities* (pp. 103-119). Malabar, FL: Krieger.

Warren, W. G. (1998). *Philosophical dimensions of personal construct psychology*. London: Routledge.

Winter, D. (1988). Reconstructing an erection and elaborating ejaculation: Personal construct theory perspectives on sex therapy. *International Journal of Personal Construct Psychology, 1*, 81-99.

Zimmerman, M. E. (1990). *Heidegger's confrontation with modernity: Technology, politics, art*. Bloomington: Indiana University Press.

CHAPTER 14

Responsive Understandings in Living Encounters: Re-Figuring Intellectual Inquiry

John Shotter

> It is not experience that organizes expression, but the other way around—*expression organizes experience*. Expression is what first gives experience its form and specificity of direction.
>
> (Voloshinov, 1986, p. 85)

> For more clearly . . . in my experience of others than in my experience of speech or the perceived world, I inevitably grasp my body as a *spontaneity which teaches me what I could not know in any other way except through it.* . . . It [my body] must teach me to comprehend what no constituting consciousness can know— my involvement in a 'pre-constituted' world."
>
> (Merleau-Ponty, 1964, pp. 93-95)

Below, I want to explore the question of whether there is somewhere else to go beyond or after social constructionism. Is there yet further progress to be made? I think there is. Indeed, it is a change of a much more radical and startling kind than any in recent years. If we are to bring something new into existence—some new practices, some radically new forms of inquiry, some new ways of being—rather than trying to move forward to formulate yet further theories or frameworks, I think we must move backward. We must come to a much greater awareness of, or sensitivity to, the very strange nature of the ways of making sense of each other, and of our surrounding circumstances, that are already occurring, spontaneously, between us and the othernesses around us now, within the present moment. Indeed, there is something very special about experiencing others' expressions and gestures (their unfolding bodily movements) in the course of their arrival. As they unfold we feel ourselves "called" to "answer" them in some way: we look in the direction they are looking, we attend to their cries, we see them interested in something and seek to find its source too.

As living, embodied beings (as "open" systems) we cannot help but be spontaneously responsive to events occurring around us, both to events that we ourselves, so to speak, "make"—by comprehensively attending to a location in our surroundings with our eyes, ears, turnings of the body, and so on—and those that just happen, that spontaneously "call" us to attend to them. As a result of being responsive in this way, strange things happen to and within us. Not only is there a rich and complex intertwining of our own outgoing responsive activities with those coming into us from our surroundings, but also within this intricate intertwining, a "space" with a "depth" (of human possibilities) to it is created around us. At the point of contact between two or more different forms of life with each other, another (collective) form of life emerges—a form of life with its own unique, horizon-bound environment (i.e., a world).

The idea of "going back" to gain an awareness of our embedding in what we might call this *primordial* "responsive order" (Gendlin, 1997), and the style of inquiry required if we are to do this, will be central to everything I want to say. For, as I see it, our current view—of ourselves as subjectivities viewing our surroundings as something objective—is an emergent outcome of other, prior, much more intricate kinds of involvement with the others and othernesses around us. It is the ceaseless flow of shifting, spontaneously responsive activities occurring between ourselves and the others and othernesses around us, which is always already there in the background to everything we do and say, that we must now attend to and describe. For these activities are the source from which all our more self-consciously controlled activities emerge and have their being; it is also the context into which they can ultimately re-enter, thus to modify it.

OUR SPONTANEOUSLY RESPONSIVE, LIVING, BODILY ACTIVITY

To make sense of the primordial responsive order already present in the background of our lives together, we need a new kind of attention to our living, spontaneously responsive, bodily activity. For life in our moment by moment living of it is very different from how we think and talk about it, after the event, in terms of the traditional Cartesian view of it as merely a passive puppet-like host inhabited and animated by an all-powerful rational mind.[1] Our lives are fuller, more multi-dimensional, more fluid, with fleeting, complexly intertwined shifts of energy than we are able, officially, to recognize. We can move in an instant from an outgoing focus on an aspect of one's surroundings at one moment, to an inner focus on supposings and ponderings, on rememberings, imaginings, and desirings the next, with each moment in some meaningful way interconnected with the next. There is something very special also about human moments of *expression*: we can see the others around us thinking, hesitating, looking, listening, wanting, trying, and so on. While the Prousts, Flauberts, and Joyces of the world might attempt to capture such moments in their novels, we do not have any established, routine ways to grasp such living moments in our ongoing, unfinished, unfolding living of them. We do not usually reflect on our expressions in the course of their expression. Indeed, we still feel that any such efforts (if made at all) rightly belong in the world of art, for they only have a point for those seeking to refine their sensibilities; they are not, and cannot be, we feel, an ordinary part of daily life. Only what can be truly shared by all—properly tested and evaluated objective knowledge—can serve that function. Thus, in scientific psychology, with its commitment to being objective, we try to capture life only in terms of its completed products, its outcomes, in terms similar to how we grasp actual objects in our surroundings. As a result, we try to understand our living activities—which are emergent, unitary wholes, articulated into "parts" only within the context of each such whole—by explaining them to ourselves in terms of a set of essentially non-living, externally related, objective parts[2] (i.e., in speculative, theoretical terms, as if beneath their everydayness was something hidden as yet utterly unknown to us). Speculative theo-

[1] No wonder the idea that our bodies could be "snatched" at any moment by another alien and free-floating mind is a powerful fantasy for us today.

[2] William James (1890) called this "The Psychologist's Fallacy:" "The psychologist... stands outside the mental state he speaks of. Both itself and its objects are objects for him. Now when it is a *cognitive* state (percept, thought, concept, etc.), he ordinarily has no other way of naming it than as the thought, percept, etc., of *that object*. He himself, meanwhile knowing the self-same object in his way, gets easily led to suppose that the thought, which is *of* it, knows it in the same way in which he knows it, although this is often far from being the case. The most fictitious puzzles have been introduced into our science by this means" (p. 196). It leads us to think that when we speak, there must a sort of "inner eye" that looks at our knowledge (inner mental representations) of syntax to guide us in formulating our utterances grammatically.

ries thus come to guide our research rather than undeniable facts of our existence.

The overall thrust of my article is to argue that this need not be so. Recent work by Wittgenstein, Bakhtin, Voloshinov, and Merleau-Ponty, along with the earlier work of Goethe, suggest to us a quite different way of orienting ourselves toward and relating ourselves to our surroundings. As a consequence, they also suggest to us a quite different way of thinking and talking about what we mean by the words "knowledge," "understanding," and "inquiry"—and many other such words related to the nature of our intellectual lives together. The trouble is that currently, we do know how to direct each other's attention to those aspects of our activities in the present moment that matter and that make a difference in our lives. We lack the linguistic means, collectively, to point out crucial features of our interactions with each other in the course of their occurrence. As Milan Kundera (1993) puts it: "When we study, discuss, analyze a reality, we analyze it as it appears in our mind, in our memory. We know reality only in the past tense. We do not know it as it is in the present, in the moment when it is happening, when it is. Remembering is not the negative of forgetting. Remembering is a form of forgetting" (p. 128).

Yet in our actual acting, the fact is that we do know in our moment by moment practical dealings with our surroundings both their subtle details and of the "mental movements," so to speak, that we make in dealing with them. Indeed, that we do know what is going in our everyday practical dealings with each other, fleeting moment by fleeting moment, is apparent to us in any conversation of importance to us—we respond to the slight hesitations of our conversational partners, to their knowing smiles, the embarrassed flickers of their eyes, a changed rate of breathing, and so on. We feel ourselves completely immersed within a continually changing emotional ambience that functions for us as a measure of the shifting direction of our conversation, where it now is and where it appears to be heading. Indeed, conversational analysts (e.g., Ochs, Schegloff & Thompson, 1996) are currently reinforcing this claim with some very detailed and intricate measurements. So although it might seem as if there is too much going on too quickly to attend to it all, the fact is that we do discriminate many such refined nuances with very great accuracy and acumen. As Wittgenstein (1953) puts it: "If it is asked: 'How do sentences manage to represent?'—the answer might be: 'Don't you know? You certainly see it, when you use them.' For nothing is concealed" (no. 435). If we fail to formulate an intelligible account of how we can and do make a unique and subtly nuanced sense to each other in a way that allows us to appreciate more explicitly our own part in the process, then that can only be due to the difficulties we face in making use of the linguistic means available to us, not in the visibility of the relevant phenomena—for, as Wittgenstein (1953, no. 435) adds, "nothing is hidden."

What follows below, then, is an attempt, drawing on the work of the above mentioned writers (and many others), to overcome this lack: to use portable words, words in a decontextualized text, to point toward aspects of lives together at crucial points from within our living of them, while trying at those points to stay within the present moment, to stay within the unceasing living flow of life.

SOCIAL INTERACTION: THE PRIMORDIAL SCENE

I look across the room at a stranger, our eyes meet, and she smiles slightly in response, or looks away again immediately. Although it is difficult to say precisely in what our sense of contact consists, our sense of being in one or another kind of contact with each other is nonetheless distinct. It is visible to us in the movement of our eyes. Each of us can see the other seeing us; we can see the other respond to our responses to them. Upon analysis, there is a sensed correlation in the interplay between our scanning of them and their scanning of us. But the character of the interplay between us is much more than merely a quantitative matter of this kind, more than merely a matter of correlations between outer features of our activities accessible to all external observers. For, just as in a handshake between friends, when I feel your hand as strong and joyous and you feel mine as limp and uncertain, so it is also from within an exchange of glances: I can gain a qualitative sense of your inner nature, a sense of who you are, while you can gain a sense of me. Just as I sense the ice on the road through the changed way my car responds to my efforts to steer it, so it is with my experience of "you." Your inner nature—your care and respect for me, your vigor and zest for life, your distractedness and disorientation at events in your life—they all become apparent to me through the slight variations in how you respond to the rhythm of my active hand movements with your's—as my inner nature becomes apparent to you in the same way. There is a certain "style" or consistency in your responsive "answers" to my "calls:" you are always just a little ahead of me, or stiffer, or slower, etc. Just as when reading we sense a meaning *through* the words we read, while the words themselves remain in the background, so the *signs* (the specific variations) in terms of which you become apparent to me also withdraw into the background. They pass unnoticed. But there is even more, something else that happens in our encounters with each other that is also utterly inaccessible to outsiders. A little world with its own requirements and understandings, a living whole that makes "calls" on us and to which we feel "answerable," emerges between us and around us. My keenness to meet you takes you by surprise. Your surprise disturbs me and I draw back a little. Our meeting becomes a little awkward. Something is needed to start us off again, a new beginning. You smile and say what a nice day it is, and let us walk along together for a bit, and I agree. The fall has begun and the brightly colored leaves set the scene for the character of our friendship. We feel comfortable with each other again.

But how are the knowings and understandings described above, which guide us in our practical doings, possible in the midst of all this fluidity? For they seem to involve the creative combining of two or more sources of activity to produce, not simply a merged average activity, but a distinct otherness located "out there," a unitary whole with its own "inner" nature, a positioned source of activity with its own unique "style" of life. I visually scan over a scene. My two eyes return to, and convergently focus on, the same rock face, up there, again and again, as well as on possible hand holds on my climb up to it from where I now stand. But in doing this, it is not a matter of me simply integrating a sequence of separate *stimuli* (static pictures) provided me by a sequence of glimpses, but of me finding ways within the continuous flux of spontaneously responsive experience to orient myself in relation to my surroundings by focusing all (or a number) of my sensory channels on certain invariances or stabilities within that flux to which I can return time and time again. I see what I touch and touch what I see, and hear the rasping sound of my fingers slipping on the rock as issuing from the point at which I can see them touching it. As Gibson (1979) points out: "Vision is a whole perceptual system, not a channel of sense. One sees the environment not with the eyes but with the eyes-in-the-head-on-a-body-resting-on-the-ground" (p. 205). And, we might add, similarly for the auditory system: it is not an isolated channel of sense either. One hears one's environment not with the ears, but with the ears-in-the-head-on-a-body-resting-on-the-ground-facing-in-a-certain-direction; thus the two systems are not in fact physically separable from each other, but reciprocally implicated in each other's operation.

Similar to my creative discovery of a set of stable "places" in terms of which to orient myself in my climb up a rock face, so the otherness of the other is made available to me in the same way (i.e., in the constancies discoverable in the variations between my many outgoing expressions addressed to them, and all the incoming responses from them addressed to me). They, (i.e., their "style" of being) is present to me in the differences between my expressions and their responses to them, as I am present to them in the same way.

But how can we make sense of such a creative process as this, in which a unitary whole is created to accommodate, so to speak, a set of otherwise unrelated fragments? Seven considerations (at least) are, I think, relevant:

1. One consideration that is crucial to the approach I shall take is Bakhtin's (1981, 1984, 1986) claim that our living relations to the others and othernesses around us are structured neither in cause and effect terms, nor in terms of sign to meaning, but dialogically (i.e., in relationally-responsive terms, in terms of a circumstance or situation "calling for" or "motivating" a response from us). As he puts it with respect to our verbal utterances:

> Language lives only in the dialogical interaction of those who make use of it...Dialogic relationships are reducible neither to logical relationships nor to relationships oriented semantically toward their referential object, [these] relationships in and of themselves [are] devoid of any dialogical element. They must clothe themselves in discourse, become utterances, become positions of various subjects expressed in discourse, in order that dialogic relations might arise among them. 'Life is good', 'Life is not good'. We have before us two judgments... Between these two judgements there exists a specific logical relation: one is the negation of the other. But between them there are not and cannot be any dialogic relationships; they do not argue with each other in any way.... Both these judgments must be embodied, if a dialogic relationship is to arise between them and toward them. (p. 183)

Thus, when these two judgments are expressed in two utterances by two different individuals, one in response to the other, then they can give rise to disagreement, to con-

tradiction, to controversy, and so on; then they are constitutive of one or another kind of relationship between the
people concerned. Indeed, more than that, as we shall see,
a unified world containing the two individuals concerned
also begins to come into existence, a world able to function
as a context in which such a disagreement, contradiction,
or controversy can make sense.

2. The dialogical is thus born in the space between the living,
bodily expressions of one individual and the spontaneous
bodily responses to them by an other. Rather than occurring in an instant, however, such dialogically structured
activity develops over time. In being neither simply caused
by an external (stimulus) event (behavior), nor due to the
reasons or motives of an individual (action), it falls into a
special, third category of activity, exhibiting an intertwined, multidimensional complexity. Its unfolding
"shape" owes its character to its continually changing
responsive relations to its surroundings as people sequen-
tially "answer" spontaneously to the "calls" coming to
them in turn from within their different involvements with
their surroundings.

3. We are always involved in the world around us in one way
or another. Not to be involved, not to be oriented toward
our surroundings, but to be totally disconnected from
them, is not, as living beings, an option for us.

4. Whatever individuals do in response to their surroundings
is both "expressive" of their attitudes or orientations to
them, as well as "calls out" an other's response. The relation
of such "expression-summoned bodily responsiveness," if
we can call it that, to us later being able to express meanings to each other, is well expressed by Mead (1934), who
notes that: "The mechanism of meaning is . . . present in
the social act before the emergence of consciousness or
awareness of meaning occurs. The act or adjustive response
of the second organism gives to the gesture of the first
organism the meaning it has" (pp 77-78). In other words,
long before anything occurs in our heads, in our conscious
experience, we can find in the very structure of our responsive bodily activities the precursors or prototypes for what
later we shall talk of in mental or cognitive terms.

5. This gives rise to another consideration of great importance—although it may seem very strange indeed to bring
it in at this point. It is the importance of the enthymeme or
enthymemic structures. In rhetoric, an enthymeme—like
the two utterances mentioned above: "Life is good" and
"Life is bad"—consists in only two propositions, and lacks
the "middle term" that joins them; if the two utterances are
to be accepted as jointly making sense, then the middle
term (the contextualizing world) must be implicitly and
creatively supplied by all those involved. Put otherwise, an
enthymeme or enthymematic structure occurs when a
speaker or performer says or does something that an other
who witnesses it responds to in such a way that both performer and audience agree to the resulting joint outcome
(Bitzer, 1959). I mention the importance of enthymemic
structures in the light of the following comment by
Voloshinov (1987):

> Whatever kind it be, the behavioral utterance always
> joins the participants in the situation together as *co-par-*
> *ticipants* who know, understand, and evaluate the situa-
> tion in a like manner... Thus, the extraverbal situation
> is far from being merely the external cause of an utter-
> ance—it does not operate on the utterance from the
> outside, as if it were a mechanical force. Rather, *the sit-*
> *uation enters into the utterance as an essential constitutive part of the*
> *structure of its import.* Consequently, a behavioral utterance
> as a meaningful whole is comprised of two parts: (1)
> the part realized or actualized in words and (2) the
> assumed part. On this basis, the behavior utterance can
> be liken to an enthymeme."[3] (p.100)

6. But how are the "middle terms" of enthymemes created?
This question leads me on to a fourth consideration: As we
have seen, dialogically structured, living activity cannot be
described in merely causal terms, nor can it be understood
logically or rationally in terms of people's reasons for so
acting. It seems to be an utterly distinct and very strange
third kind of activity, in which the individual activities
involved, although they may be very different from each
other, nonetheless form, for a moment, a single, true unity

---

[3] Here is a precise example of the previous point—that we can find in the very
structure of our responsive bodily activities, the precursors or prototypes for what
later we shall talk of in mental or cognitive terms.

of internally related parts. It is like the complex unity produced in the stranding and intertwining of the different
instruments in an orchestra playing a symphony; with each
playing its part, the unity of a dialogically-structured event
is, as Bakhtin (1984) paradoxically puts it, "plurality of
unmerged voices and consciousnesses" (p. 6)—they "combine but are not merged in the unity of the event" (p. 6).

7. But how can a unity be formed from unmerged con-
stituents. Should not we more properly call it a mixture or
an amalgam? Like splitting the atom, a contradiction in
terms would seem to be involved. What could a living unity
of unmerged entities or activities be like? How are living relations within such a unity different from the dead, mechanical, and logical relations with which we are familiar? Here,
I want to draw on Merleau-Ponty's (1962; 1964) work: he
takes the spontaneous intertwining of the two monocular
views from our two eyes as a paradigm for what can happen when two separate activities intertwine in a living relation to each other. As we know—rather than a blurred,
averaged, and still two-dimensional view—in the intertwining we become the beneficiaries of a three dimensional, binocular view of the scene before us. Indeed, from the
slight variations between the different views from the two
eyes, besides a left-right and an up-down dimension of
relation between ourselves and our surroundings, a third
relational-dimension of near and far emerges, a dimension
that allows us to orient toward and act in our surroundings
in a more refined way. The different arrival time of sounds
at our left and right ears operates in the same way, giving
us not a merged echo effect, but the directionality of the
sound.

These seven considerations bring out something of what is
so very special in our embedding within what we now might call a
"responsive order" (Gendlin, 1997). New relations that matter to us,
new features requiring our evaluative judgments, new dimensions
that both offer us certain opportunities for action while also exert-
ing certain calls upon us to which we must respond, are continually
being created, unnoticed, in our dialogically-structured encounters
with the others and othernesses around us. Although we usually
remain unaware of always being situated within such a dialogically

structured space, although the created sense of a "depth" usually remains unarticulated in the background to our lives together, it is always *from within* such a complexly intertwined space—in "answer" to the "calls" it exerts upon us—that we responsively perform our actions. The unique nature of such spaces can, thus, only be studied *from within* the practices in which they are created. Thus to investigate their nature, their structure, the calls they can exert on us, what is possible for us within them and what is not, we need some utterly new methods of investigation, quite different from the "onlooker" methods inherited from the natural sciences. Instead of dealing with regularities and repetitions, as in modernist inquiries, we must deal with quite specific "once-occurrent events of Being" (Bakhtin, 1993, p. 2), occurring in the quite distinct and specific realities of under-standing emerging between us in the many different relationships in which we become involved. It is toward the nature of these methods and their comparison with what currently we think it is to be rational that I now turn.

METHODS OF A DELICATE EMPIRICISM: "ENTERING INTO" THE WORLD OF AN OTHER

We have taken it, then, that there is something very special about us as living, embodied beings. Our living bodies are not just secondary things that our minds happen to animate, as in the modernist-Cartesian approach. Nor is the world around us just an inert world of things and objects "over there" which provide us with bodily *stimuli* that we, in perception, must discover how to *interpret*. We have also accepted above that there is something very special about those moments when we and the others and othernesses around us are in a mutually responsive contact with each other, spontaneously (i.e., immediately and unthinkingly). In such moments, as Merleau-Ponty (1964) puts it (to repeat his words from the epigraph quota-tion above), my body is "*a spontaneity which teaches me what I could not know in any other way except through it*" (p. 93). Wittgenstein (1980) expresses a similar idea in commenting, "the origin and the primitive form of the language game is a reaction" (p. 31). He goes on: "But what is the word 'primitive' meant to say here?" he asks, "Presumably that this sort of behavior is *pre-linguistic*: that a language-game is based *on* it, that it is the prototype of a way of thinking and not the result of thought" (1981, no. 541).

Thus, in what follows, we shall take what might be called *the interactive moment* as the primal scene of social life, and center all our inquiries within such moments. But in doing so, I must repeat a warning: in focusing on such moments, we must not forget the never ceasing existence of the background flow of spontaneously responsive, continually shifting activity in which all our more self-conscious activities are embedded. We must not slip back into modern ways of thinking in which it is assumed that any process, any flowing activity simply consists in a sequence of externally related, self-contained components parts, mentally integrated into a whole in some way—like the separate frames of a movie. Our task is the reverse of this. For we must differentiate the moments of interest to us from an otherwise rich and comprehensively mixed up whole, a unity that never ceases to be present to us as a unity throughout our dealings with it.

Such a shift in standpoint will, as we shall see, entail a radical change in how we think and talk about the nature of intellectual inquiries in human affairs. In contrast to modernist inquiries, rather than beginning with the formulation of speculative hypotheses meant to picture or represent the structure of "hidden" mechanisms and seeking to introduce new practices "out of the blue," so to speak, our task will be very different. We shall begin with our already existing practices, and have a much more practical aim.[4] Given the quite distinct and specific circumstances in which we are involved, in both our everyday and special practices, and the quite specific realities of understanding that have so far developed within them, our task is to discover how our already existing practices might be further linguistically articulated and discursively understood, thus to further refine and elaborate them. But, to what features of our involvements with our surroundings should we attend? What can we count on? Where are the fixities, the anchor points, so to speak, in term of which we can speak in a sharable way with each other about our activities?

As I have already noted above, both Wittgenstein and Merleau-Ponty point out to us the importance of our spontaneous,

---

[4] Given our focus on events occurring within the present moment, modernist inquiries, it can be argued, are both *after the fact* and *beside the point*. They are after the fact because in taking the modernist stance of an external observer, we divert our attention away from the fleeting complexity of those moments of responsive adjustment within which we discover, in the present, how to tailor our actions in the course of their performance to their surrounding circumstances. They are beside the point because in so hiding the unfolding relation of our performances to their surroundings, we then turn our attention in the wrong direction: we inquire into supposed occurrences inside the heads of individuals rather than attending to events actually occurring between them.

bodily reactions to events—both self-made and naturally occurring—as teaching us something new. It is, as Steiner (1989)
remarks: "The 'otherness' that enters us makes us other" (p. 189). To
their remarks above and this remark of Steiner's, I want to add another of Wittgenstein's (1953). It is simply that "our attitude to what is
alive and what is dead, is not the same. All our reactions are different" (1953, no. 284). We have not taken this simple distinction seriously enough. A quite special and distinct form of engaged, responsive understanding becomes available to us with living forms that is
quite unavailable to us with dead ones. While we can only study dead
forms from a distance, seeking to understand the pattern of events in
the past leading up the present form of their existence, with living
forms, we can *enter into a relationship* with them and, if we open ourselves to their movements, we can find ourselves spontaneously
responding to them. In other words, instead of seeking to explain a
present activity in terms of the past, we can understand it in terms
of its *meanings* for us now (i.e., in terms of the spontaneous responses it "calls for" from us in the present moment).

Totally entranced with the modernist, Cartesian tradition, we
have (in our official, intellectual dealings) ignored the knowings and
understandings available to us in this everyday way. They seem to lack
the proper stamp of Truth! Thus, when currently unsure of how to
answer the "calls" coming to us from our surroundings, we feel an
overwhelming temptation to treat our uncertainty as a "problem" to
which must find a "solution" in terms of an explanation. Whereas,
suggests Wittgenstein (1981):

> . . . the difficulty... is not that of finding the solution but rather
> that of recognizing as the solution something that looks as if it
> were only a preliminary to it... This is connected, I believe, with
> our wrongly expecting an explanation, whereas the solution to
> the difficulty is a description, if we give it the right place in our
> considerations. If we dwell upon it, and do not try to get beyond
> it. (no. 314)

In other words, when faced with a disorienting circumstance, a circumstance in which we do not know how "to go on,"
rather than turning away from it and burying ourselves deep in
thought in an attempt to mentally and imaginatively construct a way
to explain it in ways already familiar to us, we should stay "with it."
We should look it over as we look over a painting or a sculpture in
an art gallery. We should respond to it from up close, from a distance,
from this angle and that, until we can begin to gain a shaped and

vectored sense of the space of possibilities it opens up to us in the responses it "calls" from us. And we should do this in collaboration with the others involved with us in the practice in question. This kind of collaborative "surveying" of our activities and practices from within our conduct of them is a quite different kind of activity from thinking about them theoretically. It leads to a quite different way— a way I have in fact been using—for us to communicate between us about our practices. To allow ourselves to be influenced in this way is to follow an utterly different set of methods. It is to follow a set of methods first developed by Johann Wolfgang von Goethe [1749-1832].

Descartes (1637/1968) talked about us making ourselves the "masters and possessors of Nature" (p. 78). Later, Kant (1781/1970) urged that each of us must function only as "an appointed judge who compels the witness to answer questions which he himself has formulated" (p. 20), refusing to be led by nature's "lead-strings" if we are to ever follow the true path of science. Goethe, however, saw Descartes's and Kant's scientist as "the task-master of nature, [who] collects experiences, hammers and screws them together and thus, by 'insulating the experiment from man . . . attempt[s] to get to know nature merely through artifices and instruments... [and never leaves] the gloom of the empirico-mechanico-dogmatic torture chamber" (Goethe, as cited in Heller, 1952, pp. 17-18). Goethe sought a more gentle approach, a less Ramboesque way of conducting our intellectual inquiries. As he put it, he sought

> . . . a delicate empiricism which makes itself utterly identical with the object, thereby becoming true theory. . . . The ultimate goal would be to grasp that everything in the realm of fact is already theory. Let us not seek for something beyond the phenomena—they themselves are the theory" (Goethe, as cited in Brady, 1998, p. 98).

I cannot go fully into the details of Goethe's methods here. So let me try to bring out their responsive nature through a comparison between them and the sequence of steps derived from the dominance of Rampant Reason in The Classical Tradition.

The sequence of steps in the classical tradition goes like this:

1. Treat any newness or strangeness as a problem to be solved.

2. Analyze it into already known elements.

3. Find a pattern or order in them.

4. Hypothesize an agency responsible for the order (call it, say, some such mysterious "stuff" such as "The Mind").

5. Find further evidence for "The Mind."

6. Enshrine it in a theory.

7. Manipulate the strangeness (now known in terms of our theory of mind as "Inner Mental Representations") to produce an advantageous outcome.

We thus arrive at what we call a "solution" to the problem. Following Bakhtin (1984), we could call this process the continual, monological rediscovery of sameness. The sequence of steps followed in the less rampant, more delicate empiricism of Bakhtin and Wittgenstein, perhaps under Goethe's influence, goes like this:

1. Treat the othernesses one encounters as radically unknown to us—approach it not like an appointed judge, but with care, respect, and anxiety.

2. "Enter into" dialogically-structured, reciprocally responsive relations with it.

3. We must be "answerable" (partially) to its calls, just as it is (partially) answerable to ours; we must allow it to display its being to us.

4. An "it" appears between us, produced neither solely by us or by the otherness—the "it" is our it: poiesis is at work between us—the sensed creation of form.

5. The form has a shaped and vectored sense to it—we can develop a sensitivity or sensibility of the other's responsive relations to us.

6. As we continue our commerce with the otherness, there is a gradual growth of familiarity with its "inner shape or character."

7. As we "dwell on, or within" our relations with the otherness, we gain a sense of the value of its yet-to-be-achieved aspects—the prospects it offers us for "going on" with it.

As Merleau-Ponty (1962) remarks with respect to such a process:

Here there is nothing comparable to the solution of a problem, where we discover an unknown quantity through its relationship with known ones. For the problem can be solved only if it is determinate, that is, if the cross-checking of the data provides the unknown quantity with one or more definite values. In understanding others, the problem is always indeterminate because only the solution will bring the data retrospectively to light as convergent... [As] in a foreign country, I begin to understand the meaning of words through their place in the context of action, and by taking part in a communal life... [Just as] I begin to understand a philosophy by feeling my way into its existential manner, by reproducing the tone and accent of the philosopher. In fact, every language conveys its own teaching and carries its meaning into the listener's mind. (pp. 179)

In other words, rather than a solution, rather than further information, what we gain in this process is *orientation*: We gain a shaped and vectored sense of how "to go on" in relation to the otherness concerned. Indeed, rather than bringing what was "a problem" to us wholly to an end, the process above gives us only beginnings and beginnings without end—with solutions to this or that particular problem, but no overall final solutions, in principle. But gradually, with patience and persistence, we can come to feel more "at home" with what was at first a radically strange other or otherness. We can come to feel "at home" in the primeval chaos of everyday life!

CONCLUSIONS

The Ramboesque application of the classical tradition in so many spheres of our relations to the others and othernesses around us, has produced a dominant world-picture of only dead and mechanical things, in which nothing new ever occurs—the continual rediscovery of sameness. What would the world around us look like if we were to re-figure it in Bakhtin-Wittgensteinian-Goethean terms? If we were to take a number of our grand terms (like Truth, Consciousness [con=with scio=knowing], Ideas, Knowledge, and so on) and see through them a new living world of unceasing, spontaneously responsive relationships, in which unities were formed and held together for a moment by their participant parts, just for a while calling on each other and then, at the next moment, regrouping to form new unities, and so on.

What an amazing world!

The re-figuring of all of our grand terms in dialogic-poetic terms would, I think, awake us (as William Blake put it) from "single vision and Newton's sleep." This is the crucial point. If we can just desist for a while from asking questions as "appointed judges" and allow ourselves to be responsive to the others and othernesses around us, the world suddenly becomes a wondrous place. Is there still a task for university intellectuals in all of this? You bet! But rather than the noble seclusion of the ivory tower, they will have to open themselves up to world around them if they are to undertake it. Let the re-figuring begin.

REFERENCES

Bakhtin, M. M. (1981). *The dialogical imagination* (C. Emerson & M. Holquist, Trans.). Austin, TX: University of Texas Press.

Bakhtin, M. M. (1984). *Problems of Dostoevsky's* poetics (C. Emerson, Trans.). Minneapolis, MN: University of Minnesota Press.

Bakhtin, M. M. (1986). *Speech genres and other late* essays (V. W. McGee, Trans.). Austin, TX: University of Texas Press.

Bakhtin, M. M. (1993). *Toward a philosophy of the act* (V. Lianpov, Trans., & M. Holquist, Ed.). Austin, TX: University of Texas Press.

Bitzer, L. F. (1959). Aristotle's enthymeme revisited. *Quarterly Journal of Speech, 45,* 399-408.

Brady, R. H. (1998). The idea in nature: Rereading Goethe's organics. In D. Seamon & A. Zajonc (Eds.), *Goethe's way of science: A phenomenology of nature* (pp. 83-111). Albany, NY: State University of New York Press.

Descartes, R. (1968). *Discourse on method and other writings* (F. E. Sutcliffe, Trans.). Harmondsworth: Penguin Books. (Original work published 1637)

Gendlin, G. (1997). The responsive order: A new empricism. *Man and World, 30,* 383-411.

Gibson, J. J. (1979). *The ecological approach to visual perception.* London: Houghton Mifflin.

Heller, E. (1952). *The disinherited mind: Essays in modern German literature and thought.* Cambridge: Bowes & Bowes.

James, W. (1890). *Principles of psychology* (Vol. 1). London: Macmillan.

Kant, I. (1970). *Critique of pure reason* (N. K. Smith, Trans.). London: Macmillan's St Martin's Press. (Original work published 1781)

Kundera, M. (1993). *Testaments betrayed: An essay in nine parts.* New York: Harper Perennial.

Mead, G. H. (1934). *Mind, self and society.* Chicago: University of Chicago Press.

Merleau-Ponty, M. (1962). *Phenomenology of perception* (C. Smith, Trans.). London: Routledge and Kegan Paul.

Merleau-Ponty, M. (1964). *Signs* (R. M. McCleary, Trans.). Evanston, IL: Northwestern University Press.

Ochs, E., Schegloff, E. A., & Thompson, S. A. (Eds.) (1966). *Interaction and grammar.*

Cambridge, UK: Cambridge University Press.

Steiner, G. (1989). *Real presences*. Chicago: University of Chicago Press.

Voloshinov, V. N. (1986). *Marxism and the philosophy of language* (L. Matejka & I. R. Titunik, Trans.). Cambridge, MA: Harvard University Press. (Original work published 1929)

Voloshinov, V. N. (1987). *Freudianism: A critical sketch*. Bloomington, IN: Indiana University Press.

Wittgenstein, L. (1953). *Philosophical investigations*. Oxford: Blackwell.

Wittgenstein, L. (1981). *Zettel* (2nd ed., G.E.M. Anscombe & G. H. V. Wright, Eds.). Oxford: Blackwell.

CHAPTER 15

Now What?
The Personal and Professional in Constructivist Thought

Sara K. Bridges

In this volume we have seen the wide-ranging ways in which those actively involved in the constructivist psychological community view constructivism and its application to practice, notions of disorder, research and the directions constructivism may take in the future. However, as there are many connections between the different ways of viewing constructivist thought (see Raskin, Chapter 1, this volume), there are also many connections between all of the chapters that seem to run throughout this volume. In the following "coda" chapter, I will identify some of these themes both within each section and the volume as a whole, offer my thoughts on the future direction of the family of constructivist psychologies, and pose some questions in light of constructivist psychological theory, training, research and practice.

The primary theme that seems to run throughout this volume is the view that it is time to "get on with it" in terms of living constructively as psychologists. It seems that for many, talking about what constructivism is—and what it is not—is less motivating at this point in the development of the theory. During the 2000 NAPCN at New Paltz conference, I admittedly experienced the same reaction—theory is good, now let us go and live and work within this theory that we inhabit. Thus, I was excited to see so many presentations (and subsequent chapters) that addressed the need to apply more fully what it is that we do. So, would this volume be a good starting place for those new to constructivism or personal construct theory? Probably not.[1] However, this is a good place for those who want to

---

[1] For those interested in introductory writings on constructivist psychology I would suggest: Neimeyer, R. A., & Mahoney, M. J. (Eds.). (1995). *Constructivism in psychotherapy.* Washington, DC: American Psychological Association; Neimeyer, R. A., & Raskin, J.D. (Eds.). (2000). *Constructions of disorder: Meaning-making frameworks for psy-*

truly incorporate postmodern philosophy as it is represented in constructivism into their personal and professional lives. Personally, living constructively to me indicates the seamless integration of our theory of personal change and development into how we relate to others outside of our professional academic lives. For many, this happens as an unintended byproduct of finding a secure theoretical home base in constructivism. Like learning to read or ride a bicycle, for some once they have found their way to constructivism and have started to recognize the goodness of fit with their personal epistemologies, it is difficult to imagine a time when they were not living constructively (or could not read or ride a bike). For others, perhaps the journey to find a place for constructivism in their personal lives is a bit more challenging, especially when confronted with the alternative epistemological foundations of those close to them (i.e., fundamental spirituality, commitment to the way things "really" are, etc.). Regardless, the process of integration seems to be an important one, and one that is touched on by many authors in this volume. Professionally, living constructively means more fully assimilating constructivism into the ways in which we practice, construe the process of diagnosis, perform research and find personally significant ways of inviting constructivism to fit our own realities.

For the past fifty years, theorists and philosophers have been working diligently to enumerate the various ways that constructivism differs from other theories of psychology (Kelly, 1955/1991; Neimeyer, 1995; Neimeyer & Jackson, 1997). Granted there will most likely be a need for more clarification in the coming years. However, currently there is a trend looking at a constructive way of being both in the personal and professional lives of constructivist psychologists. In this volume there is a professional call to make the work that we do more actively constructive; how we practice our theory with different issues without promoting manualized or "standard" treatment protocols, how we conceptualize "disorder," how we conscientiously perform research and decide which important issues warrant our attention and how we envision the future. Additionally, I believe that many people who are drawn to the fami-

chotherapy. Washington, DC: American Psychological Association; Neimeyer, R. A., & Stewart, A. E. (2000). Constructivist and narrative psychotherapies. In C. R. Snyder & R. E. Ingram (Eds.), Handbook of psychological change (pp. 337-357). New York: Wiley; Franklin, C. & Nurius, P. S. (Eds.). (1998). Constructivism in practice: Methods and challenges. Families International Inc.: Milwaukee, WI; Kelly, G. A. (1991). The psychology of personal constructs (2 vols.). New York: Routledge. (Original work published 1955)

ly of constructivist theories find themselves living constructively in their every day lives and interactions with important others.

For some it may be desirable to form a more standardized theory of constructivism. This would certainly make it easier to describe who we "are" and what we "do" to interested others (licensure boards, students, colleagues, etc.) However, the formation of a unified singular theory of constructivist psychology appears to be antitheoretical to constructivism in general. If people are essentially in process (Kelly, 1955) and are able to fluctuate as is indicated by their experiences, it would seem that the theory of constructivism would also be open to modification as needed. Thus, it is refreshing to experience unique views of practice, diagnosis, research, and theory without having to return to a proof of the viability of the family of constructivist psychologies in general. This is not to say that core features of constructivist psychology have been abandoned. Indeed, throughout this volume the authors reiterate some of the core themes of constructivist psychology: truth is relative; reality is invented and not discovered; meaning is socially or individually constructed; and that taking a non-objectivist, non-reductionist stance when working with clients or research participants is beneficial.

After a thorough introduction to the different "varieties" of constructivism offered by Raskin (Chapter 1, this volume), we then shift into four main areas or categories represented at the 2000 conference, which are practice, diagnosis, research and future trends in constructivist psychology. Within each of these sections I have identified themes or, more loosely, "trains of thought" that tie the chapters together. I believe that these themes represent more major trends in constructivist thought and offer them in conjunction with conceptual questions for further consideration.

SECTION ONE: Constructivist Approaches to Practice

Primarily the main theme of this first section is the demonstration that theory does in fact directly contribute to practice. Constructivism has been criticized for being a strictly esoteric philosophy with limited applicability to therapy (Held, 1995). However, the chapters in this section extend the growing literature on constructivist psychotherapy and its specific application to distinct difficulties and predicaments. It should be noted, however, that none of the authors in this section suggest that there is a right way or best way to work with clients and their stories. Instead, they suggest that there are different, and perhaps more useful ways of construing the difficulties clients encounter. Simply becoming aware that there are alternatives to how they are viewing their difficulties can help clients to decide if they want to make a change and, if so, how they would like that change to look. The overarching theme that runs through each of the chapters in this section is that there is not a single correct way of viewing one's difficulties or predicaments. Moreover, there is not a single correct way of working with people as they struggle to better position themselves in life.

I am reminded here of a recent Public Broadcasting Service special called *Earth on Edge*. In general, this special looked at the state of the Earth and the environmental challenges we are facing currently and in the coming decades. Having spent the last two years in rural Northern California, I have become well aware of the debate about logging and the preservation of trees in our environment. There is very little "middle ground." People are either sitting in trees to prevent their destruction or cutting them down, which in general public opinion is seen as a "bad" thing to do. During the *Earth on Edge* program, there was a segment on the current potentially disastrous lack of water in South Africa. It appears that when Europeans first came to South Africa, they were disturbed by the lack of trees. So, as they walked about through hilly territory, filled with only small useless brush, they would spread a trail of seeds—hoping to create forests that would make this barren land more hospitable, more "homelike." However, having trees in this part of the world turned out to be less than a good thing. These invasive gluttonous creatures consumed as much water as they possibly could, very much unlike the low growing natural vegetation. By soaking up billions of gallons of water that were once present in the streambeds, the trees caused a very serious water shortage. The answer? Hire 40,000 workers and train them to cut down the trees. All of them! At the recommendation of the environmentalists! Could cutting down trees actually be an environmentally conscious activity? In this situation, yes!

What does this have to do with constructivist practice? It seems that we are finding in more and more areas of our lives that what we once thought was an objective truth (trees are good, they should not be cut down) is not always true. Perhaps this is also true for the objective ways in which people and their difficulties have been viewed. What was once clearly a "behavioral" problem (i.e., the problem with the disobedient adolescent in Eron and Lund, Chapter 2, this volume) may in fact be something more central to the core way that each person in the predicament viewed their situation and construed the intimate relationships in their lives. Allowing for alternative views of difficulties and providing space for different ways of understanding problems are truly strengths of constructivist psychology that are amplified in the first section of this volume.

In the coming decades, I see a need to take a deeper look into how we practice as constructivist psychologists. Not only in the ways in which we work with people as they strive to overcome difficulties in their lives, but also where we work with them, how we hear their stories, and the approach we take in attempting to understand them. Constructivism is beginning to address the issues of racism, heterosexism, sexism, ageism, and ableism. Constructivism is recognizing that specific attention may be needed to find ways of working with people who are not highly verbal or insight oriented.

There also may be a need to make ourselves more visible in communities where help may be needed. Constructivists have been criticized for staying in our "Ivory Towers" and not allowing our ways of practicing to reach those who could benefit from it. Becoming actively involved in communities, training, and national and local organizations are just a few steps that may help to move constructivism out of the 50-minute therapy session or academic ivory tower. One attempt by constructivists at networking with interested others has recently resulted in the formation of the Constructivist Psychology Section (CPS) of the Division of Humanistic Psychology of the American Psychological Association. (See the Appendix for more on this.)

Conceptual Questions for Consideration

1. With pockets of constructivists nestled throughout the world, how can we best train those interested in constructivist psychologies?

2. How can we help students who are looking for constructivist mentors or professors to connect with these people?

3. Is there a continued need to empirically prove the viability of constructivist therapeutic methodologies?

SECTION TWO: Constructivist Notions of Disorder

The major theme in this section is that diagnosis is often reductionistic and harmful to both our clients and to us as we attempt to fully understand them. That being said, the chapters in the section suggest different approaches for addressing the need to have a plan for what may or may not happen in therapy. For many, knowing that there is a "method to our madness" when it comes to therapy, that we have some idea of why it is that we do what we do, is connected to this planning stage. Additionally for many clients, knowing that there is a bit of structure or a plan for their therapeutic process (i.e., that they may be able to predict or anticipate the changes to come) can provide some comfort in an otherwise potentially uncomfortable position for them. Coming to a therapist for help with life's predicaments necessarily includes the therapist as a "major player" in how clients view their difficulties. Thus, the opinion of the therapist and his or her "plan" for their time together can be quite significant in how clients come to view their situations. The connection (or relationship) between the client and the therapist is a vital factor in the process of therapy.

The self-in-relation theory proposed by Surrey (1991) suggests that women, and potentially all people, can know themselves better through their connection with others. Through deeper and more meaningfully intimate relationships with others, rather then through autonomous "personal searches," we can become more familiar with our needs, strengths, abilities, and growing edges. This view of self or personal development is quite different from most traditional psychological theories that "emphasize a separate self; an autonomous, self-sufficient, contained entity" (Kerl & Duffey, 2001). The connection between the self-in relation theory with the major theme of this section is clear; we cannot simply look at individuals as the solitary keepers of "their disorders." Disorder happens in context—I cannot be abnormal without a comparison to something or someone else. Not only do we have a better sense of who we are at different points in time through our connections with others, we also have a better idea of how we are different or how the other is different from us. However, who is different from whom, and who needs to change is arguably arbitrary. This point is brought into an even clearer light in the quote offered by McNamee (Chapter 7, this volume) of Hoeg's 1995 novel *Borderliners*:

> Every person who says of something that it is good or bad or a bit better than yesterday is declaring that a points system exists; that one can, in a reasonably clear and obvious fashion, set some sort of a number against an achievement. . . . But never at any time has a code of practice been laid down for the awarding of points. (pp. 78-79)

In this situation the author is referring to a boarding school where the students were assessed by the authorities to determine their futures. However, the argument holds for diagnosis (and relationships) as well. As people in meaningful relationships, it is common to believe or be told that we are "too" something (i.e., too sensitive, too antisocial, too logical, too shy, too loud, too flirty, too emotional, etc.). In order to be "too much" of something, these statements (or beliefs) require comparison, either real or imagined. In some situations these comparisons could be starting points for meaningful change and the development of deeper and fuller relationships. In other situations these comparisons can lead to a simple reduction to feelings of inadequacy, diagnosis, or unhelpful categorization.

If diagnosis is a comparison, then the definition of "normal" needs to be made clearer, a task that is beyond comprehension. For example, even with something supposedly as easy to define as "normal" sexuality, the task is not a simple one. A colleague of mine defines one's views about sexuality in the following way: Normal is what we both do; kinky is what you do and I do not (if I hold you in a favorable light); perverted is something that neither one of us would do. Again, normalcy is relative and somewhat arbitrary, as is diagnosis.

Conceptual Questions for Consideration

1. Is there utility in the DSM for constructivist psychologists?

2. How does our disenchantment with diagnosis influence how we train students?

3. Are we doing a disservice to students by not helping them to become familiar with the language of traditional diagnosis, even if the language and the motivation behind the development of this language is unacceptable to us.

4. How can we truly communicate with other professionals without a shared language (Gergen & McNamee, 2000)?

SECTION THREE: Explorations in Constructivist Research

Following the themes set forth in the first two sections, the authors in this section challenge constructivist researchers to be true to their constructivist epistemologies—meaning that they call on

researchers to include the perspectives of their participants, to actively avoid the quantitative reduction of ideas, experiences, or meanings, and to be more personally present in the research that is conducted. Similar to constructivist therapeutic practice, conducting
constructivist research demands that the researcher (like a therapist)
allows him or herself to be part of the process, and not simply an
objective and disinterested observer. For many this goes against their
training in modernist objective research methodologies. As
researchers or scientists, the goal has been to completely remove
oneself from experiments conducted to assure that the results found
actually do measure what was intended. Yet, for decades critics of traditional modernist research methodologies have stated that it is
impossible to perform research without bias, or to pretend that the
simple act of measuring does not interfere with those being meas-
ured. Many steps have been taken to allow for the subjective views of
the participants in qualitative work (Patton, 1990). However, these
methodologies often face criticism for being "unscientific." What
would happen if, instead of vainly attempting to carry out "pure"
research, the aim for constructivist research was to include the
researcher's perspective in the research and readily admit that the
results were "co-constructed?" How does this connect to outcome
research, and how can we answer the call for empirically validated
forms of treatment for managed care providers. Or do we need to?

Empirically validated forms of treatment have been criticized
on many fronts, from the process of the research (Lampropoulos,
2000) to the goals of the research (Bohart, O'Hara, & Leitner, 1998).
However, for others, including many constructivist authors in this
section, the major criticism is paradigmatic (Bohart, 2000).
Empirically validated treatment research models require both manualization (to ensure consistency of treatment) and diagnosis (to
ensure that the treatments work, defined as a significant reduction in
diagnosis specific symptomology) (Bohart, et al., 1998;
Lampropoulos, 2000). The need for both a specific treatment (manualization) and a specific diagnosis follows the randomized clinical
trial model mandated in the medical community when testing new
medications. In the second section of this volume, the disdain for
diagnosis was made very clear. In the third section, it is apparent that
performing research that supports manualization—while imitating a
medical, objectivistic way of thinking—simply does not coincide
with constructivist epistemologies.

As constructivist researchers and therapists we are "personal scientists" along with our clients. This means that we are also working to make sense of our own worlds as we attempt to understand the worlds of our clients. To assume that we know how to "treat" one of our clients because we had been "successful" in treating similar clients previously does both a disservice to the client and to our own meaning making processes. Thus, performing research (either as personal scientists or active researchers) that leads to manualization of constructivist therapies is counterintuitive to constructivist researchers and therapists. This point was made utterly clear to me as I began my training as a psychotherapist. While working with a highly verbal and insightful client, I had found a book that I thought might be helpful to her. I photocopied the first chapter for her and said that we could talk it over during our next session if she would like. During the week between our sessions, she read the first chapter and then proceeded to locate the book in a local bookstore, buy it, and read it in its entirety prior to our next session. When we met next, she went into great detail about how much the book had meant to her, how it had changed her life and how much better she felt about herself and her difficulties. Armed with "a significant finding" and what I now knew was the perfect antidote to all aliments similar to hers, I copied that first wonder chapter again and gave this very effective "treatment" to a different client with the "same" problem. I also told her that we could discuss it during our next session if she would like and then sat back and waited for the magic cure to happen. As it turns out, the chapter also had a profound effect on this client. She returned the next week and had taken deliberate steps to highlight the sections that she "hated the most." She reported that she hated all of it, but certain sections were particularly obnoxious and she wanted to make sure we had a chance to discuss them. Thus, it would seem as a personal scientist, the results of my miracle book experiment were not very generalizable.

Conceptual Questions for Consideration

1. If we are not looking to empirically validate constructivist therapies in the medical model that has been prescribed, what kinds of outcome research would be interesting and helpful?

2. What do constructivists mean when they say that therapy works? And how can we respond to the need for accountability in therapeutic practice?

3. What new kinds of constructivist research methodologies

can be fashioned to better address constructivist meaning making processes?

4. If research is as subjective as has been suggested, can any research be applicable to anyone other than those directly involved in the research?

SECTION FOUR: New Directions in Constructivist Psychology

In this final section, the authors endeavor to find their own voices as constructivist psychologists, either by critiquing other's attempts to find "fundamental truths" in psychology or to make psychology an applied science, or by valiantly attempting to describe the "in-betweeness" of two actively involved entities. The authors allow themselves to move into the "personal" side of living constructively by exploring topics near to their own hearts. This follows the theme of the volume and of constructivism in general: our constructs are open to revision. These revisions can happen both personally and professional and it would be counter-theoretical to insist that a singular, stable, theory is necessary.

Apparently since the beginning of time, people have endeavored to understand the world around them. From the angry Gods of thunderstorms to the flatness of the earth to the multitude of "true" weight loss strategies (i.e., low fat/high carbohydrate, high fat/low carbohydrate, no sugar, grapefruit, etc.), we have learned that our once steadfast theories of how things "really are" have required adaptation. Nevertheless, there continues to be a belief that eventually all things will be "known" and that striving towards this goal will allow for a certain sense of comfort. In other words, believing that someday all truths will be revealed makes it possible for people to believe that eventually all aspects of life will be predictable. Thus, anxiety about the unknown will be eliminated. Furthermore many who are comforted by the search for an objective truth do not seem to be bothered by the fact that many of the "knowns" in the world have subsequently been shown to be untrue. Perhaps these "knowns" could be considered "knowns for now" or perhaps "knowns for me," as is suggested by the authors in this last section. Allowing for variability in theory and in personal process seems to be the cornerstone in constructivism as it currently stands and the direction we will see it take in the future.

Yet, I think a note of caution should be raised at this point. Although I believe variability in theory is a positive attribute in the family of constructivist psychologies, there still is a need to both teach others about these theories and a need to reach those less academically inclined who could possibly benefit from learning about constructivism. This is not to say that there needs to be a limit on constructivist theory variability. However, there does seem to be a need to present constructivism in an "understandable" form. Currently there is a deluge of "self-help" books (broadly defined), psychologically related talk shows, and programs available for public consumption. These avenues for self-help promote a "right way" to be more satisfied in life and make promises about the 7 or 8 or 9 easy steps it will take to get on the right track. As constructivists, I believe that many of us shudder as we peruse the "psychology" sections of bookstores or hear the "Dr. Laura's" on the radio. However, few of us are actively presenting alternatives. I am not suggesting movement towards a monumental leap onto the self-help band wagon, yet there does seem to be a need to make constructivism more accessible to non-academics and interested others. Thus, although variability is key to the continued growth of constructivist theory (and quite interesting to those already familiar with its main tenets), there is still quite a bit of room left for spreading constructivism out of university and conference settings and into a more public domain.

Conceptual Questions for Consideration

1. What is our responsibility as constructivist researchers, therapists, and theorists to move beyond our academic publishing circles and make our way of respecting each person's individual reality more commonly understood and perhaps even appreciated?

2. In what ways does the depth and breadth of constructivist theory variability bring us closer to or further from theoretical accessibility?

3. Will making constructivism more "public" in some way reduce the respect it has gained in academic circles?

4. What avenues can be created to continue the personal explorations of constructivists?

CONCLUSION
In each chapter of this volume, we have seen the authors incorporate both the personal and the professional approaches to constructivist psychology. Through clinical vignettes, personal stories or reflections, appeals for methodological changes and visions of the future, each author has endeavored to move beyond the question of constructivist viability and into broader and more meaningful applications of constructivist theory. However, as was true at the 2000 NAPCN conference, each of the authors presents constructivist theory and its application a bit differently. This is the strength of constructivist thought in general and this volume in particular. Complete integration of constructivist psychologies was not the goal of this volume or of the conference, nor will it be of future conferences or volumes. Instead, like a quilt of many colors, the beauty of constructivist thought is clearly displayed here; each chapter is enhanced by its proximity to the next chapter without needing to blend into a vast grayness of singular theoretical simplicity.

REFERENCES

Bohart, A. C. (2000). Paradigm clash: Empirically supported treatments versus empirically supported psychotherapy practice. *Psychotherapy Research, 10*, 488-493.

Bohart, A. C., O'Hara, M., & Leitner, L. M. (1998). Empirically violated treatments: Disenfranchisement of humanistic and other psychotherapies. *Psychotherapy Research, 8*, 141-157.

Franklin, C. & Nurius, P. S. (Eds.). (1998). *Constructivism in practice: Methods and challenges.* Families International Inc.: Milwaukee, WI

Kelly, G. A. (1991). *The psychology of personal constructs* (2 vols.). New York: Routledge. (Original work published 1955)

Kerl, S. B., & Duffey, T. (2001, Spring). Do relational view of self support subordinate roles? *Professional Issues in Counseling.* Retrieved July 30, 2001, from http://www.shsu.edu/~piic/spring2001/kerlduffey.htm

Hoeg, P. (1995). *Borderliners.* London: The Harvill Press.

Lampropoulos, G. K. (2000). A reexamination of the empirically supported treatments critiques. *Psychotherapy Research, 10*, 474-487.

Neimeyer, R. A., & Mahoney, M. J. (Eds.). (1995). *Constructivism in psychotherapy.* Washington, DC: American Psychological Association.

Neimeyer, R. A., & Raskin, J. D. (Eds.). (2000). *Constructions of disorder: Meaning-making frameworks for psychotherapy.* Washington, DC: American Psychological Association.

Neimeyer, R. A., & Stewart, A. E. (2000). Constructivist and narrative psychotherapies. In C. R. Snyder & R. E. Ingram (Eds.), *Handbook of psychological change* (pp. 337-357). New York: Wiley.

Patton, M. Q. (1990). *Qualitative evaluation and research methods* 2nd edition. Newberry Park, CA: Sage.

Snyder, C. R. & Ingram, R. E. (Eds.). (2000) *Handbook of psychological change.* New York: Wiley.

Surrey, J. L. (1990). The self-in-relation: A theory of women's development. In J. V. Jordan, A. G. Kaplan, J. B. Miller, I. P. Stiver, & J. L. Surrey (Eds.), *Women's growth in connection: Writings from the Stone Center.* New York: Guilford Press.

Jonathan D. Raskin is an associate professor of psychology at the State University of New York at New Paltz. He received his A.B. from Vassar College and his Ph.D. in counseling psychology from the University of Florida. Dr. Raskin's scholarship focuses on examining the implications of constructivist theories for psychology. Specifically, he has published articles and book chapters that apply constructivism to psychotherapy, abnormality, and ethics. He co-edited *Constructions of Disorder: Meaning-Making Frameworks for Psychotherapy* (with Robert Neimeyer; American Psychological Association Press, 2000). He also serves as book review editor for the *Journal of Constructivist Psychology* and is licensed as a psychologist in New York.

Sara K. Bridges received her B.A. from Indiana University, her M.S. in Marital and Family therapy from Butler University and her Ph.D. in counseling psychology from the University of Memphis. She is currently an assistant professor of counseling psychology at the University of Memphis. Dr. Bridges' research interests focus on constructivism, counselor education and training, and issues related to human sexuality. Specifically, she is pursuing a constructivist approach to sex therapy and exploring issues related to training counselors to work with the sexual concerns of their clients.

Appendix A: Constructivist Psychology on the Internet

PERSONAL CONSTRUCT THEORY

Personal Construct Psychology (PCP):
http://repgrid.com/pcp/

George Kelly:
http://www.oikos.org/kelen.htm

Personal Construct Psychology Internet Resources:
http://www.med.uni-giessen.de/psychol/internet.htm

Personal Construct Psychology Home Pages and Web Sites:
http://www.med.uni-giessen.de/psychol/pcp/home-pages.htm

Personal Construct Psychology References Database:
http://www.psyc.uow.edu.au/research/pcp/citedb/index.html

EnquireWithin-A Repertory Grid/Personal Construct Psychology Site:
http://www.EnquireWithin.co.nz

RADICAL CONSTRUCTIVISM

Humberto Maturana:
http://www.oikos.org/maten.htm

Ernst von Glaserfeld:
http://www.oikos.org/vonen.htm

Life's Natural Solutions:
http://members.ozemail.com.au/~jcull/

Towards an Ecology of Mind:
http://www.oikos.org/psicen.htm

SOCIAL CONSTRUCTIONISM

The Virtual Faculty (social constructionist global education program):
http://www.massey.ac.nz/~ALock/virtual/welcome.htm

Kenneth Gergen:
http://www.swarthmore.edu/SocSci/kgergen1/web/page.phtml?st=home&id=home

Social Construction of Reality:
:   http://www.virtualschool.edu/mon/SocialConstruction
    /index.html

Postmodernism and Social Constructionism:
Postmodern Campfire:
:   http://killdevilhill.com/postmodernchat/messages2/
    1978.html

Beyond Psychodiagnostics:
:   http://www.swarthmore.edu/SocSci/kgergen1/
    Psychodiagnostics/index.html

NARRATIVE APPROACHES

Narrative Approaches:
:   http://www.narrativeapproaches.com

Narrative Psychology Internet Resource and Guide:
:   http://web.lemoyne.edu/~hevern/narpsych.html

Depth Oriented Brief Therapy (DOBT):
:   http://www.dobt.com/

ORGANIZATIONS, THERAPY CENTERS, AND RESEARCH GROUPS:

North American Personal Construct Network (NAPCN):
:   http://www.newpaltz.edu/~raskinj/NAPCNmain.htm

European Personal Construct Association (EPCA):
:   http://www.psyctc.org/epca/

Australian Personal Construct Group (APCG):
:   http://www.bendigo.latrobe.edu.au/health/hstud/pcp/
    APCG.html

Centre for Personal Construct Psychology:
:   http://www.centrepcp.ndirect.co.uk/

Society for Constructivism in the Human Sciences:
:   http://orgs.unt.edu/constructivism/society.htm

Houston Galveston Institute:
:   http://www.neosoft.com/~hgi/

East Side Institute for Short Term Psychotherapy:
:   http://www.eastsideinstitute.org/

322

Mental Research Institute:
http://www.mri.org/

Institute for the Study of Psychotherapeutic Change:
http://www.talkingcure.com/

Taos Institute (social constructionism):
http://www.taosinstitute.org

Constructivism and Discourse Processes Research Group:
http://www.infomed.es/constructivism/

JOURNALS AND NEWSLETTERS:

Journal of Constructivist Psychology:
http://www.tandf.co.uk/journals/tf/10720537.html

Constructivism in the Human Sciences:
http://orgs.unt.edu/constructivism/society.htm

Constructivist Chronicle (NAPCN newsletter):
http://www.newpaltz.edu/~raskinj/CCIndex.html

The "Internet-ional" Personal Construct Psychology Newsletter:
http://www.med.unigiessen.de/psychol/pcp/
news.htm

Narrative Psychology Internet and Resource Guide:
http://web.lemoyne.edu/~hevern/narpsych.html

Postmodern Therapies News:
http://www.california.com/~rathbone/pmth.htm

UPCOMING CONFERENCE

North American Personal Construct Network (July 10-14, 2002)
http://www.educ.ubc.ca/napcn/

APPENDIX B: ABOUT THE NORTH AMERICAN PERSONAL CONSTRUCT NETWORK

THE ORGANIZATION

The North American Personal Construct Network (NAPCN) is a network of persons interested in Personal Construct Psychology and related constructivist approaches to psychology, relationships, and human change processes. It is largely comprised of psychologists, but there are also members from related disciplines. Those interested in personal constructivism or related areas of constructivist, constructionist, narrative, or postmodern approaches to psychology are encouraged to join.

MEMBERSHIP INFORMATION

NAPCN membership is open to anyone. An annual membership includes a subscription to the *Journal of Constructivist Psychology* (4 issues per year) and receipt of the NAPCN newsletter, the *Constructivist Chronicle*. Dues can be paid in either US or Canadian dollars. To join, complete form included in this volume, which lists 2002 dues.

NAPCN CONFERENCES

NAPCN sponsors its own conference in even numbered years. These conferences allow for constructivist scholars to gather and share ideas within an academic and collegial conference setting. In odd numbered years, NAPCN co-sponsors an international congress with the European Personal Construct Association (EPCA) and the Austral-Asian Personal Construct Association (APCA). The international congress provides a forum for an even wider array of constructivist scholars wishing to communicate with one another.

NEXT NAPCN CONFERENCE

University of British Columbia, Vancouver, Canada (July 10-14, 2002) For more, go to http://www.educ.ubc.ca/napcn/

NAPCN NEWSLETTER

NAPCN publishes a newsletter, the *Constructivist Chronicle*, twice a year. The newsletter contains conference information, updates on new books and articles related to constructivist psychology, and feature articles on events and people within the constructivist community.

324

CONSTRUCTIVIST PSYCHOLOGY SECTION
The North American Personal Construct Network (NAPCN), in conjunction with Division 32 (Humanistic Psychology) of the American Psychological Association (APA), has established a new interest section in Division 32: the Constructivist Psychology Section (CPS). Joining Division 32 and CPS entitles NAPCN members to a 15% discount on 2002 NAPCN dues! Both NAPCN and Division 32 membership forms are included in this volume.

CURRENT NAPCN OFFICERS

President:

Jonathan D. Raskin, State University of New York at New Paltz

Treasurer:

Stephanie Lewis Harter, Texas Tech University

Newsletter Editor:

Robert H. Mole, University of Calgary

Steering Committee Members:

Sara K. Bridges, Humboldt State University

Jay S. Efran, Temple University

April E. Metzler, Lehigh University

Kenneth W. Sewell, University of North Texas

Index of Proper Names

[Numbers in italics refer to listings in reference sections.]

Subject Index

Ableism, 311
Abnormality, 123-139, 274
  as deviation from the norm, 131
  difficulty explaining as physical illness, 125
  difficulty explaining as problem of psyche, 125
  discovered vs. invented, 126
  and individualism, 148-150
  as inferred rather than observed, 133
  as internal dysfunction, 127
  lack of a single definition, 125-126
  and morality, 134
Accidentalism, 77
Accommodation, 11
  according to von Glaserfeld, 11-12
Ageism, 311
Aging, 240
Alternating perception, 234, 240
American Psychological Association, 2, 311
  ethical guidelines of, 193
Anarchistic perspective, 279
Anorexia nervosa, 132
Anticipation, 278-279
Antisocial Personality Disorder, 135
Anxiety, 28, 153
Applied psychology, 265, 266, 274-276
Appreciative inquiry method, 166
Aristoteleian mode of thought, 277-278
As if posture, 165, 252n
Assimilation, 11
  according to von Glaserfeld, 11-12

Attention Deficit Hyperactivity Disorder, 151, 153. *See also* Hyperactivity
Autoethnography, 240
Autopoiesis, 12-13, 16

Behavioral theory, 125
Behavioral utterances
  as meaningful wholes, 297
Being, 210, 267, 268, 269, 276-277, 281, 282, 299
Biological model, 125
Bodily activity, 290-293
Bodily reactions, 301
Brain-injured patients
  quality of life, 159-160
Bulimia nervosa, 28

Calculative thinking, 267
Cartesian tradition, 238, 290-291, 299, 301
Case of Don, 84-96
Case of Jill, 177
Case of John, 99-100, 101, 101-102, 106-107, 110, 113-115
Case of Saul Cruz Ramos in Mexico City, 163-164
Case of the Ryan family, 66-70, 71, 74, 77-82, 83
Catholicism, 278
Catskill Family Institute (CFI), 63, 66
Causality, 253-254
  and mental illness, 254
Child sexual abuse. *See* Sexual abuse
Circumpection, 53
Civil commitment, 174
Classical tradition, 302, 304
  steps of, 302-303
Client-centered therapy, 72, 74-75
Clinical knowledge, 250

MEMBERSHIP APPLICATION

North American Personal Construct Network

Name: _____

Address: _____

_____

_____

Highest Degree: _____

Date Awarded: _____

Institution: _____

Are you a student?

_____ Yes _____ No

2002 DUES: NAPCN membership only

(Consider joining Division 32 and its Constructivist Psychology Section for discounted NAPCN rates; see below)

United States: $56 US (professional rate) / $30 US (student rate)

Canada: $85 CDN (professional rate) / $47 CDN (student rate)

2002 DUES: CPS and NAPCN membership

(Must be a member of Division 32 of the American Psychological Association for these rates; see Division 32 membership form in this volume)

United States: $66 US (professional rate) / $36 US (student rate)

Canada: $100 CDN (professional rate) / $55 CDN (student rate)

Outside North America: $76 US (professional rate) / $46 US (student rate)

Send payment to: Stephanie Lewis Harter, Ph.D.
Psychology Department
Box 42051
Texas Tech University
Lubbock, TX 79409-2051, USA.

Printed in the United States
1254100003B/102